INSIGHT GUIDE

Hawaii

Discovery
CHANNEL®

APA PUBLICATIONS
Part of the Langenscheidt Publishing Group

✳ INSIGHT GUIDE
Hawaii

ABOUT THIS BOOK

Editorial
Project Editor
Scott Rutherford
Editorial Director
Brian Bell

Distribution

UK & Ireland
GeoCenter International Ltd
The Viables Centre, Harrow Way
Basingstoke, Hants RG22 4BJ
Fax: (44) 1256 817988
United States
Langenscheidt Publishers, Inc.
46–35 54th Road, Maspeth, NY 11378
Fax: (1) 718 784 0640
Canada
Thomas Allen & Son Ltd
390 Steelcase Road East
Markham, Ontario L3R 1G2
Fax: (1) 905 475 6747
Australia
Universal Press
1 Waterloo Road
Macquarie Park, NSW 2113
Fax: (61) 2 9888 9074
New Zealand
Hema Maps New Zealand Ltd (HNZ)
Unit D, 24 Ra ORA Drive
East Tamaki, Auckland
Fax: (64) 9 273 6479
Worldwide
Apa Publications GmbH & Co.
Verlag KG (Singapore branch)
38 Joo Koon Road, Singapore 628990
Tel: (65) 865 1600. Fax: (65) 861 6438

Printing

Insight Print Services (Pte) Ltd
38 Joo Koon Road, Singapore 628990
Tel: (65) 865 1600. Fax: (65) 861 6438

©2002 Apa Publications GmbH & Co.
Verlag KG (Singapore branch)
All Rights Reserved
First Edition 1980
Twelfth Edition 2000; updated 2002

CONTACTING THE EDITORS
We would appreciate it if readers
would alert us to errors or out-
dated information by writing to:
Insight Guides, P.O. Box 7910,
London SE1 1WE, England.
Fax: (44) 20 7403 0290.
insight@apaguide.demon.co.uk

www.insightguides.com

This guidebook combines the interests and enthusiasms of two of the world's best-known information providers: Insight Guides, whose titles have set the standard for visual travel guides since 1970, and Discovery Channel, the world's premier source of non-fiction television programming.

The editors of Insight Guides provide both practical advice and general understanding about the history, culture, institutions and people of numerous destinations around the world. Discovery Channel and its website, www.discovery.com, help millions of viewers across the globe to explore their world from the comfort of their own home as well as encouraging them to explore it first-hand.

How to use this book

Insight Guide: Hawaii is carefully structured to convey an incisive understanding of the Hawaiian islands and their cultures and to guide readers through the wide range of sights and activities on offer to visitors there:

◆ To understand Hawaii, it is important to know something of its past. The **Features** section, which is indicated by a yellow bar at the top of each page, covers the islands' convoluted history and culture in a series of lively, authoritative and evocative essays.

◆ The main **Places** section, marked by a blue bar at the top of each page, provides a full run-down of all the many attractions and desti-

EXPLORE YOUR WORLD'
Discovery
CHANNEL

Map Legend

National Park
✈ Airport
Bus Station
Ⓟ Parking
❶ Tourist Information
✉ Post Office
Church/Ruins
∴ Archeological Site
∩ Cave
★ Place of Interest

The main places of interest in the Places section are coordinated by number with a full-color map (e.g. ❶), and a symbol at the top of every right-hand page tells you where to find the map.

nations that are worth seeing in Hawaii. Places of major interest on all of the islands are coordinated by number with full-color maps.

◆ The **Travel Tips** listings section, headed by an orange bar, provides a convenient point of reference for up-to-date practical information on travel, hotels, restaurants, shops, and festivals.

The contributors

This edition was supervised by **Scott Rutherford**, who lived in Hawaii for many years. It builds on the original 1980 edition and on the ten subsequent editions.

Supervising a team of Hawaii-based updaters was **Cheryl Chee Tsutsumi**, who has worked in travel journalism since the 1970s. Maui updater **Paul Wood** calls the island's Upcountry region home.

Editing the Oahu chapter was **Lance Tominaga**, editor of *Aloha* magazine. Kauai and the Big Island were updated by **Betty Fullard-Leo**, while Oahu-based **Joyce Akamine** overhauled the Travel Tips. Also contributing were **Susan Essoyan** and **Beverly Fujita**. The entire book was thoroughly updated in 2002 by Hawaii resident and author **Allan Seiden**, and edited in-house by **Sylvia Suddes** and **Jenni Rainford**.

Important contributors to previous editions of this Hawaii guide include **Kekuni Blaisdell, Susan Scott, Marty Wentzel, Jerry Hopkins, Joan Conrow, Alberta de Jetley, Ronn Ronck, Larry Lindsey Kimura**, and **Leonard Lueras**.

It's nearly impossible to take a dismal photograph in Hawaii. This fact, it should be made clear, doesn't diminish the efforts of photographers who illustrated this Insight Guide, including **Catherine Karnow, Ron Dahlquist, Galen Rowell, Frank Salmoiraghi, Scott Rutherford**, and the insightful and provoking photographs taken long ago by **Ray Jerome Baker**.

Once an independent kingdom ruled by a monarchy, Hawaii is now an American state – the 50th and most recent – but still sometimes feels a little out of synchronism with the mainland. On the same latitude as Mexico City, the state's ambiance is Asian and Pacific Islander, peppered with only a little North American quirkiness. This combination is, and has long been, an enticing one, sparking such descriptions of Hawaii as that by the writer Mark Twain as "the loveliest fleet of islands anchored in any ocean," and inspiring many visitors to come to its exotic shores.

Hawaii

CONTENTS

Hanalei Bay, Kauai.

Insight on....

Information panels

Places

Travel Tips

ALOHA

Few travelers arrive in Hawaii without preconceptions.
Inevitably, expectations pale next to Hawaii's diversity

ay the word "Hawaii" and seductive images come to mind: secluded beaches, fragrant rainforests, mountains that soar above the mists, sunsets so brilliant they blow the mind, waterfalls shimmering like silvery ribbons in valleys unmarred by human footsteps. Of all the destinations on Earth, Hawaii is certainly one of the most wondrous, with an allure that goes far beyond preconceived images and actual physical beauty.

The islands of Hawaii are home to an amazingly diverse gathering of peoples: Chinese, Japanese, Vietnamese, Koreans, Filipinos, Samoans and other Pacific islanders, Caucasians, and Native Hawaiians. Over the decades, intermarriage has diluted bloodlines, so that today a *kama'aina* (local-born or long-time resident) is more likely than not a beautiful blend of races. And as with the mixing of ethnic and cultural groups, so too with the islands' cuisines, religions, languages, fashions, music, dances, and arts. Every ethnic group that came to Hawaii has added something special, creating a cultural climate unlike elsewhere in the United States or the world.

Even Americans on the US mainland can forget that Hawaii is fully part of the United States. More than one resident, when making a business call to the mainland, has been asked if American money or postage is valid in the islands, or if Hawaii has a separate country code. (Yes to money and postage, but no to a different country code.) Of course, Hawaii is administratively as much a part of the United States as Vermont. Hawaii's residents celebrate Easter, Independence Day, Thanksgiving and Christmas. But they also enthusiastically observe holidays such as the Lunar New Year, Kamehameha Day, Samoan Flag Day, and the Japanese Obon season. Along with hamburgers and cotton candy, food booths at school carnivals peddle Japanese teriyaki, Chinese noodles, Portuguese *malasadas* (doughnuts), Korean *kalbi* (barbecue) ribs, and Hawaiian *kalua* pig and *poi*. Houses of worship in the islands range from synagogues to cathedrals to Buddhist temples, and for some Native Hawaiians, ancient *heiau*, or sacred temples.

Hawaii's economy is driven in large part by tourism, followed by the military and agriculture. Nearly 7 million people visit the islands annually, pumping more than $10 billion into the state. Hawaii adopted its nickname, the Aloha State, in 1959 when it became a state. Since then, Hawaii has also chosen an official state bird, the endangered *nene* goose; a state fish, *humuhumunukunukuapua'a*; a state mammal, the humpback whale; a state tree, *kukui*, or candlenut; a state gem, black coral; and a state flower, the yellow hibiscus. Its

PRECEDING PAGES: *pali* on Kane'ohe side of Ko'olau Range; flow from Kilauea entering the ocean, Big Island; Ha'ena Point, Kauai; evening surfing.
LEFT: hula performer with a winning smile.

official anthem, "Hawaii Pono'i", is a haunting and moving melody composed in 1874 by Henry Berger, the long-time leader of the Royal Hawaiian Band who originally titled it "The Hymn of King Kamehameha I". The song's lyrics were written by King David Kalakaua.

Each of the major Hawaiian islands has its own official flower: Oahu, *'ilima*; Maui, *loke lani*; the Big Island, *red lehua*; Kauai, *mokihana*; Molokai, white *kukui* blossom; Lanai, *kauna'oa*; and Ni'ihau, white *pupu* shell. Even the uninhabited island of Kaho'olawe has an official flower, the *hinahina*.

Oahu, the main island, is perhaps the biggest surprise. Located here is Honolulu, the state capital and home to over 800,000 people. The largest city between Asia and the Americas, Honolulu offers much of the sophistication of New York, Tokyo and Paris. Within the city proper, between Diamond Head and Pearl Harbor, are Chanel, Christian Dior and Gucci, plush hotels, and five-star restaurants known to gourmets the world over.

But just half an hour's drive from Honolulu is the Hawaii of old: majestic mountain ranges, verdant meadows, pristine beaches, and breezes scented with plumeria and *'awapuhi* (wild ginger). *Keiki* (children) fish with nylon lines tied to bamboo poles, snacking on guavas, *liliko'i* (passionfruit) and bananas plucked from roadside trees.

That precisely is the wonder of Hawaii. Two visitors arriving on the islands at the very same time may wind up having two very different experiences. There is the Hawaii of today, with its luxurious resorts, magnificent golf courses (many of which were carved from ancient lava fields), fine dining and shopping. And there's the Hawaii of yesteryear – simple, laid-back, innocent, and historical.

No matter where you go, no matter what you do, you will be touched by Hawaii's *aloha*. Translated, the word *aloha* breaks down as *alo*, to face, and *ha*, the breath of life. It is the spiritual glue that binds the islands' cosmopolitan population, whatever the ethnic or cultural background.

About the spelling of place names

Two symbols can be added to Hawaiian words to assist pronunciation: a glottal stop ('), called the *'okina*, and a macron, which is a horizontal line over a vowel, indicating that the sound is drawn out longer than is normal. *Insight Guide: Hawaii* uses the *'okina*, but not the macron. The glottal stop, which gives a "hard edge" to a vowel or separates two adjoining vowels with distinct sounds, is necessary for basic pronunciation in normal conversation, while the macron offers a more subtle, precise pronunciation.

All place names in this guide that need them use a glottal stop, with three exceptions: Hawaii, Oahu and Kauai, which can written as Hawai'i, O'ahu and Kaua'i. But the non-glottal spellings are so common and ubiquitous that most cartographers delete the glottal stop for these islands. Two islands requiring glottal stops for proper pronunciation are Ni'ihau (*nee-ee-how*) and Kaho'olawe (*kah-ho-o-lah-vay*). In this guide, we use glottal stops for these two islands. ❑

RIGHT: talking story on a local telephone.

Decisive Dates

150,000 BC Diamond Head forms through a crack in the emerged reef of Oahu.

AD 200–500 First settlers arrive in Hawaii, probably from the Marquesas Islands.

800–1200 Next significant wave of Polynesian pioneers arrive, this time from Tahiti.

circa **1750** Kamehameha (the Great) is born on the Big Island's northernmost point.

1778 In January, Captain James Cook encounters the Hawaiian islands, anchors in Waimea Bay, off the island of Kauai. He names the islands the Sandwich

Islands, after his patron, the Earl of Sandwich. In November, he returns to Hawaii from the Arctic after a fruitless search for the Northwest Passage. He anchors at Kealakekua Bay, on the Big Island.

1779 Cook is killed on 21 February in a skirmish with Hawaiians. His remains are buried at Kealakekua Bay.

1790 Kamehameha I begins unification of the Hawaiian Islands by conquering Maui and Lanai.

1791 Kamehameha completes conquest of the Big Island.

1795 On Oahu, Kamehameha's forces drive the army of Kalanikupule over Nu'uanu Pali. The great warrior king now rules all the major islands except Kauai.

1810 Kauai's chief, Kaumuali'i, finally surrenders to Kamehameha without a battle.

1812 Sandalwood trade booms.

1819 Kamehameha I dies in Kailua-Kona, on the Big Island. His son, Liholiho, becomes Kamehameha II, and Kamehameha's wife, Ka'ahumanu, becomes kuhina nui, sharing power as regent. They pave the way for the introduction of Christianity in the islands by abolishing the ancient kapu system.

WESTERN INFLUENCES

1820 The first contingent of Protestant missionaries arrives in Hawaii. The kingdom's capital and royal court are moved to Lahaina, on Maui.

1823 Liholiho and his favorite wife, Kamamalu, sail to England to meet King George III.

1824 Liholiho and Kamamalu are stricken with the measles and die in London.

1825 Kauikeaouli becomes Kamehameha III. Whaling industry begins a 40-year boom.

1831 Lahainaluna Seminary (now the oldest school west of the Rocky Mountains) welcomes its first students from both the mainland and Hawaii.

1835 First Hawaiian sugar plantation is established at Koloa, Kauai.

1842 Kawaiaha'o Church dedicated in Honolulu.

1845 Hawaii's capital is moved back to Honolulu from Lahaina. First legislature in Hawaii convenes. The king announces plans for a constitutional government.

1848 Kamehameha III enacts the Great Mahele, dividing land among the crown, chiefs and commoners.

1852 The king unveils a new liberal constitution. About 300 Chinese immigrants are brought in to work in the cane fields.

1854 Kamehameha III dies.

1855 Alexander Liholiho becomes Kamehameha IV.

1863 Kamehameha IV dies, and Lot Kamehameha takes the throne as Kamehameha V.

1869 "Big Five" company Alexander & Baldwin founded.

1872 Kamehameha V dies, abruptly ending the Kamehameha dynasty. He leaves no heir.

1873 Lunalilo is elected king.

1874 Lunalilo dies on 3 February. Nine days later, Kalakaua is elected king. The new monarch visits Washington, DC, to push for a reciprocity treaty with the United States. The first such treaty is ratified, allowing Hawaiian goods, particularly rice and unrefined sugar, entry into the United States tax-free.

1878 Thousands of immigrant plantation workers arrive, primarily from Portugal and Asia.

1881 Kalakaua embarks on a round-the-world trip.

1883 No doubt inspired by the lavish lifestyle he encountered on his global tour, Kalakaua holds an elaborate coronation ceremony at 'Iolani Palace, nine years after his ascension to the throne.

1885 Japanese sugar laborers arrive.

1887 Hawaiian League is formed by powerful haole businessmen. Kalakaua signs the Bayonet Constitution, which greatly limits his power.

1889 Robert Wilcox leads an unsuccessful revolt against opponents of the king.

1890 Kalakaua heads for California, hoping rest will improve his deteriorating health.

1891 Kalakaua dies in San Francisco. His sister, Lili'uokalani, is named queen.

END OF THE MONARCHY

1893 Anti-royalists launch a successful coup. Lili'uokalani is asked to abdicate the throne, and a self-proclaimed provisional government is established, led by Sanford B. Dole. President Grover Cleveland sends a representative to investigate the situation, who recommends that the monarchy be restored.

1894 The provisional government declares itself to be the Republic of Hawaii, with Dole as president.

1895 Supporters of the queen stage a counter coup, but are defeated. Lili'uokalani is arrested and brought to trial. She is found guilty of treason and confined for nine months in 'Iolani Palace.

1898 The US Congress passes a resolution to annex Hawaii as a territory, and President William McKinley signs the legislation to annex Hawaii.

1900 Hawaii becomes a territory of the United States, with Sanford Dole as its governor. Construction of a naval base at Pearl Harbor begins.

1902 First transpacific telegraphic cable linking Hawaii and California is laid.

1903 Prince Jonah Kuhio Kalaniana'ole begins a term as Hawaii's delegate to Congress that lasts until his death in 1922.

1906 Immigrants from the Philippines arrive to work on the sugar plantations.

1917 Queen Lili'uokalani dies.

1919 Dredging of the channel and construction of facilities at Pearl Harbor are completed.

1922 James Dole's Hawaiian Pineapple Company buys the island of Lanai.

1929 Inter-Island Airways (now Hawaiian Airlines) starts passenger service between the islands.

1935 Congress passes an act allowing workers to organize into unions and engage in collective bargaining. Over the next 30 years, unions in Hawaii grow.

1936 Pan American Airways launches transpacific passenger service to Hawaii.

PRECEDING PAGES: an *ali'i* feather cape, early 1900s.
LEFT: the Earl of Sandwich. **RIGHT:** a descendant of the *ali'i*, or Hawaiian aristocracy.

1941 Japanese fighter planes bomb Pearl Harbor, propelling the United States into World War II.

1942 Americans of Japanese ancestry form the 442nd Regimental Combat Team, the most highly decorated American military unit during World War II.

STATEHOOD

1959 Hawaii becomes the 50th state in the union.

1974 George Ariyoshi becomes the first Japanese-American governor in the US.

1978 Last scheduled passenger ship flying an American flag between mainland and Hawaii arrives.

1986 Hawaii's first ethnic Hawaiian governor, John Waihe'e, takes office.

1989 Japanese investment in Hawaii real estate exceeds US$7 billion. Residential and commercial property in the state reaches inflated values.

1993 100th anniversary of the monarchy's overthrow. President Bill Clinton and Congress apologize for this.

1994 Filipino-American Ben Cayetano is elected the state's governor.

1998 Jack Lord, of *Hawaii Five-O* fame, dies in Honolulu. Ni'ihau Ranch ceases operation.

2000 Sugar plantations close on Maui, the Big Island, Oahu and Kauai. Only a few of the dozens of plantations remain: pineapple on Maui and Oahu, sugar on Kauai and Maui.

2001 Terrorist bombings in New York and Washington DC cause a downturn in Hawaii's tourist trade. ❑

"*On Sunday the 17th, by eleven o'clock* AM, *we were safely moored in company with the Discovery... The bay where we lay at anchor, called by the natives Karakakooa, is a convenient harbour, and having suffered much in our masts and rigging, we were happy at last to find so proper a place to refit...*

After we were moored, the ships continued to be much crowded with the natives, and surrounded by a vast multitude of them... We were struck with the singularity of this scene, and particularly pleased with... this important new discovery... in consequence of not having succeeded in finding a northern passage homeward...

KARAKAKOOA, *in OWYHEE.*

Before we had been long at anchor, the Discovery *had so many people hanging on one side that she was seen to heed considerably... Captain Cook communicated his sentiments to Pareea, who instantly cleared the ship of her incumbrances... From this circumstance it appeared to us that the chiefs of this island exercise a most despotic power over the commonalty..."*

Official British Admiralty comments about the arrival
of Capt. James Cook at Kealakekua Bay, on 17 January 1779

S. Leroy d'après J. Arago.   Gravé par Lerouge.

ÎLES SANDWICH. UN OFFICIER DU ROI EN GRAND COSTUME.

BEGINNINGS: ANCIENT HAWAII

Thousands of centuries passed after the islands' creation before the first life took root. People, however, arrived just 15 or so centuries ago

Each year the speckled plover wends its way southward from its summer grounds in Siberia and Alaska, flying southwest as far as the Marquesas Islands, Tahiti, and New Zealand. For thousands of miles, save for a stop in Hawaii and other more obscure landing spots, the plover's wings beat rhythmically through Pacific winds until the bird finds a perch in central or south Pacific. Once there, it spends between nine and ten months fattening up on crustaceans, snails, and insects, then returns to Alaska and Siberia, when these destinations are at their warmest.

Ancient seafaring Polynesians from the islands around Tahiti no doubt observed the movements of this bird. They knew that such a fragile bird had to be going somewhere, coming from somewhere. This curiosity may have led to Hawaii's discovery, over 2,000 miles (3,200 km) north of Tahiti.

In seaworthy, double-hulled canoes embellished with '*aumakua* – carved images of their family gods – these Polynesian islanders set out on epic ocean journeys, perhaps motivated by the plover heading north. The reasons for setting off into the unknown were probably many: seeking refuge from persecution and conquering enemies, escaping the pressures of overpopulation, or simply wanderlust, intrigued about what lay beyond the horizon.

The first European to find the Marquesas Islands, Portuguese explorer Pedro Fernandez de Quirios, believed that there was no possibility of Polynesians traveling eastward very far against the prevailing trade winds. Such a journey, however long or short, would have "required instruments of navigation and vessels of burden, two things of which these people are destitute."

These "destitute" Marquesans, however, were but the last chapter of an island-hopping migration of peoples that had begun thousands of years earlier, probably in Southeast Asia. By AD 400, Marquesan canoes had sailed as far east as Easter Island, 2,500 miles (4,000 km) away. In time they also reached New Zealand and Hawaii. The British explorer and navigator Captain James Cook, who first sailed to the South Pacific in 1768 to observe the transit of Venus, watched with a seaman's respect as Tahitians took visual bearings on stars, using no instruments, to plow ahead into uncertain seas.

The first Polynesians reaching Hawaii, located in latitudes high above the familiar stars, had not just ventured into the unknown, but had, in the words of contemporary American author and ecologist Kenneth Brower, literally "left their universe." They had none of Cook's navigational instruments and charts, relying instead upon an inner sense, an internal navigation system programmed by intuition, knowledge, and experience. The European explorers, too, ventured into an unknown, but it was a reasonably comfortable one referenced on a round planet consisting of magnetic poles and invisible lines of longitude and latitude. Wherever he was, however mysterious and far from home, the European navigator had a piece of paper with directions for guidance.

The Polynesian navigator's view of the world was more limited. Not dependent on inscribed lines of latitude and longitude, he used an eclectic mix of information and clues to chart a steady course, studying the behavior of birds like the plover, dolphins, and the color of the ocean and the clouds.

Most obvious, of course, were the stars. The early Polynesians did not use just one star, or even a dozen stars. They used hundreds of stars that were woven into a memorized tapestry of mnemonic chants that detailed hundreds of known course settings throughout the Pacific.

Based on observational and astronomical data accumulated over the years, it seems that

KAPU AND TABOO

Hawaiian life was regulated under systematic laws known as *kapu*. The English word "taboo" comes from the Tongan word "tabu".

LEFT: a helmeted warrior in a feather cape, drawn by a French artist in 1819. The helmet offered little head protection, however. Note the extensive tattoos.

Polynesians made the incredible 2,000-mile (3,200-km) journeys to Hawaii by fixing on two key stars – Sirius and Arcturus. Astronomers at the Bishop Museum in Honolulu note that "Sirius, the brightest star in the sky, passed almost directly over Tahiti and Raiatea (also called Hawa'iti). The present position of Sirius with respect to the equator has changed very little from that of the days of Polynesian voyaging. Arcturus, called Hokule'a by the Hawaiians and noted for its bright redness off the Big Dipper's handle, presently passes over the northern end of the island of Hawaii. At the time of the great voyaging it passed over the island of Kauai."

in Hawaii has been confirmed by carbon dating, and by comparison of fishhooks and adzes found in Hawaiian and Marquesan sites dating from approximately the same period. These new Hawaiians lived in relative isolation for several centuries after the first migrations, but about 650 or 750 years later, sometime between 800 and 1200, Polynesians from Tahiti began arriving over a period of two centuries on the islands they referred to as Hawaiia, or Burning Hawaii, believed to be a reference to Hawaii's volcanoes.

Scholars have speculated that this second wave of Polynesians subjugated the earlier Marquesans as slaves, or perhaps drove them far-

Some of the most skilled Polynesian navigators did not use the stars at all. Perhaps because their boats were considerably smaller than the large European sailing ships, the Polynesians "felt" the ocean more, sensing its subtle moods and messages, just as a sports car driver today feels the road better than a bus driver. The Polynesian navigator felt the ocean, literally, in the direction of swells and in the subtle interference of waves that were reflected off distant islands.

Discovery of Hawaii

The first discoverers and settlers of Hawaii are believed to have arrived sometime between AD 200 and 500. Evidence of Marquesan landfalls

ther north in the Hawaiian chain until they were completely eliminated. The Tahitian immigration to Hawaii ended and the settled newcomers lived in isolation for several centuries, developing into the Hawaiian culture that would later greet Captain Cook.

Conquered Marquesans may have been the *manahune*, or *menehune*, mentioned in early Hawaiian and Tahitian chants. The term *manahune* was used derisively in the Tahitian homeland to refer to slaves or plebeian castes, but its meaning changed through the centuries to mean, probably sarcastically, the mysterious gnomes who lived on the Hawaiian Islands during the Tahitian migrations of the 12th to 14th centuries.

Offspring of Tahiti

Both Marquesans and Tahitians brought with them a similar language, as well as foods, myths, traditions, and gods. It was the Tahitian, however, who is credited with bequeathing the name "Hawaii", which was first given to the largest of the islands, now commonly called the Big Island, and later to the complete chain of islands. As the Polynesian bard Kamahualele chanted centuries ago, "Behold Hawaii, an island, a people/The people of Hawaii are the offspring of Tahiti."

Sir Peter Buck, the eminent half-Maori ethnologist who once served as the Bishop Museum's director, explained the origin of the

relationship is exemplified by the ancient name of a channel located south of Maui, between the smaller Hawaiian islands of Lanai and Kaho'olawe. The channel's Hawaiian name is Kealaikahiki. By substituting the letter k in the word with t, the word *te-ala-i-tahiti* is formed, which translates as "the pathway to Tahiti," or "the pathway to foreign lands."

Early life

When the first Polynesian canoes landed on Hawaiian shores, probably on or near the southernmost point of the Big Island, the islands were almost an unspoiled paradise. Although much

VOYAGES OF THE *HOKULE'A*

In the constellation Bootes, the star Arcturus is a zenith star for Hawaii, meaning that it passes directly overhead daily. In Hawaiian, the star is called *Hokule'a* – star of gladness.

In the 1970s, a Polynesian-style voyaging canoe was built to recreate the journeys of ancient Polynesians to Hawaii. It was named *Hokule'a*. Navigation by Mau Piailug and Nainoa Thompson, his student, used only the stars and ocean swells. Since then, *Hokule'a* has made several successful voyages between Hawaii and southern Polynesia. *Hokule'a* was joined in the 1990s on expeditions by a sister canoe, *Hawai'iloa*. Unlike *Hokule'a*, made from modern materials, *Hawai'iloa* is constructed of materials closer to those used by early Polynesians.

When not out exploring, *Hokule'a* is berthed at Honolulu's Hawaii Maritime Center.

word Hawaii in his book, *Vikings of the Pacific*, published in 1938. He noted that in ancient times "the headquarters of the Polynesian main body was established in the largest island of the leeward group of Tahiti, named Havai'i after an ancient homeland."

As Tahiti-based fleets set out to settle the Society Islands, Samoa, Tonga, Fiji, Hawaii, and New Zealand, they established colonies often named after their home island. Dialectal differences resulted in today's place name variations. An even more persuasive Hawaii-Tahiti

LEFT: masked canoe rowers, sketched in 1779 by an artist with Captain Cook. ABOVE: a gourd mask.

of the land was barren and dusty, some 2,200 kinds of plants unique to the Hawaiian Islands managed to thrive among the scrub. The islands' undisturbed shoreline reefs and lagoons, fern forests, alluvial plains, and well-watered valleys and highlands were rich with indigenous flora and fauna. Symbols so prominent in 21st-century Hawaii – coconuts, orchids, sugar-cane, pineapples – were introduced to Hawaii from elsewhere.

When the first Marquesans arrived, they found nearly 70 varieties of indigenous Hawaiian birds, about two dozen of which are now believed to be extinct. But neither amphibia (frogs, newts, and the like), nor reptiles, nor mosquitoes, lice, fleas, flies, or gnats were to be found. And for nearly 1,000 years, until mariners began arriving from the East and West, most fatal or even debilitating diseases were also absent.

The *malihini*, or newcomer, Polynesians found only two mammals in Hawaii: the hoary bat, which had somehow migrated from either North or South America, and the monk seal, a relative of seals found in the Caribbean and the Mediterranean. The hoary bat, known as the *'ope'ape'a* to Hawaiians, still haunts the nights of Big Island's Kilauea Crater area. The

make *kapa* (bark cloth), and the *ti*, a relative of the lily whose roots and leaves are still used as wrapping and matting, and for making hula skirts and a liquor called *'okolehao* (lit. iron bottom).

Most of what we now know regarding ancient Hawaiian life is from poetic oral traditions, known in the local language as *mele*. In these *mele*, the Hawaiians' *kupuna*, or ancestors, passed on to their descendants all they knew of their history. Various aspects of physical and spiritual life, from the trivial to the momentous,

POETIC RAPTURE

Where is Kumukahi?
He is at Hau'ula.
He has settled down,
enraptured by a statue.

— The Legend of Halemano

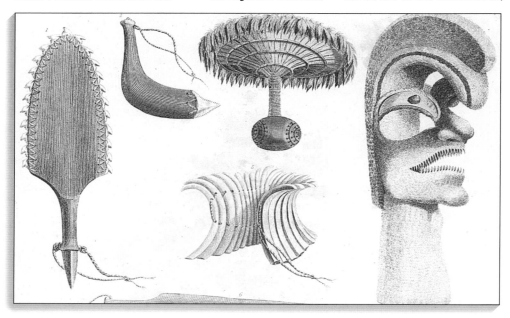

monk seal, nearly slaughtered into extinction for its valuable skin and oil during the 1800s, now rarely ventures near populated islands.

Introduced plants and animals

The arriving Polynesians upset Hawaii's ecological balance with dogs, pigs, chickens, and, probably unintentionally, the first stowaway rats. To supplement their diet, the first Hawaiians also introduced taro, a starchy tuber from which the grey, pasty mush called *poi* is made. Also introduced were coconuts, bananas, yams, *kukui* (candlenuts), wild ginger, breadfruit, and sugar-cane. Then came utility plants like the *wauke*, or paper mulberry, which was beaten and sun-bleached to

were reported in this unwritten literature, which consisted of family genealogies, myths, and day-to-day accounts of human experiences.

Other insights about early Hawaii come from the initial observations made by foreign explorers such as James Cook, George Vancouver, and Otto von Kotzebue. Additionally, there are the important memoirs of early Hawaiian scholars, notably John Papa Ii (1800–70), Samuel Kamakau (1815–76), Kepelino Keauokalani (1830–78), and David Malo (1793–1853).

Another source has been the antiquities and folklore collected by Abraham Fornander (1812–87), a surveyor, editor, and judge. Fornander, who was married to a Hawaiian woman, spoke and wrote the Hawaiian language fluently. He wrote a history of the islands entitled, *An Account of the Polynesian Race: Its Origins and Migrations*. He also collected and translated many Hawaiian chants into English.

According to the information offered by these chroniclers, the people of Hawaii developed one of the most complex non-technological cultures ever encountered by early Europeans.

Kapu life

Hawaiian life was simple and straightforward, regulated under systematic laws known as *kapu*, a variation of the Tahitian word *tapu*, from dancers. The labor and working class, *maka'ainana* or commoners, worked the land. At the very bottom were the social outcasts, the slaves or *kauwa maoli*. Sometimes the unfortunate *kauwa* were marked by tattoos on their foreheads, and they were often summarily conscripted as sacrificial victims by the priestly *kahuna*.

Under this hierarchy, the tightly circumscribed *kapu* and bloodlines could not be crossed. A typical penalty for a *kapu* violation was execution by stoning, clubbing, or strangulation; sometimes violators were buried or burned alive. Sometimes a *kapu*-breaker was singled out as a convenient sacrificial victim for a god,

where the word "taboo" originates. At the time of the first contact with Europeans, Hawaiian society was feudal and defined mostly by island, with two or three *mo'i*, or kings, struggling for control of each island. Ranking below the kings were hereditary groups of *ali'i*, or noblemen. Nearly on the same level as *ali'i* were the *kahuna*, a prestigious group including priests, healers, and astrologers. Lower down was a small class of craftsmen and artists, *kanaka wale*, who made the canoes, calabashes and *lei* (garlands). This class also included fishermen and hula

LEFT: articles of ceremony from early Hawaii.
ABOVE: an 1873 engraving of female surfers.

but usually he was sacrificed as a lesson to others. The Hawaiian scholar and historian David Malo has recounted that a person could be put to death for allowing his shadow to fall upon the house of a chief, or for passing through that chief's stockade or doorway, or for entering the house before changing his *malo* (loincloth). He could also be executed because he appeared before the chief with his head smeared by mud. Other common *kapu* declared that women could not eat pork, coconuts, bananas, and shark meat, nor could they eat with men.

Certain seasons were established for the gathering or catching of scarce plants or animals for food, probably as conservation measures.

Sometimes sporting chiefs declared certain surfing-spots *kapu* for their own exclusive use. Some *kapu* were instigated by Machiavellian chiefs, priests or influential court retainers under the guise of religion, or to tyrannically oppress a person or group of people. Many of the laws, however, were simply to protect resources and assure social stability.

Kapu violators had a place where they could seek sanctuary, whatever their crime. These places of refuge, called *pu'uhonua*, had to be reached by the transgressor before he was caught. The odds, of course, were against the transgressor. A good example of a *pu'uhonua* is

located on a lava promontory at Pu'uhonua O Honaunau National Historical Park, on the Big Island's Kona coast. This *kapu* system affected every aspect of Hawaiian life, from birth to death, until it was abolished in 1819 by King Kamehameha II and the queen regent, Ka'ahumanu. But until its abolition, *kapu* protected the powers of Hawaiian kings.

Worship

Hawaiians generally worshiped privately and at small shrines they built in their homes or outdoors, but the focal points of most major religious observances were large open-air temples known as *heiau*. Ruins of these *heiau* can be

seen throughout Hawaii. In most cases, what remains today are rudimentary platforms, terraces and walls made of large lava stones. In ancient times, they housed *kapa*-covered oracle towers, sacrificial platform-altars, carved stone and wooden sculptures, images of gods made of thatch and feathers, sacred stones, rough-hewn monoliths, groupings of wood and stone sub-temple structures, and often a disposal pit for decayed human, animal, or plant offerings.

The most complex temples were those built by Hawaiian chiefs to initiate a war. These *heiau waikaua* (war temples), also called *luakini*, were kept spiritually "alive" by periodic human sacrifices. Once it had been decided to wage war and proper sacrifices had been made to Ku, the war god, the high chief would call for his *kilo lani* (astrologer) to determine the most auspicious day to do battle. Exceptional power might be elicited from the gods by sacrificing an enemy chief at the *luakini*.

War and arts

Given the generally clannish and feudalistic structure of ancient Hawaiian society, wars were frequent. Periodic and courtly sham battles were held between friendly chiefs to keep young warriors prepped and alert. This system of fore-arming and forewarning was reminiscent of European days of chivalry.

The ritual aspects of Hawaiian wars quickly gave way to brutality. There might be some opening decorum, gladiator-style, in which two renowned warriors would fight to the death in front of opposing armies. But more often than not, the two armies would meet on an impromptu or chosen battleground, usually during daylight hours and following an exchange of verbal taunts and insults, and commence battle.

Common Hawaiian weapons included spears up to 18 feet (5 meters) in length, shorter javelins, assorted daggers (some lined with shark teeth), stone-headed clubs, serrated shark-tooth clubs, a variety of sennit-and-stone tripping weapons, slingshots, strangling cords, and any and all objects (rocks, boulders, branches) that could be spontaneously introduced into the fray by resourceful warriors.

But life in ancient times was not an endless cycle of war-making, oppression, and workaday drudgery. Hawaiians developed unique forms of recreation, including such diversions as kite-flying, puppet theater and staged dances, numerous games of skill and chance, archery (used to kill rodents), tobogganing on *holua* sleds that were raced down specially prepared hillside runways; and surfing, known as *he'e nalu*.

The Hawaiians also created the most exquisite variety of fine artwork and personal adornments found anywhere in Polynesia. Wood and stone sculpture was graphic and bold, while Hawaii's delicate featherwork is still considered to be the finest example of this art to be found. James Cook, in describing Hawaiian featherwork, observed that "the

Hawaiian *kapa*, the soft bark-cloth fashioned from bast of the paper mulberry, also represents a major artistic achievement. Strips of bark were first soaked, then beaten until they were smooth and paper thin. The cloth was then decorated by bamboo stamps with intricate designs carved on them, inked by dyes made from the leaves, bark, fruit, and roots of various plants.

Perhaps the most diverse art practiced by the Hawaiians was body adornment in the form of necklaces, headbands, and anklets made of flowers, nuts,

FEATHERY PATIENCE

A chief's feather cloak could take decades to complete, requiring some 450,000 feathers plucked from an estimated 80,000 birds.

surface might be compared to the thickest and richest velvet." His lieutenant, James King, suggested that the "feathered cloak and helmet… in point of beauty and magnificence, is perhaps nearly equal to that of any nation in the world."

It would be impossible today to duplicate one of these cloaks, because most of the birds whose feathers were plucked for use have since become extinct. In old Hawaii, the king commissioned specially selected groups of royal feather-pluckers who stalked and snared their preferred prey with nets and long sticky wands.

LEFT: wooden image of *Kakailimoku*, the war god.
ABOVE: admiring a temple's carved deities.

seeds, shells, ivory, teeth, turtle shells, human hair, and other natural materials. Tattooing, too, was popular, often as an expression of mourning. Both men and women tattooed their bodies with a variety of designs: some were of a topical nature, but there were also repetitive motifs, usually geometric patterns. The design was rubbed into the skin with small sharp needles made of fish and bird bones, or shells.

Tattooing is still practiced in other parts of Polynesia and has long been popular in nautical circles. In Hawaii, tattooing was condemned by the missionaries and had largely disappeared until the late 1980s, when it was revived as a way of asserting native Hawaiian identity. ❑

ARRIVAL OF CAPTAIN COOK

Captain James Cook was noted for his sensitivity to the cultures he encountered during his global explorations. Still, after his arrival, Hawaii changed immensely

Hawaii's modern era began in 1778, with excitement and terror, when Hawaiians on the island of Oahu saw two strange, white-winged objects moving at sea. These floating islands, as the Hawaiians were to describe them, were the British ships HMS *Resolution* and HMS *Discovery*, commanded by Captain James Cook.

En route from the South Pacific to the north – and, it was hoped, an elusive Northwest Passage – Cook and his crew, which included an astronomer and artist assigned to the expedition by the British Admiralty, had accidentally become the first known non-Polynesians to land on the Hawaiian islands. It was a formidable find, the last significant land on Earth to be found by Europeans. In his ship's log, Cook later suggested that finding Hawaii was "in many respects the most important discovery made by Europeans throughout the extent of the Pacific Ocean." Cook marveled at the existence of the Polynesian settlements: "How shall we account for this nation spreading itself so far over this vast ocean...?" Cook named these isles the Sandwich Islands, in honor of Cook's patron, the Earl of Sandwich, First Lord of the Admiralty.

Oahu was the first island to be sighted, but Cook passed by and continued on to the northeast, making landfall on 21 January 1778 at Waimea, on Kauai's west coast. After five days of replenishment and sightseeing, including a visit to impressive Waimea Valley, strong winds at night blew his ships away from Kauai and nearer to the smaller island of Ni'ihau. There, Cook's men received salt and yams from the islanders in exchange for goats, pigs, and the seeds of melons, pumpkins, and onions. Western flora and fauna were thus introduced.

Also introduced, against Cook's explicitly posted orders, were syphilis, gonorrhea, and other European diseases. All too aware of the effects of introduced diseases on indigenous peoples, Cook had told his men clearly that no Hawaiian women were to be allowed on board the ships, nor any person "having or suspected of having the venereal disease or any symptoms thereof, shall lie with any woman" under threat of severe lashing at the ship's masthead.

Thomas Edgar, master of the *Discovery*, said his men employed every devious scheme possible to get women on board the ships, even "dressing them up as men." But he noted also that the Hawaiian women "used all arts to entice them into their houses and even went so far as to endeavour to draw them in by force."

In February, Cook left Hawaii to continue his search for the Northwest Passage, taking his two ships far above the Arctic Circle. As winter again approached, Cook returned to Hawaii, sighting Maui in November. For two months, the *Discovery* and *Resolution* charted the islands, first Maui then the Big Island. Coming around the Big Island's southern tip from the east, Cook anchored along the Kona coast in a bay called Kealakekua, the "pathway of the god." It was exactly one year since his first landfall in Kauai.

LEFT: the British navigator James Cook. **RIGHT:** Cook receives special offering at his Kealakekua welcome.

If Cook was impressed a year earlier by the way Hawaiians on Kauai had prostrated themselves in his presence, he must have been even more impressed by his reception at Kealakekua Bay; Cook's second coming was monumental. He arrived at a propitious time: the *makahiki* celebration, an annual tribute to the god Lonoikamakahiki – and Cook's auspicious arrival was identified by the Hawaiians as Lono's return. Consequently, Cook was afforded the greatest welcome ever accorded a mortal in Hawaii.

One of Cook's lieutenants estimated that 10,000 Hawaiians turned out in canoes, on surfboards, swimming in the bay, and waiting on shore to greet the return of Lono. Cook wrote, "I have nowhere in this sea seen such a number of people assembled in one place; besides those in the canoes, all the shore of the bay was covered with people, and hundreds were swimming about the ship like shoals of fish." John Ledyard, an American adventurer who had signed on board the *Resolution* as corporal of the marines, reported later that two officers counted from 2,500 to 3,500 canoes afloat in Kealakekua's waters. Ledyard and others also described unusual white *kapa* (bark cloth) banners held aloft on crossbars – an ancient symbol of Lono – which resembled the ships' masts and sails. Ledyard

An OFFERING before CAP.ᵗ COOK, in the SANDWICH ISLANDS.

THE *HAOLE* ARRIVE

"The ship was first sighted from Waialua and Wai'anae (on Oahu) sailing for the north. It anchored at night at Waimea, on the island of Kauai, that particular place being nearest at hand. A man named Moapu and his companions who were fishing with heavy lines saw this strange thing move by and saw the lights… they hurried ashore and hastened to tell Ka'eo and the other chiefs of Kauai about this strange apparition.

"The next morning the ship lay outside Ka'ahe at Waimea. Chiefs and commoners saw the wonderful sight and marveled at it. Some were terrified and shrieked with fear. The valley of Waimea rang with the shouts of the excited people as they saw the boat with its masts and sails shaped like a gigantic stingray. One asked another, 'What are those branching things?' and the other answered, 'They are trees moving on the sea.' A certain *kahuna* named Kuohu declared, 'That can be nothing else than the heiau of Lono, the tower of Keolewa, and the place of sacrifice at the altar.' The excitement became more intense…"

– Samuel M. Kamakau
19th-century Hawaiian author and historian

wrote that when Cook went onshore, the masses of Hawaiians "all bowed and covered their faces with their hands until he was passed."

There were extravagant ceremonies held in Cook's honor, including one at a sacred temple, or *heiau*. Cook and his men tried their best to please the Hawaiians with tours of their ships, a flute and violin concert, and a fireworks display. All the while, Cook readied his ships for a voyage to Asia, and after two weeks, they set sail. But three days later, just off the Big Island's north shore, a fierce winter storm damaged the *Resolution*'s foremast. Cook returned to Kealakekua to make essential repairs.

Death of Cook

Cook found that the *makahiki* festival at Kealakekua was finished, and because of a *kapu* put on Kealakekua Bay by King Kalaniopu'u, the area was nearly deserted. The Hawaiians who remained were not as generous in their tribute, and in fact were surprised that a god's property could be badly damaged within his own domain.

The Hawaiians grew increasingly bold, taking objects from the ships that pleased their fancy, particularly things made of metal. When they took the *Discovery*'s cutter, Cook went ashore with nine marines to take Kalaniopu'u hostage in exchange for return of the boat, a

strategy that had worked before on other Pacific islands. A scuffle broke out, and a large party of over 200 Hawaiian warriors attacked Cook's landing party. Five of the marines escaped, but four others, as well as Cook himself, died. The British ships fired on the Hawaiians, who retreated.

Two delegations of concerned Hawaiians later returned parts of Cook's body "cut to pieces and all burnt," wrote James King, Cook's second lieutenant. One bundle of Cook's bones, wrapped in fine *kapa* and a cloak made of black and white feathers, included "the captain's hands (which were well known from a remark-

---

WERE THE SPANISH FIRST?

Spanish ships may have landed in Hawaii up to two centuries before Cook. Historians offer unexplained artifacts, including a map taken by the British in 1742 from a captured Spanish galleon. The map was "a chart of the northern Pacific which marked the track of the round trip between the Philippines and Acapulco." It showed islands in approximately the same latitude as Hawaii. Additionally:

• The galleon trade between Mexico and Manila began in 1556, lasting 200 years. Odds that a galleon would happen onto Hawaii, at the same latitude as Mexico City, are good.

• Early Western visitors reported island residents with distinctly Caucasian features.

• Hawaiian feather cloaks and helmets — not found elsewhere in Polynesia — with a Spanish look and usually of red and yellow, the royal colors of Spain, were found in Hawaii.

---

able cut), the scalp, the skull, wanting the lower jaw, thigh bones and arm bone; the hands only had flesh on them, and were cut in holes, and salt crammed in; the leg bones, lower jaw and feet, which were all that remained and had escaped the fire, he said were dispersed among other chiefs."

What remained of Cook was buried at Kealakekua Bay, and in late February of 1779, the *Discovery* and *Resolution* set sail, passing Maui, Molokai and Oahu before anchoring again briefly at Waimea, on Kauai. ❑

LEFT: the warrior's helmet appears Spanish in style.
RIGHT: this Spanish map may show Hawaii as Los Mojas.

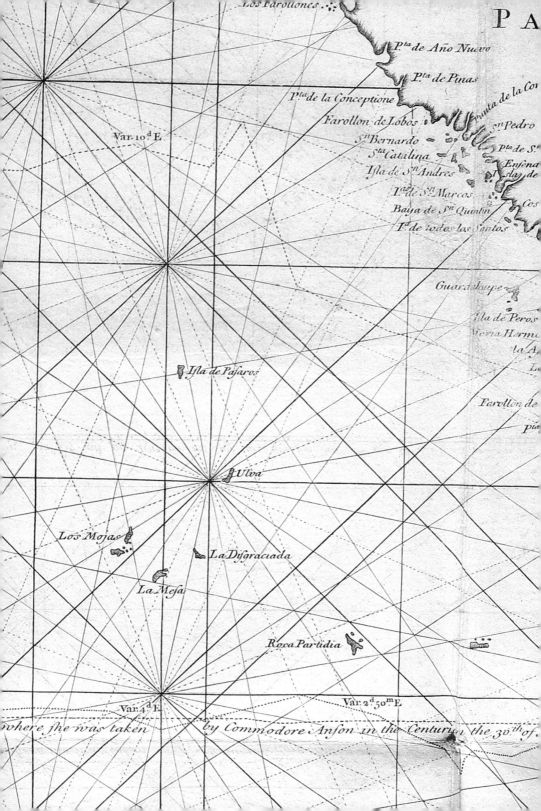

Los Farollones

P A

P.ta de Año Nuevo

P.ta de Pinas

P.ta de la Conceptione

Punta de la Co

Farollon de Lobos

S.n Pedro

S.n Bernardo

P.ta de S.

S.ta Catalina

Ensena

Isla de S.n Andres

sla de

I.de de S.n Marcos

Cos

Baya de S.n Quintin

I.s de todos las Santos

Guardaluipe

Isla de Peros

Var. 10.d E.

Maria Herma

la A.

Le

Farollon de

pia

Isla de Pajaros

Ulva

Los Mojas

La Disgraciada

La Mesa

Roca Partidia

Var. 4.d E.

Var. 2.d 50.m E.

where she was taken   by Commodore Anson in the Centurion the 30.th of

Lauvergne del

SCÈNE DE DANSE

SOUVENIR.

ALOHA OE

(My love to you.)

MARCH.

The Queen Kapiolani. *The Princess Liliuokalani.*

Composed and arranged by

J. THOMAS BALDWIN.

Incorporating the popular Song "Aloha Oe"

BY THE

Princess Liliuokalani

And performed by

BALDWIN'S BOSTON CADET BAND

AT THE

Grand Reception given by the City of Boston to

Queen Kapiolani and Princess Liliuokalani

May 12th 1887.

THE HAWAIIAN MONARCHY

The monarchy of Hawaii began with Kamehameha the Great, who united the Hawaiian islands. It ended with the overthrow of Queen Lili'uokalani

It would be over five years after Cook's death before other Europeans visited Hawaii. In 1785, a China-bound trading ship stopped for supplies, and in the following year, four ships from England and France visited the islands. They were followed by Russian, Spanish and American ships. Soon frigates, sloops and schooners laden with American furs began dropping anchor in Hawaii. Most were bound for Macau, Shanghai, and Guangzhou (Canton), where the furs would be traded for silks and tea.

Kamehameha I (1795–1819)

Often mentioned in the logs and diaries of visiting ships' captains and merchants was Kamehameha, which means "the lonely one." A distinguished warrior and one of King Kalaniopu'u's nephews and chief subordinates, Kamehameha (pron. *ka may-ha may-ha*) had impressed Cook at Kealakekua Bay. Cook's lieutenant, James King, wrote that Kamehameha's hair "was now plaisted over with a brown dirty sort of paste or powder, and which added to as savage a looking face as I ever saw, it however by no means seemed an emblem of his disposition, which was good natured and humorous, although his manner showed somewhat of an overbearing spirit, and he seemed to be the principal director in this interview."

Kamehameha was a careful observer of the *haole* (Caucasians). He had been wounded by a gun on the beach when Cook was killed, and it was evident to Kamehameha that one man with a small brass cannon could have a great advantage over several warriors with clubs and spears. By 1789, Kamehameha's own large double canoe was carrying a swivel gun mounted on a platform strapped across the hulls.

A 10-year civil war involving Kamehameha and others erupted on the Big Island in 1782. When the timing seemed astrologically and mil-

itarily propitious, Kamehameha conquered Maui and Lanai in 1790. He then returned to the Big Island to deal with the continuing civil war there. Keoua, his chief rival on the Big Island, was displeased at how the inheritance was divided.

In the meantime, Kamehameha lost Maui, whose own chief then invaded Kamehameha's

Big Island domain with a fleet of war canoes. Kamehameha repelled the Maui invaders, assisted by the swivel guns and military expertise of Englishmen John Young and Isaac Davis, who had been taken in by Kamehameha as advisers and later made high chiefs. Keoua, Kamehameha's Big Island rival, however, was not yielding easily.

Kamehameha took no chances. He built an immense *heiau* (temple) to his war god near Kawaihae in Kohala – it still stands – and invited Keoua to meet him there. When Keoua arrived, Kamehameha had him killed.

Kamehameha was now king of all the Big Island. He recaptured Maui, then Molokai. In the

PRECEDING PAGES: French seamen enjoy an Oahu hula extravaganza. **LEFT:** Royalty were not above music and performances. **RIGHT:** Kamehameha the Great, looking uncomfortably dressed.

meantime, a small civil war had broken out on Oahu, and Kamehameha took advantage of the disorder to land with his fleet in southern Oahu in 1795. In a mighty display of military strength, Kamehameha and his warriors drove Oahu's remaining army up Nu'uanu Valley and over the edge of Nu'uanu Pali, a precipitous cliff. With Oahu's conquest – and the ritual sacrifice of it's king, Kalanikupule, to Kamehameha's war god – Kamehameha was monarch of all of Hawaii, except Kauai and Ni'ihau, more than 70 miles (110 km) west of Oahu.

In 1796 and 1809, Kamehameha assembled invasion fleets destined for Kauai and Ni'ihau,

Kamehameha the Great died after a long illness in 1819, near a favorite *heiau* known as Kamaka Honu – the Eye of the Turtle – in what is now Kailua-Kona town on the Big Island. He was about 63 years old. So that nobody could defile them or use their powerful *mana* (spirit), Kamehameha's bones were hidden in a secret place somewhere on the Kona coast.

Kamehameha II (1819–24)

Kamehameha's son and successor, Liholiho, was not a strong and commanding ruler like his father. But Ka'ahumanu, the favorite of Kamehameha the Great's many wives, was intelligent,

the most distant of the main islands. The channel from Oahu to Kauai is treacherous, and the invasion attempts were foiled by the weather and disease. In 1810, Kauai's king peacefully yielded to Kamehameha. The islands were unified under King Kamehameha I, or Kamehameha the Great.

Although Kamehameha retained the traditional ways, he also learned those of the Europeans whose ships he supplied with provisions. Hawaii's sandalwood proved a lucrative trade for Kamehameha, and he directed commoners by the thousands to harvest it for shipment to Asia. Exports continued until there were no more sandalwood trees in the islands. In the meantime, agriculture suffered from neglect.

CIVILIZED MISSIONARIES

Rev. Hiram Bingham, unofficial leader of the first group of Christian missionaries to Hawaii, wrote of his followers' impressions: "The appearance of destitution, degradation, and barbarism among the chattering, and almost naked savages, whose heads and feet, and much of their sunburnt skins were bare, was appalling. Some of our number, with gushing tears, turned away from the spectacle. Others, with firmer nerve, continued their gaze, but were ready to exclaim, 'Can these be human beings? Can such things be civilized?'"

fearless, and powerful. Upon Kamehameha's death, she made it clear to Liholiho that it was his father's wish that she be the *kuhina nui*, the joint ruler or queen regent of Hawaii.

One of Ka'ahumanu's first actions was to abolish the ancient *kapu* system. Urged on by Ka'ahumanu, Liholiho sat down with her at a feast, violating the *kapu* that prohibited men and women from eating together. Ka'ahumanu and Liholiho then ordered that all the *heiau* and carved wooden idols be destroyed. The social and cultural shock to Hawaiians was enormous, leaving an overwhelming spiritual vacuum.

The vacuum didn't last long. The first party of 14 New England missionaries arrived in 1820 aboard the American brig *Thaddeus*, ready to fill the religious void. Had the timing of the *kapu* collapse and the arrival of the missionaries not been so coincidental, the history of post-contact Hawaii could have been very different.

Although Ka'ahumanu and Liholiho had reservations about these overdressed *haole*, they let the American missionaries preach at Kailua-Kona and Honolulu for a one-year trial. The missionaries never left, and their descendants garnered land and power.

The English had retained an interest in Hawaii since Cook's first contact, and in 1822 Liholiho received a gift from King George IV: a small schooner named the *Prince Regent*. Delighted, Liholiho left Hawaii the next year on a British whaling ship to visit King George and negotiate a treaty. Liholiho and his entourage were royally feted in London, but before he could meet with King George, he and his queen, Kamamalu, caught the measles and died. Before setting sail for England, Liholiho had dictated a will that designated his younger brother Kauikeaouli, who was Kamehameha the Great's sole surviving son, as his logical successor.

Kamehameha III (1825–54)

The early years of Kauikeaouli – Kamehameha III – would better be called the reign of Ka'ahumanu. Kauikeaouli was only 10 years old when his brother Liholiho died. As *kuhina nui*, Ka'ahumanu exerted a strong influence on both the boy king and the Hawaiian people, most of whom were still disoriented and adrift after the demise of the *kapu* system.

LEFT: Queen Ka'ahumanu in an 1816 sketch.
RIGHT: Hawaii's first royal coat-of-arms.

Half a year after Liholiho left on his ill-fated trip to England, Ka'ahumanu had announced a system of civil laws obviously based on the Congregationalist missionaries' teachings. In fact, the Congregationalists had cultivated considerable spiritual and political influence over Ka'ahumanu, eventually converting her to Christianity. Ka'ahumanu became one of the Congregationalists' most enthusiastic converts. Another convert to Christianity was an *ali'i* peer, the Big Island high chiefess Kapi'olani.

In 1824, Kapi'olani (not to be confused with her niece and namesake, the future Queen Kapi'olani) hiked to the mouth of Halema'uma'u

PRECURSOR OF HAWAII'S COAT OF ARMS
Prepared in London in 1843–44 at the order of Timothy Haalilio and the Reverend William Richards

in the Kilauea caldera. There, at the edge of the fire goddess Pele's domain, Kapi'olani defiantly renounced her. She lived to tell the tale, and at the Hilo Congregationalist mission, 90 impressed Hawaiians instantly became new converts.

Encouraged by the royal support, missionaries built churches and schools throughout the islands. Even more, as "messengers of Jehovah," the missionaries used their court influence to veil Hawaiians with everything Puritan. Bare skin on women in any degree – much less nudity – was condemned, and women were draped in dresses mostly ill-suited to the tropics. The ancient and sacred *hula*, a dance of communication and poetry, was outlawed as lewd and lascivious.

Equally high on the agenda was putting the Hawaiian language into romanized script. The missionaries' intent in doing so was evangelical, no doubt, but teaching Hawaiians to read and write gave them a new tool with which to communicate their own histories and thought, especially as the missionaries had suppressed traditional storytelling methods like the *hula*.

When Ka'ahumanu died in 1832, Kamehameha III took full control of the government in a reign noted for a couple of frivolous early years of horseracing, gambling, drinking, and dancing. His half-sister, Kina'u, the *kuhina nui* and successor to Ka'ahumanu, managed state

matters during his bouts with the bottle. The missionaries continued to consolidate power, accepting government appointments.

In the mid 1820s, just as the sandalwood trees had all but disappeared in the islands, whaling became Hawaii's major source of revenue, with Honolulu and Lahaina among the Pacific's most important ports. Whaling kept Hawaii's economy above water for over 30 years. At its peak in 1846, 429 ships were anchored in Maui's Lahaina Harbor.

The missionaries, of course, protested the extracurricular activities of sailors on liberty. One visiting preacher in the early 1840s complained that Lahaina had become "one of the breathing holes of hell… a sight to make a missionary weep." Attempts by the missionaries to quench liquor and prostitution were not well received, and the homes of several preachers in Lahaina were bombarded with cannon by angry sailors from aboard the safety of anchored ships.

Perhaps Kamehameha III's most significant act was an irreversible edict issued in 1848, which became known as the Great Mahele. Under subtle pressure by missionary advisers and businessmen, the king divided Hawaii's land ownership – previously the pleasure of the royalty – among the monarchy, government, and common people, thus allowing working-class Hawaiians to own property for the first time.

Two years later, foreigners also were permitted land ownership. Within a few years, the *haole* had accumulated large estates of land; by 1886, about two-thirds of all government lands sold had been bought by resident *haole*. Hawaiians, unfamiliar with land ownership, had done little to thwart the foreigners' acquisitions.

By the late 1850s, whales had been hunted nearly to extinction, petroleum and coal were replacing whale oil, and the United States was sinking into a civil war. The boom days of the Hawaiian Islands were over.

Hawaii's business and political interests turned from whaling to a new commodity, sugar. During California's gold rush in 1849, a handful of small sugar planters in Hawaii had made great profits when Kaleponi – California – turned to Hawaii for its sugar supply. Sugar's potential looked sweet, especially for those with the land under the cane. Whereas whaling had been mostly a merchants' boom, sugar would be a land barons' boom. But sugar plantations are labor intensive, and the local pool of laborers was almost nil, as the population had been devastated by disease. More pragmatically, Hawaiians saw little merit in the low-paying, backbreaking work of harvesting sugar-cane, especially as the islands offered plenty of traditional foods.

For sugar to become a major industry, thousands of laborers needed to be imported. The first group of 293 Chinese arrived in 1852, followed over the decades by Japanese, Portuguese, Filipinos, Norwegians, Germans, Koreans, Puerto Ricans, Spaniards, and Russians. A significant percentage of Hawaii's ethnic mix today descends from those early immigrant laborers.

The 30-year reign of Kamehameha III, the longest of any Hawaiian monarch, was one of considerable change and adjustment, and often stability and growth; foreign ways were also adopted. The king established a supreme court, an upper house of royalty and a lower house of elected representatives. Kamehameha III had no children and named a nephew, Alexander Liholiho, as his successor.

Kamehameha IV (1855–63)

Alexander Liholiho, grandson of Kamehameha the Great, had a certain dislike for America, and

AMERICAN MEMORY

In America, a train conductor in New York City mistook the future Kamehameha IV for a servant and ordered him out of the railway car. That unpleasant memory of America lingered long.

titute Hawaiians, many of who were still suffering from introduced European diseases.

In 1863, after the death of his son, Kamehameha IV died aged 29 during an asthma attack. Some Hawaiians said that he simply drank himself to death, while others said that he died of a broken heart.

Kamehameha V (1863–72)

A believer in the strong, autocratic style of Kamehameha the Great, Lot Kamehameha, an

during his short reign, he shifted Hawaii closer to the British Empire in both spirit and policy.

Educated by Americans at an elite royal school, Kamehameha IV and a brother had visited Europe and America in 1849 and 1850. Their experiences in Europe, especially England, were enjoyable and enriching, but not so in America.

Alexander Liholiho was not a mover and shaker, but he left behind a legacy of concern for Hawaiians. One that remains today is the Queen's Medical Center, established by him and his wife, Queen Emma, in 1859 to care for sick and des-

elder brother of Kamehameha IV, refused to take an oath to uphold the liberal constitution of 1852. He believed that it weakened the powers of the Hawaiian monarchy, making it vulnerable to overthrow by non-royalists, a forethought that later turned out to be true.

In 1864, Lot declared a special convention to revise the constitution. This convention accomplished nothing, so the king offered a new constitution that abolished the matriarchal office of *kuhina nui*, set up a one-chamber legislature for nobles and elected representatives, and required that persons born after 1840 pass literacy tests and meet certain property qualifications before being allowed to vote or serve in the legislature.

LEFT: a view of old Lahaina, on Maui, around 1870.
ABOVE: Kamehameha IV and Kamehameha V.

His act was in effect a bloodless but effective coup d'état. This strengthening of the monarchy led to increasing resentment among non-royalists – mostly foreign businessmen – and added fuel to the fire that would later bring down the monarchy.

Mark Twain wrote of Kamehameha V: "There was no trivial royal nonsense about him. He dressed plainly, poked about Honolulu, night or day, on his old horse, unattended; he was popular, greatly respected, even beloved." A bachelor, Lot left no

ROYAL RUMBLE

Queen Emma's backers rioted in protest after Kalakaua's selection. Several people were injured, one fatally, in a free-for-all fight inside and outside the election courthouse.

heir and named no successor. When he died aged 42, the 77-year-long dynasty of Kamehameha the Great ended.

William Lunalilo (1873–74)

Under the constitution of 1864, the legislative assembly unanimously elected Prince Lunalilo as king in 1873. It was a popular decision with the Hawaiians, who had already voted for him a week before. As popular as Lunalilo – or Prince Bill – was with the people, he was an alcoholic and ineffective in leadership. Thirteen months later he died without an heir. The kingdom's legislative assembly once again went about the sticky business of electing a new sovereign.

Kalakaua (1874–91)

There were two contenders for the throne: David Kalakaua, who had lost to Lunalilo in the previous election, and Queen Emma, widow of Kamehameha IV. After a spirited campaign, the assembly handily elected Kalakaua as king of Hawaii in 1874. Kalakaua's ancestors had been high chiefs on the Big Island.

Ruling with a flourish and style that earned him the nickname "the Merrie Monarch", Kalakaua ignored the calls for annexation and devoted his energy to fashioning his kingship in the courtly tradition of European monarchs. He built himself the magnificent 'Iolani Palace; embarked on a trip around the world; became the first monarch to circumnavigate the globe; and presented gala horse races, grand balls, and old-style Hawaiian feasts. During his reign, Kalakaua openly clashed with educators and Christians about restoring Hawaii's rapidly disappearing cultural traditions.

In 1874, the same year he ascended the throne, Kalakaua traveled to Washington, DC, hoping to negotiate a reciprocity treaty with the USA. He and his entourage were grandly received by President Ulysses S. Grant and a joint session of the Congress. Newspaper reporters described the state banquets arranged for Kalakaua as the most lavish they had ever seen in the nation's capital. Kalakaua subsequently received strong personal support from Grant. By the following year, the US Senate approved a treaty giving Hawaii "favored nation" duty concessions and thus eliminating tariffs on sugar. While the treaty was a triumph for the new king, it also gave America a lock on the islands, presaging its future interest in Pearl Harbor as a military base, and preventing Kalakaua from using Hawaii's location to gain concessions from Britain or France.

Perhaps most importantly for Hawaii's immediate future, the treaty gave the sugar-growers increased economic confidence and security. And, as would later become clear, the agreement gave the growers disproportionate political and social leverage, eventually weakening the Hawaiian monarchy's power.

A string of scandals began to taint Kalakaua's reign, to the self-righteous delight of the foreign business community. In 1887, an armed insurrection led by a *haole* political group called the Hawaiian League forced Kalakaua to accept a new "Bayonet Constitution" that seriously constrained his powers. This new constitution required that voters own at least $3,000 worth of property or have an income of at least $600 a year, requirements that effectively eliminated most Hawaiians from the political franchise. Power conclusively shifted to Hawaii's land-owning and predominantly white minority.

Two years later, a fiery part-Hawaiian revolutionary named Robert Wilcox staged a counter coup against the businessmen. He and about 150 armed followers loyal to the kingdom swash-

they didn't agree with his dubious money-raising schemes, usually concocted by Spreckels.

In 1891, while visiting California in an effort to restore his failing health, Kalakaua died in a San Francisco hotel suite. Before leaving Hawaii, Kalakaua had appointed his sister, Princess Lydia Kamakaeha Lili'uokalani, as regent during his absence. She became Hawaii's first and only reigning queen.

Lili'uokalani (1891–93)

Lili'uokalani was a staunch royalist. Right from the start, she made it clear that she planned to restore monarchical power and the rights of

buckled their way past the King's Guards and occupied 'Iolani Palace. But Wilcox's coup d'état failed miserably. Within hours, he and the other revolutionaries were flushed out with rifle fire and crude dynamite bombs laced with twenty-penny metal spikes. Seven of his men were dead and another 12 wounded.

For the remainder of his reign, Kalakaua was, for the most part, a figurehead monarch. Often at the service of the sugar baron and poker partner Claus Spreckels, who had arrived in Hawaii in 1876, Kalakaua dismissed cabinets when

---

LEFT: King Kalakaua, the Merrie Monarch and Hawaii's last king. **ABOVE:** US Marines from the *Boston*.

native Hawaiian people. Weary of the plodding cabinet government created by the Bayonet Constitution of 1887, she announced in 1893 that she would issue a new constitution placing power firmly back in the hands of the monarchy.

Pro-annexation, anti-royalist forces planned to overthrow the monarchy, to be followed by annexation negotiations with the United States. In January 1893, they launched their revolt after first enlisting John B. Stevens, the US minister in Hawaii. An ardent supporter of the pro-annexation movement, Stevens ordered the landing of Marines from the visiting gunship USS *Boston*, ostensibly to protect American lives and property – but without authorization from

Washington. That afternoon, some 160 armed Marines positioned artillery pieces and Gatling guns at strategic points in Honolulu, and by the next day, "without the drawing of a sword or the firing of a shot," a self-proclaimed government led by Sanford Dole was in power. Lili'uokalani had no choice but to abdicate her throne.

She believed that the American government, learning of the coup, would reinstate the monarchy. "I yield to the superior force of the United States of America," she protested to Sanford Dole, "to avoid any collision of armed forces and perhaps the loss of life. I do this under protest, and impelled by said force, yield my

authority until such time as the Government of the United States shall, upon the facts being presented to it, undo the action of its representatives and reinstate me in the authority which I claim as the constitutional sovereign of the Hawaiian Islands."

Unlike his predecessor, newly elected President, Grover Cleveland did not support the coup, and he dispatched a special investigator to Honolulu to investigate. The investigator arrived in Hawaii to find American flags flying above Hawaii's public buildings. He ordered the flags taken down and the Marines withdrawn. He reported to Cleveland that "a great wrong has been done to the Hawaiians." Cleveland sent a message to Congress stating that the unauthorized use of American troops in Hawaii was "an act of war against a peaceful nation." Congress, lobbied by the sugar interests, ignored Cleveland.

In 1894, the provisional government established itself as the Republic of Hawaii. Sanford Dole was named president. President Cleveland sent a representative to Hawaii seeking the reinstatement of Queen Lili'uokalani, but Dole and his cabinet refused to step down. Lili'uokalani and her supporters planned a counter-coup, to be led by the indefatigable Robert Wilcox. The government arrested the royalists, including Queen Lili'uokalani, for treason. The queen denied guilt, but bombs and arms were found in her Washington Place garden.

Lili'uokalani was placed under house arrest and a week later she gave up the throne. She was found guilty of high treason and sentenced to five years of hard labor and fined $5,000. The penalties were never enforced, but she remained imprisoned at 'Iolani Palace until later that year.

Fully assimilated

In November 1897, Cleveland lost the presidential election to William McKinley, and in 1898, McKinley signed annexation papers. Two years later, Hawaii was an American territory. Sanford Dole was its first territorial governor. Lili'uokalani and Dole publicly reconciled in 1911 at the opening of the Pearl Harbor naval base. In 1917, during World War I, Hawaii's last monarch raised the American flag over Washington Place for the very first time. Seven months later, she died at the age of 79. ❑

HISTORICAL HINDSIGHT

Hawaii is ours. As I look back upon... this miserable business and as I contemplate the means used to complete the outrage, I am ashamed of the whole affair.

Pres. Grover Cleveland, in his memoirs

Overawed by the power of the United States... the people of the Islands have no voice in determining their future, but are virtually relegated to the condition of the aboriginals of the American continent.

Queen Lili'uokalani, in her memoirs

LEFT: Queen Lili'uokalani, 1893. **RIGHT:** an 1897 German cartoon satirizes Hawaii's marriage to Uncle Sam.

MODERN HAWAII

First it was sugar that defined Hawaii's economy. Pineapples came along and helped out, as did the military. Now, tourism is the state's financial anchor

At the start of the 20th century, it looked as if the schemes of the business and land barons had finally come to pass. Sugar was soon joined by a new commodity, pineapple. James Dole (a relative of Sanford Dole) successfully began marketing Hawaii-grown pineapples on the US mainland. Hawaii would soon be the world's major supplier of pineapple.

The tenacious effort of anti-royalists, businessmen, landowners, and sugar barons to bring Hawaii under the umbrella of the United States was finally consummated two years after annexation, when President William McKinley made Hawaii an American territory in 1900.

Territorial status certainly sealed the future of the monarchy. There would be no return. The territory's governor and judges were now appointed by the American president. The governor, in turn, appointed local administrators.

The rise of sugar

With Sanford Dole leading the territorial government, just about all of the new territory's banking, commerce, and transportation remained under the continuing control of five large *haole* corporations built largely on sugar: Castle and Cooke, Alexander and Baldwin, C. Brewer, Theo. H. Davies, and American Factors (now called Amfac). By intention and default, they controlled Hawaii's politics and government.

Sugar's future remained of paramount importance. Because it was now part of the US, Hawaii was classified a domestic producer and thus no longer subject to import tariffs. Greater profits could be anticipated, and the plantations could grow. But expansion of the sugar plantations required more labor. Since Hawaii had no large pool of ready local labor – Hawaiians were now too few in number and, besides, few of them saw much merit in working the hot, dusty cane fields – workers had to be imported.

PRECEDING PAGES: Hawaii wouldn't be Hawaii without a Hula show in Waikiki. **LEFT:** surfer on Waikiki beach, early 1900s. **RIGHT:** a U.S. representative accepts the territory of Hawaii from President Sanford Dole.

Before, as an independent kingdom and republic, there had been no restrictions on immigration to Hawaii, and so the sugar barons had brought in tens of thousands of workers from Asia, first from China and then from Japan. Later, workers came from Portugal, Puerto Rico, Korea, and the Philippines. But now as an American territory,

immigration quotas were determined in Washington. Immigration from Asia was curtailed. With their traditional labor sources evaporating, Hawaii's sugar plantations were nevertheless in luck with a new source of labor: the Philippines, under the American flag since the 1898.

At this time, Hawaii was very much a Republican territory, governed by an entrenched oligarchy of businessmen intent on preserving their power. Hawaii was a place of well-defined social hierarchies. White men owned the plantations and held supervisory positions, while immigrant laborers ranked low. The first generation of immigrant laborers, indentured and mostly from Asia, buttressed this rigid plantation hierarchy.

The new Americans

But as Hawaii swaggered into the 20th century, something happened that was not at all anticipated. Those first-generation Chinese, Japanese, and Filipinos who had worked hard and quietly on the plantations decided to stay in Hawaii after their labor contracts ended. They had children. These plantation babies were by birth American citizens. Unlike their parents, they were not foreigners, nor newcomers, nor strangers in a strange land. Hawaii was home.

As this second generation of Asian immigrants grew up, the power of the Big Five corporations, Republican politicians, and missionary land-

regular inter-island mail routes. The first flight between Hawaii and another destination outside of the chain had been almost completed four years earlier when a US Navy seaplane coming from California ran out of fuel 300 miles (480 km) from Hawaii. Two years later, the first civilian flight to reach the islands ran out of fuel and crashed into a mesquite tree on Molokai.

A more reliable air connection with the US mainland arrived on an April morning in 1935, when a 19-ton Pan Am Clipper landed at the fleet air base in Pearl Harbor, completing an "exploratory" flight from San Francisco that took 19 hours and 48 minutes.

Hawaiian Pineapples. District of Wahiawa, Island of Oahu.

owners was challenged, their footing further undermined by an economic depression that boosted the confidence of labor movements. By pushing Hawaii to become a territory, and by admitting tens of thousands of immigrants, the ruling powers had been hoist by their own petard.

In 1935, 10 years after a violent strike by cane laborers in Hanapepe, Kauai, left many Filipino workers dead, legislation passed by the US Congress made it legal for workers to organize into unions and engage in collective bargaining.

Air transport between islands arrived in 1929, when Inter-Island Airways, now Hawaiian Airlines, connected the islands with amphibious aircraft. Five years later, the new airline began

Seven months later, a second Pan Am aircraft touched down with a cargo of mail, then continued an island-hopping route to Manila, creating the first Pacific air connection between North America and Asia. Less than a year later, the *Hawaii Clipper* skimmed across Pearl Harbor's waters with a cargo of seven paying passengers – a new kind of tourist with money to spend.

World War II

Early on Sunday morning, 7 December 1941, two waves of Japanese aircraft – 360 planes in all – dropped below cloud cover and attacked every major military installation on Oahu. The Japanese attack devastated the US Pacific fleet.

There were 2,323 Americans killed. Japanese casualties were less than 100. Most of the ships at anchor in the harbor were severely damaged if not sunk. Some 68 Oahu residents were killed or injured. Japanese submarines sank cargo and passenger vessels in local waters. They also surfaced to shell Hilo, Nawiliwili, and Kahului harbors.

The same day as the attack on Oahu, President Franklin Roosevelt declared war on Japan. Later in the morning, Hawaii was placed under martial law. The state remained under mar-

JAPAN EXPANDS

Japan had been expanding its control in Asia for 50 years. Now the Pacific was next, including Pearl Harbor, home of the US Pacific fleet since 1908.

In Hawaii, the AJA population was far too prominent to be confined, not only because they were a majority percentage of Hawaii's population, but also because they were a major thread in Hawaii's social and cultural fabric.

Eventually, AJAS of military age were permitted to enlist in the army. A volunteer group from Hawaii was assembled into a single unit called the 100th Infantry Battalion, later expanded into the 442nd Regimental Combat Team with over 1,000 volunteers. Not trusted to

tial law until 1944, during which time military courts completely replaced all civilian jurisdiction in Hawaii. The US Supreme Court ruled after the war that this was an unconstitutional move.

At the beginning of the war, the largest ethnic group in Hawaii was of Japanese ancestry. On the mainland, Americans of Japanese ancestry (AJA) were confined in desert internment camps, a policy that was entirely racial and not substantiated by claims of national security. (Americans of German and Italian ancestry were, however, left alone.)

LEFT: pineapples and plantation workers, 1910.
ABOVE: an American destroyer explodes, Pearl Harbor.

fight soldiers of their ancestral homeland (Americans of German or Italian descent faced no such restrictions), the Japanese-American soldiers were shipped to Europe. Suspicions about loyalty vanished when the 442nd became the most decorated American unit in World War II. Returning home to Hawaii, many AJAS used veterans' benefits to pay for college, turning later to law and politics and becoming the core of another shift in Hawaii's structure.

After the war, a succession of workers' strikes established unions as one of Hawaii's major political and economic forces. They solidified their power in 1952 with a six-month work freeze on Hawaii's docks that nearly devastated the territory's economy, almost completely dependent on shipping. Hawaii's business and political *ancien régime*, however, were sore and sour losers, accusing the unions of being part of the Marxist plague. But the Republican Party, which had been entrenched since well before anyone alive could remember, was knocked out of power in 1954 by a decidedly different incoming group of territorial legislators – half of whom were AJAS – that were supported by the now-powerful labor unions.

PARANOID PINEAPPLES

In the 1950s, Hawaii's activist unions were closely scrutinized and accused of being revolutionary tools of an unproven Communist conspiracy.

eventually overcame Congressional reluctance. It has been suggested that southern congressmen were against admitting Hawaii as a state dominated by, for heaven's sake, non-Caucasians.

A deal was finally struck linking Hawaii and Alaska for statehood, and in 1959 Hawaii became the 50th American state. Statehood was ratified by Hawaii's voters 17 to 1. Only the precinct of Ni'ihau, the privately owned island off of Kauai, peopled by native Hawaiians, voted against it. In most elections, Ni'ihau's people

Statehood push

Between 1903 and 1957, 22 bills addressing statehood for Hawaii failed Congressional votes in Washington. Unlike mainland areas annexed as territories, there had been no provisions in Hawaii's territorial legislation for eventual statehood. And in any case, territorial status had suited the sugar interests just fine.

But in 1934, Congress had given Hawaii's sugar barons a kick in the *'okole* (buttocks) by grouping Hawaii along with foreign producers of sugar. Exports to the mainland plummeted. Statehood would be necessary to sustain Hawaii as a leading sugar producer. The Big Five and other interests pushed for statehood and

voted against the Democratic Party leanings of the rest of the state.

Until this time, Hawaii had rarely been thought about by mainland America. It was, after all, a long, expensive boat journey away. Statehood was one of those historical pivots, like Cook's visit and the overthrow of Lili'uokalani, that irrevocably changed Hawaii's destiny and direction.

At the time of statehood, the tallest building in Hawaii was 10-story-high Aloha Tower, and Waikiki was peppered here and there with just a few hotels. Defense and agriculture, primarily sugar and pineapple, were Hawaii's two main sources of revenue.

That same year, a regular commercial jet service was inaugurated by Qantas between Australia, Hawaii, and San Francisco, cutting travel time to California from nine propeller hours to less than five hours by jet. A few months later Pan Am connected Honolulu with the Pacific Coast and Tokyo, Japan.

The commercial jet's ability to maintain a constant turnover of visitors made mass tourism a very promising enterprise. The jets brought an increasing numbers of visitors, and the once-stately, low-rise Waikiki hotels soon found themselves surrounded, and dwarfed, by bigger and taller hotels.

office buildings and high-rise condos. Small, quiet rural towns – Kailua, Kane'ohe, Mililani, Hawaii Kai, Makakilo – turned into bedroom communities for Honolulu-bound commuters.

In the early 1980s, tourism overtook government and military spending in economic importance. Agriculture slipped to a distant third. Some of the lost agricultural revenues were replaced by the exponential growth of *pakalolo*, or marijuana, cultivation, which illegally flourished in Hawaii's forests, sugar-cane fields and backyards. Since then, an aggressive eradication effort, involving aerial herbicide spraying, has cut production substantially.

The neighboring islands, too, got a jolt. To make room for blossoming resorts, agricultural land was converted into resort developments, especially on Maui and Kauai. On the Big Island, resorts were built on barren lava. Former sugar-plantation workers became hotel staff.

Hawaii's urban center since the end of whaling, Honolulu simply exploded as new mainlanders and businesses arrived. Some peripheral neighborhoods expanded in population by up to 600 percent. And in the areas where it couldn't spread out, Honolulu shot up in wall to wall

LEFT: a Honolulu newspaper announces statehood.
ABOVE: Maui's resorts epitomize Hawaii's tourism.

Yen for money

In the 1980s, Hawaii's tourism entered a period of unparalleled expansion, fueled in part by the philosophy of using plastic money instead of cash. Additionally, an influx of Asian capital, mostly from an over-heating Japanese economy, injected the state with a building flush that would later prove to be over-extended. Huge "fantasy resorts," developed to suit upscale tastes, became the new resort paradigm. Designed to keep visitors and therefore money on the property for their entire visit, the resorts themselves, not Hawaii, became the destination.

By the late 1980s, Japanese investors (highly leveraged by inflated stock and real-estate) had injected $15 billion into Hawaii's economy. The Japanese bought heavily into hotels and resorts, acquiring 30 percent of all hotel rooms in Hawaii, and 70 percent of those costing over $100 a day. There was some backlash against such a concentration of foreign ownership. But the Japanese kept the hotels under American management – thus successfully deflecting the worries of labor unions and local residents – and spent tens of millions of dollars to upgrade tired hotel properties. Throughout the islands, hotel standards increased.

Thirty percent of the home purchases in 1987/88 east of Diamond Head involved Japan-

Kaiser. At the time, it was the highest price ever paid – and in cash – for an American residential property.

In the economic downturn that followed the collapse of Japan's "bubble" economy, property values fell, aggravating economic instability. The Kaiser estate was ultimately foreclosed, a symbol of the economic events of the 1990s.

While immense profits were made in the 1980s by some Hawaii residents with upscale property to sell, many others were pushed out of their homes and neighborhoods where families had lived for generations. When low-income retired people started being evicted

ese, who often bought at prices much higher than appraised values. Property assessments and taxes in some neighborhoods increased by as much as 100 percent in less than a year. A number of elderly Waikiki residents were displaced by higher rents when their apartment buildings were bought out by Japanese.

Billionaire Genshiro Kawamoto went Hawaii house-hunting in the late 1980s, saying that he was looking for a place "to keep a change of clothes in." For six months he drove around Honolulu looking for the right place. He ended up buying 160 homes for $80 million cash before he found the perfect closet: a $40-million estate once owned by the industrialist Henry

from apartments they had rented for years, Hawaii's welcome of the yen wavered.

"I'd like to send a message back. Enough," Frank Fasi, then mayor of Honolulu, stated. "We don't want you and we don't need you... I don't want Honolulu to become a suburb of Tokyo." Fasi even journeyed to Tokyo to scold the Japanese. Many disagreed with the mayor, including the governor of Hawaii, but Fasi's actions reflected a growing resentment of perceived Japanese condescension towards Hawaii, of Hawaii as a Japanese playground and a high-yield, low-risk investment for those with yen.

The situation was compounded when the Japanese, unaccustomed to the dictates of a multi-ethnic society, purchased property and attempted to exclude Americans. In one instance, for example, a Japanese investor in a planned golf course blurted out that it would be exclusively for Japanese nationals, an illegal action in the United States (but not in Japan.)

The infusion of yen into Hawaii skidded to a halt in the early 1990s, when the over-leveraged Japanese investors lost their shirts as Japan's stock and real-estate markets crashed. The yen that once dominated investment was humbled.

NO *KAPU* ON BEACHES

All of Hawaii's shoreline up to the high-tide mark is public property and it must be accessible to the public. Access can't be restricted.

until only one had it all. The missionaries and sugar barons took it from the Hawaiians, and now everybody wants to take it from everyone else – or at least own some of it.

About half of Hawaii is owned by the state, county, and federal governments. Of the remaining land, three quarters is owned by a collection of less than 40 owners, mainly descended from the early Protestant missionary families with names like Bishop, Campbell, and Wilcox. These private landowners collectively own 60

"The Japanese will have learned some lessons. Too much money coming in at one time will create …animosity," the Japanese consul general in Honolulu said. "We can't have quick money, one-night stands. There's got to be respect for local customs and the way of life here."

Land issues

The one common denominator of human history in Hawaii is the acquisition of land. The Tahitians took the land from the Marquesans. The Hawaiian kings took it from one another

percent of Molokai, and 40 to 50 percent of Oahu, Maui, the Big Island, and Kauai. Nearly all of Lanai and Ni'ihau are privately owned by single families.

Land ownership in Hawaii involves both "fee simple" purchase, where the land is included in a real-estate transaction, and leasehold, in which the land is held for a set period, generally ranging from 20 to 50 years. Many of Hawaii's larger hotels have been built on leased land, particularly in Waikiki. Through the 1970s many private homes and condominiums were also built on leased land, although since that time most have been sold to homeowners and converted to fee simple ownership.

LEFT: students display the Hawaiian flag in solidarity.
ABOVE: agricultural land is diminishing in the islands.

The swirl of money and resort development in the 1980s rekindled concerns about the land, and about Hawaii's priorities. The state's over-heated real-estate market peaked in the early 1990s and then stagnated, along with the state's economy. The question of land, unfortunately but inevitably, has the potential to polarize and divide ethnic interests in the islands.

In 1993, the land issue came to the forefront during a four-day centennial remembrance of Queen Lili'uokalani's overthrow. With 'Iolani Palace covered in black bunting, it was not a time of celebration and festivities. Then Governor John Waihe'e, the state's very first governor of

Hawaiian ancestry, issued executive orders that only the Hawaiian flag, not the American, fly over state office buildings during the four days.

There is no dispute that the overthrow of Queen Lili'uokalani was illegal under international law. In fact, the sovereignty of the islands had earlier been recognized by both the United States and the European powers. The immediate events of the overthrow were orchestrated by local businessmen and a representative of the United States whose actions, which included the dispatch of American troops from a visiting ship to sustain the coup, were taken without the authorization of the American president. This was sustained by congressional inaction.

On the centennial of the overthrow of the Hawaiian monarchy in November 1993, then President Bill Clinton formally apologized on behalf of the US government for its role in the 1893 coup in Hawaii. The joint Congressional resolution that he signed also acknowledged the illegitimacy of the 1898 annexation.

The centennial of the overthrow offered a platform for the numerous Hawaiian sover-eignty groups seeking a redress of the islands' annexation. Some of the groups want control over certain Hawaiian lands. Others advocate complete secession from the United States.

One of the most outspoken sovereignty groups, Ka Lahui Hawaii (The Hawaiian Nation), demands a "nation within a nation." It would allow Hawaiians to control their own lands, determine their own government, estab-lish their own laws, and set their own taxes – an arrangement already guaranteed by legislation with Native American peoples on the mainland. Hawaiians, however, have never been classified as Native Americans.

Ka Lahui Hawaii wants the Hawaiian nation established on about 1.5 million acres (600,000 hectares) of land – 200,000 acres (80,000 hectares) of existing Hawaiian homelands and an additional 1.2 million acres (480,000 hectares) of land possessed by the monarchy at the time of Queen Lili'uokalani's overthrow. This land was ceded by Sanford Dole's republic to the United States and returned to the state in 1959.

A common theme among all the sovereignty groups is the question of *'aina*, or land. For the resolution of land use and responsibility is crucial to making sovereignty, in any form and to any degree, succeed.

In 1994, Filipino-American Ben Cayetano was elected governor. The 1990s were not kind to Hawaii. The retrenching of the Japanese econ-omy left the state without a reliable inflow of cash investment. Severe economic problems in 1997 and 1998 across most of Asia also affected tourism in Hawaii. By 1999, with the boom on the mainland also leading to increased visitor numbers in Hawaii, tourism seemed poised for a slow rebound, but the terrorist attacks on New York and Washington DC in 2001 were an obvi-ous setback to the Hawaiian tourist industry's lengthy recovery process.   ❑

LEFT: members of Ka Lahui Hawaii are outspoken.
RIGHT: a jugglers' commune on the Big Island.

NATURAL HISTORY

Today, Hawaii appears to be the proverbial paradise with its diverse and lush flora and fauna. Ironically, most of what one sees has been recently introduced by humans

Many millions of years ago, lava from the fiery interiors of the earth rumbled and surged, blasting through a jagged vent 15,000 feet (4,550 meters) below the ocean's surface. A fraction of an inch at a time – 2 to 3 inches (5 to 8 cm) a year – the Pacific Plate of the earth's crust crept northwest, rafting the volcano that had formed away from the hot spot and allowing a new sea mount to build under the water. A number of islands broke the ocean's surface, grew, then eroded away into atolls, while at the same time newer islands formed. Eons later, a line of subterranean mountains, some surfacing to 15,000 feet (4,550 meters) above sea level, stretched majestically in a row across 1,600 miles (2,500 km) of the Pacific Ocean, from the Big Island of Hawaii to Kure Atoll.

Over the centuries, floating seeds, fish, and marine larvae drifted to the islands on ocean currents. Winds carried fern spores, tiny seeds, and insects. Birds, sometimes full of fertile eggs or viable seeds, landed here, often propelled by storm winds. These isolated colonists adapted to suit their environment, making them unique, or endemic, to Hawaii. The process, scientists theorize, began more than 50 million years ago on what are now the atolls of the northwest islands of the Hawaiian archipelago.

Some 30 miles (50 km) southeast of the Big Island's southernmost point, far beneath the surface of the ocean, a new island – Lo'ihi – is forming over the hot spot in the earth's crust. Such eruptions, which begin on the ocean bottom, are the first stage in building Hawaii's broad shield volcanoes; they slowly grow as a thin layer of lava covering earlier layers. Underwater, lava hardens into pumice – light rocks full of gas bubbles – and pillow lava, or rock hummocks with rounded, smoother shapes.

Lo'ihi is predicted to jut from the ocean as a new shear-sided, cliff-rimmed island some tens

of thousands of years from now. Depending on the forces of nature – or on the whim of the volcano goddess Pele – it may eventually connect with Hawaii above sea level, making the Big Island even bigger.

When seamounts break the ocean's surface, the lava erupts in fiery fountains, flowing from

craters and rifts in the mountain's sides. Five such seamount volcanoes formed the island of Hawaii: Kilauea, Mauna Loa, Hualalai (all have been active within the past 200 years), Mauna Kea, and Kohala, the oldest volcano on the Big Island. Basaltic lava from ancient and more recent eruptions is the most common rock in the Hawaiian chain. A drive around the Volcano area and Ka'u reveals two types of hardened lava: *paho'eho'e* and *'a'a*. Both have the same chemical composition. Paho'eho'e, because it retains more gas, is hotter when it erupts, producing a fluid flow that hardens to smooth, ropy lava. 'A'a, on the other hand, hardens to rough, chunky and sharp lava.

PRECEDING PAGES: stormy waves, Hanalei Bay, Kauai; Haleakala volcano, Maui. **LEFT:** waves probably carried the first forms of life to the Hawaiian islands.
RIGHT: a new fern leaf begins to unfold.

Eventually, the tops of the volcanoes collapse, creating wide depressions called calderas. On the Big Island, Kilauea (which is currently erupting) and Mauna Loa have calderas. When lava from these active volcanoes reaches the sea, you can witness the awesome process of island-making.

Hot lava pouring into the ocean turns shore waters into churning cauldrons, giving rise to towers of steam and cloud build-up. Sulfur dioxide released by active calderas, combines with rain from these clouds, falling as dilute sulfuric acid. Chlorine gas freed from

FOURTH IN AMERICA

Consisting of 132 islands, atolls, reefs, and shoals, Hawaii ranks fourth in the United States in coastline.

growing at the edges, circling the island like underwater lei. As an island erodes and sinks on its journey to the northwest with the shifting tectonic plate, the coral grows upward, searching for the sunshine that is so crucial to its survival. Reefs growing along the edges of middle-aged islands like Maui, Molokai, Lanai, Oahu and Kauai are called fringing reefs. The island of Hawaii's fringing reef is only now just beginning.

As the Pacific Plate continues to sink, lagoons tend to form between the reef and its island. These barrier reefs can be seen

boiling sea water mixes with the sulfur, giving the area a chemical odor. It's a primordial scene not to be missed, but it can be dangerous. Once the volcano-building stops, other forces take over. Wind and sun eat away at the land, surf carves the coastlines, and rain cuts valleys and ridges into the new mountains. Volcanic rocks break down and gradually turn into soil. Plants arrive, then animals. Eventually, humans take over. What was once just a hot spot on the ocean floor is now fertile, life-supporting land.

Like the creatures that populate them, islands become middle-aged, grow old, and die. This aging process is visible in the Hawaiian Island chain. After new islands form, coral reefs start

in some of the older Hawaiian islands of the northwest chain. Eventually, the island in the center vanishes underwater, creating an atoll – a coral reef enclosing a lagoon. The coral reef rises above the ocean unevenly, forming numerous low islands in a circular shape. Kure, at the northwest end of the Hawaiian chain, is such an atoll.

Forces of erosion have turned gentle slopes similar to those found on Mauna Loa into breathtaking ridges like those of Kauai's Na Pali coast. The towering north shore cliffs of Molokai are the tallest ocean cliffs in the world, rising nearly 2,000 feet (600 meters) above the sea. Sandy beaches, rocky shores, and crater-shaped bays line other coastal areas throughout the state.

Climate

Ecosystems in Hawaii are many and varied, depending not only on the location of the islands on the earth's surface, but also on the topography of the land and the amount of wind, rain and sunshine in each area.

Because Hawaii is in the sub-tropics, seasonal differences are slight. Temperatures are relatively stable, varying from an average of 80°F (25°C) around the coastal areas in winter months to 88°F (31°C) in the summer. At higher elevations, the difference increases. On the same latitude as Mexico City, Hong Kong, and Cairo, Hawaii's longest day is 13 hours and 20 minutes compared to Seattle's 16 hours; the shortest day in Honolulu is 10 hours and 50 minutes, while Seattle's is 8 hours and 20 minutes.

In general, rainfall in the islands is sparsest in leeward areas – central mountains drain the northeasterly trade winds – and atop the highest mountains. The average annual rainfall ranges from less than 10 inches (25 cm) to more than 430 inches (10 meters).

Weather develops as the tradewinds carrying clouds across the ocean ascend the mountains and the air is cooled. Condensation causes rainfall on the windward side of the mountain ranges, leaving little moisture to fall as the depleted winds pass over the leeward side of each island. The climates of the islands mimic climates of much larger continents, with tropical rainforests, grasslands, deserts, and even areas of tundra represented on a smaller scale.

Ecosystems of Hawaii

Narrow bands around each island where land and ocean meet are called coastal vegetation zones. Here, hundreds of plant and animal species live, each having adapted in its own way to this unique environment. Humans have settled in coastal zones for so long that it's sometimes hard to find a place that hasn't been drained, dredged, or filled. The landscapes seen around the islands have been radically altered by humans. This isn't necessarily bad; it's just different from what was once there.

Even with so much human influence, researchers recognize 150 different plant communities in Hawaii, named according to elevation, moisture, and vegetation. Within each

of these, the plants and animals interact with one another and their environment to form ecosystems. In some areas, preserves – rainforests or shifting sand dunes that might hide traces of former lives, the bones of extinct birds, or ancient Hawaiian burial grounds – have been set aside. In these ecosystems, native species are protected.

A wetland is one kind of ecosystem. The term wetland refers to areas where water dominates the environment and its plants and animals. Wetlands can contain salty, brackish (salt and fresh), or fresh water, and can be up to 6 feet (2 meters) deep. Anything deeper is a lake. Hawaii's bogs, estuaries, swamps, and streams contain

unique scenery, plant life and bird life well worth checking out, as most remaining wetlands in the state are now protected preserves.

Forests contain dozens of ecosystems. Hawaii's forests are divided into dryland, medium-wet, and rainforests. Before humans came to Hawaii, dryland forests covered the leeward side of the larger islands and nearly all of Lanai and Kaho'olawe.

Ancient Hawaiians cleared much of this land for agriculture; later settlers finished the job. Today, dryland forests are rare. Researchers believe that in the past, the islands were wetter, with extensive dryland forests producing and holding moisture.

LEFT: lava fountain, Kilauea, Big Island. RIGHT: tourism has affected the ecology of Hanauma Bay.

Medium-wet forests, growing between 2,000–9,000 feet (600–2,700 meters), have the largest number of native tree species of all ecosystems in Hawaii, even the rainforests, which grow in the elevation zone just above the medium-wet forests. Hawaii's rainforests receive at least 100 inches (254 cm) of rain per year. During the winter, clouds often engulf these forests, producing thick, cool mists. The two native trees seen most often in both types of forests are *koa* and *'ohi'a-lehua*, which support Hawaii's famous forest birds, the honeycreepers and their relatives.

Above the forests are alpine zones where few plants grow. Some desert-type plants like

the islands was a slow process. If today's Hawaiian islands are between 1 million (Big Island) and 7 million years-old (Kauai), then just one plant had to establish itself every 15,000 years to account for today's mix of native plants. The best places to see these plants and animals are in Hawaii's national parks, wildlife refuges, and the state's marine conservation districts, where all reef-life is protected from fishing.

Most marine life encountered is native, or endemic, except for several species of snappers, imported by the state from Tahiti in the 1950s as game fish. All sea turtles in Hawaii are native,

Hawaii's famous silverswords thrive in these high, dry, alpine areas, along with some insects. In some of these alpine areas, on the Big Island's Mauna Loa and Maui's Haleakala, for example, snow falls in winter.

Plants and animals

The Hawaiian Islands began as barren lava rock, thousands of miles from the nearest land. Today the islands are lush with plants and teem with animal life; some of these are native, but most have been introduced by people.

Hawaii's native species are the plants and animals that managed to establish themselves without human interference. This colonizing of

and are endangered and protected by law. It is illegal to ride or chase these harmless creatures.

Hawaii's only native land mammal is the Hawaiian bat. Because of their night-time habits and secretive natures, bats are extremely difficult to find, even for researchers.

Native marine mammals include whales, dolphins, and monk seals. These are also protected by federal laws. With only about 1,600 of them left, Hawaiian monk seals are in extreme danger of extinction. If you see one resting on a beach, which is normal behavior for them, back off quietly and consider it a lucky day.

Only a few of the flowers and trees seen while driving along Hawaii's highways are native.

Seven kinds of hibiscus are native, but with 200 species of hibiscus in the world and more than 5,000 hybrids, the ones you see are often not Hawaii originals. Pandanus, also called screwpine or *hala*, are roadside native trees. *Koa* (popular for furniture) and *'ohi'a lehua* are native trees common to parks and preserves.

Since many of their seeds float, beach plants are often native, including beach morning glories and beach *naupaka*, thick green bushes with white flowers.

POLYNESIAN PESTS

Stowaways on Polynesian canoes included geckos, skinks, rats, house flies, fleas, and lice. Geckos are welcome in island homes because they eat insects, but the other immigrants are unwanted pests.

think of as native to Hawaii are actually aliens, introduced by those early settlers. Some common plants on this list are coconut palms, bananas, bamboo, ti, ginger, breadfruit, taro, sweet potatoes, yams, sugar-cane, mountain apples, and bottle gourds.

Candlenut trees, called *kukui* in Hawaiian, were also introduced, but this is still Hawaii's official state tree, partially due to the fact that the nut had so many uses in early Hawaii. The meat could be burned for light

Introduced species

Starting around AD 500, Polynesians brought with them the plants and animals they needed to live in their new home. Although keeping these species alive through such voyages was a tricky business, the immigrants managed to shuttle at least 27 kinds of plants and several kinds of animals – some wanted, some not – to Hawaii.

Even though this happened centuries ago, these species are considered alien because humans had a hand in their introduction. As a result, a few plants and animals that many might

LEFT: the humpback whale winters in Hawaiian waters.
ABOVE: the extinct *'o'o*, and the once-endangered *nene*.

or ground up for seasoning food. The nut itself was used for body adornment. Kukui products are still common: the oil from the nuts is used in cosmetics, and the nuts themselves are polished to make necklaces and bracelets. It's easy to spot the abundant kukui trees in a forest: their leaves, which look as if they've been dusted with flour, are very pale next to others.

Sugar-cane is another introduced Polynesian plant. Ancient Hawaiians used sugar-cane as a sweetener, for famine food, and as medicine. The leaves were used for hats and thatching. For decades, sugar-cane has been Hawaii's leading crop. It still is today, although high labor costs and competition from other sweeteners have caused a dramatic and continuing decline in the industry. One acre of land yields more than 11 tons (9,900 kg) of cane, giving Hawaii the highest yield per acre in the agricultural world. However, it is widely believed that by about 2010 sugar will no longer be grown here, although it will hopefully be replaced by alternative crops.

Ancient Hawaiians brought animals such as pigs, dogs, and chickens to the islands as food stock. Left to run loose in the forests, pigs and dogs wreaked havoc on native species, and continue to do so today. Pigs eat native plants, and wild dogs kill native birds, most of which nest on the ground.

Hawaii's landscape changed forever when those first Polynesian explorers landed with their plants and animals, but that was only the beginning. Since Captain Cook's arrival, plants and animals have streamed into the islands from all around the world. Today, these post-contact introductions are more common than both native and Polynesian-introduced species.

Since these aliens often out-compete or eat native species, the flood of introductions is causing the extinction of many endemic plants and animals. Hawaii has the dubious distinction of having more plant and animal species on the endangered species list than any other American state. Part of this phenomenon can be attributed to its isolated position on the globe, as a lack of natural enemies allowed more species to adapt and survive in the islands than in other places. Obviously, introduced species aren't all bad. The exotic plants provide Hawaii with stunning flower lei, sweet-smelling parks and gardens, and highways lined with color.

The mass of brilliant color along the roadsides comes from, among others, bougainvilleas and plumerias, native to tropical America. Other common aliens are ironwood and silk oaks from Australia, banyan trees from Asia, and Cook's pines from the South Pacific's Cook Islands. Orchid growers in the state, especially on the Big Island, have made Hawaii world-famous for orchid hybrids. Hawaii has just three native orchids, a minute number compared to the over 30,000 species which make up the entire family.

Many food plants that people associate with Hawaii are foreign. Among these are coffee (Africa), pineapples (Brazil), mangos (India), guava (Mexico to Peru), papaya (tropical America), and lychee (China).

While many alien fruits and flowers are welcome, many alien animals are not. Cockroaches, mosquitoes, centipedes, goats, sheep, and wild cats have caused environmental disasters and human misery. Mongooses, for example, were imported from India via Jamaica by sugar growers to eat rats, but they preferred eating native birds and their eggs. It was realized too late that mongooses hunted during the day, while rats were active at night.

While residents and visitors welcome some non-native creatures, such as mynah birds and red-crested cardinals, state officials vigilantly guard against pests such as snakes, particularly the brown tree snake from Guam, which has virtually extinguished avian life on that Pacific island. (The snake hitchhikes in the wheel wells of commercial and military aircraft flying to Hawaii from Guam.) Strict laws, for the most part, have been successful. Outside the zoo, only a few illegal snakes have been found. However, there is growing concern about the brown tree snake.

Quarantine laws have kept Hawaii rabies free, and the once-endangered *nene*, the Hawaiian goose, is now often seen in the wild at Volcano on the Big Island and Haleakala on Maui. ❑

LEFT: Norfolk pines were introduced as windbreaks.
RIGHT: the heliconia flower, also introduced by humans.

HAWAII'S DISAPPEARING FLORA AND FAUNA

No doubt both the Polynesians and Europeans had good intentions, but both groups introduced plants and animals that have decimated Hawaii's own.

The Hawaiian monk seal *(left)* is a shy creature, keeping to itself in the uninhabited islands and atolls of northwestern Hawaii. Only occasionally does it make an appearance on one of the main islands, usually Kauai. It is one of only two indigenous mammals in Hawaii; the other is the hoary bat. The Polynesian rat, first introduced by ancient Polynesians, is considered by some to have evolved enough to be considered a Hawaiian species.

AVIAN DISAPPEARANCE

Many species of Hawaii's native birds, evolving through the centuries with few natural predators, have all but disappeared. The mongoose, introduced to combat rats brought centuries earlier on Polynesian canoes, prefers eggs and has decimated native birds. Other introduced species threaten Hawaii's birds. The mynah, introduced by Europeans, is a pushy creature, and it has forced many other bird species from their habitat. Snakes are not found in the wild in Hawaii. Yet. But a serious threat to both indigenous and introduced bird species is the brown snake from Guam, arriving as a stowaway on commercial and military aircraft.

FLORA

Prior to the arrival of people, it is estimated that the level of endemic (found nowhere else) plant species was higher in Hawaii than anywhere else on the planet. Today, the flora that we associate with Hawaii – plumeria, hibiscus, pineapples, bananas, guavas – are all introduced species. Hawaii's indigenous plants are fighting for survival, and many are already extinct.

▷ NOT ENOUGH TO CROW ABOUT
Hawaiian crows probably won't survive, despite conservationists' efforts. There are around 2 dozen birds remaining, not enough for a strong gene pool.

△ SILVERSWORD
The silversword, related to the sunflower, is uniquely adapted to high-altitude life and the fragile soils. People and ants threaten them.

▽ TOO MANY PIGS
Pigs, introduced by Polynesians, and goats and cattle, introduced by Europeans, have destroyed Hawaii's native plant species.

IDYLLIC HAWAII'S BENIGN EVOLUTION

Statistically, a new species became established on Hawaii every 15,000 years. Hawaii's extreme remoteness gave those animal and plant species that arrived a unique environment in which to grow and evolve. By the time the first humans arrived 1,500 years ago, nearly 9,000 kinds of flora and fauna unique to the islands had evolved, including the silversword *(above)*.

With the absence of mammals, plants did not develop defenses such as thorns and toxins, nor did birds develop behavior that protected them from predators. When people introduced numerous animal species – from birds to grazing cattle – Hawaii's indigenous species were poorly equipped for survival.

Indigenous plants and birds today are found only in mostly inaccessible places: on the cliffs of Molokai's north shore, in the boggy highlands of Kauai, and in the restricted and fenced-in Kipahulu Valley of eastern Maui.

△ RAT REJECTION
Another introduced mammal, the mongoose, has decimated many of Hawaii's indigenous birds. Brought by Europeans to control rats, it preferred birds – it is a day mammal and rats prefer the night.

◁ *NENE*, HAWAIIAN GOOSE
The *nene*, or Hawaiian goose, is found on the Big Island, Maui, and Kauai, usually at higher elevations. Unlike other goose species, the *nene* lacks webbed feet; it has claws that are more useful on the volcanic slopes.

▷ HAWAIIAN STILT
Like most of Hawaii's native birds, the Hawaiian stilt lacks the necessary defensive behavior against introduced predators. Found only in a few inland wildlife sanctuaries, such as on Maui's central isthmus, the stilt is a delightful if rare sighting for the birdwatcher.

▷ PROTECTED BY SHYNESS
The reclusiveness of the Hawaiian monk seal (hence, the "monk") has probably assured its species survival. Rare is the sighting of a grown monk seal, much less a pup seal *(right)*. Wisely, they prefer uninhabited islands.

SPIRIT OF THE ISLANDS

Although Hawaiian culture long ago yielded to outsiders, underlying all modern
society in Hawaii is a foundation of revived ancient values

In Hawaiian tradition, the land, or *'aina*, is mother. *'Aina* literally means "that which feeds." The land doesn't belong to people; Hawaiians belong to it and are part of it. If separated from the land, Hawaiians and their culture tend to drift and lose meaning. The sheltering home, the trees outside, the earth beneath – all are alive and aware. The shapes of the clouds, the cries of birds at night, the sounds of waves on the reef – all have messages for the Hawaiian people. Hawaiian tradition involved constant communication with other living beings, with the land, rocks, clouds, sea, and spirits of ancestors.

Today on these islands that were an independent nation over a century ago, *kanaka maoli*, as native Hawaiians call themselves, have the shortest life expectancy of all ethnic groups. They have the highest mortality rates for heart disease, stroke, cancer and diabetes, the highest infant mortality, and the highest rates of suicide, accidents, and substance abuse.

Forty percent of the population of Oahu Prison is *kanaka maoli*. Hawaiians make up less than two percent of the graduating class at the University of Hawaii and have the highest drop-out rates in the school system, the lowest family median incomes, and the highest rates of homelessness. Hawaiians are at the bottom of the heap in their own homeland, displaced by the fracturing of an intense connection with land and tradition.

'O ke au i kahuli wela ka honua. 'O ke au i kahuli lole ka lani. The opening lines of "He Kumulipo," the chant describing the origins of the cosmos, literally mean "at the time of the hot earth, turning against the changing sky." But the *kaona*, the hidden meaning of the words, is of the mating between the sky-father, Wakea, with the earth-mother, Papa, out of which came everything in the cosmos.

PRECEDING PAGES: ancient petroglyph cave on the Big Island. **LEFT:** the taro plant is one of the god Kane's many forms. **RIGHT:** often found at traditionally sacred sites are offerings of lava wrapped in *ti* leaves.

According to "He Kumulipo," the *kalo*, or the taro plant, was one of the early children of the earth-mother and the sky-father. But this *kalo*-child was born deformed and died. From its burial place sprouted the taro plant, which became a staple food of Hawaiian life. Clustered around the central plant – the *makua*, or parent – are

'oha (offshoots), and around them, little *keiki* (children). Collectively, this complete plant is called *'ohana*, also the Hawaiian word for family.

The next child born was Haloa, the first human ancestor. But since the taro plant is the *hiapo*, or eldest sibling of humans, it is the superior. It is also another form *(kinolau)* of Kane, one of the highest gods. When eating taro, one is eating the god Kane, taking in his godly *mana*, or power.

'Aina, the land

Before Westerners arrived, Hawaiians had no ownership of land. They had access to all of the natural resources except those few areas that were *kapu*, or taboo – certain fishing grounds during certain seasons, for example. The chiefs or king held the land as proxy for the gods, administering it on earth. Islands were usually divided into *ahupua'a*, large wedges of land extending from the mountain peaks to the coastline and into the water beyond. An *ahupua'a* typically contained ridges on both sides of one or several valleys, forested uplands, a length of shoreline, and the adjoining ocean. In short, it was self-sustaining. The fisherman worked not only for himself, but for everyone; likewise the farmer and the woodsman. Of necessity, good interpersonal relationships, with sharing and exchange, were paramount, .

existed, but this was not the rule and there were no separate dwellings for them. Everyone slept in the big sleeping house, or *hale noa*. Because of the communal arrangements, *kanaka maoli* children learned early about sex and childbirth.

Children were taught about the three *piko*, or centers and were secure knowing that through the three *piko* they were firmly attached to this present life, to the earliest ancestors, and to the lives of unborn generations.

The *piko waena* is the navel, the memory of the link between mother and child in the womb. More, it is a connection with everything in this physical world. It also covers and is related to

'Ohana, the extended family

Practically all the inhabitants of an *ahupua'a* were blood relatives, an extended *'ohana*. Because there was no private ownership and no property to inherit, there was no need for households with a father, a mother, and their children. In the *'ohana*, all the men and women in the middle generation were *makua* (parents) and one mated with whomever one desired. All youngsters were *kamali'i* (children); all elders were *kupuna* (grandparents). There was no difference between parents, aunts, and uncles, and there was no word for cousin. Members of the same generation were all siblings. In the *'ohana* of ordinary farmers and fishermen, couples certainly

OF HAWAII'S PEOPLE

It is the meeting place of East and West, the very new rubs shoulders with the immeasurably old… you have come upon something singularly intriguing. All these strange people live close to each other, with different languages and different thoughts; they believe in different gods and they have different values; two passions alone they share, love and hunger. And somehow as you watch them, you have an impression of extraordinary vitality.

William Somerset Maugham
The Trembling of a Leaf, 1921

the *na'au* (the intestines), the organs of knowledge, wisdom, and feeling.

The second *piko* – the fontanel, the opening between the bones of a child's skull that closes as the child matures – is the *piko po'o* (head center). Through this *piko*, the personal spirit connects with the spiritual world of the ancestors back to the beginning of time, to the natural world about us as *'aumakua*, the ancestral and guardian spirits, and into the future, where the personal spirit will continue to live in different forms forever. The third *piko* is the *piko ma'i*. *Ma'i* are the genitalia, the organs of procreation. This *piko* connects us with our children and

Traditionally, *kanaka maoli* see sex everywhere in nature, and the link between creation and procreation is direct and obvious. In the morning, the wind blows the *pali* mists in a shimmering curtain of rain down island valleys – the rain is the semen of Wakea, the sky-father, impregnating Papa, the earth-mother. This is a common belief and image in many of the world's cosmologies. The opening lines of Queen Lili'uokalani's haunting "Aloha 'Oe" speak of the proud rain on the cliff creeping into the forest, seeking the bud of the *lehua* – the male seeking the female. There are songs about *maile* (rainforest vine) wrapped around a flower

their descendants into the limitless future. In the here and now, *kanaka maoli* are in human form, but they have existed in many previous forms and will exist in many more in the future. Time in this human form is short; after death, *kanaka maoli* join ancestors, assume spiritual form, and come back to families as *'aumakua*. Sometimes they return in the form of a bird, sometimes a fish, or a turtle, shark, tree, rock, breeze, cloud, or even a new child born into the family. The *'aumakua* protects loved ones by warning, guiding and informing them.

LEFT: a *lu'au* of Hawaiians. **ABOVE:** Penis of Nanahoa (Ka Ule o Nanahoa), a phallic stone on Molokai.

lei, male entwined with female. Most *kanaka maoli* songs and chants celebrate the same thing: the joining of male with female. The cosmos was created, and continues to be created, by the mating of Papa and Wakea, "the hot earth turning against the changing heaven." Hawaiians see sexuality as a central fact of nature: from mating comes new life.

When a relationship goes out of balance, the ideal is *ho'opono pono*, a process of guided reconciliation that seeks to achieve both understanding and forgiveness. However, complex psychological issues are often at work here, and the *kanaka* may instead opt for a less harmonious solution of rage and violence.

Hawaiian Gods

From their South Pacific homelands, early Polynesian seafarers brought north with them the foods that had sustained them back home. By doing so, they also brought to Hawaii the great gods of Polynesia: Kane, Ku, Lono, and Kanaloa. As the Polynesians knew well, the gods were essential for human achievement in the new homeland.

Polynesian gods were never distant and abstract. Rather, they moved through the waters and on the earth, and they could take on many forms, including plants. Thus, the Polynesians knew that by bringing

taro, one of the god Kane's forms, to Hawaii, they carried with them Kane himself. With 'uala, the sweet potato, they brought Lono. 'Ulu, breadfruit, and niu, the coconut, bore Ku, and with mai'a, the banana, came Kanaloa.

Kane, the supreme god, was the procreator, the ancestor of all chiefs and commoners, the male (kane) power who dwells in eternity – the god of sunlight, fresh water and forests. Kane was not fond of human sacrifices. An owl was one of his assumed forms.

Hawaiians prayed to **Ku** for rain and growth, and for successful fishing and sorcery, but he was best known as a patron god of war. Resplendent images of Ku, whose combative title was "The Island Snatcher," were carried on the war canoes of Kame-

hameha the Great. According to oral traditions, these fearsome images – wrought of red i'iwi feathers embellished with mother-of-pearl eyes and mouths of jagged dog teeth – would utter dreadful cries during battle.

Lono was a god of thunder (lono means "resounding"), clouds, winds, the sea, agriculture, and fertility, but his personage could assume dozens of forms, including a fish or a man-dog being. Hawaiians never appealed to benevolent Lono with human sacrifices. Most notably, he was honored during the annual makahiki harvest festivals of November, December, and January, when his image was carried by chiefly retainers on their tribute-and-tax-collecting tours of the islands.

It was during makahiki that Captain James Cook's arrival on the Big Island was greeted joyously by Hawaiians gathered at Kealakekua Bay. Some theorize the Hawaiians mistook his visit for the return of Lono.

Kanaloa, lord of the ocean and the ocean winds, was often embodied in the octopus and squid, but also in other natural things, such as the banana. He was a companion of Kane, and according to some, the two traveled together, "moving about the land and opening spring and water holes for the benefit of men."

Coming to Polynesia from distant, unknown places, these four gods had been created before all other gods. They created the universe from the earth, a calabash, by tossing the calabash's cover up to form the sky, sun, and moon. Seeds in the calabash became stars. The pantheon of Hawaiian deities is extensive, ranging from the four great gods to the lesser specialized gods, such as Pele, the volcano goddess, and Laka, goddess of hula.

For the contemporary traveler to Hawaii, Pele is the best known of the lesser gods. As the fire goddess, she is responsible for the current eruptions of Kilauea. A common misconception is that Pele created the Hawaiian islands. The islands had already surfaced when Pele, driven by wanderlust, arrived from Tahiti in a great canoe provided by the god of sharks. From Ni'ihau, she traveled down the island chain looking for a suitable home, which were within active volcanoes.

On the Big Island, she sought out the reigning fire god, Aila'au, hoping to settle in with him. But he had heard of her awesome power and the blazing firepits she dug. As she approached Kilauea, he ran away, leaving her to build a soaring palace of fire that endures in legend and in periodic eruptions on the Big Island to this day. ❏

Talking story and fighting

One way of maintaining balance is by *mo'olelo*, or talking story. A visitor may simply see this as locals sitting and chatting. In fact, talking story builds trust and emphasizes things in common. This is not to suggest that the traditional *kanaka maoli* world was without violence. Oral history holds that the high *kahuna* Pa'ao brought a strict new religion from Tahiti in about the 13th century, increasing the power of the *ali'i*, or royal elite, meting out harsh punishments for the

WISHING DEATH

Na kanaka ku'u wale aku no i ka 'uhane… The people freely gave up their souls and died.

— *1840s saying about Hawaiians dying from depression.*

fought to restore balance, *pono*, particularly as a growing population forced people into closer proximity with one another. In earlier times, warfare had important elements of ritual, as the warrior classes tested their strength against each other but rarely disrupting the commoners. When James Cook arrived in 1778, there were indeed bloody conflicts between Kamehameha and other high chiefs. Commoners were conscripted into their armies. But the first Westerners in Hawaii may have exaggerated warfare's

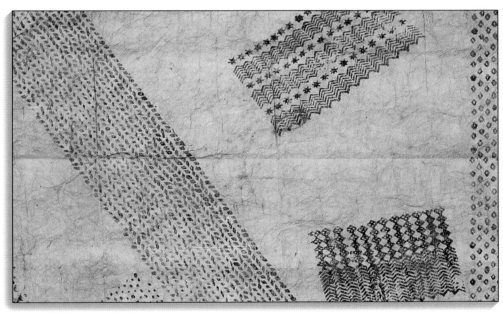

breaking of new *kapu*, and introducing new rituals, including human sacrifice. Rivalry increased between chiefs for political control. But the traditional culture of the *maka'ainana* (lit. the eyes of the land, or commoners) continued much as it had before the arrival of Pa'ao. *Maka'ainana* probably didn't pay much attention to the new hierarchy or the religious rituals, being absorbed rather with work, *'ohana* and *'aumakua*.

Why was there warfare in a society dedicated to maintaining harmony and proper relationships? To some degree, one could say wars were

importance in Hawaiian society, misunderstanding its role. The arrival of Westerners intensified the bloodshed; gunpowder tipped the balance of power. Introduced values about the acquisition of material goods – the sandalwood trade, for example – became goals of war. The natural world was now one of "natural resources" and no longer an extension of *'ohana*, of family.

Personal power

Mana (special spiritual or personal power) derives from two main sources. One source is rank at birth. *Ali'i* (royalty) are born with more *mana* than commoners. Higher-born *ali'i* have more *mana* than lesser-born. The other is train-

LEFT: image of Kamehameha's war god, Kukailimoku.
ABOVE: 19th-century *kapa*, or bark cloth.

ing: a skilled carver, fisherman, chanter, navigator, physician, or dancer gradually acquires this kind of *mana*, as ability is refined. These skills require long apprenticeship, and one's specialized knowledge shouldn't be too readily shared with others lest its power be diminished. *Huna* – certain confidential, secret aspects of the skill – requires the understanding of how numerous forces interact, the maintenance of certain kinds of protocol, and the observance of strict kinds of behavior.

At all levels of society, *kanaka maoli* believe in balance and protocol. Preparing and consuming a meal has to be done in a certain way.

Preparations for the treatment of someone who is ill, such as the gathering of *la'au lapa'au* (medicinal plants), must be completed at a certain time of day with certain rules, prayers, and thoughts. Chants, dances, and rituals have to be conducted impeccably. There is a right way to do everything, and even the smallest daily activity is enmeshed in a web of belief and practice.

The chants used in ritual, prayer, and *hula*, if the words and songs are uttered properly, carry with them considerable power. Hawaiians don't merely petition the gods and hope they'll act; Hawaiians participate by their way of asking. The belief, the ritual, and the result all become one process. And prayers are two-way communications between humans and gods. Responses are received and interpreted in whatever form they may come: patterns in the fire, images in a dream, a sudden gust of wind, a grumble of thunder, a thought that seems to come from nowhere. But of course, nothing comes from nowhere; everything has causes and exists for a reason.

This careful attention to detail and procedure led to a pursuit of excellence stretching beyond what was just necessary to survive, resulting in creations that were extraordinary by the standards of any society.

Kanaka maoli wa'a (sailing canoes) were until very recently the swiftest sailing craft on the ocean. Dazzling feather capes and *lei* (garlands) were admired by jaded Europeans of the time. *Kanaka maoli* agriculturists developed more than 300 varieties of taro, many of them for dyes and medicines as well as food.

Walled *loko i'a* (fish ponds) extended from the shores and efficiently raised fish that fed on algae. Stone-faced terraced and irrigated pondfields *(lo'i)* filled the valleys, growing shrimp and fish as well as prodigious amounts of taro and other crops. Hawaiians were master agriculturists, botanists, herbalists, and craftsmen, fulfilling all needs and creative efforts and expressions entirely from plant materials.

To be or not to be

The *kanaka maoli* sense of balance requires being in the natural environment. The depletion of fishing grounds and the loss of lands destroyed traditional sources of livelihood, which had imparted meaning to the world.

Contemporary Hawaii is promoted as one of the world's most ethnically diverse and harmonious societies. Should the *kanaka maoli* attempt to fit in as just another ethnic group? Some advocates of Hawaiian sovereignty believe it's almost impossible to be both *kanaka maoli* and part of modern America. When immigrants come to Hawaii from, say, China and Portugal, and their children forget their ancestors' culture, the Chinese and Portuguese cultures still exist in their homelands. For *kanaka maoli*, the Hawaiian islands are the only homeland. If *kanaka maoli* language and culture die here, they're gone from the earth, and *kanaka maoli* vanish as a people. ❑

LEFT: offering to the gods at a sacred birth place, Oahu.
RIGHT: outrigger canoe practice.

LIFE IN THE ISLANDS AND SYMBOLS OF THE LAND

While the Westernization of the Hawaiian islands has been thorough, it is still possible to intimately explore and experience ancient ways and textures.

After the arrival of Europeans in Hawaii, a process that sociologists call "dualism" occurred, in which two distinct cultures and economies exist simultaneously. Eventually, however, Western processes and values supplanted those of traditional Hawaii. Nonetheless, one may witness the ways and places of old Hawaii even today. Archeologists, anthropologists and sociologists have undertaken exacting reconstructions and preservation of sacred temples and villages. Travelers can immerse themselves in ancient ambiance at Pu'u Kohola, Lapakahi, and Pu'uhonua 'O Honanunau, all on the Big Island; Kane'aki and Pu'u 'O Mahuka *heiau*s (temples) on Oahu, and Pi'ilanihale *heiau* on Maui, and 'Ili'ili'opae on Moloka'i.

ANCIENT WAYS

In ancient Hawaii, the *'aina*, or land, was considered the property of the gods, held in trust by a chief or king. He in turn allocated land to support the *ali'i* (royalty), who allowed *maka'ainana* (commoners) to cultivate it. The commoners, protected by the *ali'i*, turned over much of the food grown to the *ali'i*. Although living in a feudal society, commoners were not indentured to the *ali'i*, and could leave if they wanted.

The land itself was divided into wedge-shaped parcels called *ahupua'a*, which usually extended from the coast up into a mountain valley; ideally, they were self-sustaining in seafood, produce and water.

Life was satisfactory, but it wasn't especially idyllic. Warfare was common, and commoners had to be careful not to violate *kapu* – the taboos that were law. Surfing the chiefs' waves or trespassing through sacred temples could result in death. But whether a violator of *kapu* or a warrior escaping an enemy, a person could find safety in a *pu'uhonua*, a place of refuge. Here, absolution by a *kahuna*, or priest, cleansed transgressions or assured sanctuary.

△ AHU'ENA *HEIAU*
This reconstructed *heiau*, or temple, is right on the harbor waterfront in Kailua-Kona. Originally a place of human sacrifices, it was restored by Kamehameha the Great as his personal *heiau*.

△ MODERN CARVINGS
Craftsmen still carve the sacred images called *ki'i akua*. A good place to watch them being made is at Waimea Falls Park, on Oahu's North Shore.

◁ WEATHERED IMAGE
The wood of carved *ki'i akua* is untreated, and so takes on a timeless cast in the tropical weather. This one is from Pu'uhonau 'O Honaunau National Historical Park, on the Big Island.

OF ROYAL STONES AND PETROGLYPHS

In central Oahu are the birth stones of Kukaniloko *(above)*. This clearing in a pineapple field has been sacred to Hawaiians as far back as the 1100s.

The wives of high-ranking chiefs gave birth on the stones' gently curved surfaces. Attendant chiefs, high priests, and physicians would gather in a ceremony marked by chants and offerings. The *ali'i* child would be named and the umbilical cord – *piko* – would be cut.

Hawaiians would place the severed *piko* in a hole carved into the rock, essentially a simple petroglyph, or *kaha ki'i*. This *piko* hole could be just a couple of inches in diameter and an inch or so deep, or it could be quite elaborate. The *piko* hole for a male child might have circles carved around it; that of a female infant would be adorned with a semicircle.

Piko were put where *mana*, or spirit, was strong, such as at Kukaniloko. It was hoped that the child might be influenced by the *mana*, and maybe even absorb some of it. Sometimes a representation of the family's *'aumakua* (family or personal god) would be carved into the rock adjacent to the *piko* hole.

On the Big Island, the Kona and Kohala districts offer several easily accessible petroglyph sites, such as at Puako. As most of them are at ground level, take extreme care and don't walk on top of them.

△ REFUGE GUARDIANS

Fearsome *ki'i akua*, images or idols were used to protect and impress. These are at Pu'u 'O Honaunau, a reconstructed place of refuge on the Big Island and a National Historical Park.

▽ POUNDED CLOTH

Tapa, or cloth made from bark, was used for clothes.

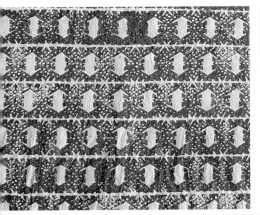

△ NAUTICAL PROTECTION

Kiha Wahine, the Lizard Woman, protected the voyaging canoe *Hokule'a* during its voyages to the South Pacific in the late 1990s. Kamehameha the Great usually carried an image of the war god on his war canoes – for protection, good luck, and to instill fear in his enemies. It worked.

HAWAII'S PEOPLE

*Hawaii has an extraordinary ethnic and cultural mix; its people originate from
as far afield as Asia, Europe, North America and the South Pacific*

Over the decades, Hawaii has received waves of immigrants from various cultures. Except for the Native Hawaiians, who were here first, and the Caucasians, who came to convert or build business empires, or in later years to settle in "paradise", most of Hawaii's ethnic groups came to work on sugar-cane or pineapple plantations and stayed to raise families. According to the 2000 census statistics, which used "self-defining" categories, Caucasians make up about 33 percent of the state's 1.2 million people. Japanese follow with 17 percent, then the Filipinos at 14 percent. The rest comprise Chinese, Koreans, African-Americans, Samoans, Vietnamese and a mix of Pacific islanders and other Asian races.

The Hawaiians

Indigenous Hawaiians are now among the most inconspicuous people walking the streets of Hawaii. In the century following first contact with Europeans, most of Hawaii's native people died from epidemics of introduced diseases: cholera, influenza, mumps, measles, whooping cough, and smallpox. Gonorrhea caused steril-ity; syphilis resulted in stillbirths.

The statistics astound. Hawaii's aboriginal population had shrunk from an estimated 300,000 at the time of Captain Cook's 1778 visit to about 40,000 in 1893, when the Hawaiian monarchy was overthrown. And many of those 40,000 were *hapa*-Hawaiian, or part-Hawaiian. By the mid-19th century, a hauntingly intangi-ble but real disease killed many more thousands of Hawaiians: sheer psychological depression. *Na kanaka ku'u wale aku no i ka 'uhane* – The people freely gave up their souls and died.

Given the degree of inter-racial mixing over the past two centuries, it's difficult to know how many full Hawaiians remain. According to state health department estimates, there are approx-imately 9,100 Hawaiians of unmixed ancestry,

LEFT: the late Aunty Edith Kanakaole performs a hula amidst a koa forest.
RIGHT: backing the message in a colorful fashion.

or just under one percent of Hawaii's total pop-ulation, including military. Those of partial Hawaiian ancestry number roughly 200,000. The most Hawaiian of islands is Ni'ihau, a pri-vately owned island off Kauai's west coast with a population of 200 – all Hawaiian. Molokai has the next largest percentage of part Hawaiians of

about 45 percent of its population. Lanai, another mostly privately owned island, is next with just under 10 percent.

The Hawaiians have made a comeback, it might be argued, by marrying into other racial groups and thus sustaining some of the blood lines. Equally if not more important is the revival of the Hawaiian culture, nearly extinguished by Protestant missionaries in the 19th century.

A *malihini*, or newcomer, might point out that part-Hawaiians are also part something else, but part-Hawaiians, whatever their other ancestry, almost unanimously think of themselves as Hawaiian first. It's a point of pride, if not of status, to be a *keiki o ka 'aina*, a child of the soil.

Many Hawaiians are aliens in their own land, and alienation cultivates difficult problems. Hawaiians and part-Hawaiians make up the largest number of inmates in county jails and the state prison. They account for the greatest percentage of welfare recipients, the majority of school dropouts and juvenile delinquents, and have the highest rate of illegitimate children.

But Hawaiians are taking strong political and social positions in support of Hawaiian rights and self-government. Their claims for autonomy and sovereignty have substantive and irrefutable historical standing, but pragmatically, the state of Hawaii will not be turned back *in toto* to the

Hawaiians. Some critics of the movement even worry that the more reactionary factions could lead to an ethnocentric, if not anti-*haole* (Caucasian), racism.

The Chinese

"The ball at the Court House on Thursday night last, given to their majesties the King and Queen by the Chinese merchants of Honolulu and Lahaina, was the most splendid affair of its kind ever held in Honolulu… We have heard but one opinion expressed by those present (which includes all Honolulu and his wife), and that was that the Celestials have outshone the 'outside barbarians' in fete-making for the throne."

According to this newspaper report, the party hosted by Chinese business leaders in 1856 to honor the marriage of King Kamehameha IV and Queen Emma took Honolulu by storm.

At the time of the ball, Hawaii's Chinese community numbered maybe 600 persons. It marked the entry of local Chinese into the highest circles of society. The king was so pleased that one of the Chinese sponsors married the foster sister of the future King Kalakaua, later becoming the first and only full-blooded Chinese to be appointed to the Hawaiian royal court.

Hawaii's Chinese didn't always have it so good. In the 1890s, jealous American business-

THE REAL CHARLIE CHAN

During the 1910s and 1920s, downtown Honolulu was the turf of Chang Apana, a Hawaiian-Chinese police detective. Known to the local Chinese as Kana Pung, Apana retired in 1932 after 34 years of distinguished service as a police officer and detective. At his impressive funeral the following year, the Royal Hawaiian Band marched in his cortege.

Apana was the inspiration for Charlie Chan, a fictional character of the American writer Earl Derr Biggers. In 1925, with the publication of Biggers' novel *House Without a Key*, the whimsical Inspector Chan assumed a place in fictional history. "Ah so," Chan would say in non-Chinese Japanese. Biggers wrote many installments of *The Adventures of Charlie Chan* and dozens of specials, such as *Charlie Chan in Shanghai*. Projecting dubious ethnic stereotypes, Chan was nevertheless of Hawaii.

men, in an attempt to restrict the inroads that enterprising Chinese were making into local commerce, initiated successful legislation that restricted the freedom of Chinese immigrant laborers. Nevertheless, over the decades the Chinese have become one of Hawaii's most prominent, influential, generous, and financially successful ethnic groups.

From the sandalwood trade of the early 1800s, the Chinese were well-acquainted with Hawaii, known to them as Tan Heung Shan, or the Country of the Fragrant Tree. The first Chinese laborers here arrived in 1852, 195 workers from Guangdong and Fujian provinces in southeastern China. Before they left China, they had signed five-year contracts promising them $36 a year, sea passage, food, clothing, and housing.

Many of those first Chinese were intent on finishing their contracts and returning to China with money. Others married local women and, with their savings, set up shops in Honolulu and Lahaina, the boom towns of the mid 1800s. The Chinese often found a niche in retail, especially as they were not welcome in the sugar industry except as laborers.

Most Chinese who used to live in Honolulu's so-called Chinatown (near the harbor) left downtown long ago, taking their new-found affluence to other, ritzier sectors of the community, espe-

China Group) was crucial to the future success of China's revolutionary movement against foreign powers. Because Chinese patrons in the islands contributed generous support to Dr. Sun's cause, Hawaii became known in some Chinese circles as the cradle of the Chinese republic.

The Japanese

When Hirohito, the late Emperor of Japan, arrived in Hawaii in 1975, his aircraft landed at Honolulu International Airport from a southeasterly approach, rather than the standard northwesterly. The reason: the emperor's pilots wanted to avoid flying over Pearl Harbor and

cially after World War II. But a few persistent old-timers stayed behind, where they still mind Hong Kong-style acupuncture clinics, market food stalls, noodle factories, and restaurants.

It was in Chinatown where Honolulu schoolmates Ho Fon and Dr. Sun Yatsen met to plan a Chinese revolution. Dr Sun Yatsen, considered the father of modern China by both Communist and Nationalist Chinese, founded his original revolutionary group in Honolulu in 1895. That secret society, first known by the Chinese-Hawaiian name Hsing Chung Hui (Revive

LEFT: tinted photograph of a traditional Chinese shop.
ABOVE: sumo, early 1900s, and Big Island farmer.

subjecting him to reminders of the war fought in his name 35 years earlier. Meeting him at the airport was an "aloha" delegation that included three US congressmen of Japanese descent, the recently elected Japanese-American governor of Hawaii, and an American of Japanese ancestry, then president of the University of Hawaii.

Along the highway from the airport to downtown and Waikiki, Hirohito and his entourage rolled past dozens of businesses with Japanese names, fleets of fishing sampans wriggling with fresh tuna for Hawaii's sashimi-crazy households, and opulent Buddhist and Shinto temples and shrines. To say that the Japanese have succeeded in Hawaii is an understatement. From

World War II until the present day, their political and social power has been considerable.

This Japanese rise to prominence began with humble origins. It wasn't until 1868, during the first year of Japan's reformist Meiji Era, that an "official" group of immigrants from Japan put into Hawaii. These *gannenmono*, or first-year men, arrived at Honolulu on board the British sailing ship *Scioto*. Carrying three-year laborer contracts, all were quickly assimilated into local plantations, earning about 12 cents a day or, according to one account, about twice what they could make in Japan. By 1885 that income quadrupled to about 50 cents a day.

islands, or more than twice the number of Hawaiians, Caucasians, or Chinese in Hawaii. Until the mid-1970s, the Japanese remained Hawaii's largest ethnic group.

The Japanese, like nearly all of Hawaii's *non-haole* laborers, suffered from racial and economic prejudices under Hawaii's plantation elite. And when Japan attacked Pearl Harbor, a small number of local Japanese-Americans were forced into internment camps on the mainland.

In Hawaii, where AJAS (Americans of Japanese ancestry) made up 40 percent of the population in the early 1940s, internment of all AJAS was out of the question. But under martial law,

ANNOUNCEMENT

Due to censorship imposed on the alien controlled press, the Japanese section of the Kwazan has been abandoned. We will hereafter publish only the English section of our paper; until further notice.

buted and discussed. Waichi Ouye is leader for Honohina Club and Hatsuo Fuji is leader for Ninole Club.

————0————

Read The Kwazan

GOING FOR BROKE

Although the Japanese-Americans of Hawaii were not interned *en masse* as on the US mainland, nearly 1,500 were still forcibly sent to mainland internment camps. Still, second-generation *(nisei)* Japanese-Americans volunteered by the hundreds for the army.

After stalling, the government finally created an all-*nisei* unit in 1942, the 100th Battalion. A year later, so many *nisei* had volunteered that a larger unit was formed, the 442nd Infantry Regiment. Both units were sent to Italy in 1944, where they fought together as the 442nd Infantry Regiment, nicknamed "Go For Broke."

Fighting in Italy and France, the *nisei* units won seven presidential unit citations and 6,000 individual awards, the most highly decorated unit in the American military during World War II. Their casualty rate was over three times the military's average.

Strict emigration laws in Japan, however, made it difficult for more Japanese to come to Tenjiku, or the Heavenly Place, as Hawaii was called. A little diplomacy was called for on this matter. So in 1881, King Kalakaua visited Japan on the first leg of a tour around the world. He initiated treaty discussions with the Japanese and actively pursued the Japanese immigration issue until it was given sanction. In 1885, a group of 943 immigrants – 676 men, 159 women and 108 children – arrived in Honolulu.

Life was often miserable in the plantation camps, but Japanese continued to arrive in ever-increasing numbers. By 1900, there were 61,000 Japanese workers and dependents in the

Japanese language schools and radio stations were shut down; Buddhist, Shinto and Zen temples were closed; and Japanese newspapers were strictly censored. Still, not a single case of Japanese-American disloyalty or sabotage occurred during the war.

Japanese *nisei* (second-generation Japanese-Americans) by the hundreds volunteered for military duty, but were turned away initially. Eventually and reluctantly, the War Department relented and in 1942, an all-*nisei* battalion of national guardsmen and draftees was created.

Regardless of ethnic background, nearly everyone in Hawaii lives a little bit of the Japanese lifestyle, knowingly or not. Few are the homes where shoes aren't removed before entering, and many are the *kama'aina* (long-time residents) who order sushi or sashimi without thinking twice. All residents of Hawaii are very much at home with things Japanese. The thump of *mochi* pounding or of drums for the Buddhist *bon odori* that honors souls of the dead are common sounds in Hawaii's diverse neighborhoods.

The Filipinos

The first Filipinos to call Hawaii home were acrobats and musicians who swept into Honolulu after a performing tour of China and Japan. In true Filipino spirit, they set to work entertaining Oahu's residents for two weeks in 1888 while waiting for their ship to San Francisco.

"The Filipino troupers pleased their Hawaiian audiences, and the spell of Hawaii upon the performers was even more potent: so much so that when sailing time came and their manager refused to pay their salaries until arrival in San Francisco, they returned to their lodgings and took up their abode in Hawaii. Four of the 12 young men found immediate employment in the Royal Hawaiian Band of King Kalakaua."

It is the sugar industry more than anything that gets the credit for making Hawaii the largest Filipino community in the world outside the Philippine archipelago. Immigration of Filipinos as laborers began in 1906 with the arrival of 15 Filipino laborers to work on a sugar plantation. For the next 40 years, Filipinos poured into Hawaii at a pace exceeded only by Japanese.

More than 125,000 Filipinos were recruited by the labor-hungry sugar companies, mostly in northern Ilocos. Of them, however, only 10,000 were women, and another 7,000 children. Not keen on being bachelors, about half of the men returned home to find wives and begin lives anew with money earned in the fields. Most who remained in Hawaii either married women from other ethnic groups or endured an extended if not eternal bachelorhood.

Tired of the plantation hierarchy and inequalities, the Filipinos organized into labor unions. The Filipino Federation and Labor Union, for example, was well-organized and actively agitating for employee benefits as early as 1919. And although some of their early labor-management confrontations ended in violence, death,

and defeat, *bum-by* (by-and-by), to use a favorite Filipino expression, their tenacity and eventual successes nurtured a collective dignity. Eventually, unions attained legal status and protection.

Filipino celebrations follow Roman Catholic observances, including an exotic candlelight festival held every spring on the Feast Day of Santa Cruz. The biggest annual event is the June Fiesta Filipina, which takes place at various locations throughout the islands. You'll find people in traditional garb enjoying Filipino music and food.

Filipino cuisine hasn't captivated island palates as have the cuisines of Korea, China,

Thailand, and Japan. But for complete menus à la Manila or Zamboanga, stroll into one of several eateries around town and wish the proprietor a sincere *mabuhay* (hello).

The Koreans

"In Hawaii you rarely ever see a group of Koreans, but you see a Korean in every group." This comment by a Honolulu-born Korean businessman is a contemporary comment on Hawaii's highly mobile and adaptable Korean community. Unlike the more clannish Japanese and Chinese, Hawaii's 20,000-plus Koreans have rapidly fanned out into society. Their "outmarriage" rate, for example, has been as high as

Left: notice in Japanese-language newspaper, World War II. **Right:** Filipina immigrant in gown, early 1910s.

80 percent for both men and women, an inter-racial marriage statistic second only to part-Hawaiians. In the United States, Honolulu is second only to Los Angeles in the number of native-born Korean residents. Both long-established and recently immigrated Koreans have capitalized on their verve, ambition, and versatility to achieve business and social successes in Hawaii. Their overall education and income levels, for example, are the highest per capita of any ethnic group in Hawaii. Although they are less than three percent of the local population, Koreans have introduced considerable spice and fire to the islands. "It's the *kim chee*,"

jokes a man who recently married a Korean woman, and became enamored of her country's pickled vegetables. Whether in the land of Morning Calm or in Hawaii, Koreans are a down-to-earth lot, without the communicative vagueness of their Asian neighbors. Koreans speak their minds and, since Korea was opened to the West, they have been dubbed the Irish of Asia: being highly sociable people, they enjoy a drink or two.

They've adapted well to Hawaii, but many of their traditions elude the younger generation. *Halmoni* (grandmothers) who first came to Hawaii as "picture brides" still try to arrange marital matches in the traditional Korean way, but second- and third-generation children

usually have other ideas. The *haraboji* (grand-fathers) still gather at community centers to spend long hours deep into clacking rounds of an ancient Korean board game, *changgi*, or Korean chess.

In the islands, probably the most popular nickname for Koreans is *yobo*. Literally, yobo means "my dear" and is a way of addressing one's husband or wife. It is also the informal equivalent of "hello" or "hey there," when used to catch one's attention. Early Korean immigrants would address one another *yobo-seyo*, or simply *yobo*, which is not quite as polite. This term stuck as an island nickname.

Koreans first arrived as laborers in 1903. Over the next two years, more than 7,000 Koreans, most of them young men (10 for every Korean woman), signed up to work in Hawaii. But in 1905, Korea's emperor cut off all labor emigration after hearing that Korean laborers had been mistreated on hemp plantations in Mexico. Not until the Japanese annexed Korea and allowed a thousand Korean picture brides to join their "picture grooms" did Korean immigration to Hawaii resume.

When Japan invaded Korea in 1910, Hawaii became a source of pro-Korean revolutionary support. In fact, most of the Korean social societies still in Hawaii began as anti-Japanese and restore-the-homeland groups, and some of them are highly secretive. Dr. Syngman Rhee, an American-educated diplomat, turned to Koreans in Hawaii for revolutionary support against the Japanese occupation. After Japan's defeat in World War II, Dr Rhee returned to Korea triumphant as the first president of the Republic of Korea. Following a Korean military coup d'état that deposed him in 1960 at the start of his fourth term, he fled to Hawaii, dying in exile in 1965.

The Samoans

Samoans, the newest of Hawaii's immigrants, come from the six isles that make up the territory of American Samoa, a 80 sq-mile (200 sq-km) group located about 2,600 miles (4,200 km) due southwest of Honolulu.

American Samoa's ruling chieftains officially ceded their islands to the United States in 1899 and for the first half of the 20th century, American Samoa was managed by the US Navy. After World War II, it was put under US Department of the Interior jurisdiction, which appoints its governor and lieutenant governor, and oversees the election of a bicameral legislature and Congressional delegate.

Some 500 Samoans had trickled into Hawaii after World War I, the majority of them to join a Mormon community in La'ie, based on Oahu's windward shore. In 1952, after Samoan immigration to America was liberalized, a group of 900 Samoan men, women and children – about half of them Samoan-American navy men and dependants being transferred to Pearl Harbor – boarded a navy

SUMO SAMOANS

Samoan Americans from Hawaii have become quite successful in Japan in sumo. Some have even become Japanese citizens.

then helped himself to the breadfruit, mangos, and bananas growing on their private property.

Perhaps of all the Asian-Oceanic ethnic groups, Samoans have best retained their traditional cultural touchstones. When a Samoan "community" problem arises, elected chiefs, some of whom represent the various expatriate Samoan clans in Hawaii, call a special *fono*. At these councils, the chiefs establish policy, mediate in the case of intra-Samoan grievances, and, if they feel a Samoan problem requires

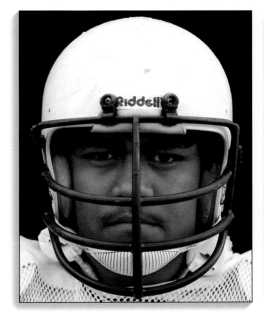

transport ship and set off for the Hawaiian islands. In 1952, these emigrants from American Samoa represented 6 percent of American Samoa's total population.

In Samoa, life is communal and sharing precedes possession. Many of these Polynesian newcomers found it extremely difficult adapting to the faster lifestyles of modern Hawaii. As a place with mostly Western inclinations regarding possession and ownership, many Hawaii residents didn't understand when a neighborly Samoan bade them *talofa* (a Samoan aloha) and

LEFT: Koreans who immigrated to Hawaii, him in 1904, her in 1914. ABOVE: Samoans are Hawaii's newcomers.

government attention, draft mutually agreed-upon statements for the proper outside individual or agency.

Most Samoan gatherings, however, are of a more celebratory nature: a wedding, or the investiture of a new chief, or Flag Day, an annual holiday that celebrates the raising of the American flag over Eastern Samoa.

Out come the *kava* cups and the colorful *lava-lava* sarongs and *puletasi* dresses, and the finely woven *lau hala* mats to be spread out on the ground. Joined by expatriates from Tonga, Fiji, Tahiti, and the Marquesas, the Samoans get together in fine *fia-fia* (feasting) fashion – *fa'a Samoa*, the Samoan way.

The Caucasians

As some Hawaiians explain it, their ancestors called the first Europeans *haole* because they could not believe that men with such pale skins and frail bodies could be alive. *Haole*, from *ha*, which means breath or the breath of life, connects with *ole*, which connotes an absence of the breath of life or, more simply, without life. Originally applied to any outsider, *haole* now refers to Caucasians, sometimes with neutral meaning, occasionally with negative meaning. Since the time of Cook, it has been fashionable in Hawaii for both *haole* and non-*haole* to put down *haole*.

For many years, the term was more of a slur than a synonym for Caucasian. *Haoles*, whether a *malihini* (newcomer) or *kama'aina* (long-time resident, old-timer), are now the fastest-growing ethnic group in the islands and are replacing the Japanese as the islands' main political force.

Since World War II, most *haole* coming to the islands more or less assimilated into the local lifestyle and rhythms, or at least made an attempt to. In recent years, however, new arrivals sometimes seem more interested in fashioning Hawaii into their own image of a paradise, or at least bringing a West Coast (from where a good percentage originate) attitude with them. It is not a new phenomenon. Since the first Polynesians arrived, every group has brought cultural baggage.

One distinct *haole* group that deserves special mention is the Portuguese, or *Portagee* in the local pidgin dialect, who immigrated in large numbers when Hawaii was still a kingdom, mostly to work in the cane fields.

As early as 1872, there were perhaps 400 or so Portuguese in Hawaii, most of them sailors who had left whaling ships for the landed life. These Europeans were well-received by both Hawaiians and *haole* merchants and planters, so in 1878 the Hawaiian government and sugar barons conducted an official labor recruitment campaign in Portugal's Azores and Madeira islands. Twenty years later, almost 13,000 Portuguese had made the rough voyage from their Atlantic islands to the Hawaiian Islands.

Many became *luna*, or foremen, on the sugar plantations, gaining a mid-level power foothold much more quickly than the Asian immigrants who worked alongside them. By the 1930s, the Portuguese community boasted a territorial supreme court chief justice, a territorial secretary and an acting governor, and the Catholic vicar apostolic of the Hawaiian Islands.

The Portuguese also introduced a small four-stringed instrument, known as the *braquino* or *cavaghindo* in Portugal, called the *'ukulele* in Hawaiian. The Hawaiian word *'ukulele* literally means "leaping flea," and the story goes that it came from the Hawaiian nickname of Edward Purvis, an English expatriate who arrived in Hawaii in 1879. Purvis made friends with newly arrived Portuguese immigrants, and he soon learned to play the *braquino* with entertaining finesse. Purvis was small in stature and quick with his hands, so his Hawaiian friends nicknamed him *'Ukulele*, the Leaping Flea.

Local Portuguese, although more than two generations removed from the old country, still celebrate Portuguese traditions and religious festivals. In the spring months, a series of post-Easter *festas* are known as the Seven Domingas, or Holy Ghost festivals. During the seven weeks of *festa*, families participate in prayer and celebration. Traditional delicacies are prepared, such as baked *pao dolce* (sweet bread) and hot fried *malasadas* (a delicious light Portuguese doughnut). ❏

LEFT: Hawaii's ethnic mix amongst newsboys, 1916.
RIGHT: Hawaiian couple.

'OLELO HAWAII – THE LANGUAGE

It may take a while to catch the local linguistic nuances. Not only is there English,

but also Hawaiian and that special local style, pidgin, a mixture of many tongues

Until the 1970s, most linguists agreed that the Hawaiian language stood little chance of survival. In the background, however, local people of all persuasions could be heard chattering in pidgin English, a hybrid island language that flits in and out of conversations like a sassy mynah bird. A typical after-work

conversation between people of Hawaiian, Chinese, Japanese, Korean, Filipino, or Samoan backgrounds might include an invitation like this: "Hey, pau hana like go my hale for grind? Get plenty 'ono pupu – even pipikaula and poke in da fridge." Translation: "Hey, after work would you like to go to my house to eat? We've got plenty of tasty appetizers, even some beef jerky and raw fish marinated with seaweed in the refrigerator."

Today, pidgin continues to predominate among locals, but increasingly, true, grammatically correct Hawaiian is heard among part-Hawaiian members of many families and other individuals at social get-togethers. The startling

change can be credited to a renaissance of pride in being Hawaiian and the establishment of language immersion schools (funded by the Hawaii Department of Education with assistance from the Office of Hawaiian Affairs), where all classes are taught in the native language. Today, not only children take classes to *'olelo* (speak) Hawaiian, their parents do so too, in order to keep up with their multilingual kids.

Even a straightforward conversation in English will be peppered with Hawaiian words that are known to all residents of the islands, and that sometimes better describe something than an equivalent word in English. *Pau hana*, used in the example above, could superficially be translated as "after work". Yet, in Hawaiian it has a richer meaning and texture that, nonetheless, defies description. You have to be in the islands for a while for the subtleties to take effect.

To describe the Hawaiian language in English is problematical because it is a language of emotion, poetry, and nature-related sound and nuance. It is an ancient language that was not transliterated until after 1820, when American missionaries arbitrarily chose 12 English letters to represent the Hawaiian sounds they thought they heard. While any transliteration of one language into the letters and sounds of another isn't perfect, the romanization of Hawaiian works well, mostly.

A language of the Pacific

For hundreds of years, the language had thrived expressively and melodically as the exclusively spoken tongue of a Polynesian people who were rich in an unwritten literature that included complicated poetic chants detailing history, genealogies, and mythologies set to memory and passed orally from generation to generation.

Historians have not determined all of the intricacies of the development of the Hawaiian language, but a fairly clear picture has emerged regarding its relationship to other languages. Hawaiian belongs to the Austronesian (formerly called Malayo-Polynesian) language family.

LEFT: translation not needed. **RIGHT:** newspaper, 1835.

These were the languages spoken by seafaring peoples who settled over a broader area of the globe than was covered by any other group until the 18th and 19th centuries, when Europeans began extensively exploring beyond their known world.

Hawaii is the furthest point of Austronesian expansion to the north, with Easter Island the eastern extent and New Zealand the most southern. From these points westward, Austronesian tongues are spoken through the Pacific to Indonesia, Malaysia, the Philippines, and parts of Taiwan. The furthest western point is the island of Madagascar off the coast of Africa.

More specifically, Hawaiian is classified as a Polynesian language closely related to the language spoken in Tahiti, the Marquesas, and the surrounding island groups of the South Pacific. Early ancestors of the Hawaiian race originated from these groups, sailing their outrigger canoes from Southeast or Indo-Malay Asia around the north coast of New Guinea, through the islands of Melanesia and into Polynesia.

Variations in the core language evolved along the way, but certain words and verbal inflections continue to reveal the ancient ties between them. Instead of the Hawaiian term *i'a* for fish, people

KE KUMU HAWAII.

HE PEPA HOIKEIKE I NA MEA E PONO AI KO HAWAII NEI.

"O ka pono ka mea e pomaikai ai ka lahuikanaka; aka, o ka hewa ka mea e hoinoia'i na aina."

Buke 1.   HONOLULU, OAHU, MEI 13, 1835.   Pepa 14.

HE ZEBERA.

SOME HAWAIIAN IN DAILY USE

aloha: love, farewell, greetings
kokua: help, assistance, as in "Please *kokua*"
mahalo: thank you

ali'i: ancient royalty, nobility
malihini: newcomer to the island, visitor
kama'aina: island-born, long-time resident
kanaka: man, person, Native Hawaiian
wahine: woman, wife
'ohana: family
keiki: child, children
haole: a foreigner, usually Caucasian
hapa: half, part, as in *hapa-haole*

'aina: land
heiau: traditional Hawaiian temple
lanai: porch, balcony, verandah
puka: hole, opening

makai: towards the ocean
mauka: towards the mountains

kapu: taboo, out of bounds, don't trespass
'ono: delicious, as in "'*Ono* food"
pau: finished, as in "I'm *pau* for today"
pau hana: end of work
pupu: hors d'oeuvres, snack

of Southeast Asia say *ika* or *ikan*. Instead of *hale* for house, they say *fare*, *'are* or *vale*. Instead of *maka* for eye, they say *mata*.

By 1819, Calvinist Christian missionaries had succeeded in converting several adventurous Hawaiian seamen who had sailed on various trading ships to America's east coast.

The first missionaries to Hawaii knew that the Hawaiian language was a spoken language only, but they were eager to set it to writing to facilitate the translation of the Bible.

By 1923, three years after their arrival, the various missionaries arbitrarily established the Hawaiian alphabet.

ABOUT THE SPELLINGS OF PLACES

Two symbols can be added to Hawaiian words to assist pronunciation: a glottal stop (*'*), called an *'okina*, and a macron, which is a horizontal line over a vowel, indicating it is drawn out. *Insight Guide: Hawaii* uses the 'okina, but not the macron. The 'okina, which gives a "hard edge" to a vowel or separates two adjoining vowels with distinct sounds, is necessary for basic pronunciation in normal conversation; the macron offers a more subtle pronunciation.

All place names in this guide that need them use a glottal stop, with three exceptions: Hawaii, Oahu and Kauai, also written as Hawai'i, O'ahu, Kaua'i. But the non-glottal spellings are so common and ubiquitous that most cartographers delete the glottal stop for these islands. Two islands requiring glottal stops for pronunciation are Ni'ihau *(nee ee how)* and Kaho'olawe *(kah ho o lah vay)*. We use these forms.

Some missionaries, for example, argued that the *k* sound was closer to *t*, or that the flapped *r* sound was more of an *l* sound. When the final vote was taken, *k* was adopted over the *t*, and *l* was chosen over the flapped *r*. The consonants were established as *h*, *k*, *l*, *m*, *n*, *p*, and *w*, while the vowel sounds were recorded as the five distinctive *a*, *e*, *i*, *o* and *u* sounds of Western romance languages. These 12 letters remain the official Hawaiian alphabet today.

For some time after Westerners began settling in the islands, Hawaiian continued to be spoken and written in government, business, and social circles of the Hawaiian kingdom. For years, it was used almost exclusively in newspapers.

Then, as the missionary influence became stronger and foreigners took over the governing of the islands, the use of Hawaiian fell into disfavor. It was declared forbidden in public schools in 1896, and by the beginning of the 20th century, it had been replaced by English on the floor of the territorial legislature.

Many Hawaiian households suppressed the use of the language in an attempt to conform to the standards of the day, and the art of chanting, which is the oral preservation of history and genealogy, diminished. The last Hawaiian language newspaper, *Ka Hoku O Hawaii (The Star of Hawaii)*, printed in Hilo on the Big Island, stopped its presses in 1948. In 1992, a monthly paper called *Na Maka O Kana*, aimed at Hawaiian-language students and published by the University of Hawaii, Hilo, began to offer news about sports, movies, and other activities in the Hawaiian language.

In the 1980s, it was estimated that only 2,000 native speakers of Hawaiian – about 300 of them residents of the privately owned island of Ni'ihau – remained in Hawaii. Today, the picture has brightened considerably. In 1979, the state legislature approved funding for the Office of Hawaiian Affairs (OHA), run for and by Hawaiians for the betterment of Hawaiians. The OHA assists the Department of Education in running language-immersion schools for children from kindergarten through 12th grade. Slowly, besides a few remaining *kupuna*, or elders, who are fluent enough to teach their native tongue, a younger generation of teachers is emerging.

Pronunciation guidelines

Every letter in Hawaiian is generally pronounced distinctly. Vowels have one sound, as in Spanish, and with none of the laziness found in English vowels: *a* sounds like ah, *e* like ay (as in hay or hey), *i* like ee, *o* like oh, and *u* sounds like oo. Likelike Highway, for example, is correctly pronounced *lee-kay lee-kay*, not *like-like*. Keep these simple rules in mind when you see signs such as Kalaniana'ole Highway or Kapi'olani.

Glottal stops, called *'okina*, often separate strings of vowels and indicate that each vowel should be pronounced distinctly. For example, Ka'a'awa makes considerable sense, but Kaaawa not so much. ❑

MUSIC AND HULA

The missionaries nearly erased the ancient forms of music and dance from the islands. They failed, and today both the old and new forms are celebrated

Few other types of music have girdled the earth more smoothly, more often, and more completely than Hawaiian music, and few musical genres have remained so popular with so many for so long. Say "Hawaiian music" to a banker in Bangkok, an army captain in Amsterdam, or a housewife in Minneapolis, and all get the same romantic, dreamy look. They're thinking of swaying palms and hips… the hula… the sultry slack-key guitar… a chilling, tremulous falsetto voice… the sassy plunky-plunkiness of a *'ukulele*… the keening notes of a steel guitar.

Hawaii has been described as a melting pot, historically quick to accept whatever comes to its golden shores. Nowhere is this phenomenal rate and degree of cultural assimilation more apparent than in the music. Listening to Hawaiian music is like listening to the islands' history.

In ancient times, Hawaiian music sounded simpler, consisting of long, monotonous chants recited either without accompaniment or against a percussive background of drums made from coconut trees, gourds, bamboo rattles and pipes, sticks, and pebble castanets. The ritualistic aspects of the music were complex and played a vital part of daily life and a significant role in religious beliefs and services. Chants, for example, were the means of establishing contact between humans and god. Entering a hula school was equivalent to entering a monastery. Today, the hula is both a spiritual and an artistic expression of Hawaiian culture.

Legends say that the goddesses of dance were Laka and Hi'iaka. (If not actually worshipped, both are still revered today.) At first, both men and women performed the dance, but only men could perform the hula during temple worship services. It was believed that by pantomiming an action, that action could be controlled in the future. Thus there were many dances for desired events, such as a successful hunt, fertility, or other successes. The hula later engulfed all of

PRECEDING PAGES: a blend of Hawaiian, Chinese, French and German ancestry. **LEFT:** 'ukulele player in Palolo Valley, Oahu. **RIGHT:** tattooed dancer in bark-cloth skirt.

Hawaiian society and became many things – teaching tool, popular entertainment, and a basic foundation for *lua*, an art of self-defense known only to early Hawaiians. As the dance became widespread and society increasingly complicated, wars and governing duties kept the men too busy for the years of training required

to be a performer. Thus, the women began to share equally in the performance of the hula.

Then an odd thing happened. After uncounted hundreds of years, King Kamehameha II overthrew the *kapu* (taboo) system in 1819 and with it went the ancient religion, of which hula was a part. This left the Hawaiian people spiritually disoriented, and ripe for newly arrived, enthusiastic Christian missionaries from New England.

These devout and dedicated settlers built churches amidst the Hawaiian huts, held services, and sang hymns. Hawaiians had never heard melody and four-part harmony before, and they collected by the hundreds outside the small churches to listen to these exotic combinations of sound. Thinking that the quickest way to a Hawaiian's soul might be through the ears, the missionaries enrolled the Hawaiians in church choirs. Progress was slow; the broader tones required by church hymns were new to Hawaiians, so the songs had to be learned by rote as the missionaries sang the hymns, called *himeni* by the Hawaiians, over and over and over again, and the Hawaiians copied as best they could.

Hawaiian music's other most dominant influence came in the

POOR TRANSLATION

Hula dancers became the rage in vaudeville and were called "cootch" dancers because many performers — few of them were actually Hawaiian — adapted the movements freely and lasciviously.

Hawaiians began doing the same with their music, and before the 1870s ended, they were composing lyrics and music simultaneously.

Berger also served as inspiration and teacher for two generations of Hawaiian musicians, some of whom later went on to local, if not national, stardom.

Other influences arrived: the guitar, for instance, was brought by early whalers or perhaps by traders from Mexico and California, but not, as is popularly believed, by Mexican cowboys,

Royal Hawaiian Band, H

form of a single man and reflected a Hawaiian king's wish to be Westernized. King Kamehameha V decided that he wanted a royal band like those in Europe, and so the brisk, mustachioed Heinrich Berger was imported from Germany in 1868 to be bandmaster. Berger, who is known today as the father of Hawaiian music, served as director of the Royal Hawaiian Band from 1872 until 1915. During this time, he conducted more than 32,000 band concerts, arranged more than 1,000 Hawaiian songs, and composed 75 original Hawaiian songs, including several still popular today. He also reversed the traditional order of the *mele*, or song, by composing the music before the words.

who arrived later in the early 1830s. In time, the traditional style of playing changed as the Hawaiian musicians loosened their strings, and tunings became whatever the player wished them to be. This style of playing came to be known as *ki ho'alu*, or slack key, and is as uniquely Hawaiian as flamenco is Spanish.

From Madeira came a small, four-stringed instrument called the *braquino*, or *cavaquinho*. It was brought to Hawaii by laborers imported to work in the sugar-cane fields, in 1878. As with so much else in Hawaiian musical history, there is disagreement as to how the *braquino* became *'ukulele*, which is Hawaiian for "jumping flea" *(see page 94).*

Scholars also continue to argue about who invented the steel guitar. Some say a Hawaiian student discovered the sound when he dropped his pocket knife upon the strings of a guitar, and holding it there with one hand, plucked the strings with the other, moving the steel knife to "slide" the sound. Others think the inventor once visited India, where he could have seen a stringed instrument, the *gottuvadyam*, played in a similar fashion. While the steel guitar has since been much identified with country-and-western music, it remains the single most identifiable part of the Hawaiian instrumental sound.

Royal inspiration

The descendants of the ancient *ali'i* ruling Hawaii in the final years before annexation to the United States were among the most talented and prolific composers of song that the island culture ever produced. The best known of these was King David Kalakaua, a complex and jovial man whose reign was also an inspiration for a genuine renaissance of music and dance.

Kalakaua was a gifted politician, world traveler, and patron of the arts. He promoted the *'ukulele* and steel guitar, and formed his own musical group, entering into competitions with relatives and friends. He collected the legends and myths of Hawaii into a definitive and literate book, and co-wrote with Heinrich Berger Hawaii's national anthem, "Hawaii Pono'i," a song that's still sung at ball games and public assemblies. The hula, long suppressed by the Christian missionaries, was revived under his personal direction. Much music is played today on the birthday, 16 November, of this bewhiskered king; the state's biggest hula competition, the Merrie Monarch (named for his nickname) takes place annually on the Big Island. His sister, Lili'uokalani, came even closer than the king to understanding and synthesizing ancient Hawaiian and Western musical traditions and form. Probably the most gifted Hawaiian of her class and time, she composed a song that has appeared in at least half the Hawaiian movies ever made, and it has been a certifiable "hit" for about 80 years, "Aloha 'Oe."

The sound of Hawaiian music changed again after Lili'uokalani's kingdom was wrenched away by aggressive sugar growers and Hawaii

became a territory of the United States. This focused mainland interest toward Hawaii, and in 1915 a group of Hawaiian musicians, singers, and dancers were the runaway sensation of the Panama-Pacific International Exposition in San Francisco, sparking a craze that swept North America and spread to Europe. Soon after, the best or most adaptable Tin Pan Alley song writers were writing so-called Hawaiian music, too.

Even if most of those new songs had little to do with true Hawaiian musical tradition – and often double-talk served as Hawaiian, as in "Yaaka Hula Hickey Dula" (a hit for Al Jolson) – the influence was immediate and significant.

The craze propelled authentic Hawaiian musicians across America for many years. They, in turn, accepted the phony Hawaiian songs to satisfy requests, eventually turning them into Hawaiian "classics." At the same time, they began arranging traditional, more authentic Hawaiian songs with the newly popular jazz beat that they heard everywhere they went.

In Hawaii, the first hotels were going up in Waikiki, and dance bands were formed for the growing number of tourists. Ragtime, jazz, blues, Latin, and foxtrot rhythms were interspersed with Hawaiian themes and English lyrics. The purists were appalled, as always, but by 1930 the *hapa-haole* (half-Caucasian) song was an

LEFT: Heinrich Berger and the Royal Hawaiian Band, 1910. **RIGHT:** *Hula halau* on Oahu, 1852.

entrenched and accepted part of Hawaiian music, soon to become a staple on what was eventually the most widely heard radio program in the world. In 1935, Hawaii's music caught the ears of West Coast listeners via "Hawaii Calls," a radio program broadcast from under a banyan tree in Waikiki and other locales. Today, many of the more than 300 Hawaiian musicians who were on the program are legends of Hawaii's musical past, among them Danny Kaleikini, Alfred Apaka and Benny Kalama.

HOLLYWOOD AWAKENS

Bing Crosby introduced two *hapa-haole* classics, "Sweet Leilani" and "Blue Hawaii," in a single film, in 1937. "Sweet Leilani" won the Oscar for best song, and so Hollywood began churning out musical romances.

From 1930 to 1960 is regarded as Hawaiian music's "golden age," as the music of the islands circled the world on television and in radio and film. Then came the Beatles, changing Hawaiian music just as they changed so many things. In fact, they nearly killed it. For 10 years, young Hawaiians were uninterested in the traditional island sound. Hawaiian music on local radio dropped to a low 5 percent. Rock dominated, and middle-of-the-road singers like Kui Lee and Don Ho emerged

Then Hollywood called. The hula was revived again and cleaned up a bit for Hollywood as authentic island practitioners were featured in many films: the swaying hips and graceful limbs of the grass-skirted dancer would be the foremost symbol of Hawaii's image of carefree sensuality.

When a songwriter urged visitors to Hawaii to keep their eyes on the hands, it was good advice, for the hands tell the story in hula. When the singer says, "Lovely hula hands/graceful as the birds in motion," the arms are extended and the hands move gracefully to simulate the wings of swooping birds. In "The Hukilau Song," which is about fishing, the hands throw out and pull in the net.

as the only Hawaiian stars, rendering songs such as "One Paddle, Two Paddle," "Days of My Youth," and "I'll Remember You."

In the 1970s there came another Hawaiian renaissance, as people with Hawaiian blood discovered an ethnic awareness and pride. So pervasive and energetic was this second cultural rebirth that all the traditional Hawaiian arts experienced a rich revival. The music became more "contemporary", a word used by the musicians themselves. Politically-relevant lyrics were added along with new rhythms, new instruments, and greater amplification, thus attracting the attention of young Hawaiians who had turned away from their heritage for so long.

Traditional sounds are revitalised

At the same time, there was renewed interest in the more traditional Hawaiian sounds. Some composers wrote songs about the kings and ancient gods. In the 1970s, Hawaii acknowledged its roots. Guitarist Keola Beamer gained recognition during this period, honing his techniques on an album called *Hawaiian Slack Key in the Real Old Style*. Beamer says, "There's power in our music which is drawn from the environment. If you sit and watch a waterfall or listen to the trade winds for awhile, you begin to feel a rhythm. You can be far away from Hawaii and hear a song and instantly be transported."

The Royal Hawaiian Band, still performing after all these years, appears in several public concerts each week, notably at noon nearly every Friday at the 'Iolani Palace Coronation Bandstand. Popular radio stations KDNN (FM 98.5) and KINE (FM 105) broadcast contemporary and traditional Hawaiian music. New generations of young entertainers continue to emerge, sending out Hawaiian vibes to the mainland, Japan, and beyond, combining music with showmanship that draws on early Hawaiian traditions. On stage, composer, chanter, dancer and singer Keali'i Reichel stands barechested, hair streaming about his shoulders,

Music is a vital part of Hawaiian daily life and songs have been written about the most mundane subjects, for example, "The Hasegawa General Store" and "Bottles and Cans", a song about Maui's Makawao dump. The sound of the 'ukulele has given birth to a raucous, backyard style of playing called *cha-lang-a-lang*.

Music is everywhere in Hawaii. Hawaiians believe that music is not just a means of communicating with the gods, but is a gift from the gods, so they in turn give it freely, whether walking along the street or lazing at the bus stop.

carved bone fishhook nestled at his neck. His body tattoos run from his ankle to disappear under his brief *malo* (loincloth). In the bright spotlight, he sings in sweet, resonant tones, switching from ballads like "Ku'u Pua Mae 'Ole" (about lasting romance and calming waters), to a poetic chant "Maika'i Ka 'Oiwi O Ka'ala" with *ipu* (gourd) accompaniment, to a whimsical novelty, "The Toad Song." His albums "Kawaipunahele" and "Lei Hali'a" have been met with critical acclaim. Reichel explains why he believes his music has such appeal: "In order to compose music, words, poetry, you have to be inspired; you have to speak from experience."

LEFT: Makaha Sons of Ni'ihau at Makua Beach, Oahu, 1979. **ABOVE:** hula dancers relax after a performance.

Sisters are doing it

Female vocalists, too, have made waves beyond local shores. Ever since Lehua Kalima, Angela Morales and Nalani Choy won a local song contest in the 1980s with an original composition called "Local Boys," their blend of pop, folk, country, and traditional Hawaiian music has delighted listeners in the United States and Japan. Na Leo Pilimehana's album "Anthology I" reached number 10 on the Billboard Magazine World Music chart and continues be a local favorite. The trio's album "Colours" is packed with songs that are personal renderings with such titles as "Taro Patch

Twist", about a planter in Waipi'o Valley who likes to dance in his taro patch, and "The Rest of Your Life", a love song accompanied by the Galliard String Quartet.

Henry Kapono, one of the islands' most prolific chroniclers of the Hawaiian experience, explores his Hawaiianness with a Jamaican beat. And then there's Moe Keale, popular singer and 'ukulele virtuoso who played with the "Sons of Hawaii," led by Eddie Kamae and the late, legendary slack-key guitarist Gabby Pahinui. Keale, who has performed in New York, Chicago, Los Angeles, San Francisco, Seattle, Hong Kong, and Canada, appears regularly in Waikiki.

"Music," he says, "is not something you just hear with your ears. It's something you hear with your heart. I can tell when Hawaiian music is being played right, because it makes me cry."

The sounds of Hawaii may not be the same as they were before Western contact – they might include touches of reggae, folk, country or classical – but they still evoke sentiment and nostalgia in the moonlight on many a balmy island night. On any island, anywhere, whether real or not.

Return of hula

Not since the early 1800s, when missionaries labeled many hula dances obscene and banned them, have such powerful and erotic movements been seen in Hawaii. Indeed, suppression of hula had been so successful that by the 1850s it had nearly disappeared. Forty years later, after King Kalakaua revived the hula, much had already been lost forever. Today, hula retains much of its serious heritage. Contemporary students heed ancient ritual religiously, although none is asked to give up sex to be a hula performer, as was true in ancient times. Different *hula halau* (hula schools) compete fiercely. Hula masters, or *kumu hula*, are revered figures. And with the male hula now in a period of rich revival, the dance has become a symbol of the islander's newly rediscovered sense of Hawaiian identity.

Hawaii's most prestigious hula event is the Merrie Monarch Festival, which pays homage to King David Kalakaua. It has been held every April since 1964 at the Edith Kanaka'ole Stadium in Hilo. The highlight of the week-long festival, which includes a parade and music celebrations, is the two-day competition of *kahiko*, or ancient hula, and *'auwana* or modern hula.

Every island has its signature hula events. On Oahu, the Queen Lili'uokalani Keiki Hula festival draws 500 children to perform in July, and in the same month, the Prince Lot Hula Festival plays out under the giant monkey pod trees of Moanalua Gardens. At Princeville, Kauai, local entertainers meet mainland musicians at the Prince Albert Hula Festival every May. On Maui, Na Mele O Maui Song Contest and Hula Festival takes place annually in Ka'anapali. ❏

LEFT: children performing the hula. **RIGHT:** state *keiki* hula (children's hula) champions.

AN ART OF FLOWERS, FEATHERS AND ALOHA

Found throughout Polynesia, lei *were once nearly sacred symbols. Today,* lei *retain some of that aura, but are also used to convey* aloha *and respect.*

In ancient times, *lei* were offered to the gods during sacred dances and chants, taking the form of head wreaths and necklaces, as well as the long, open-ended strands of *maile* (vines) that are draped around the necks of grooms and prom escorts today.

Lei are made of flowers, leaves, shells, and paper, and of anything else that can be fashioned by five basic techniques. If a *lei*-maker uses *wili paukuku*, she is winding roses and begonias in a certain style. *Humuhumu* is a *lei* sewn onto a backing. *Wili* is a *lei* that is wound or twisted, *hili* is braided with leaves and *haku* is braided with flowers. *Kui* is strung on a thread.

Before needle and thread were introduced to Hawaii, stiff grass blades from Nu'uanu Valley were used as needles, and strands of banana bark were utilized as string. For the more elaborate feather *lei* reserved for the royalty of old Hawaii, strips of *olona* bark were twisted into a cord that was flexible and strong enough to invisibly secure hundreds of feathers.

Prices may range today from less than $5 up to $50 for the fragrant *maile* and multiple strands of *pikake*. Many *leis*, like the woven ginger *lei* or the complex maunaloa orchid *lei*, are intricate works of art. Others, such as a simple plumeria *lei*, can be strung by anyone with a needle and thread.

△ **FOR THE TOURISTS**
Makers of *lei* produce hundreds if not thousands of *lei* daily for the islands' tourism industry. Most common is the plumeria *lei*.

▽ **ECLECTIC DIVERSITY**
Nearly any flower or nut can be fashioned into a *lei*, including bougainvillea, ginger, and plumeria with its luscious scent.

▽ *LEI* HULU
Red and yellow feathers were used in the *lei* of royalty. *Lei hulu* also means a dearly beloved child or person.

> **A KINGLY *LEI***
On Kamehameha Day, the Honolulu statue of Kamehameha the Great, who unified the Hawaiian islands, is draped with a floral cape of scores of long *lei*, or *lei ali'i*, a *lei* for royalty or the chief.

▽ ***LEI* FOR HULA**
The hula, both traditional and modern, uses *lei* as important adornment. Often in hula, *lei* are not made from flowers, but rather leaves and other parts of flora considered to impart importance.

△ **AROUND THE NECK**
A *lei* for the neck is known as *lei 'a'i*, also an expression for necktie or scarf.

◁ **EQUESTRIAN *LEI***
A *pa'u* rider and horse on Kamehameha Day are exquisitely adorned with *lei*. (A pa'u is a skirt or sarong for female horseback riders.)

DRAPED BY *ALOHA* AND RESPECT

In Hawaii, as in some other Pacific island cultures, a *lei* is a special symbol or gift given as a sign of respect, welcoming (or departure), or good feeling. *Lei* are also draped over the statues or images of important people in Hawaii's history, such as Kamehameha the Great *(above)*, Queen Lili'uokalani or Father Damien.

Each island has its own special material for making *lei*. The delicate orange *'ilima* blossom represents Oahu. Feathery red *lehua* blossoms from gnarled *'ohi'a* trees symbolize the island of Hawaii. Pink *lokelani* (an introduced Castilian rose) make up Maui's *lei*, while Molokai is adorned by silver-green leaves from the *kukui* tree and decorated with tiny white blossoms.

Oblong leaves and dark berries from the *mokihana* tree are fashioned into a *lei* for Kauai. On Lanai, *lei* are woven from slim strands of *kauna'oa*, an orange, mossy beach vine. Even uninhabited Kaho'olawe has a *lei* from *hinahina*, a beach plant with narrow green leaves and little white flowers. Ni'ihau is the only island not represented by a flower, but by shells: the rare and very tiny *pūpū* that are treasured by *kama'aina* as much as valuable gems.

FOOD OF AN ECLECTIC SORT

With ethnic influences from Polynesia, China, Japan, Korea, Portugal and North America, Hawaii's cuisine is among the world's most eclectic

Island menus read like a United Nations lunch order: *sushi*, pasta, crispy *gau gee*, *kim chee*, tortillas, tandoori chicken, *wienerschnitzel*, spring rolls – you name it, they eat it. Within a relatively small geographical area, visitors find a universe of dishes served in surroundings both down-home and haute, from neighborhood delicatessens hawking lox and bagels to candlelit lairs of *chateaubriand* and chocolate mousse.

Hawaii has many to thank for its tasty diversity. To begin with the Chinese, who taught islanders that rice goes just as well with eggs at breakfast as with lunch and dinner. Supermarkets of all stripes stock supplies of *cilantro* (Chinese parsley), lemongrass and ginger, and restaurants turn out everything from Mandarin, Sichuan, and Cantonese to Mongolian barbecue and stir-fry. For an energizing assault on the senses, go to a house of *dim sum*, where pushy waitresses load your table with little plates of bite-sized dumplings until hands are held up in surrender.

From the Japanese came the gifts of *shoyu* (soy sauce), *sashimi* (thinly sliced raw fish), and *tempura* (battered, deep-fried vegetables and meats, introduced to Japan from Portugal, actually). Almost every street has a sushi bar for swigging *sake* while chefs with lightning-fast hands fashion edible fantasies out of rice, seafood and *wasabi* (hot green-horseradish). Japanese culinary sensibilities are best summed up by the *bento*, a lunch box with tidy compartments for morsels of chicken, shrimp, pork cutlets, fishcake, pickled plums, rice, and other artful treats.

Wafts of garlic and grilled specialties lure hungry diners through the doors of Hawaii's Korean restaurants, which generally assume the form of Formica-tabled eateries. Therein await *kim chee* (pickled vegetables), *kalbi* (marinated short ribs), *jun* (foods fried in an egg batter), and the musical *bi bim bap*, which is a bowl of rice, with vegetables, fried egg, and a sweet sauce.

LEFT: Hawaii is a fruit-lover's paradise, with pineapples, mangos, and nectarines to name just a few.
RIGHT: lunch offerings.

A more recent influx of people from Thailand has introduced spring rolls, *mee krob* (noodle salad), and a coconut milk/hot pepper-flavored dish called Evil Jungle Prince, best followed by Thai iced tea with sweetened condensed milk. Vietnamese food – less spicy than Thai – is particularly popular for its *pho*, a broth with

noodles and beef or chicken slices. Portuguese influence makes itself known in *pao dolce* (sweet bread), *chorizo* (spicy sausage), *vinha d'alhos* (marinated meat) and a robust bean soup, while from the Philippines comes *lumpia* (fried spring rolls), *pancit* (noodles, vegetables and pork), *pork guisantes* (pork rump), *bagoong* (fish sauce) and *bitsu bitsu* (sweet potato scones).

Stir into to this pot the creativity of classically trained chefs from France, Switzerland, Germany, North America, and Italy who have been imported to work in some of Hawaii's upscale restaurants. The state's continental ideas of the 1970s have evolved into today's more health-conscious cooking, but without too much effort you can still find an authentic veal *scaloppini* or a slab of salmon drenched in dill sauce.

The most recent take on island food is called Hawaii Regional Cuisine – a variation of what's known elsewhere as Pacific Rim Cuisine, New Australian Cuisine, or fusion cuisine – which begins with a sort of culinary word association. Think of a papaya and one thinks of the prolific trees of Puna on the Big Island. Onions conjure up images of cool upcountry Kula on Maui, where the sweetest variety is grown. Guava thrives in Kilauea on Kauai, and Molokai is known for its potatoes, while fresh fish are pulled from the clear waters around all the islands.

she mingled in flavors of Filipino, Chinese, Japanese and Hawaiian dishes."

Inevitably, the blending of cooking styles occurred in Hawaii's plantation villages. When Japanese contract laborers were imported in the 1880s, they lived side-by-side with Hawaiian and Chinese workers in simple, single-walled wooden houses. The Chinese built community cookhouses, the Japanese added mom-and-pop tofu (soybean curd) factories. People grew their own *bok choi* and lemongrass in backyards.

When Hawaii's classically trained chefs saw they could infuse their own food with an exciting new range of flavors by learning Hawaiian-

The regional cuisine movement gained momentum in 1992, when a dozen curious, creative and congenial chefs began getting together to share their ideas as well as their wish lists for a wider variety of fresh produce and other more varied ingredients. In the kitchens of their own elegant restaurants, their sous-chefs and *garde-mangers* were feasting on interesting, flavorful treats they had learned to make at home.

Alan Wong, whose Oahu Restaurant is the perennial winner of the in-state Hale 'Aina Award for Best Restaurant (five out of six times from 1996–2001), explains, "While I was growing up in Hawaii, my grandfather cooked Chinese and my mother cooked Japanese, but

style cooking from each other, while supporting local agriculture, they gave their group a formal name, Hawaii Regional Cuisine, Inc.

Their presence has made a difference on Hawaii's culinary scene. Today, any number of farmers are growing crops to the specifications of chefs who visit the fields and make known what they want for their own restaurants. Tomatoes are vine-ripened; arugula and baby lettuces fill Upcountry fields on Maui and the Big Island. Many hotels grow their own fresh herbs. One hotel in Waikiki has its own rooftop hydroponic garden, and a Maui resort harvests fresh tropical fruit and other produce from an organic garden that surrounds its parking lot.

A host of other professional chefs were inspired by the original daring dozen, and Hawaiian regional cuisine has become a palate-pleasing password even beyond island shores. Who hasn't seen or heard of Hawaii's own Sam Choy, or the equally renowned Roy Yamaguchi, both of whom own several restaurants, have published cookbooks, and host their own television cooking shows? The current pantheon of greats includes George Maurothalassi-tis, Peter Merriman, Padovani and David Paul, each with their own signature restaurants.

> ### PERPLEXING *POI*
>
> A staple of the traditional diet, *poi* is a thick, viscous paste-like food. It is made from the taro root.

Passion and pineapple

Local products have become as intrinsically linked to Hawaii's lifestyle as the ebbing and flowing of the tides. Residents and visitors alike have easy access to an abundance of fresh fruit, and we're not just talking pineapple and coconut. Equally common are the tiny apple banana, the golden papaya, the pungent *liliko'i*, and the guava, a yellow lemon-sized gem with a shockingly pink interior.

The lychee, prized for its juicy white flesh, can be spotted hanging in grape-like clumps on trees

Enthusiastic practitioners of Hawaii regional cuisine collaborate closely with farmers and fishermen to get the products they need, then infuse those foods with cooking techniques from around the world. The result is a menu that reads like this: *'ulu* (breadfruit) *vichyssoise*, Manoa greens with Waimea vine-ripened tomatoes and Puna goat cheese, *tempura*-style Keahole shrimp and apple banana, sesame-cured boar loin with guava dressing, and a slice of *liliko'i* (passionfruit) chiffon pie. If so inclined, enjoy the meal with a wine from Tedeschi.

in Manoa Valley, while *poha* (cape gooseberry) thrives on bushes near Kilauea Volcano. The markets of Honolulu's Chinatown district are a good source of these and lesser-known fruits, like the tamarind, kumquat, starfruit, *rambuton* (sweet white fruit in a red, spiky shell), and *cherimoya* (with tart white flesh).

Visit Hawaii during the summer and you'll discover the joys of the mango. When mango trees start to blossom in May, it's as big a deal as seeing the first whales of winter. By July, the fruit is weighing down the branches, and neighbors distribute free bags of sweet, juicy mangoes. Leftovers that aren't picked drop on the road, get squashed by traffic, and ferment.

LEFT: the day's catch of tuna, Hilo.
ABOVE: planting taro, used for *poi*, and ripening bananas.

Ocean harvests

What is harvested by land is matched only by the bounty of the sea. The king and queen of Hawaiian fish are the *mahimahi* (dolphin fish) and *'opakapaka* (pink snapper), but *ulua* (jack crevalle), *ono* (wahoo), *'ahi* (yellow-fin tuna), and *onaga* (red snapper) are equally impressive, whether blackened Cajun-style or baked in wafer-thin layers of crispy phyllo pastry.

Locals have been known to scamper crab-like across shorelines, hanging on when the big waves roll in, in order to pick a bunch of quarter-sized shells off the lava rocks. Called *'opihi,* limpets are Hawaii's answer to French *escargots*

promoting its own special grade of lamb. Lanai axis deer has become a popular entrée laced with plum sauce, and Molokai venison makes for a tasty stew or toothsome sausage.

If all of these choices sound a little overwhelming, start with the basics. Try a plate lunch, the statewide institution defined by a few simple elements. You'll get a paper plate loaded with "two scoop rice" (No, not "two scoops of rice") plus a mound of heavily mayonnaised macaroni salad. Order one with *teriyaki* beef, breaded pork, or chicken *(katsu)*, fried fish or Spam, a passion among locals. Plate lunches are sold at carryout diners or lunch trucks.

and are rarely found on restaurant menus. More accessible is *tako* (octopus), a chewy delicacy that often shows up raw and marinated in *poke* (seasoned raw fish). In the world of aquaculture, scientists and entrepreneurs on the Big Island and north shore of Oahu are creating miniature oceans in tanks teeming with prawns, lobsters, abalone and other fishy delicacies.

Two-scoop rice

Hawaii's homegrown extends to grain-fattened beef, grass-fed lamb, and free-range game. *Paniolo* (cowboys) on Maui and the Big Island saddle up in the pre-dawn mist to round up the beef that settles onto dinner plates. Ni'ihau is

Next, try some snacks – maybe shave ice, a snowcone soaked in neon-colored tropical syrups like mango, guava and coconut. Those in the know order it with vanilla ice cream and sweet *azuki* beans on the bottom. Or munch on some *manapua*, the tennis ball-sized steamed Chinese dumpling filled with pork or curried chicken. Enjoy a bowl of *saimin*, an Asian noodle soup topped with an encyclopedia of garnishes like sliced *char siu* (roast pork), fishcake, and green onions. Or pick up a bag of crack seed, pickled plums and *pipi kaula* (beef jerky). ❏

ABOVE: locals at a *lu'au*, 1910. **RIGHT:** preparing the pig, a staple of all *lu'aus*, at Kona Village Resort, Big Island.

The *Lu'au*

I t's late afternoon when the *lu'au* table is finally set under the big banyan tree. The salmon has been chopped *lomilomi* style, with onions and tomatoes, and it sits next to a big bowl of *poi*, or pounded taro root, a staple of the old Hawaiian diet. Aunties chatter as they carry out the rest of the dishes: *laulau* (pork and fish steamed in ti leaves), *poke* (seasoned raw fish), yams, squid *lu'au* with coconut milk and taro tops, *haupia* (coconut pudding), and fresh fruit.

The boys have already pulled out the pig from the *imu* (underground rock oven), and now the moist, smoky meat is shredded and piled on a big platter as the centerpiece of the meal. Friends and family pick up a plate.

If you're lucky, you might just stumble upon the real thing at a community benefit, or be invited to one by an island friend. More likely though, the *lu'aus* you'll discover will be the commercialized variety, complete with the comic hula and *maitais*. While purists may find this a shallow version of the real thing, the *imu* ceremonies, hula, Hawaiian music, kalua pig and other culinary specialties and good cheer are all rooted in Hawaiian tradition. If you can let go of any prejudices about "authenticity," you're very likely to have a rollicking good time.

These modern *lu'aus* are a far cry from the *aha 'aina*, or feasts of old, when women dined separately from men and were prohibited from eating some of the choicest of *lu'au* fare. Finally, after 1819, when Liholiho (King Kamehameha II) abolished the old *kapu* (tabu) system of restrictions, *lu'aus* became a lively tradition enjoyed by all. Today, an Island wedding, baby's first birthday, or junior's graduation just wouldn't seem the same without a backyard bash for friends and family.

The most popular way of preparing food in old Hawaii was to *kalua* the meat, chicken, dog or fish in an earthen oven lined with stones. Today, the heart of any *lu'au*, commercial or private, continues to be the preparation and unearthing of the *imu*. Although dog is no longer part of the menu, current *lu'au* food is reasonably authentic, except for such items as macaroni and potato salads or *teriyaki*-beef, added to suit all tastes.

You'll still find pig roasted to flaky tenderness in the *imu*, accompanied by *poi*, sweet potatoes, marinated lomi salmon with chopped tomatoes and onions, and sometimes *'opihi*, a Hawaiian shellfish plucked from wave-washed rocky shorelines and eaten raw as a special delicacy. For uninitiated taste buds, it's best to sample *poi* with salty kalua pig or *lomilomi* salmon to enhance the flavors and textures. Many *lu'aus* ladle out chicken long rice, a dish of chicken cooked with translucent noodles made of rice flour and garnished with green onions. Frequently you'll find *laulau*, little green bundles of taro leaf, which taste like spinach, steamed with pork and fish. For dessert, coconut cake is a new addition, but *haupia*, a coconut-milk pudding, has long been served as a sweet finale.

The entertainment at one of these modern feasts is like taking a mini-tour through the island cultures of Hawaii, Tonga, Samoa, New Zealand, and Tahiti. Hawaii's contribution includes the haunting chants

that perpetuate the genealogies and legends of the past, as well as the graceful hula. Some *lu'aus* include pageantry with participants dressed like early Hawaiian royalty.

Whether a visitor will get his money's worth from a commercial *lu'au*, which might cost from $40 to $60 minimum, depends upon the individual, and the *lu'au*. If ready to throw yourself into the spirit of the night by donning your most colorful aloha shirt, taking off your shoes, and getting up on stage to learn a Tahitian *tamure* while your traveling companions cheer, and if you find unfamiliar foods intriguing, you'll have a good time. *Lu'au* range from tacky to traditional, and you'll just have to look around for your style. ❏

THE HAWAIIAN ISLANDS

*A look at all the islands and important destinations, with
cross references to detailed and comprehensive maps*

Pull out a map and run a finger along the islands of Hawaii, strung across the Pacific like a series of jade stepping stones. The islands line up oldest to youngest, with the youngest, the Big Island, in the southeast and the oldest islands – or what's left of them – 1,500 miles (2,400 km) away to the northwest. The oldest are atolls and shoals now, home to seabirds and the occasional Hawaiian monk seal.

Scientists say the Hawaiian islands are "drifting" northwest on a tectonic plate a few inches per year, and as each island drifts, it is also eroding and sinking under its own weight. Oahu, for example, has sunk over 1,000 feet (300 meters) since its birth three million years ago. Remaining stationary beneath the tectonic plate is a hot spot, where magma leaks through to create the islands.

This well-defined and orderly progression gives each of Hawaii's seven inhabited islands distinct geographical dispositions. The island chain encompasses a total of 6,423 sq miles (10,335 sq km) of land area, roughly the size of Connecticut and Rhode Island combined. The Big Island, aptly enough, accounts for close to two thirds of that. Hawaii ranks 40th among the states in population, with approximately 1.2 million people – about 75 percent of whom reside on Oahu.

Kauai is the oldest of the main islands, its ancient shield volcano deeply eroded into primal contours. Next comes Oahu, its two extinct volcanoes nearly unrecognizable as such. Younger still is Maui, a coupling of old and new, the older West Maui volcano worn down but Haleakala still looking like the active volcano it was (and maybe still is). Molokai, Lanai and Kaho'olawe hover off Maui's west side as small volcanic siblings. And then, visible from Haleakala's summit, is the Big Island, formed by five volcanoes and with a landscape still smoothly contoured and pristine – and still growing. Some 18 miles (29 km) off the Big Island's South Point is Lo'ihi, a gestating island that has yet to see the sun. Lo'ihi (meaning "long, tall") has given scientists a prime opportunity to study island formation. It is about 3,000 feet (900 meters) below sea level. Experts predict that a momentous event will occur about a thousand lifetimes from now.

Notes on directions

Islanders share a common vernacular for directions – the two most common are *mauka* and *makai*. *Mauka* means "upland or towards the mountains," and *makai* means "towards the sea." In Honolulu, directional words take on an even greater sophistication. Directions are also given in relation to Diamond Head, the volcanic tuff east of Waikiki, and to *'Ewa*, a district west of Pearl Harbor. ❏

PRECEDING PAGES: dusk on Lumaha'i Beach, Kauai; ferns on the Big Island; hiking atop Haleakala, Maui; eyes on Waikiki Beach, Oahu.
LEFT: two of many waterfalls on Kauai.

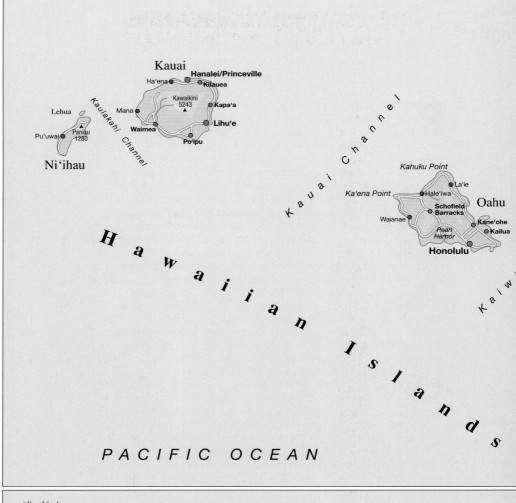

Kauai

Ha'ena · Hanalei/Princeville
· Kilauea
Kawaikini
5243 ▲ Kapa'a
Mana · Lihu'e
Waimea
Po'ipu

Lehua
Pu'uwai · Paniau
1280
Ni'ihau

Kaulakahi Channel

Kauai Channel

Kahuku Point
La'ie
Ka'ena Point Hale'iwa
Schofield Oahu
Barracks
Waianae Kane'ohe
Pearl Kailua
Harbor
Honolulu

H a w a i i a n   I s l a n d s

Kaiwi

PACIFIC OCEAN

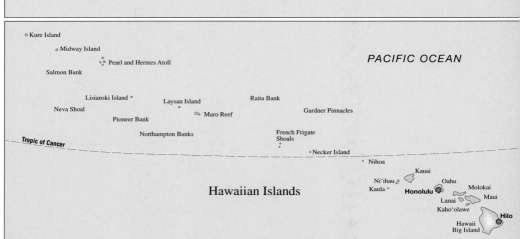

· Kure Island
· Midway Island
· Pearl and Hermes Atoll
Salmon Bank

PACIFIC OCEAN

Lisianski Island ·
Laysan Island
· Raita Bank
Neva Shoal Maro Reef Gardner Pinnacles
Pioneer Bank
Northampton Banks French Frigate
Shoals

Tropic of Cancer

· Necker Island
· Nihoa

Kauai
Ni'ihau
Kaula · Oahu
Honolulu Molokai
Lanai Maui
Hawaiian Islands Kaho'olawe
Hawaii Hilo
Big Island

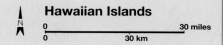

Hawaiian Islands

0 ——————————————— 30 miles
0 ——————————————— 30 km

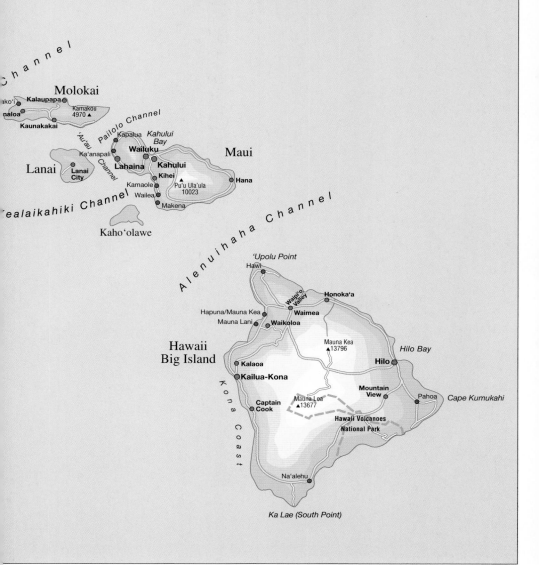

PACIFIC OCEAN

Channel

Molokai

ako'i
Kalaupapa

naloa

Kamakou
4970 ▲

Kaunakakai

Pailolo Channel

Kapalua

'Au'au

Kahului
Bay

Ka'anapali

Wailuku

Maui

Lanai

Lahaina

Kahului

Lanai
City

Channel

Kihei

Pu'u Ula'ula
10023 ▲

Hana

Kamaole

Wailea

ealaikahiki Channel

Makena

Kaho'olawe

Alenuihaha Channel

'Upolu Point

Hawi

Waipi'o
Valley

Honoka'a

Hapuna/Mauna Kea

Waimea

Mauna Lani

Waikoloa

*Hawaii
Big Island*

Mauna Kea
▲13796

Hilo Bay

Kalaoa

Hilo

Kailua-Kona

Kona Coast

Mountain
View

Mauna Loa
▲13677

Pahoa

Cape Kumukahi

Captain
Cook

Hawaii Volcanoes
National Park

Na'alehu

Ka Lae (South Point)

OAHU

Most of Hawaii's residents live on Oahu, hence its urban prominence. Still, much of the island remains rural and wild

Scour the globe and you won't find another island quite like Oahu. One old-time *kama'aina* compares Oahu to, of all things, a Chinese restaurant. "There are plenty of enticing options, there's something to suit everyone's tastes, and yet after you leave you somehow wind up hungry for more." Oahu's pleasures are diverse. Where else can you find monstrous surfing waves, a billion-dollar skyline, high tea at the beach, striptease at a downtown bar, and waterfall-defined, mist-shrouded, rainbow-blessed mountains? Every day, more than 70,000 visitors explore the island coast to coast, tip to tip, from Wai'anae in the west to Makapu'u in the east.

Like hazy Polynesian tales about the lost lands of Mu and Hawaiki, the meaning of the word *o'ahu* evaporated long ago. Nowadays, it is often, probably incorrectly, said to mean "the gathering place," but that was, perhaps, an early tourism catchphrase. In ancient Hawaii, scholars note, Oahu did not have a large population, and the powerful chiefs "gathered" not on Oahu but on the Big Island and Kauai.

Today, however, there is no doubt that Oahu is a gathering place. Its 800,000-plus residents make up around 75 percent of the state's population. Honolulu is the seat of island and state government, and in terms of geographical reach, it is the longest city in the world. Technically, the city and county of Honolulu are one and the same, covering all of Oahu and extending 1,400 miles (2,200 km) northwest up the Hawaiian chain to Kure Atoll, near Midway Island.

Both downtown Honolulu and Waikiki lie on Oahu's southern coast, backed up against the Ko'olau Range. Waikiki is nearly a separate destination in itself, and many visitors to Hawaii never leave it except to reach the airport on the other side of Honolulu. Still, only the fool would fly to one of the most remote island chains in the world just to sit in Waikiki. On the other side of the Ko'olau mountains is the windward side, green and wet. There are several commuter bedroom communities here, but farther north, the narrow corridor between mountain and ocean becomes exceedingly rural. Cresting the northern tip of the island, the highway shifts westward along the North Shore, whose waters are placid in summer but violent in winter with surfing's best waves. Between the North Shore and Honolulu on the southern coast is the fertile central plateau, and home to much of the state's military activity. On the south coast and to the west of Honolulu and Waikiki is Pearl Harbor, encircled by housing developments. West through the 'Ewa plains leads to the dry and sunny Wai'anae Coast, with its windward and coastal valleys, probably Oahu's most "local" area. ❑

LEFT: Oahu's North Shore, above Waimea Bay.

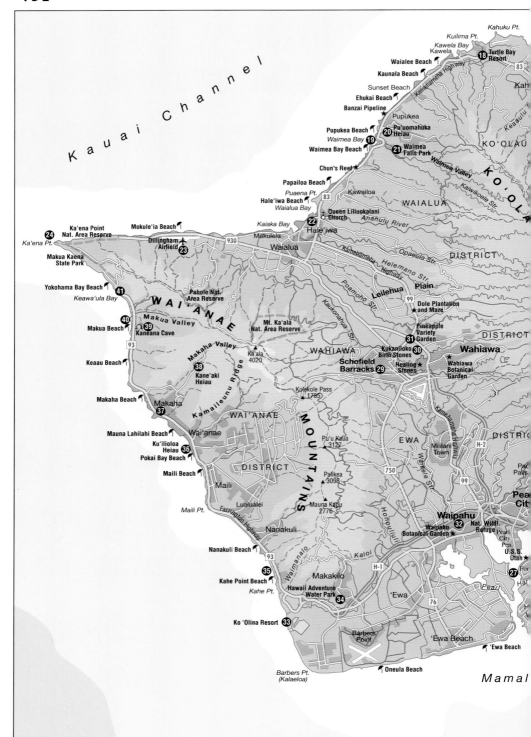

Oahu

0 ____ 4 miles
0 ____ 4 km

N

Makahoa Pt.

PACIFIC

OCEAN

Mokuauia I., (Goat I.)

Kukuihoolua I.
La'ie Pt.
Mokualai I.
★ **15** **16** Polynesian Cultural Center
La'ie
Pounders Beach
Kokololio Beach

Kaipapau Pt.
Hau'ula **Hau'ula Beach**
Aukai Beach
Kalaipaloa Pt.
Makao Beach

Mamalu Bay
Sacred Falls **Punaluu Beach**
State Park
14

Kahana Bay Beach
Kahana
DISTRICT *Bay* **13** *Mahie Pt.*
Kahana *Ka'a'awa Pt.*
Ka'a'awa **Ka'a'awa Beach**
Turnover **Kanenelu Beach**
▲ 633
Pu'u Pauao
2685

Kahana Valley
State Park
Pu'u Ohulehule
▲ 690
Moli'i
Fishpond **12** Mokoli'i I.
Pu'u Kaaumakua **11** (Chinaman's Hat)
2681 ▲ Kualoa Regional *Kealohi Pt.*
Park

Kipapa Str. **Waiahole Beach**
Waiahole
Waiaha *Str.* ⌒ *Kapapa I.*
Senator Fong's *Kekepa I.* *Moku Manu I.*
Plantation & Gardens **10** *Ahu o Laka I.*

Waiawa Str. Eleao *Mokapu Pt.*
▲ 2654 Ahuimanu
Kahaluu
KO'OLAUPOKO *He'eia*
Fishpond **9** Mokuoloe I. Mokapu
Kaloi Str. (Coconut I.)
Valley of the Temples **8** Byodo-In *Kane'ohe* *Mokolea Rock*
Temple ★ *Bay*
Pu'u Kawaipoo Haiku- *Kapoho Pt.*
2441 ▲ Gardens ★ **7** *Kailua Bay*
Keaiwa Heiau Kane'ohe
State Recreation Area **5** **6** **Kailua Beach**
H-3 **Kailua** *Popoia I.*
Halawa *Lanikai*
Heights *Mokulua Islands*
Aloha H-3
26 Stadium DISTRICT *Kaelepulu*
U.S.S. Arizona Memorial & 63 *Pond*
U.S.S. Bowfin Museum Maunawili *Waimanalo Bay*
Moanalua 61 Olomana Peak **Bellows Field Beach**
Salt Gardens 1643 ▲
Lake HONOLULU
25 Kalihi Waimanalo **4** **3** **Waimanalo Beach**
Pacific Queen Emma Mt. Tantalus
War Mem Summer Palace ★ 2013 ▲ Lyon Arboretum *Manana Island*
Keehi Tantalus-Round *(Rabbit Island)*
Lagoon Top Drive ★ RANGE *Kaohikaipu I.*
Honolulu ✈ H-1 Punchbowl Crater *Manoa* 72
National Nat. Mem. Sea Life Park **2** **1** **Makapu'u Beach**
Airport Falls of Clyde ★ Cemetery ★ DISTRICT *Makapu'u Pt.*
Sand I. Aloha Tower Maunalani Hawaii Kai *Maunalua*
Heights Koko Crater
Honolulu 92 1208 ▲ **Sandy Beach**
Waikiki Beach Waikiki Shell **Halona Blowhole**
ay Waikiki Diamond Head *Portlock*
Aquarium ★ ▲ 761 **Waialae Beach** 72 *Koko*
Diamond Head Beach *Maunalua Bay* *Hanauma Bay* *Head*

Ka i w i   C h a n n e l

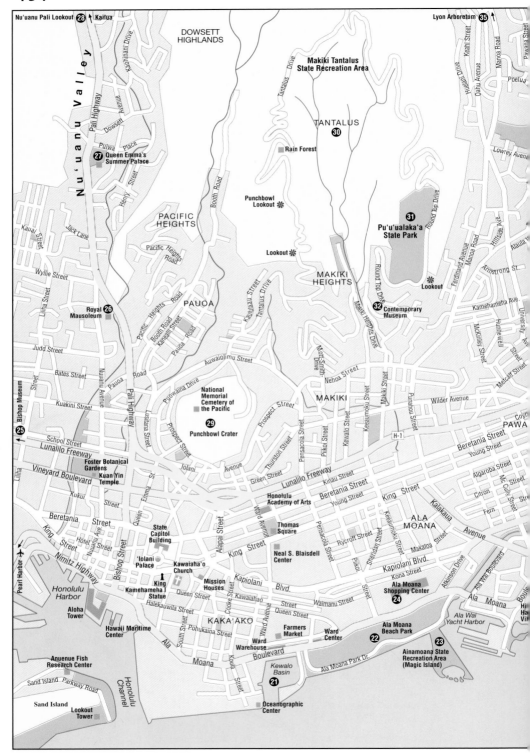

Nu'uanu Pali Lookout **28** ↑ Kailua

Lyon Arboretum **35** ↑

DOWSETT
HIGHLANDS

Nu'uanu Valley

Pali Highway

Kahihani Avenue

Dowsett

Makiki Tantalus
State Recreation Area

Tantalus Drive

TANTALUS
30

Pulwa Place
27 Queen Emma's
Summer Palace

Rain Forest

Henry Street

PACIFIC
HEIGHTS

Punchbowl
Lookout ❀

Pu'u'ualaka'a
31 State Park

Round Top Drive

Lowrey Avenue

Kauai Street

Wyllie Street

Pacific Heights
Road

Lookout ❀

MAKIKI
HEIGHTS

Lookout ❀

Lilha Street

Royal **26**
Mausoleum

PAUOA

Booth Road

Kanealii Street

Pauoa Road

Auwaiolimu Street

Kalihauai Street

Tantalus Drive

Round Top Drive

32 Contemporary
Museum

Kamehameha Ave.

Judd Street

Bates Street

Pacific Heights Road

MAKIKI

Makiki Street

Keeaumoku Street

Wilder Avenue

University Ave.

Huntwell

McKinley Street

Metcalf Street

Kuakini Street

Nuuanu Avenue

Pali Highway

Lusitana Street

Pauoa Road

Pujowaina Street

Prospect Street

National
Memorial
Cemetery of
the Pacific

Prospect Street

Nehoa Street

Mott-Smith Drive

Makiki Heights Drive

Punatou Street

Coyn
PAWA

Bishop Museum
25

School Street

Lunalilo Freeway

Foster Botanical
Gardens

Iolani

Green Street

Avenue

Thurston Street

29 Punchbowl Crater

Pensacola Street

Pikoi Street

Kewalo Street

H-1

Beretania Street

Young Street

Algaroba Street

Mc Cully Street

Citron

Fern

Vineyard Boulevard

Kuan Yin
Temple

Kukui
Street

Emma St.

Lunalilo Freeway

Kinau Street

Beretania Street

Young Street

King Street

Keeaumoku Street

Kalakaua

ALA
MOANA

Avenue

Beretania
Street

Hotel

Nuuanu

King Street

Bishop Street

State
Capitol
Building

Honolulu
Academy of Arts

Ward Avenue

Alapai Street

King Street

Thomas
Square

Neal S. Blaisdell
Center

Rycroft Street

Pensacola Street

Pikoi

Sheridan Street

Kona Street

Makatoa

Atkinson Drive

Ala Wai Boulevard

Pearl Harbor ✈

Nimitz Highway

'Iolani
Palace

Kawaiaha'o
Church

King
Kamehameha I
Statue

Mission
Houses

Kapiolani

Kawaiahao Street

Blvd.

Waimanu Street

Kapiolani Blvd.

Ala Moana
24 Shopping Center

Ala Moana

Boule

Hi
Ha
Vil

Honolulu
Harbor

Aloha
Tower

Queen Street

Halekauwila Street

South Street

Cooke Street

Queen Street

KAKA'AKO

Farmers
Market

Ward
Center

Ala Moana
Beach Park

Ala Wai
Yacht Harbor

Hawaii Maritime
Center

Pohukaina Street

Ward
Warehouse

22

23 Ainamoana State
Recreation Area
(Magic Island)

Anuenue Fish
Research Center

Ala

Moana

Boulevard

Koula Street

Kewalo
Basin

Ala Moana Park Dr.

Sand Island Parkway Road

Honolulu
Channel

21

Sand Island
Lookout
Tower

Oceanographic
Center

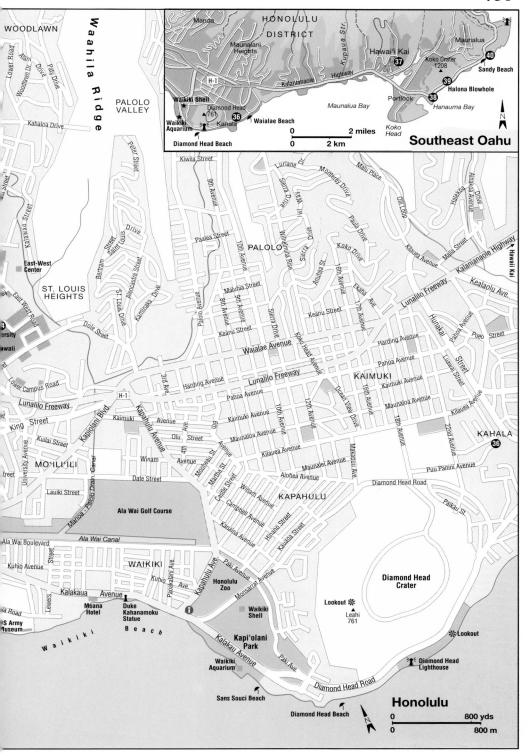

WOODLAWN

Waahila Ridge

HONOLULU DISTRICT

Manoa

Maunalani Heights

Hawai'i Kai

Maunalua

Koko Crater 1208 ▲

40

Sandy Beach

PALOLO VALLEY

H-1

Kalanianaole Highway

37

39 Halona Blowhole

Waikiki Shell ★

Diamond Head ▲761

Portlock

Maunalua Bay

38

Hanauma Bay

Koko Head

36

Waikiki Aquarium

Kahala

Waialae Beach

Diamond Head Beach

0   2 miles

0   2 km

N

Southeast Oahu

Kiwila Street

Lurline Dr.

Monterey Drive

Malu Place

Aliiolani Avenue

Halekoa Drive

9th Avenue

PALOLO

Sierra Drive

Aliei (W)

Paula Drive

Koko Drive

Olu Loop

Peter Street

Paalea Street

10th Avenue

Wilhelmina Rise

16th Avenue

Kilauea Avenue

Malia Street

Hawaii Kai

East-West Center

Bertram Street

Saint Louis Drive

Blencastle Street

Kamiloiki Drive

Malubia Street

9th Avenue

8th Avenue

Sierra Drive

Anulani St.

Ekaha Ave.

17th Avenue

Lunalilo Freeway

Kealaolu Ave.

Kalanianaole Highway

ST. LOUIS HEIGHTS

St. Louis Drive

Keanu Street

Harding Avenue

Pahoa Avenue

Hunakai Street

Pueo Street

Dole Street

Keanu Street

Waialae Avenue

Koko Head Avenue

Pahoa Avenue

KAIMUKI

Kaimuki Avenue

Luawai Street

Lower Campus Road

Harding Avenue

Lunalilo Freeway

3rd Ave.

Pahoa Avenue

12th Avenue

16th Avenue

Maunaloa Avenue

18th Avenue

22nd Avenue

Kilauea Avenue

Lunalilo Freeway

H-1

Kaimuki Avenue

10th Avenue

Ocean View Drive

KAHALA

King Street

Kuilei Street

Kapahulu Avenue

Kaimuki Avenue

Maunaloa Avenue

Kilauea Avenue

36

University Avenue

Olu Street

4th Avenue

Maunalei Avenue

Makapuu Ave.

Puu Panini Avenue

MO'ILI'ILI

Winam

Date Street

Martha St.

Alohea Avenue

Diamond Head Road

Lauiki Street

Castle Street

Winam Avenue

Campbell Avenue

Hinano Street

KAPAHULU

Kaloa Street

Paikau St.

Ala Wai Boulevard

Ala Wai Golf Course

Ala Wai Canal

Kanaina Avenue

Kuhio Avenue

WAIKIKI

Kalakaua   Avenue

Lewers

Paokalani Ave.

Kapahulu Ave.

Paki Avenue

Monsarrat Avenue

Diamond Head Crater

Kuhio   Ave.

Honolulu Zoo

Waikiki Shell

Lookout ☀

Leahi 761

Moana Hotel

Duke Kahanamoku Statue

ℹ

Kapi'olani Park

☀ Lookout

US Army Museum

B e a c h

W a i k i k i   B e a c h

Waikiki Aquarium

Kalakau Avenue

Paki Ave.

Diamond Head Lighthouse

Sans Souci Beach

Diamond Head Road

Diamond Head Beach

N

Honolulu

0   800 yds

0   800 m

HONOLULU

This city seems out of place in the middle of the Pacific Ocean. But, then again, maybe not. Many residents originate from sea-faring nations, creating an ambiance that is distinctively island-style

Map, page 141

Honolulu – the word rolls off the tongue like a soft wave breaking off Waikiki. There's no mystery about this word's origin: *hono*, a bay, and *lulu*, protected. It explains why Honolulu has been the commercial, political, and cultural center of the Hawaiian Islands since the 1800s. Until Pearl Harbor was made navigable in the mid-19th century, Honolulu Harbor was the only protected body of water of its size within 2,000 miles (3,200 km) of Hawaii.

Less than a 15-minute drive from Waikiki, downtown Honolulu is a walker's delight. A stroll through downtown can consume hours or days with its grid of side streets, shops, and oddball bars. The key to unlocking Honolulu is to treat it not like a city, but like the small gem that it is. Putter around serendipitously. Remember, you're on Hawaiian time now – take it slow and easy.

Palace in paradise

Grand old **'Iolani Palace ❶** (open Tues–Sat, 8.30am–2pm; entrance fee; tel: 522-0832) is the only royal palace on American soil. It was built in a style its architects called American Composite or American Florentine. Completed in 1882 during King Kalakaua's reign, it took three years and $350,000 to finish.

King Kalakaua and his successor-sister, Queen Lili'uokalani, lived in the palace, holding royal court from 1882 until 1893, when a group of American businessmen staged a coup d'état and abolished the monarchy. 'Iolani – Hawaiian for heavenly hawk – was renamed the Executive Building after the monarchy's overthrow, but the humiliation did not end there. In 1895, following a futile counter-revolution led by royalists, Lili'uokalani was convicted of high treason and was returned to 'Iolani Palace, where she spent most of the year living on the second floor under house arrest as a prisoner of the provisional government.

In the years that followed the coup, the palace was used as a capitol for the provisional, territorial, and state governments of Hawaii. In 1969, the state legislature and administration moved out of the palace and into the new capitol building and grounds just *mauka* (towards the mountains) of the palace. The state and a private non-profit-making group then began a $6 million effort to restore the palace to its former splendor. Original furnishings were tracked down and recovered and the palace proper now glows as it did when Kalakaua and Lili'uokalani hosted formal banquets and grand balls. 'Iolani's splendor includes Corinthian columns, etched-glass door panels, chandeliers, the mirrored and gilded Throne Room, and the spectacular three-story *koa* (an indigenous hardwood) stairwell with carved balusters. Also back in operation are the first flush toilets known

LEFT: downtown Honolulu.
BELOW: front entrance of 'Iolani Palace.

Every year in June, the festive King Kamehameha festival opens with a colorful lei-draping ceremony at the statue of Kamehameha the Great, with leis as long as 18 feet (5 meters).

BELOW: 'Iolani Palace and yet another rainbow.

to have been installed in any palace anywhere in the world, and Hawaii's first internal telephone and electric-light systems. 'Iolani Palace officially reopened to visitors in 1978. A new 10-year restoration program began in 2002.

On the palace grounds are several other intriguing sites. The **Coronation Stand**, for example, was built in 1883 for King Kalakaua and Queen Kapi'olani's coronation ceremony. The stand's foundation was rebuilt in 1919, but the copper dome is the original and now shelters free public concerts (every Friday at 12 noon) by the Royal Hawaiian Band.

The **'Iolani Barracks** is a stone structure that served as headquarters and home to the Royal Household Guards from 1871 until the overthrow of the monarchy. The small building now includes a gift shop and the palace ticket office.

The **Royal Burial Ground and Tomb** is an inconspicuous, grass-covered mound surrounded by *ti* plants in the *Diamond Head-makai* (towards Diamond Head and toward the ocean) corner. It was the site of the first Royal Mausoleum, built in 1825 to house the remains of King Kamehameha II and Queen Kamamalu, who died of measles when they visited England in 1823. Later Hawaiian *ali'i* (royalty) were also buried there. But in 1865, with the tomb overcrowded with royal remains, all were moved to a new Royal Mausoleum in Nu'uanu Valley.

On the *makai* (toward the ocean) side of King Street, across from 'Iolani Palace, is the **King Kamehameha the Great Statue ❷**. Although this heroic bronze probably bears little resemblance to Kamehameha the Great, it's a Honolulu monument and a prime spot for camera-wielding tourists. The statue shows the king holding a barbed *polulu* (spear) in his left hand as a symbol of peace and his right arm outstretched in a welcoming gesture of *aloha*. Hanging from the king's shoulders is a large feather cloak and on his head is a *mahiole*, or feather helmet.

Around his loins and chest he wears a feather *malo*, or loincloth, and a sash. When the Hawaiian kingdom's 1878 legislature commissioned this statue, King Kalakaua chose John Timoteo Baker, a local businessman and close friend, to serve as its primary model, as he was regarded to be the most handsome man in court circles. Baker was mostly Anglo-Saxon, and only about one quarter Tahitian.

Photographs were taken of Baker and others wearing ancient clothing, and these plus copies of painted likenesses of Kamehameha were sent to Thomas B. Gould, an American sculptor in Florence. Unveiled during Kalakaua's coronation in 1883, the statue is a copy of the original, which is in Kapa'au, on the Big Island.

Just behind the Kamehameha statue is the old **Judiciary Building**, which also has a royal history. It was originally designed by an Australian architect, Thomas Rowe, to be King Kamehameha V's palace. The king's household plans changed, however, and by the time the building was completed in 1874, it was used instead as a courthouse and legislative building. The building – also known as Ali'iolani Hale (*hale* means house, and *ali'iolani* translates as "chief of heavenly repute") – now serves as the home of the state's supreme court.

Kawaiaha'o Church

In a *Diamond Head* (towards Diamond Head) direction up King Street from the Judiciary Building is Hawaii's most famous Christian structure, **Kawaiaha'o Church ❸**. On Sunday mornings, or when the church's Hawaiian choir is in rehearsal, the royal palms and hala trees in its grounds seem to swell and sway with the lyrics of *"He A-kua he mo-le-le* – God is Holy," or with *"E Ha-wai-i e ku'u o-ne ha-nau e,"* the opening words of "Hawai'i Aloha," which translates as, "Oh, Hawaii, my own birthplace, my own land."

Map, page 141

Sculptor Gould's first statue of Kamehameha was cast in Paris in 1880, then shipped from Germany to Hawaii. The ship carrying it caught fire and sank off Port Stanley in the Falkland Islands. The statue was later recovered, and is now in Kapa'au, on the Big Island.

BELOW: John Timoteo Baker in photo pose, and Kawaiaha'o.

For years this was the gathering place of missionaries and Christian Hawaiian *ali'i*. Even today, the church often serves as a meeting place where matters of serious Hawaiian interest are discussed. Designed by Rev. Hiram Bingham, who led the first Congregationalist mission to Hawaii in 1820, Kawaiaha'o Church was constructed in the late 1830s and early 1840s of some 14,000 large coral blocks cut from nearby reefs. Although the present Kawaiaha'o structure was dedicated in 1842, it was preceded by four thatched churches also built under Bingham's direction, the first in 1821.

Kawaiaha'o, the "water used by Ha'o," was named after an ancient sacred spring near the **News Building** ❹ – home of the *Honolulu Advertiser* – at the corner of South Street and Kapi'olani Boulevard. Ha'o, according to oral traditions, was an ancient queen of Oahu. This is also where Liholiho, Kamehameha IV, and Lunalilo formally ascended the Hawaiian throne.

In the church grounds there is a cemetery for early missionary *haole* (Caucasians) and faithful Hawaiian members of the congregation. It is estimated that as many as 2,000 Hawaiians were buried here in the 1800s, many the victims of diseases unwittingly introduced by the early sailors and settlers. Missionaries and their descendants were buried at the back of the church, while native Hawaiians and others were segregated in death on the harbor-side of the church.

One Hawaiian, however, received special exemption from Kawaiaha'o's congregation: King William Lunalilo, the popular "Prince Bill" whose Gothic tomb stands just to the right of the churchyard's main entrance. Lunalilo, who died in 1874 after a one-year reign, requested on his deathbed that he be buried "among his people" at Kawaiaha'o, away from the "clannish" Kamehameha kings and queens who rested in vaults at the Royal Mausoleum in Nu'uanu.

BELOW: tomb of Lunalilo, and urban rider takes a break.

Another edifice on Kawaiaha'o's grounds that merits closer study is **Likeke Hale**, an adobe schoolhouse built around 1836, where early Congregationalist missionaries taught Hawaiian children the *palapala*, or Bible, and literature in general. Built of mud, limestone, and coral, Likeke Hale is the only survivor of the many adobe structures that were constructed in Hawaii during the early 1800s. It is still used today for Sunday-school classes and smaller church meetings.

The Mission Houses museum complex

Just over a hedge and a narrow road from the schoolhouse is the yard where the missionaries lived, prayed and, in 1822, printed the first of their many 19th-century writings. The **Mission Houses ❺**, now a museum complex (open Tues–Sat 9am–4pm; 553 S. King St; entrance fee; tel: 531-0481; www.lava.net/~mhm), the oldest surviving Western-style structures in Hawaii. The main white Frame House still stands as prim and true as the day it was erected in 1821 of New England timbers, which were cut and fitted in Boston and shipped to Hawaii aboard the brig *Thaddeus*. It is the oldest wooden house in Hawaii, and was for many years home to several prominent missionaries. The Coral House, where the first printing in the north Pacific was made, was built in 1823. A third building, the Chamberlain House, used as a storehouse and home for the mission's purchasing agent, was built in 1831. All three structures belong to the Hawaiian Mission Children's Society, an exclusive *kama'aina* (long-time resident) club made up of missionary descendants.

From the front entrance of Kawaiaha'o Church, *mauka* across King Street is **Honolulu Hale ❻**, the city's California-Spanish-style city hall built in 1927. Adjacent at a red-brick structure in a burst of Americana with white pillars is

Map, page 141

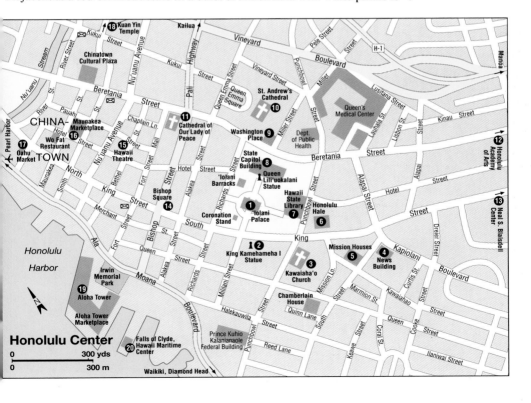

Honolulu Center

0   300 yds
0   300 m

what a few locals facetiously call Honolulu's Monticello because, from a distance and with considerable imagination, it looks similar to Thomas Jefferson's historical Virginia home. This structure, opposite the Mission Houses, was dedicated in 1916 as the Mission Memorial Building to honor the original New England missionaries. Since 1947, it's been used as a city hall annex. *'Ewa* is the Greco-Roman **Hawaii State Library** ❼ (478 S. King St; open Mon, Fri, Sat 9am–5pm; Wed 10am–5pm; Tues, Thur 9am–8pm; free; tel: 586-3500), which has an extensive Hawaiian and Pacific Isles collection. Built between 1911 and 1912, it was restored and modernized in the late 1980s.

State capitol and surroundings

Behind 'Iolani Palace is contemporary Hawaii's center of power – the **State Capitol Building** ❽, dedicated in 1969 and completely renovated in the mid-1990s. The structure's architectural lines were designed to suggest Hawaii's volcanic and oceanic origins. Its high and flaring support pillars, it has been said, represent royal palms. Paneling made of *koa* in offices and conference rooms gives the structure a distinctly Hawaiian touch. On the *makai* side of the building stands a majestic, bronze **statue of Queen Lili'uokalani**, the last monarch of Hawaii *(see page 45)*. An outstretched hand holds fresh flowers, placed there daily by admirers and supporters.

On the *mauka* side of the capitol, along Beretania Street, fly the American and Hawaiian flags, and a blue, red, and starred governor's flag. Visitors to the islands are sometimes surprised to see the British flag in the upper left corner of Hawaii's red, white, and blue flag, designed in 1816 for Kamehameha the Great. It is thought that this flag includes the Union Jack out of consideration

BELOW: *pau* riders on the state capitol grounds.

for the British sea captain George Vancouver, who presented Hawaii with its first flag when Kamehameha temporarily placed his islands under the protection of Great Britain. Other historians say Kamehameha adopted the Jack-and-Stripes flag so that Hawaiian ships at sea would look both American and British, thereby discouraging pirates from pillaging his kingdom's vulnerable vessels.

On the same side, take a moment to study the bronze **sculpture of Father Damien Joseph de Veuster**, the self-sacrificing priest who lived and died among sufferers of leprosy (now called Hansen's disease) at Kalaupapa, Molokai in the 1870s and 1880s. This blockish statue, create by Venezuelan sculptor Marisol Escobar, is a duplicate of one that stands in Statuary Hall at the US Capitol building in Washington, DC. Unveiled in 1969, the statue ignited controversy because the bold and tragic likeness was based on a photograph taken of the priest shortly before he died of Hansen's disease in 1888. At the time, his formerly handsome features were grossly disfigured. Controversy regarding the statue has subsided, but Escobar's Damien remains a powerful artistic statement, and a telling memorial.

Set back off Beretania Street is a tidy white mansion, **Washington Place ❾**, the official residence of Hawaii's governor since 1921. It was previously the home of Lydia Kapa'akea Dominis, the *ali'i* who would later rule as Queen Lili'uokalani. This gracious structure, rendered in what was called a Greek Revival form of architecture, was built in 1846 for the American sea captain John Dominis, who moved to Hawaii from New York in 1837. Dominis was lost at sea shortly after he finished building this home, but his widow and young son, John Owen Dominis, continued to live in the mansion.

After her husband's death, one of the first things Captain Dominis's widow did was to rent out several rooms in the house to Anthony Ten Eyck, then Amer-

Map, page 141

Statue of Father Damien, State Capitol Building.

BELOW: interior of Washington Place.

ican commissioner to Hawaii. Ten Eyck established his legation in the house, and by late 1847 an American flag was fluttering over the house's front lawns.

John Owen Dominis and Lydia Kapa'akea, the future Queen Lili'uokalani, were married in 1862, taking up residence at Washington Place with Dominis's mother. They lived there until 1891, when Lili'uokalani ascended the throne and moved into 'Iolani Palace, naming her husband the Prince Consort of Hawaii.

When Dominis died later that year, Washington Place became the queen's property, but she didn't return there until her regime was toppled in 1893. Until Lili'uokalani's death in 1917, at age 79, Washington Place remained a center of courtly social proceedings. Many of the distinguished visitors were treated to a private concert by Lili'uokalani, who liked to sing in her Music Room at a massive *koa* grand piano. Named after George Washington, the building is the oldest continually occupied residence in Honolulu. Now the home of Hawaii's governor, plans are underway to restore portions and open the building to the public.

Peek in next door at **St. Andrew's Cathedral ⑩**, an English-Norman structure built at a snail's pace between 1867 and 1958 of imported English sandstone. Only another block *'Ewa* up Beretania Street is the **Cathedral of Our Lady of Peace ⑪**, built by Roman Catholic missionaries from France. This coral building at the top of the Fort Street Mall was dedicated in 1843. Father Damien was ordained here in 1864.

Culture to the east

Down Beretania Street from Washington Place and the Capitol, towards Diamond Head, is the **Honolulu Academy of Arts ⑫** (900 S. Beretania; open Tues–Sat 10am–4.30pm; Sun 1–5pm; entrance fee; tel: 532-8701). Built in 1927, the acad-

Lili'uokalani in her younger years as a princess. She became queen in 1891.

BELOW: front entrance of Washington Place.

emy houses galleries of Asian and Western art, plus inner courtyards rich in flora and sculpture. There are works by Modigliani, Picasso, Gauguin, van Gogh, Pissaro, and Rodin, and one of the finest Oriental collections in America, including writer James Michener's collection of Japanese woodblock prints. A block *makai* of the academy is the **Neal S. Blaisdell Center** ⓭, named for a former Honolulu mayor who served from 1955 to 1968. The complex encompasses an 8,000-seat arena, 2,100-seat concert hall, and a spacious exhibition hall. Performances of the Honolulu Symphony are first rate, with international stars of the classical world taking part in the symphony season (Sep–May).

Big business and wealthy families

Anchoring downtown is **Bishop Square** ⓮, a refreshing plaza with fountains at the intersection of Bishop and King streets. Named after Charles Reed Bishop, who established both the Bishop Estate and the Bishop Museum, **Bishop Street** carries financier and fun-seeker alike past the graciously porticoed suites of the "Big Five" *kama'aina* corporations – conglomerates built on sugar in the 19th century by business and missionary families. Today, a bronze statue of the royalist Robert Wilcox shares their turf. Every Friday is Aloha Friday, when nearly every man on the street – Big Five type, banker or otherwise – wears a crisp aloha shirt. A necktie on Friday is truly an odd sight, as is a sports coat or sweater.

Be sure to check a special events listing before heading downtown. You just might be able to catch a show at the historic **Hawaii Theatre** ⓯, located at the corner of Bethel and Pauahi streets, two blocks *'Ewa* of Bishop Street. The 1,400-seat theater, which opened in 1922 and closed in 1984, reopened in 1996 thanks to a $30-million restoration effort that returned the old theater to its

Map, page 141

The Neal Blaisdell Center, then known as the Honolulu International Center, opened in 1964. Its debut act was the surfing music duo, Jan and Dean.

BELOW: slow day at Bishop Square.

original glory: gold metallic leaf adorns the columns and grillwork moldings inside the theater; the lobby has new marble floors and counters. Lionel Walden's *Glorification of the Drama*, a stunning mural that presides over the proscenium arch, has been fully restored. Today, the theater is a downtown hot-spot showcasing a wide range of musical and theatrical acts.

Chinatown and Hotel Street

Historic buildings vie with rising glass towers throughout Honolulu. Perhaps the most interesting of the historic structures outside of the capitol district are in an area near the harbor. This brick-rococo neighborhood is a pleasant four-block stroll from the Federal Post Office Building, down Merchant Street, Honolulu's old "Financial Boulevard." Many of the structures in this area escaped the demolition ball: some have been restored, while others add a seedy edge to parts of Chinatown.

Between Bethel Street and Nu'uanu Avenue are two immense stone lions flanking **Hotel Street** that announce **Chinatown**, an area bounded by the harbor waterfront and Nu'uanu, Beretania and River streets. In the late 1860s, Chinese plantation workers, after paying off their indentured labor contracts, gathered here and established new lives.

In 1900, a twelve-block area in Chinatown burned down when a fire, set by the board of health to eradicate bubonic plague, went out of control. Once the rambunctious venue for sailors on liberty and characters on the loose, if not on the run from the law, Hotel Street is being transformed, mostly for the better, in a long-evolving urban renewal effort. Most of the area's unseemly past has been scrubbed over or pushed out, although several peep shows and bars still remain.

BELOW: century-old architecture near Merchant Street.

Just beyond them, however, Chinatown comes into its own in a medley of Asian markets, noodle factories, shops, and art and antique galleries. Side streets cutting across Hotel Street and extending from King Street to Beretania tempt the curious. The **Maunakea Marketplace** ⓰ (1120 Maunakea St.; open Mon–Sat 6am–6pm; Sun 6am–3.30pm) is a modern, open plaza nestled amidst the old – look for the clock tower with Chinese numbers. Down on King Street, towards the waterfront, the **Oahu Market** ⓱ will rekindle a traveler's Asian memories with its early-morning hubbub of mongering and bargaining.

Hotel Street ends at River Street, which parallels the lower **Nu'uanu Stream** descending from the Ko'olau Mountains. On the *mauka* side of Chinatown, on Vineyard Boulevard, is the **Kuan Yin Temple** ⓲, where Buddhist and Daoist images gleam and a 10-foot (3-meter) statue of Kuan Yin, the Buddhist goddess of mercy, dominates. A quiet respite is found beneath hardy tropical trees in the vast **Foster Botanical Gardens** (50 N. Vineyard Blvd.; open daily 9am–4pm; entrance fee; tel: 522-7065) on Vineyard Boulevard just beyond the Kuan Yin Temple. Several plants, such as the fragrant and ever-blossoming cannonball tree, are the only specimen of their genus and species in Hawaii.

Along the harbor

Towards the waterfront, Fort Street Mall empties into **Ala Moana Boulevard**, an oceanside artery that starts as Nimitz Highway near the Honolulu International Airport and turns into Ala Moana ("ocean street") when it reaches downtown. Near here stood the old "fort" – Ke Ku Nohu, *circa* 1816 to 1857 – that gave Fort Street its name. Cross Ala Moana, hop on the elevator to the top of the **Aloha Tower** ⓳ (observation deck open Mon–Fri 9am–4pm; Sat 9am–10pm;

Map, page 141

The herb garden at Foster Botanical Gardens was the site of Hawaii's first Japanese language school. During Japan's attack on Pearl Harbor, an errant shell exploded in a classroom of students.

BELOW: Hotel and Front streets in 1893, and Kuan Yin Temple.

Sun 9am–6pm) and watch a fabled Hawaiian sunset disappear triumphantly into Pacific waters over Honolulu Harbor. This pleasing 1925 structure is only 10 stories high – or 184 feet (56 meters) – but it was once the tallest building in Hawaii. Aloha Tower is now dwarfed by the skyscrapers of downtown Honolulu.

As recently as the 1950s, Aloha Tower smiled down upon Hawaii's famous "Boat Days," when luxury Matson liners would arrive and depart at piers 10 and 11 in a hail of flowers and *hapa-haole hula*. On and off the ships would go huge steamer trunks and travelers in white linen suits and ribboned hats. At pier side, local boys would dive for coins tossed into the water. Something of that spirit has returned as increasing numbers of cruise ships make Honolulu port-calls, with Boat Day arrivals reinstituted in the process. The half-hour long mix of hula, music, confetti launches and waterboat displays provide a festive atmosphere, with Aloha Tower as the centerpiece of an open-air shopping, restaurant, and entertainment complex. For the Boat Day schedule, call 528-5700.

A museum after King Kalakaua's boathouse

Immediately adjacent to Aloha Tower is the **Hawaii Maritime Center** ㉚ (open daily 8.30am–5pm; entrance fee; tel: 536-6373), a museum modeled after the boathouse of King Kalakaua. Completed in 1988, the features exhibited depict Hawaii's 2,000-year-old seafaring heritage, from ancient Polynesian canoes to modern surfboards, sleek passenger liners and military submarines. Docked next to the Hawaii Maritime Center is the *Falls of Clyde*, the world's only surviving full-rigged, four-masted sailing ship. Built in Scotland (Clyde is the name of the river running through Glasgow, Scotland) in 1878, it spent 20 years in the India trade before entering the Hawaii trade routes. Its last voyage was in 1921.

Aloha Tower.

BELOW: Aloha Tower Marketplace and downtown view from Aloha Tower. **RIGHT:** Boat Day in the 1920s.

Next to the *Falls of Clyde*, and so small you might miss it, is the ***Hokule'a***, a double-hulled, 60-foot (18-meter) modern replica of an ancient Polynesian voyaging canoe. Several times since the 1970s, including a 1999 voyage to Easter Island, it followed long-established Polynesian ocean routes between Hawaii and the South Pacific. Only traditional navigation techniques – stars, ocean swells, rhythm – are used to make the *Hokule'a*'s modern-day voyages.

European explorers didn't find Honolulu Harbor for more than 14 years after Captain Cook's arrival in 1778, probably because the navigable channel leading into the harbor was only about 550 feet (165 meters) wide, and also because in those early post-contact days the Big Island and Maui were greater centers of Hawaiian power than Oahu. However, in late 1792 or early 1793, Captain William Brown, then busy in both the Pacific Northwest-China fur trade and a new Hawaiian gun trade, accidentally came across this inlet. He described it in his logbook as "a small but commodious basin with regular soundings from 7 to 3 fathoms clear and good bottom, where a few vessels may ride with the greatest safety." Brown named it Fair Haven, a term that is almost synonymous with the Hawaiian name, Honolulu. While Oahu's chiefs had always preferred Waikiki, with the arrival of sailing vessels and a new concept called money, other *akamai* (smart) Hawaiians, including Kamehameha, began moving to Honolulu's harbor. In Kamehameha's hands, Honolulu became the most important stopover point in the mid-Pacific ocean, with hundreds of ships making use of the harbor every year.

Although Kamehameha eventually returned to the Big Island around 1812, he closely monitored commerce at Honolulu until his death in 1819, as did his sons, Kamehameha II and Kamehameha III. Later, during the whaling era, the Kamehamehas moved Hawaii's capital to the booming town of Lahaina, on

Map, page 141

BELOW: bow of the *Falls of Clyde*.

Map, page 134

TIP

In Honolulu, locals speak of a place as being *'Ewa* or *Diamond Head* of something else, not east or west. For example, Waikiki is *'Ewa* of Diamond Head. You'll catch on.

BELOW: yachts in a trans-Pacific race. **OPPOSITE:** painting textiles.

Maui. Eventually the Hawaiian elite recognized that the future would play out in Honolulu, and in 1845, Kamehameha III moved back to Honolulu where he officially declared it as the capital of the Hawaiian Kingdom, in 1850.

Toward 'Ewa

From Aloha Tower, heading *'Ewa* along the Nimitz Highway leads towards the airport and *'Ewa*; and traveling *Diamond Head* on Ala Moana Boulevard leads to Waikiki. Nimitz Highway is an unattractive gateway to Waikiki, a mess of traffic amidst light industry and warehouses – an unfortunate introduction to Oahu's beauty, partly revealed on the crowded H-I Freeway that also links the airport to Waikiki.

One notable site just *mauka* of Nimitz and *'Ewa* of Chinatown is an area called Iwilei (pronounced *ee-vee-lay*), formerly the locale of the Dole Pineapple Cannery. Alas, Hawaii's pineapple industry isn't what it was. The cannery operation shut down in the early 1990s, and the site is now a failed visitor attraction known as **Dole Cannery Square** (650 Iwilei Rd; open Mon–Sat 9am–6pm; Sun 9am–4pm), a shopping complex that features a free video presentation retelling the history of pineapple in Hawaii. Dole Pineapple's famous "pineapple" water tank, which for years stood as a landmark above the facility, has been taken down, although plans to rebuild it are reportedly on the drawing board.

Toward Waikiki and Diamond Head

Along Ala Moana Boulevard, past the **Prince Kuhio Kalaniana'ole Federal Building**, the harbor and ocean disappear behind walls and buildings. But a mile or so farther on are a few file-it-away spots worth a visit. **Kewalo Basin ㉑**, where Honolulu's fishing fleet return with the day's catch, offers fresh seafood and a departure point for coastal cruises and sport fishing. Opposite Kewalo Basin and on the other side of Ala Moana Boulevard are two popular shopping, restaurant and cinema malls, **Ward Warehouse** and **Ward Centre**. On the *makai* side, just past Kewalo Basin, begins the **Ala Moana Beach Park ㉒**, 100 acres (40 hectares) of open space and beaches with good swimming and decent surfing beyond the reef. The adjacent artificial peninsula, known locally as **Magic Island ㉓**, or **'Ainamoana State Recreation Area**, is popular with joggers, cyclists, skaters, and walkers.

Directly *mauka* from Magic Island is the **Ala Moana Shopping Center ㉔**, Hawaii's largest shopping mall, with more than 200 stores and eateries. The latest renovation and expansion (completed in 2000) added Neiman-Marcus to a roster of top-end retailers.

On the extreme *Diamond Head* end of Ala Moana Beach Park, a bridge rises over the wide **Ala Wai Canal** and into Waikiki and its concrete corridors. To the left of the Ala Wai Bridge is the canal itself (*ala wai*, or freshwater way), a favorite training area for outrigger canoe paddlers. Oceanside, bobbing and tacking hither and thither in snappy trade winds, are dozens of spindly sailing craft at the **Ala Wai Yacht Harbor** and yacht basin, towered over by the Hawaii Prince and Renaissance Ilikai hotels. ❑

WAIKIKI

Map, page 157

There's nothing else like it anywhere in the Pacific Ocean: a perfect beach with crystal-clear water, a backdrop of lush mountains laced with clouds and rainbows, luxurious hotels, and some pure schlock

A t 500 acres (200 hectares) in size, it covers less than 1 percent of Oahu's land area, yet Waikiki pumps $4.5 billion into Hawaii's economy annually, representing 40 percent of the state's total tourism dollars. It provides 40,000 jobs tending to Oahu's 76,000 tourists daily, while somehow finding the room to house its 20,000 residents.

World-famous Waikiki Beach, actually a series of connecting beaches – Sans Souci, Queen's Surf, Kuhio, Waikiki, DeRussy and Duke Kahanamoku – extends for more than a mile in a broad crescent of sand. The city has spent millions upgrading Waikiki beachfront promenade, adding landscaped gardens, statues, historic monuments and tourist facilities. Additional upgrades to Kapiolani Park, Fort DeRussy and along the Ala Wai Canal have greatly enhanced Waikiki's appeal, with new commercial development underway along Kalakaua and Kuhio avenues, Waikiki's two main thoroughfares. Plans have also been announced for the revitalization, by 2005, of central Waikiki's hotel district, centered on Lewers St.

Early Hawaiians named this 1.5-mile (2-km) long coastal strip *Waikiki,* or spouting water, because its inland section was a wetland nurtured by mountain streams and springs. As early as the 1400s, Hawaiians capitalized on this water with a sophisticated irrigation system that fed aquaculture ponds and taro fields.

Until the 1920s, when completion of the Ala Wai Canal diverted water from the swamps and created dry land for future hotels, Waikiki's somewhat smelly interior was still a boggy place of fish ponds, taro patches, and rice paddies populated by quacking waterfowl and other damp creatures. The area's beaches, coconut groves, and fish-rich reefs, however, have long made this area a favorite spot among *ali'i,* or the Hawaiian royalty. All Hawaii's royals had homes here, as did the island's ruling chiefs before them.

In the 1860s, a dirt road was built to link Waikiki's cool surf with hot and dusty Honolulu. Two decades later, a mule-drawn omnibus began making daily round trips to Waikiki; by 1888, a regular tram service was initiated. Most island visitors stayed with friends or in one of downtown Honolulu's hostelries – notably the long-gone Hawaiian Hotel, on Hotel Street – until the 1880s and early 1890s, when a few Waikiki beach cottages were converted into guest bungalows.

In 1884, Allen Herbert opened one of these bungalows near Diamond Head and named it **Sans Souci** (French, lit. "without a care"). Five years later, Herbert hosted one of early Waikiki's most famous visitors, the noted Scottish author Robert Louis Stevenson.

Even today, those same heavenly sunsets take place off Sans Souci Beach, where the New Otani Kaimana

PRECEDING PAGES:
Waikiki and
Diamond Head.
OPPOSITE:
catamaran captain.
BELOW:
high-handed beach
art, Waikiki style.

"If anyone desires such old-fashioned things as lovely scenery, quiet, pure air, clear sea water, good food, and heavenly sunsets hung out before his eyes... I recommend him cordially to the 'Sans Souci'", wrote author Robert Louis Stevenson.

BELOW: Waikiki beauty queen.

Beach Hotel has replaced Stevenson's bungalow. Waikiki's first world-class hotel, the Moana, a gleaming structure full of steamer-set tourists, opened in 1901 *(see page 158)*.

Whether looking at Waikiki through the windows of an air-conditioned tour bus or while breaking in new flip-flops on flashy Kalakaua Avenue – or on its parallel artery, **Kuhio Avenue** – Waikiki is upbeat, a place full of surprises. Take, for example, the **Stones of Kapaemahu Ⓐ**, four imposing boulders at Kuhio Beach adjacent to the Honolulu Police substation. Approach the stones with respect, because according to Hawaiian oral traditions, they possess the *mana*, or spiritual powers, of four *kahuna* – priests or wizards – who were renowned throughout Polynesia for their wisdom and healing abilities. These four wizards – Kapaemahu, Kahaloa, Kapuni and Kinohi – came to Oahu from Tahiti in the 16th century, then left. A metal plaque notes that "before vanishing, the wizards transferred their powers to these stones."

A stone's throw away is the bronze **Statue of Duke Kahanamoku Ⓑ**. The statue includes a bronze surfboard representing Duke's classic 24-foot (7.2-meter) long *koa* board. Short boards are the norm today, but some of the old long boards still in use can be found nearby in storage racks wedged between the Moana Hotel and the Honolulu Police substation. Apart from being the Honolulu sheriff, Duke Kahanamoku was a swimming medalist and a world-record holder in three Olympics. Most importantly, he brought surfing into the modern age and introduced it – and Hawaii – around the world. Behind the statue, beach boys paddle oversized surfboards out to surf spots like Queens, Populars, or Canoes. A statue of King Kalakaua graces Gateway Park, at the *'Ewa* end of Waikiki, while another under the banyans outside the zoo honors Mahatma Gandhi.

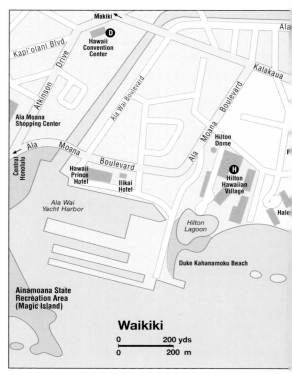

Waikiki

0   200 yds

0   200 m

A block *'Ewa* (to the west) from the twin 40-story towers of the Hyatt Regency Waikiki (a top-floor ocean view to die for) is the **International Market Place** ⊙. This acre or so of souvenir shops and kiosks selling everything from shave ice to gold jewelry was a pleasant, open place full of birds, a banyan tree and a good share of curious local folk. In recent years, however, with Waikiki space becoming an increasingly precious commodity, the Market Place has become rather over-crowded and tacky. It remains a worthwhile stop on any itinerary however, and it's still a challenge to leave its premises without purchasing some curious trinket.

In the early 1990s, there was talk of replacing the Market Place with a massive convention center. However, the $350-million **Hawaii Convention Center** ⊙ – which was completed in late 1997 – was built on the outskirts of Waikiki, on the *mauka* (towards the mountains) side of the Ala Wai Canal and bordered by Atkinson Drive, Kapi'olani Boulevard, and Kalakaua Avenue.

Visiting Hawaii several years ago, Russian poet and journalist Yevgeni Yevtushenko wrote *The Restaurant For Two*, about a small tree-house office in a banyan tree at the entrance to the International Market Place. He wrote of "mermaidenly thighs… heedless brown hands… pilings of palm… baked shark's fin steeped in pineapple… the samba's throb… and flat champagne." Then, he recalled, a man stepped up to the banyan tree, threw a switch and turned on "the bird song tape-recorded to lend the illusion of Paradise." Such is the artificial charm of Waikiki.

Three landmark hotels

Since the mid-1950s, hotels in Waikiki have risen in unrelenting waves of concrete and steel, a Great Wall of Waikiki. At last count, there were more than 30,000 hotel rooms in Waikiki. However, for most of the 20th century, three

Map, page 157

TIP

If you are renting a car, know that Honolulu's roads can be a little confusing. Entrances and exits for the H-1 freeway defy logic – they often don't come in pairs – and the routes into Waikiki are convoluted and fussy.

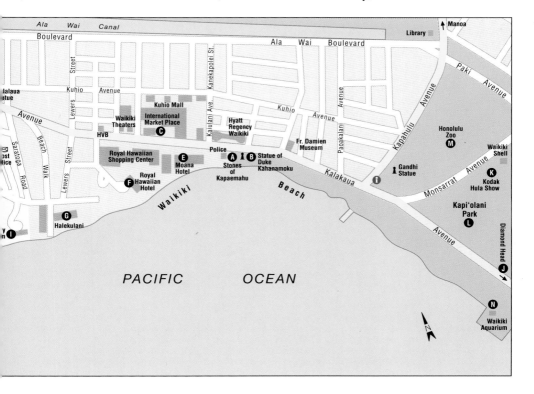

From the Banyan Courtyard, Hawaii Calls' MC *would end the show with "All of us wish you were here with us here in Hawaii on this beautiful day. Come over and see us sometime! Aloha, aloha nui loa."*

BELOW: dusk's twilight over Waikiki and Diamond Head.

Waikiki hotels anchored the beach, luxurious locales that are still regarded with respect by *kama'aina* (long-time residents) who knew them way back when.

The **Sheraton Moana Surfrider Hotel** ⓔ, on the beach along Kalakaua Avenue near the Duke Kahanamoku statue, is the *tutu-kane,* or granddaddy, of them all. At its center is Hawaii's first luxury hotel, the **Moana**, which is what it is commonly called even today. Opened in 1901 with 75 rooms, it offered Hawaii's first electric elevator, and a 300-foot (90-meter) wooden pier with a bandstand at its far end; unfortunately, the pier was dismantled in 1930. In 1918, two wings were added, forming the **Banyan Courtyard**, still popular today for its ambiance and nightly music beneath a banyan tree planted in 1885. Another extension was added in 1952, and in 1969 the **Surfrider Tower** was built.

From 1935 to 1972, the Moana's Banyan Courtyard was known internationally as the favorite home of *Hawaii Calls,* a Hawaiian music program hosted by Webley Edwards and once regarded as the most widely listened-to radio show on Earth. Some 1,900 shows, carried by as many as 600 radio stations around the world, were broadcast live from Hawaii.

In 1989, after a two-year, $50 million restoration by its Japanese owners, the Moana Surfrider reopened its doors looking as charming as it did when it first opened nine decades earlier. On the hotel's second floor, above the open-air lobby, is a museum with artifacts and nostalgic photographs.

When the Matson Navigation and Territorial Hotel companies unveiled the $4 million **Royal Hawaiian Hotel** ⓕ in 1927, Honolulu's *kama'aina* elite shifted their focus from the Moana to this Moorish-Spanish-style structure just down the beach. Social Honolulu and San Francisco were atwitter as the Royal Hawaiian's completion date neared. An advance *Honolulu Advertiser* story promised

that the Royal's opening would be "one of the greatest social events in the history of Hawaii… There will be softly thrumming music upon the air. There will be the powerful fragrance of flowers. There will be the pomp and brilliance of social glory." And indeed there was; 1,200 guests turned out to witness a "semi-barbaric pageant" produced by Princess Abigail Kawananakoa, the hotel's first official guest and wife of the late Prince David Kawananakoa. The princess's pageant, which began in waters offshore Waikiki, was a splendidly campy restaging of the 1795 landing at Waikiki of the conquering Kamehameha the Great. From the Royal's pink balcony, the princess hand-directed the movement of a fleet of 15 outrigger canoes and dozens of Hawaiians in warrior regalia.

During the next 15 years, the six-story, 400-room Royal Hawaiian became the place in Hawaii where the Hollywood likes of Mary Pickford, Douglas Fairbanks, Al Jolson, and Ruby Keeler joined various Duponts, Rockefellers, Fords, and presidents and royalty over green turtle soup Kamehameha, medallions of sweet breads Wilhelmina, gourmandise, and moka in the tapestry-filled Persian Room, now known as the Monarch Room.

With Hawaiian standards flying above its pink bell towers, and bush-jacketed bellhops tending to guests' needs, the Royal cruised through the Great Depression. But in 1941, World War II hit Pearl Harbor, and barbed wire was rolled across the sands of Waikiki. Few of the world's big spenders could dance during blacked-out nights amidst beach sentries carrying M-1 rifles and the like. So the Royal mothballed its tapestries and was leased to the US Navy until 1945. Postwar, the Royal prospered once again in the late 1940s and into the mid-1950s, and in 1959 was purchased by Sheraton, which, in 1975, sold it to the Japanese conglomerate, Kyoya although Sheraton continued to manage the hotel.

Map, page 157

BELOW: opening night at the Royal Hawaiian, 1927.

Duke Kahanamoku

I n his lifetime, he was an Olympic champion, a Hollywood celebrity, a local sheriff and one of Hawaii's pre-eminent ambassadors of goodwill. Duke Kahanamoku's most enduring legacy, however, lives on through thousands of surfers in Hawaii and all around the world. Through it all, Kahanamoku was first and foremost a beachboy. He helped popularize surfing in places like California, Australia, and New Zealand. Kings and queens once governed Hawaii's lands, but it was a Duke who ruled its ocean waves.

A full-blooded Hawaiian, Duke Paoa Kahanamoku was born in Honolulu in August 1890. The Kahanamoku family moved to Waikiki three years later, and young Duke was never far from the beach he would help make famous. In 1911, in his first timed swims, he broke three free-style world records at Honolulu Harbor. Kahanamoku, in fact, shattered the 100-meter record by 4.6 seconds. When word was sent to Amateur Athletic Union (AAU)

officials in New York, they replied sternly, "Unacceptable. No one swims this fast!"

A year later, at the Summer Olympics in Stockholm, Kahanamoku made believers the world over by capturing the gold medal in the 100-meter free-style, and a silver medal as part of the American 200-meter free-style relay team. The handsome Olympic star became an international celebrity. In the 1920 and 1924 Olympics, Kahanamoku again came home a medalist.

In the 1920s, Kahanamoku tried his hand at acting. In all, he appeared in nearly 30 movies, sharing the screen with Hollywood giants like Dorothy Lamour, Ronald Coleman, and another Duke, John Wayne.

Kahanamoku's most impressive performance, however, came in 1925, when he used his longboard to rescue eight drowning men off Newport Beach, in California. The local police chief called his act of heroism "the most superhuman rescue act and the finest display of surfboard riding that has ever been seen in the world."

After returning to Oahu, he married Nadine Alexander in 1940 (who died in 1997 at the age of 92.) Kahanamoku was elected Honolulu's sheriff and was re-elected 12 times, finally giving up his office in 1960 when the position was abolished.

In January 1968, Kahanamoku suffered a heart attack in the parking lot of the Waikiki Yacht Club and died at the age of 77. An estimated 10,000 people attended his funeral at Waikiki Beach. From outrigger canoes, family and friends scattered his ashes in the waters off Waikiki Beach. Reported the *Honolulu Star-Bulletin*: "There is a strange sound in the booming surf in Waikiki today, like the anguished cry of a mother at the loss of her favorite son."

In 1990, on the centennial anniversary of his birth, an imposing bronze statue of Kahanamoku, sculpted by local artist Jan Fisher, was unveiled at Waikiki Beach. Some beachboys lament the fact that statue is facing *mauka* instead of the ocean. In truth, perhaps only the Duke could safely ignore the rule of the surf never to stand with one's back to the ocean. ❑

LEFT: Duke Paoa Kahanamoku taught surfing to anyone who was willing. Waikiki Beach, 1939.

The **Halekulani** , *'Ewa* along the beach, was another pioneering hotel in Waikiki, where in the early 1900s, American author Jack London drank hard, chain-smoked, and spun stories on his typewriter. It was here, too, where writer Earl Derr Biggers created the fictional detective Charlie Chan. The Halekulani's bar, The House Without A Key, takes its name from the title of the first Charlie Chan novel, published in 1925. Originally opened in 1907 as the Hau Inn, the Halekulani (lit. "the house befitting heaven") was the last of the low-rise hotels on Waikiki Beach. The original bungalows have now been replaced with 450 modern but exquisite rooms (undeniably Waikiki's finest) in wings that are terraced back from the beach. Beneath the same *hau* tree that gave shade to London and Biggers, Hawaiian music and hula usher in the sunset.

Map, page 157

Waikiki for free

You'd be hard pushed to find such an eclectic range of creations in any other urban square mile of Hawaii state. They include the 9 x 28 ft (3 x 8 meter) fresco mural *Early Contacts of Hawaii with Outer World*, at the Waikiki branch of First Hawaiian Bank (2189 Kalakaua Avenue) by artist Jean Charlot, and small parks decorated with bronzes of King Kalakaua, Princess Kaiulani, Duke Kahanamoku and Mahatma Gandhi.

Like your art big? Then check out the larger-than-life *kahiko* (traditional) hula dancers at the landscaped Ala Moana gateway to the **Hilton Hawaiian Village** . Then wander through the Village's landscaped grounds, enjoying the collection of rare birds and the king's ransom of giant *koi* (Japanese carp). Beachside, look up at the 30-story rainbow murals (the largest in the world) that make the Rainbow Tower a Waikiki landmark.

BELOW: double the wild Waikiki fun.

Diamond Head's distinctive uplifting shape came from the steady trade winds 150,000 years ago that piled erupting ash higher on the ocean, or leeward, side of the tuff cone.

BELOW: view of Waikiki from atop Diamond Head.

Accommodations can be costly in Waikiki, but some of the best things to do here are actually free:

• The **US Army Museum** ❶: (Open Tues–Sun 10am–4.30pm; tel: 438-2819), at Fort DeRussy on Kalia Road, displays warfare artifacts including weapons of ancient Hawaii, the American Revolution, Spanish-American War, World Wars I and II, and the Korean and Vietnam wars. Even for the pacifist, this is an interesting and underrated museum, located inside Battery Randolph, a massive bunker built in 1911 with walls on its seaward side made of 22 feet- (6.6 meter-) thick concrete. When the military tried to demolish the football-field-size bunker in the late 1960s, they couldn't do it, and hence the museum. The battery had two disappearing 14-inch (35 cm) shore guns, cut up in the late 1940s, that could fire a 1,600-pound (726-kg) shell 14 miles (22 km) out to sea.

• **Diamond Head** ❶: You can actually drive into this extinct volcanic tuff cone and hike up the inner walls to its seaside rim 761 feet (231 meters) above the beach. It's well worth the short but steep hike. The view of Waikiki and Oahu's south shore is one of the island's best, and atop one of the abandoned World War II gun emplacements is a comfortable picnic spot. Inside the crater itself is a air traffic-control facility of the Federal Aviation Administration. *Mauka* outside the crater is a state-of-the-art film studio operated by the state, which would dearly love to see another long-term project, such as *Magnum P.I.* or *Hawaii Five-O*, in production here to boost tourism and the local economy.

Diamond Head is a nickname given the crater in 1825 by British sailors who mistook worthless calcite crystals found on its slopes for diamonds. Its original Hawaiian name was Lae'ahi, which means "brow" *(lae)* of the yellow-fin tuna *('ahi)*. Hawaiian legends say that the fire goddess Hi'iaka, Pele's younger sister,

noticed the resemblance between Diamond Head's profile and that of the *'ahi* and named it Lae'ahi, which in later years was inexplicably shortened by map-makers to Leahi. Its steep slopes were favored for *holua* sliding, a tropical form of tobogganing over dry ground.

Long before this tuff cone became Hawaii's most famous landmark, Lae'ahi was the site of the Papaenaena *heiau*, an important temple. According to historical accounts, some of the last human sacrifices ordered by Kamehameha the Great took place at this *heiau* following the decisive Battle of Nu'uanu Valley, in 1795. Early descriptions indicate that the *heiau* was located just beneath Diamond Head's jutting brow and slightly to its Waikiki side.

• **Hula Show ⓚ**: Corny and camp but also downright fun, this touristy hour-long performance takes place (Tues, Wed and Thur 10am) on a lawn adjacent to the **Waikiki Shell** amphitheater at Kapi'olani Park. Male and female hula dancers perform in front of a thatch hut to music sung and strummed by *tutu wahine* (grandmothers) in bright *holoku* – loose, seamed dresses – and flower-banded *lauhala* hats.

• **Kapi'olani Park ⓛ**: This complex of beaches, grassy picnic and play areas, amphitheaters, jogging courses, gardens, a zoo, and aquarium was dedicated on 1 June 1877, Kamehameha Day, as Hawaii's first public park. Opening day was celebrated with a slate of high-stakes horse races held on a new track laid out just below Diamond Head. King Kalakaua named the park after his wife. The park's Kamehameha Day races early in the 20th century, outlawed by temperance and anti-gambling forces. Kapi'olani Park remains one of Oahu's favorite recreational areas, and whether you're seeking tennis, soccer, kite flying, surfing, or long tranquil walks under monkeypod and ironwood trees, you'll find it here.

Map, page 157

Picture-postcard perfect at the Hula Show.

BELOW: a float in the Kamehameha Day parade, Waikiki.

Map, page 157

In 1927, world swimming records were set at the Waikiki Natatorium by Buster Crabbe and Johnny Weissmuler, the future Hollywood Tarzan.

BELOW: outdoor tidal pool at the Waikiki Aquarium. **OPPOSITE:** tourist boys and rental classic.

Kapi'olani Park is also the finishing point for one of the running world's biggest and best-known marathons. The Honolulu Marathon takes place each December and draws competitors from around the world. The race, which was first run here in 1972, draws more than 30,000 runners annually, many of them from north Asia, and particularly Japan, where marathon-running has become extremely popular.

Across the street at **Queen's Surf Beach** – named for Lili'uokalani's beach house that once stood here – beach boys gather for volleyball, and to listen to impromptu conga drum, guitar, and flute concerts held under a banyan tree, especially at sunset. The nearby **War Memorial Natatorium**, built to commemorate World War I veterans, is now partially restored. Designed by the same architect who did the beautiful California Academy of Sciences in San Francisco, the natatorium was dedicated in 1927 as a world-class swimming facility. Although the pool, long in a state of disrepair, was approved for an $11-million restoration program in the 1990s, that plan drew substantial opposition from the community and sparked legal challenges. To date, only the decorative arch and entry have been restored.

Beasties galore

At the **Honolulu Zoo**  (open daily, 9am–4.30pm; entrance fee), you can enjoy the typical antics of assorted primates, lions, elephants, giraffes, and hippos. The zoo is the only place in Hawaii where you can see a live snake: there are no wild snakes in Hawaii, and strict control is maintained on their import.

Except for sea birds, virtually all the birds seen nowadays in Hawaii are introduced species. This is probably the only place a visitor – and most residents – can see indigenous mountain birds, including the exquisite *'apapane* (Hawaiian honeycreeper) at the Manyara Bird Sanctuary and the South American Aviary.

The Tropical Forest section is filled with flowering plants, trees and gardens, and there is a Children's Zoo where kids can pet a llama or touch a monitor lizard.

Over the past decade or so, the zoo has made significant improvements, including the opening of the expansive African savanna exhibit, the Karibuni Reserve.

Yet more exotic creatures can be found just a few minutes away at the **Waikiki Aquarium** (2777 Kalakaua Ave; open daily, 9am–5pm; entrance fee), established in 1904. Affiliated with the University of Hawaii since 1919, the Waikiki Aquarium is the third-oldest aquarium in the US. Probably the rarest inhabitants here are the monk seals. The monk seal and hoary bat are the only two mammals known to have been native to Hawaii when the first Polynesian settlers arrived. A complete renovation of the Waikiki Aquarium in 1993 included a new habitat for the seals and an indoor shark tank. There are also fascinating exhibits on the nautilus and the spawning of the *mahimahi*, perhaps the most popular fish for eating in the Hawaiian islands.

If you're still feeling energetic, it's possible to continue walking around the front of Diamond Head – there are spectacular views from the road overlooking the ocean – and into Kahala. It's a hike, definitely, and most definitely none of the millionaires in Kahala will invite you inside their mansions for a cool drink. Too bad. ❏

HONOLULU NEIGHBORHOODS

Map, page 134

Hugging the foothills, valleys, and coastline surrounding downtown Honolulu are a number of interesting neighborhoods. Some are working-class, like Kaimuki, while others, such as Kahala, are ritzy

Nestled against the Ko'olau Mountains that rise behind them, the neighborhoods of Honolulu skirt around the hullabaloo of Waikiki and downtown Honolulu, weaving through pristine valleys, ridges and coastal flats. Ranging from working class to million-dollar class, they extend from Kalihi, then into the tropical wetness of Nu'uanu, over the heights of Tantalus, into the lush valley of Manoa, through upscale Kahala and into the suburbia of Hawai'i Kai.

Kalihi

Kalihi provides a glimpse of a long-established working-class neighborhood, complete with small-town bakeries, restaurants, and an uninspired commercial district that offers little of interest to the visitor aside from the Bishop Museum.

From downtown, proceed *'Ewa* up North King Street to the venerable **Kaumakapili Church**, across the street from the Tamashiro fresh seafood market. This Congregational church was originally built in 1837 at the corner of Beretania and Smith streets downtown, but after it burned down during the big Chinatown fire of 1900, it was rebuilt on this busy Kalihi corner. Kaumakapili was the common man's counterpart to downtown Honolulu's Kawaiaha'o Church, which was used mostly by royalty.

Further *'Ewa* of North King Street, then *mauka* up Kalihi Street and across the H-1 Freeway, is the world's greatest repository of Pacific and Polynesian research and artifacts: the **Bernice Pauahi Bishop Museum** ㉕ (1525 Bernice St; open daily 9am–5pm; entrance fee; tel: 847-3511). Established in 1889 by Charles Reed Bishop, it was a memorial to his wife Bernice, a princess and the last of the Kamehameha family.

The Bishop Museum is considered one of America's most important multi-disciplinary museums, a Smithsonian Institution in microcosm. Besides housing the world's most comprehensive Hawaiian and Polynesian collections, the museum maintains natural history collections of nearly 20 million animal and plant specimens. (It also manages a planetarium and astronomical observatory, the *Falls of Clyde*, a four-masted sailing ship in Honolulu Harbor, and the adjacent Hawaii Maritime Center.) In the museum's cavernous *koa*-paneled Hawaiian Hall (1903) are carved and feathered icons, capes and other remnants of pre-contact Hawaii; brilliant regalia from the time of Kamehameha the Great; the monarchical crowns, thrones, and court costumes used in 'Iolani Palace by King Kalakaua and his sister, Queen Lili'uokalani; and important pieces reflecting the experiences of Hawaii's many immigrant groups. The stone Bishop Hall (1891), was the boys' department of the Kamehameha Schools until 1941.

PRECEDING PAGES: Hanauma Bay. **OPPOSITE:** cozy Kahala bungalow. **BELOW:** beneath cloud-capped pali.

Much of Hawaii's land is privately owned by just a few estates. The Bishop Estate, Hawaii's largest private estate, owns nearly a tenth of Hawaii's land, including much of the land beneath hotels, homes, and condo buildings.

Appropriately, the most Hawaiian center of learning in Hawaii is located in Kamehameha Heights, just above the Bishop Museum: **Kamehameha Schools**, a private complex of elementary and secondary schools for students of Native Hawaiian ancestry. It is supported by income earned by the multi-billion dollar estate of the Princess Bernice Pauahi Bishop.

Nu'uanu

Even the name is beautiful – **Nu'uanu**, meaning the "cool height." Although residents of other valleys – Manoa comes to mind – might differ, there was no doubt among early *haole* (Caucasian) settlers that Nu'uanu was the best place to live. Nu'uanu was the first suburb in which they built their Victorian mansions with broad lanai, and where they planted the monkeypods, banyans, Norfolk Island pines, bamboo, eucalyptus, African tulips, and golden trees that now tower over the valley's indigenous ferns, hibiscus, koa, and ginger. Many of these estates are still occupied by wealthy missionary descendants, but most have been sold or leased to institutions, churches, or Asian consulates.

Before stalking through the valley's lush rainforest, listen for the "oms" vibrating out of the **Soto Zen Mission** of Hawaii (1708 Nu'uanu Avenue), a duplicate of a major Buddhist *stupa* at Bodhgaya, India, where Gautama Buddha gave his first sermon. This temple's Indianesque towers would appear most at home on a Himalayan crag, but a few Japanese influences – gardens of tinkling water, sand, and bonsai – give its authenticity away. Built in 1952, the temple is somewhat similar to an even larger shrine, the nearby and hard-to-miss **Honpa Hongwanji Mission** (1727 Pali Highway), which was built in 1918 to commemorate the 700th anniversary of the Shin Buddhist sect.

BELOW: main hall of Bishop Museum.

The man who invented baseball

Just *mauka* is the old **Oahu Cemetery**, where many names of rich or famous *haole* residents can be seen on tombstones. One in particular merits the attention of serious American sports fans: the layered, pink granite tomb with the inscription, "Alexander Joy Cartwright Jr. Born in New York City April 17, 1820. Died in Honolulu July 12, 1892." This austere monument, located at the center of the cemetery, marks the remains of the man who invented the game of baseball. After inventing the game – the first baseball contest played under Cartwright's rules took place in 1846 in Hoboken, New Jersey – Cartwright drifted west and eventually ended up in Hawaii. He founded Honolulu's first volunteer fire department and served as its fire chief from 1850 to 1859.

Only a few hundred yards further up Nu'uanu Avenue is the **Royal Mausoleum** ㉖, where the bodies of Kamehameha II, Kamehameha III, Kamehameha IV, Kamehameha V, Kalakaua, Queen Lili'uokalani, and other members or favored friends of those royal Hawaiian families are buried. The only two Hawaiian monarchs not buried here are King Lunalilo, who at his own request was buried in the grounds of Kawaiaha'o Church, and Kamehameha the Great, whose bones were hidden away in a secret burial place on the Big Island. The mausoleum, which lies on a 3-acre (1-hectare) site chosen by Kamehameha V, was prepared in 1865 to replace an overcrowded royal burial tomb on the grounds of 'Iolani Palace.

Nearby, below lush stands of plumeria, ti, ginger, kamani and palms, gushing Kapena Falls join Nu'uanu Stream. On the mausoleum side of the falls, below the Pali Highway that curves and buzzes with traffic overhead, are three Oahu petroglyph sites, where ancient Hawaiians carved several primitive human and dog figures and other unexplained symbols into large stones alongside the

Map, page 134

Nu'uanu Valley is thick with plants and trees today, planted decades ago by residents of the valley. Before this, Nu'uanu had no dense vegetation.

BELOW: early 1900s photograph of Nu'uanu Valley.

stream. The dog figures are thought to be images of a ghost dog, Kaupe, who, according to oral traditions, once haunted this valley.

A logical traffic flow leads back onto the **Pali Highway** *mauka* up to Hanaiakamalama, the "foster child of the moon" and better known as **Queen Emma's Summer Palace** ㉗ (2913 Pali Highway; open daily 9am–4pm; entrance fee; tel 595-3167). This royal bower with a ginger- and ti-lined driveway was built in the late 1840s and later sold to John Young II, an uncle of Queen Emma and son of Kamehameha the Great's chief *haole* adviser, the Englishman John Young. Queen Emma and Kamehameha IV in turn bought it from Young and named it Hanaiakamalama after a favorite Hawaiian demigoddess. Until Emma's death in 1885, the royal family used this home as a summer retreat, salon, and courtly social center. In 1890, the summer palace was bought by the Hawaiian government, and since 1911 it has been part of a public park. The Daughters of Hawaii organization has maintained the former royal home as a museum since 1915.

The palace's rooms have been restored with many of the royal family's belongings. Among the items are a spectacular triple-tiered *koa* sideboard of Gothic design presented to Emma and Kamehameha IV by Britain's Prince Albert; a heavy gold necklace strung with tiger claws and pearls given to Emma by a visiting maharajah; and various opulent wedding and baby gifts, which were given to the royal family by England's Queen Victoria, who was the Hawaiian Prince Albert's godmother. Among the most fascinating Hawaiian pieces is a stand of feather *kahili* (royal standards) in the queen's master bedroom. Behind and around the corner from the palace, off Pu'iwa Road, is a lovely little retreat, Nu'uanu Valley Park, favored by lovers and daydreamers who like to lounge under its gigantic trees.

BELOW: Nu'uanu tea party, 1908.

Continue the journey through the valley with a drive through the hanging vines, bamboo, wild ginger, jasmine, and cool air of Nu'uanu Pali Drive. Along this wending path you'll spot stately kama'aina mansions hidden away in the bushes, and, on rainy days, dozens of tiny waterfalls run wherever wrinkled Ko'olau ridges let them flow. **Waipuhia Valley Falls**, on the left side of Nu'uanu Valley just before you reach the Pali Lookout, is nicknamed "Upside Down Falls" because its waters are often blown straight back up a cliff and turn into mist before they can reach the precipice below. Waipuhia means "blown water."

The **Nu'uanu Pali Lookout** ❷ lies above a well-marked road spur just off the Pali Highway, and it is one of the most popular scenic attractions on Oahu. Although it can get crowded, it's still an impressive spot, offering panoramic views of the *pali* and the Windward Coast. Gale-force winds rush up this Ko'olau palisade and literally stand one's hair on end. The view from the lookout is spectacular: sawtooth peaks rise behind and below like a great rampart, green and yellow banana groves ripple far below like breezy stands of wheat, and tiny ships at sea seem to be steaming toward an unreachable horizon. From here, the Pali Highway continues down to the windward side and the bedroom communities of Kailua and Kane'ohe.

Punchbowl and Tantalus

Another relaxing Honolulu adventure includes two areas above town wedged between Nu'uanu and Manoa valleys, commonly known as Punchbowl and Tantalus-Round Top. **Punchbowl Crater** ❷, once a site of human sacrifices, was known to Hawaiians as Puowaina, or "the hill for placing [of sacrifices]." Like Diamond Head and Koko Head craters, Punchbowl emerged during Oahu's most recent eruption phase about 150,000 years ago. It was pushed upward by volcanic action through a vast coral plain that had built up around this side of the Ko'olau Mountains.

Today, Punchbowl is the site of the **National Memorial Cemetery of the Pacific**, where more than 40,000 war veterans and family members are buried. The small, flat, white headstones, set level with Punchbowl's expanse of grass, stretch across the crater's 112-acre (45-hectare) floor.

Perhaps the most famous person buried here was not a conventional war casualty. Rather, he was a journalist whose ability to write about the average foot-slogging GI during World War II made him one of the most widely read combat correspondents. Ernest Taylor "Ernie" Pyle was killed by Japanese gunfire on a small Pacific islet. Pyle's burial here was allowed because he had served in the US Navy during World War I. Cemetery officials have estimated that as many as 50,000 people a month visit his grave.

From Punchbowl's mountain-side entrance, Puowaina Drive crosses a bridge over Prospect Street and drifts along a steep valley through Papakolea, one of Oahu's few Hawaiian homestead communities. At the top of Puowaina Drive, turn right onto Tantalus Drive, a winding mountain road that twists through some of Oahu's largest *kama'aina* estates. **Tantalus** ❸ has some of the coolest and most panoramic vantage points

Map, page 134

If for some reason you find yourself touring Oahu and making a stop at Nu'uanu Pali Lookout while wearing a skirt, do hold down that skirt because of the updraft.

BELOW: memorial at Punchbowl.

on this side of the island. Hike one of the many marked trails near the mountain's 2,013-ft (610-meter) peak into groves of bamboo and fern. At the top, Tantalus Drive connects with Round Top Drive, which descends down the *Diamond Head makai* (ocean side) to Makiki and Punahou.

There are at least a dozen knock-out viewpoints on Tantalus, but locals seem to agree that the best one, a panorama extending from Diamond Head to Pearl Harbor and the Wai'anae Mountains, is from **Pu'u'ualaka'a State Park ㉛**, on Tantalus's Diamond Head flank. A few hairpin turns below this peak is a straight stretch of Round Top Drive beside a lava rock wall, with an unobstructed postcard view of Diamond Head, the University of Hawaii, and lush Manoa Valley. Down below in Makiki Heights is the **Contemporary Museum ㉜** (2411 Makiki Heights Drive; open Tues–Sat 10am–4pm; Sun noon–4pm; entrance fee; tel: 526-0232), a beautifully maintained contemporary art museum, with a gift shop and an appealing café that is a good place for lunch.

Makiki

Honolulu's "three Ms" – Makiki, Mo'ili'ili, and Manoa – occupy areas just *mauka* of Ala Moana and Waikiki. Descending from the Ko'olau, Manoa Valley is a lush retreat favored by *kama'aina*; Makiki and Mo'ili'ili lie at its mouth.

Makiki, named after a type of stone used as weights for octopus lures, is largely a residential neighborhood of flats and heights just below Round Top. It's a nice warm-up for the pleasantly cool and neighborly charms of adjacent Manoa. Makiki is an early example of what other parts of Honolulu have come to look like, as Oahu's hillsides have been developed in the 1980s and 1990s. Condominium sprouting is at its vertical best (or worst) here.

After they were tossed from power in the Philippines, Ferdinand and Imelda Marcos found themselves in exile, living in a pleasant Makiki villa with stunning views of Honolulu.

BELOW: University of Hawaii campus.

Manoa

Manoa Valley ㉝, meaning "vast," has long been preferred by islanders as a residential refuge from the heat and hassle of Honolulu's coastal flatlands. Indeed, residents of both Manoa and Nu'uanu consider their valleys the closest one can get to Eden – both are verdantly green and consistently wet – and still manage to be near shopping centers and bus routes.

At the mouth of this easy-going vale is the center of higher education in Hawaii, the large **University of Hawaii ㉞** Manoa campus, attended by some 18,000 full-time students. This institute has the academic and post-adolescent aura typical of any university in the world, except that its student body, like Hawaii itself, is generally more colorful and casual – loud T-shirts, shorts and sandals – and more ethnically mixed than the typical university campus. The university's sports teams are nicknamed the Rainbows.

At the **East-West Center** – a federally funded institute on the university campus that promotes understanding in the Pacific Basin – are a Thai pavilion personally presented and dedicated by King Bhumibol Adulyadej of Thailand in 1967; a Center for Korean Studies building hand-painted in the busy and intricate style of Seoul-area Yi dynasty palaces; and the center's main building, Jefferson Hall, which is fronted by large Chinese dog-faced lions and backed by a Japanese garden rich in sculptured grass, bonsai trees and a lily pond full of nibbling *koi* (Japanese carp).

Half a mile or so beyond Punahou School and beyond the university is the junction of Manoa and East Manoa roads. Branching left, Manoa Road leads to the back of the valley and the University of Hawaii's **Lyon Arboretum ㉟**, established in 1907. Nearly 6,000 plants grow on the arboretum's 120 acres (48

Map, page 134

BELOW: rainbow of Mo'ili'ili.

Map,
page 134

TIP

The drive between
Hanauma Bay and
Sandy Beach is
stunning. It is also the
perfect time to watch
the road, not the
scenery, as the road is
narrow and twisting,
with many blind spots.

hectares), rising from 300 ft (90 meters) to 1,800 ft (550 meters) above sea level. Tropical and native Hawaiian plants, conservation biology, and Hawaiian ethnobotany are the major themes here. Cool **Manoa Falls**, accessed via a nearby trail, is fed by 160 to 200 inches (4,065–5,080 mm) of rain a year.

Mo'ili'ili

The town of **Mo'ili'ili** – its name translates to "pebble lizard," a mythical beast destroyed by Hi'iaka, Pele's younger sister – is a busy area of university-related haunts like pubs, cheap eateries, and a cinema showing art and independent films. Adjacent to Mo'ili'ili is **Kaimuki** ("the ti oven"), mentioned in ancient Hawaiian chants as a place where mysterious *menehune* people toasted ti leaves. Its character seemingly frozen somewhere in the late 1950s, Kaimuki is a wonderful urban spot rich in red dirt, mango trees, and a virtual United Nations of restaurants and shops.

Kahala and Hawai'i Kai

Continuing towards Koko Head, Kaimuki descends down into the high-status, high-priced neighborhood of **Kahala** ❸. Following Hawaii's statehood in 1959, this part of the island became increasingly residential as Honolulu proper began running out of living space. Until then, the area was mostly noted for vegetable gardens and piggeries. Today, Kahala is a gracious residential area with one of Oahu's most desirable postal codes. At the end of ritzy Kahala Avenue is the Kahala Mandarin Oriental, formerly known as the Kahala Hilton. Built in 1959, the hotel has become the Hawaiian escape for those with money and status. A walk along Kahala Beach toward Diamond Head leads past immaculate beachfront estates. In the other direction is the Wai'alae Country Club.

Further along Kalaniana'ole Highway, toward Oahu's southeastern tip, is the vast bedroom community of **Hawai'i Kai** ❼, created by the late billionaire industrialist Henry J. Kaiser during the early 1960s. The development included converting Kuapa, once Hawaii's largest fishpond, into a marina for Kaiser's master-planned suburb, now home to more than 30,000 people. Check out the variety of water activities, from parasailing to snorkeling, offered by Reef Adventure, located in Hawaii Kai's Koko Marina complex (tel: 396-6133), which will take you out into the neon-blue waters of Maunalua Bay.

Southeast coast

Hawai'i Kai disappears as the Kalaniana'ole Highway cuts over a saddle ridge at **Koko Head** – named either for the red earth common in the area or for the blood *(koko)* of a man bitten by a shark long ago – and peaks above **Hanauma Bay** ❽. The remnant of an eroded extinct volcanic tuff cone, Hanauma ("the curved bay") is now an emerald-blue cul-de-sac filled with protected but bold Hawaiian fish that seduce snorkelers. Elvis Presley's 1961 movie *Blue Hawaii* helped make Hanauma Bay popular. Too popular, in fact. As many as 10,000 people visit the bay on any given day. Restrictions on parking and vehicular access, as well as beach usage, have eased the congestion somewhat. Despite the crowds, worldly snorkelers still proclaim this bay to be unsurpassed.

After Hanauma Bay, the feeling of a city evaporates. At the next cliffside turn, *makai* of Koko Crater, tourists wait at a parking lot lookout to hear the **Halona Blowhole** ❾, a lava formation that does a brief geyser-like wheeze when incoming sea swells push up through its underwater entrance. Appropriately, *halona* means "peering place." Take a pass. Just beyond, before you round Makapu'u Point to Oahu's windward side, is **Sandy Beach** ❿, a local favorite for body surfing, people watching and, in season, an occasional whale sighting. ❑

OPPOSITE: couples.

WINDWARD SIDE

In Hawaii, "windward" means mountainous, wet and lush. Oahu's windward coast follows the rule, even in suburban Kailua and Kane'ohe, by offering primal contours and rural textures

Map, page 132

Beyond Koko Head and Sandy Beach, the highway cuts inland, northward, and upwards. At the crest, windward Oahu unfolds in one of the more beautiful Hawaiian vistas. Continue northward from Sandy Beach along winding Kalaniana'ole Highway and watch for this scenic lookout at the top of the rise and on the ocean side of the road. Directly below the lookout's parking area is **Makapu'u Beach Park ❶**, bounded by rough open seas, sheer lava-rock cliffs, and hill-sized dunes. Makapu'u is prized for its bodysurf-ing waves. Lifeguards are stationed on the beach, but inexperienced bodysurfers should take extreme caution when in the water. The rocky summit on the right is **Makapu'u Point**, where a white lighthouse is perched on the craggy black-lava palisade. A paved road leading up to the lighthouse is closed to automobiles but is accessible by foot; the view of the coastline is well worth the hike, especially during whale-watching season in winter.

Off Makapu'u are two small tuff-cone islands – a small, greenish-black one in the foreground called **Kaohikaipu Island**, and a larger, adze-shaped one named **Manana** but more commonly known as **Rabbit Island**, not because of its slight rabbit's head shape, but because it was formerly a rabbit-raising farm. The 67-acre (27-hectare) island is now a state-protected (and off-limits to people) sanctuary for seabirds.

On Makapu'u's *mauka* (mountain) side, if wind conditions are amenable, brilliantly colored hang gliders may be seen floating in thermal currents that sweep up the face of sheer 1,200-ft (360-meter) cliffs. Below that neck-twisting focal point are perhaps more intelligent animals: the false-killer whales, dolphins, penguins, sea lions, and other aquatic creatures at **Sea Life Park ❷**, smaller, but similar to such complexes in Florida and California. Among the highlights is a 300,000-gallon (11,350-hectoliter) Hawaiian reef tank, filled with sharks, rays, sea turtles, and teeming fish of every color. The park also maintains a wildlife rehabilitation unit, and is called upon when marine animals are found in distress.

Northward

For the next 30 miles (50 km) or so, prepare to be over-whelmed literally and psychologically by the majestic **Ko'olau Mountains**. Like a massive curtain that parts now and then to expose lone spires, fluted columns, crystal falls and deep green valleys, these sheer cliffs dwarf everything in their vicinity. Meaning "windward," the Ko'olau wear mist as a *lei* (garland), rainbows like jewels, and rainfall like running tears, or as the Hawai-ians like to poetically say, *lei i ka noe*. On and on they stretch, from Makapu'u nearly to the North Shore, like a chain of otherworldly cathedrals crowned by mist.

PRECEDING PAGES: riding horses in the hills near Kualoa. **OPPOSITE:** snorkeling in Kane'ohe Bay. **BELOW:** a hang glider's view of Sea Life Park.

An overlooked gem

If you're looking for a beach with plenty of empty space, an awesome mountain *pali* (high-cliff) backdrop, and warm waters to soak in, **Waimanalo Beach ❸** has few peers. It's one of those gems often overlooked by visitors. **Waimanalo ❹** is as local a town as anywhere in Hawaii, a place where the rural Hawaiian lifestyle is sustained. Perhaps the area's most notable resident was Gabby Pahinui (1921– 1980), one of Hawaii's finest musicians. Another famous Waimanalo product is Chad Rowan, a sumo star who competes in Japan under the name Akebono (Sunrise). In 1993, he became the first *gaijin* (foreigner) to ever ascend to the rank of *yokozuna*, or grand champion, in sumo.

Beyond Waimanalo and **Bellows Air Force Station** rises 1,643-ft (499-meter) **Olomana**, a modest spire that nevertheless might look more appropriate covered with snow in the Swiss Alps. Named for a giant who jumped from Kauai to this peak, Olomana casts morning shadows over **Maunawili**, an emerald vale where two parting lovers inspired Queen Lili'uokalani to write her timeless song *Aloha 'Oe*. But just minutes past Olomana, Maunawili, and the fragrant cow paddocks and banana groves are Oahu's second and third most-populated towns – Kailua and Kane'ohe – which unfurl in a hybrid of modern suburbia and natural setting.

If you're entering **Kailua ❺** around sunset, pause for a moment under the banyan tree on the corner of Oneawa Street and Ku'ulei Road. Scores of mynah birds will be gathering to roost for the night, kicking up a squawking fuss. A fine beach stretches the length of **Kailua Bay**, but the most convenient access to this swathe of residential sand is at **Kailua Beach Park ❻**, just before the cul-de-sac community of **Lanikai**. Blessed with fine winds and water, Kailua ("two seas or currents") is the site of international windsurfing competitions.

Celebrities such as James Cagney, Henry Fonda, and Chet Atkins used to drive to Waimanalo from Waikiki just to hear Gabby Pahinui play his guitar.

BELOW: Waimanalo Beach.

Kane'ohe ❼ town is a bedroom community for Honolulu and the nearby marine base, with residential subdivisions that hug shimmering **Kane'ohe Bay**. The large Kane'ohe Marine Corps Air Station dominates scenic Mokapu Peninsula. Just offshore, Mokuolo'e, better known as Coconut Island, is the site of the Hawaii Institute of Marine Biology, run by the University of Hawaii.

Stunning Kane'ohe Bay is a popular recreation area, protected by outlying reefs and good for most watersports. Several catamarans offer day trips to the bay's central sandbar. Kane'ohe means "bamboo husband." One interpretation says that a woman of ancient times compared the cruelty of her husband with a sharp bamboo knife; others suggest the name refers to one of his physical attributes.

Attractions for culture-vultures

Cultural attractions in the area include the serene **Byodo-In Temple ❽** (47-200 Kahekili Hwy; open daily 9am–4.30pm; entrance fee), a termite-proof cement replica of Kyoto's famous Byodo-In Temple of Equality. It is the major structure in the **Valley of the Temples Memorial Park**. A 7-ton bronze bell, 2-acre (0.8-hectare) reflecting lake, peacocks, swans, ducks, meditation niches, and tinkling waterfalls enhance its imported architecture.

Of cultural and historical importance is a series of ancient fishponds that pepper windward shores north of Kane'ohe. The splendid **He'eia Fishpond ❾**, on the Kane'ohe side of **Kealohi Point**, is Oahu's biggest. It has a wall 12 ft (3.6 meter) wide and 5,000 ft (1,500 meter) long, and once enclosed an area of 88 acres (35 hectares). In recent years, land developers have proposed turning this classic example of Hawaiian engineering into a small-boat marina, but conservastionists, historians, and archeologists are fighting these plans.

Map, page 132

Oahu once had nearly 100 fishponds used by Hawaiians to grow seafood. Now, only five are left intact. Four are on this windward coast: He'eia (north of Kane'ohe), Kahalu'u, Moli'i (off Kualoa Point), and Huilua (Kahana Bay). The fifth is at Oki'okiolepe, in Pearl Harbor.

BELOW: Byodo-In Temple.

Another worthwhile stop is **Senator Fong's Plantation and Gardens** ❿ (47-285 Pulama Rd; open daily 9am–5pm; entrance fee), a 725-acre (293-hectare) attraction owned by former US Senator Hiram Fong and his family, with gardens of exotic flowers, scenic views of windward Oahu, and guided tram tours.

A rural lifestyle prevails in the Waiahole and Waikane valleys. Although taro is the main crop, there are also orchid and anthurium nurseries and vegetable farms. In 1976, the state government bought 600 acres (240 hectares) of the **Waiahole Valley**, which was threatened with suburban development, and zoned it in a secure agricultural designation, to protect it from speculative developments.

Kauhi, a demigod from Tahiti, was imprisoned on the rock by followers of the goddess Pele. One day, Kauhi saw Pele's sister, Hi'iaka, and fell in love with her. Trying to break out of his prison, he was frozen into stone in his present crouching position. It's now commonly called Crouching Lion.

Waterfowl heaven

At **Kualoa Regional Park** ⓫, heads usually crane seaward for lingering looks at a small, distinct island known to Hawaiians as **Mokoli'i** ⓬ (the little *mo'o*, or lizard), which, long ago, was nicknamed Chinaman's Hat. At low tide, one can easily wade out on the reef to this island, bask under palm trees, and photograph the graceful Hawaiian stilts *(ae'o)* and frigate birds *(iwa)* that soar overhead. On shore, the 124-acre (50-hectare) **Moli'i Fishpond**, easy to spot with a 4,000-ft (1,200-meter) long retaining wall, has been in cultivation for 800 years. This is also a very good place to see endangered Hawaiian waterfowl. Kualoa has long been sacred to the ancient Hawaiians and was favored as a royal residence.

Inland is the **Kualoa Ranch**, the largest of the few working cattle ranches still left on Oahu. In recent years, the enterprising owners have developed it as a popular tourist destination, offering activities like horseback riding, snorkeling, jet-skiing at the beach park just across the street, plus helicopter tours that take in this spectacular stretch of coast and mountains. Equally impressive is a catamaran sail to Kane'ohe Bay's sweeping sandbar. Set in the midst of the bay's waters and backed by the towering *pali*: this is Hawaii at its most beautiful. For information call Captain Bob's Picnic Sail (tel: 942-5077).

Beyond Ka'a'awa is **Mahie Point**, which overlooks the *hala* (pandanus or screwpine) groves, reedy lagoons, and whistling ironwood that rim the silent beauty of **Kahana Bay** ⓭. There is a rock formation at the Point called **Kauhi**, although it is generally better known as Crouching Lion after an entrepreneur renamed it to give his nearby restaurant a romantic name. From a certain angle, the rock does look like a lion. Local legend disagrees *(see margin)*.

Straw baskets bulging with plump papayas, avocados, and Chinese bananas hanging inside weathered wooden stands compete with hanging shell chandeliers for the traveler's dollar along this stretch to **Hau'ula**. Nearby **Sacred Falls Park** ⓮ is known as **Kaliuwa'a Falls** in Hawaiian. Kaliuwa'a, the "canoe leak," was said to be a hangout of the legendary pig god Kamapua'a, who could assume the form of a man or pig, depending upon his intentions. Due to a landslide that claimed eight lives in 1999, the trail to Kaliuwa'a has been closed indefinitely. However, helicopter tours still offer visual access to the area.

Further north is **La'ie** ⓯, a predominantly Mormon community with the chaste-looking **Mormon Temple**, built in 1919 by descendants of missionary Mormons

living in this area since 1864. The temple is closed to non-Mormons; however, there is a visitor center that is open to all. Also in La'ie are the Hawaii campus of **Brigham Young University** and the **Polynesian Cultural Center** ⓰, which manages to educate visitors in the history and culture of the Pacific islands despite its theme-park presentation. Your hosts are native islanders whose enthusiasm and warmth are infectious, and the activities range from serious to comical, with plenty to keep you occupied; an IMAX theater adds a high-tech element to the experience. The center's main shows – performed nightly by young Mormon students from Fiji, Samoa, Tahiti, Tonga, the Marquesas, New Zealand, and Hawaii – are designed, according to brochures, to give visitors a "pure cultural view of Polynesia." Just north of the cultural center is **La'ie Point**, at the end of Anemoku and Naupaka streets and where windward waters running hard from the north pound two little offshore isles – **Kukuiho'olua** and **Mokualai** – with a frightening and beautiful force, especially in winter.

A floundering tourist attraction sits at the north side of Kahuku town: the **Kahuku Sugar Mill**, until 1971 an operating mill that converted sugar-cane into molasses. For several years the mill was a theme park and then reopened as a small shopping center. More interesting is **Kahuku** ⓱ itself, a town where workers' cafés, grocery stores, karate *dojo,* and tiny homes survive much as they did when residents awoke to the mill's morning steam whistle. A walk around this village, where ferns and orchids hang in bleach-bottle planters, is usually highly rewarding.

Aquaculture is very big business in the Kahuku area. Shrimp, shellfish, and edible seaweed are all cultivated in large ponds. Roadside stands offer the freshest and best catches of the day. ❏

Map, page 132

BELOW: the Polynesian Cultural Center has been charming tourists since 1964.

Map, page 132

NORTH SHORE

The ground along the North Shore fairly rumbles in winter as the world's finest surfing waves arrive from the north. The North Shore is also a rural counterpoint to Oahu's urbanized southern coast

A drive along the North Shore is as far away from Waikiki as one can get without leaving Oahu. The syrupy smells of plumeria and coconut oil are replaced by the salty aroma of the pounding surf, and Waikiki's concrete wall of hotels gives way to the raw, unencumbered beauty of the North Shore.

Oddly enough, the first major landmark encountered on the North Shore, continuing from the windward side, is a hotel: the **Turtle Bay Resort ⓲**, which sits on a dramatic point extending into the ocean, with dramatic vistas of storms and waves. A few miles farther, the world's finest surfing waves crash onto offshore reefs and sandbars: Sunset, Rocky Point, Banzai Pipeline, Waimea Bay, Chun's Reef, Hale'iwa, and Avalanche. For most of the year, **Waimea Bay ⓳** is often as placid as a lake, but in winter when storms in the Arctic send wave pulses across the Pacific, Waimea Bay and the North Shore take on a mesmerizing fury. In December 1969, more than 30 homes between Kahuku Point and Hale'iwa were reduced to tinder as monstrous 50-ft (15-meter) waves pounded the North Shore. The most jaded surfer will agree that a tubing, top-to-bottom wave off one of those reefs generates enough adrenaline to keep anybody going through at least a few nervous lifetimes, especially when Waimea

BELOW: Waimea Bay, looking westward towards Ka'ena Point.

Bay is breaking with waves so big that hundreds of people line the road like spectators at a gladiator show. The waves are so thunderous that the ground trembles underfoot. Only the best surfers paddle out towards the 20- to 30-ft (10-meter) winter swells lifting like glossy black holes on the blue-gray horizon.

A good place to take in Waimea Bay, most of the North Shore, and the distant Wai'anae Mountains is from the **Pu'uomahuka Heiau State Monument** , on a 250-ft (75-meter) bluff above the **St. Peter and Paul Church**. Turn off from the main road onto Pupukea Road, at the fire station and supermarket.

At the very top of the bluff, on a marked side road, is an ancient *heiau*, or temple. It is one of Oahu's largest, and Hawaiians still leave offerings for the gods, usually lava stones wrapped in ti leaves, on its walls. It was known as Pu'uomahuka, the hill of escape, although historically not for some. In May 1792, two crew members (some accounts say three) of Captain George Vancouver's ship HMS *Daedalus* were offered in sacrifice at this *heiau* after being captured while filling water barrels at the mouth of the Waimea River. One theory behind the murders is that the Hawaiians had an insatiable desire to procure guns and ammunition.

When Vancouver was informed of what had happened, he pledged to track down and punish the culprits, and eventually he did. Three Hawaiians were executed with a pistol by their own chiefs in full view of islanders and crewmen. There is some debate as to whether the trio were the actual offenders. Some historians believe Oahu's wily ruler, Kahekili, rounded up three innocent people and "sacrificed" them to assuage the British captain. Whatever the truth may be, the *heiau* is a somber, foreboding place.

Where Waimea River enters Waimea Bay, look for the entrance to **Waimea Valley**, home of **Waimea Falls Park**  (59-864 Kamehameha Highway; open daily 10am–5.30pm; entrance fee; tel: 638-8511) on the *mauka* (mountain) side of the road, opposite the beach park. Located at the end of the valley, this 1,800-acre (728-hectare) botanical garden offers historical and cultural demonstrations, and a breathtaking diving exhibition from 55-ft (16.5-meter) cliffs. With outdoor recreational activities in demand, the park has added kayak expeditions, mountain-bike tours, and all-terrain vehicle rides to its menu. It's a nice place for a picnic or carefree exploration of the area's natural beauty. The park has 6,000 varieties of native and imported plants.

Summer and shave ice

Further westward along the North Shore's surfing grounds, a small cement bridge funnels traffic over a little stream into **Hale'iwa**  (House of the Frigate Bird), an artsy and funky outpost – but the biggest town on this side of Oahu – where people of all ethnic backgrounds and lifestyles mingle. An eclectic mix of trendy cafés, art galleries, boutiques, and shops mix with remnants of the old plantation days. Fujioka's Supermarket is one of the town's more familiar establishments. Founded in 1910, the family-run business carries the usual groceries and knick-knacks, along with, as a sign of the times, the North Shore's finest selection of wines and imported cigars.

Banzai Pipeline.

In 1899, Hale'iwa, not Waikiki, opened the island's first hotel: the Victorian-style Hale'iwa Hotel, now long gone.

BELOW: cooling off near Waimea Falls.

Map,
page 132

*Ka'ena Point, Oahu's
northernmost tip.*

BELOW: coast near
Mokule'ia Beach.

Summer festivals in Hale'iwa

A good time to visit Hale'iwa is in the middle of summer, at the height of the
Japanese *Obon* season, when the **Hale'iwa Jodo Mission** has its annual festival
with a unique *toronagashi*, with dozens of flickering lanterns – each a farewell
light for an ancestor's spirit – floating on the dark sea to the east side of **Kaiaka
Bay**. Hale'iwa also hosts the **Hale'iwa Festival** in July and the **Hale'iwa Taro
Festival** in September, two annual celebrations which offer a hometown glimpse
into Hawaiian culture. And no summer excursion to Hale'iwa would be complete
without a stop at Matsumoto General Store (66-087 Kamehameha Hwy; open
8.30am–6pm), locally famous for its refreshing shave ice that comes in a rainbow
of flavors. At the bottom of a proper shave ice are *azuki* beans and ice cream.

Upon leaving Hale'iwa, there are two options: continue south down the Kamehameha Highway through central Oahu and back to Honolulu, or go further east
past the taro and banana patches to the old plantation town of **Waialua**.

Beyond Waialua, on the *mauka* side of Farrington Highway, is the **Mokule'ia
Polo Farm**, Hawaii's most exclusive athletic facility, where visiting teams from
North America, Australia, England, and Ireland battle through chukkers of com-
petitive polo (most Sundays between late February and July) against local pony
teams; bring a picnic and settle in. Further down the road is the **Dillingham Air
Field ㉓**, where commercial glider pilots and paying passengers loop in thermal
air currents rising alongside the 2,000-ft (610-meter) Wai'anae *pali* (high cliffs).
At the end of the road beyond Mokule'ia, a foot trail continues on to **Ka'ena
Point ㉔**, which is being returned to its natural state through conservation efforts.
Beyond by foot is the Wai'anae Coast. In winter, waves as high as 50 ft (15
meters) have been witnessed off Ka'ena Point. No one has surfed them. Yet. ❏

Surfing

Some historians believe that a primitive form of surfing originated somewhere in the Pacific around 2000 BC. It is likely that when the first Polynesians migrated to the Hawaiian Islands around AD 400, they were already well-versed in the sport.

Early Hawaiians called surfing *he'e nalu*, which literally translates as "wave sliding". Hawaiian chants dating from the 15th century recount surfing exploits, indicating that *he'e nalu* had become so developed that competitions were held among famous surfers, usually royalty, or *ali'i*. These were widely heralded affairs, sometimes pitting chiefs against each other; crowds of supporters would indulge in high-stakes gambling by placing property bets on a favored wave rider.

One Hawaiian legend tells the story of Kawelo, whose wife was taken by his brother, the ruling chief 'Aikanaka. Full of anguish, Kawelo was plotting his revenge when he suddenly noticed a crowd on the beach, enjoying *he'e nalu*. Overcome with desire, Kawelo at once forgot completely about his wife and 'Aikanaka and headed for the beach to engage in his favorite pastime. No wonder one long-time surfer says, "Perfect waves are miracles. When they come, everything else stops, including romance."

WAVES OF CHANGE

Gone are the days when *ali'i* rode on large *koa* boards weighing 150 lbs (70 kg). Also gone are early 20th-century Waikiki-style boards made of California redwood. And just as extinct are the balsa "pig boards" that were popular in the early 1950s. Thanks to modern technology, today's surfboards are made of foam and fiberglass, and can weigh less than 5 lbs (2 g). The serious surfer today maintains not just one surfboard, but an all-purpose "quiver" of boards, ranging in function and size. Short-boards are slightly more than 6 ft (2 meters) in length, while long-boards (more buoyant and stable, they permit the surfer to perform more creative maneuvers) are about 9 ft (3 meters) in length.

RIGHT: women surfed in ancient Hawaii as they do today. Surfer in Waikiki, 1915.

Learning to surf is relatively easy. There is a handful of surfing instruction schools on Oahu, but one can usually get informal lessons from willing beachboys in Waikiki.

Of course, you can't become a true surfing aficionado without first knowing the language. Here are a few local slang terms to be mastered:

- **breaks**: waves.
- **gonzo**: highly enthusiastic, raring to go.
- **hang ten**: usually performed on long boards, this maneuver entails placing all 10 toes over the nose or front of the board.
- **lull**: when waves aren't coming in.
- **rights/lefts**: the direction a wave breaks as you face the shore.
- **sets**: groups of arriving waves.
- **wipe out**: crash and splash, and it should be only on a big, big wave.

The best time to watch big-wave surfing is in November and December, when the **Triple Crown of Surfing** is held on Oahu's North Shore. The Triple Crown consists of three separate competitions featuring professional surfers from around the world. ❑

CENTRAL OAHU

Map, page 132

Central Oahu is wedged between the mountains of the old Wai'anae and Ko'olau volcanoes. At the southern end of this fertile land of pineapples is Pearl Harbor, Hawaii's number-one visitor site

Urbanized travelers who are so inclined will find the freeways slicing across central Oahu to their liking. Indeed, with all the housing subdivisions sprouting up in parts of Oahu's interior, a mainlander could feel quite at home. From Waikiki and downtown Honolulu, travel west along the Lunalilo Freeway, more commonly called the H-1, then cut north on the H-2 freeway. But before heading into central Oahu itself,there are several places of interest worth a visit.

Ancient Moanalua

Just off the H-1 freeway is **Moanalua Gardens ㉕**, a tranquil retreat graced with huge, umbrella-like monkeypod trees. A popular picnic spot and site of the annual Prince Lot Hula Festival, the gardens are privately owned but are open to the public. Behind is **Moanalua Valley**, an even more spectacular wilderness area where there are tall white hibiscus trees shading a stream, and Hawaiian petroglyphs and an ancient medicinal pool surrounded by colorful morning glories, gardenias, ferns, and fragrant vines. The valley is also privately owned, and is open to hikers who call in advance (tel: 833-1944). The Moanalua area was likely named for two ancient encampments where travelers between Honolulu and 'Ewa could rest. A nearby field called Pueohulunui (lit. "much-feathered owl") was said to be a place where owls from Kauai and Ni'ihau arrived for a big battle.

In the early 1970s, Moanalua Valley was the focal point of a bitter controversy between the state government and local activists. The state's plans for a freeway connecting central and windward Oahu called for a portion of that freeway to wend through the valley. However, petroglyphs were discovered within the encroachment area, and the valley was entered into the National Register of Historic Places. In 1977, a US Supreme Court ruling forced the state to reroute the freeway to circumvent the valley. The resulting H-3 Freeway, completed in 1998, winds its way through the lush heart of Halawa Valley, descending to the Windward Coast at Kane'ohe.

Conspicuously set on a ridge overlooking the freeway is the **Tripler Army Medical Center**, a pink structure built in 1948 and the largest military hospital in the Pacific. The 14-story hospital was named after General Charles Stuart Tripler, a major-general who served as army medical director of the *USS Potomac* in the Civil War. He also wrote the army's first standard manual on the medical examination of military recruits.

As you approach Pearl Harbor, you'll easily spot the 50,000-seat **Aloha Stadium ㉖**, Oahu's prime but plagued-by-rust outdoor venue for major sports and special events like the annual State Fair. Home of the annual Pro Bowl football game, which features National

OPPOSITE: preparing shave ice, not to be confused with a snowcone.
BELOW: sugar-cane fields of central Oahu.

Football League all-stars, the stadium was built in 1975 and can be realigned into baseball or football configurations. Concession workers sell Chinese crack seed and *saimin* noodles along with the usual hot dogs and burgers.

Aloha Stadium's parking lot is the site for one of Oahu's biggest attractions, when some 30,000 residents and visitors flock to the **Aloha Flea Market** (open Wed, Sat and Sun 6am–3pm; entrance fee), Honolulu's largest swap meet. Here are row upon row of vendors hawking everything from aloha shirts to zucchini.

Just *mauka* (towards the mountains) of the stadium is **Stadium Mall**, a retail complex, unremarkable except that it is home to **The Ice Palace**. Yes, there is ice skating even in the balmy Hawaiian islands, and it's a favorite activity for many youngsters. The Ice Palace occasionally hosts hockey competitions.

Beyond the stadium lie the east, middle, and west lochs of Pearl Harbor – named for the pearl oysters once found here – and the towns of **'Aiea** and **Pearl City**, known mostly for their shopping centers and housing subdivisions.

'Aiea is the only town or city in the United States whose name is made up entirely of vowels.

Day of Infamy

Pearl Harbor ㉗ has been well-known since the morning of 7 December 1941, when Japanese dive-bombers devastated the US Pacific fleet anchored in the harbor. The ***USS Arizona* Memorial** ㉘ (visitor center open daily, 7.30am–5pm, tel: 422-0561; www.nps.gov.usar, shuttle boats to the *USS Arizona* run between 8am–3pm, weather permitting), the famous monument to that "day of infamy," as President Roosevelt called it, is a radiant memorial straddling the hulk of the *USS Arizona*, which lies immediately below the surface, still leaking oil.

The hull is the tomb of 1,100 men who died when a series of Japanese torpedoes and aerial bombs sank the battleship. The memorial, designed by Honolulu archi-

BELOW: a veteran at the Arizona Memorial, and Japanese tourists.

tect Alfred Preis, was made possible in part by a benefit concert staged in 1961 by Elvis Presley. A museum, bookstore, and film occupy visitors awaiting a US Navy launch to the memorial, which is the most popular free attraction on Oahu, with more than a million visitors annually. Waits of one to two hours are not uncommon.

Map, page 132

Just a few minutes' walk from the Arizona Memorial visitors' center is the *USS Bowfin* **Submarine Museum and Park** (open daily, 8am–4.30pm; tel: 423-1341; entrance fee), a privately operated attraction well worth a look. Would-be submariners and the curious can check out defused torpedoes, descend into and walk through a completely refurbished World War II diesel-electric submarine, the *USS Bowfin*, which is credited with 44 ship sinkings in nine patrols. A shuttle links the *Bowfin* to the *USS Missouri* (open 8am–4.30pm; entrance fee; tel: 422-1600), the decommissioned World War II battleship aboard which Japan's surrender was signed.

Another monument, considerably lower in profile and cost, can be found on **Ford Island** alongside the rusting hulk of the *USS Utah*. Civilians, however, can visit the site only if accompanied by a member or dependent of the US military. At neighboring **Hickam Air Force Base**, a plaque marks where the *Apollo 11* astronauts first touched earth after their walk on the moon in 1969.

Commissioned on 7 December 1942, the Bowfin was later mothballed in the Middle Loch of Pearl Harbor until it was brought out of retirement.

Central plateau

On the drive north and inland on the H-2 freeway, Oahu's central plateau rises gradually until it reaches the **Schofield Barracks ㉙** army post and **Wahiawa**, the highest residential community on Oahu. Wahiawa (lit. "place of noise") can be bypassed altogether by staying on Highway 90, which separates the town from Schofield Barracks. But military buffs will enjoy a stop at Schofield's

BELOW: inside the Arizona Memorial.

Map, page 132

TIP

Throughout the islands you will encounter *leis* or ti-covered objects at sacred sites. These are religious offerings of Native Hawaiians and should be left undisturbed. They are not tourist souvenirs.

Tropic Lightning Museum (open Tues–Sat 10am–4pm), which houses artifacts, photographs, and archival materials documenting the history of Schofield Barracks and the famed "Tropic Lightning" 25th Light Infantry Division.

Others might care to stop in Wahiawa to take a look at the visually unspectacular **Healing Stones**. The stones sit on a simple altar inside a concrete shelter on California Street. Until the late 1920s, pilgrims regularly visited these stones, which, according to legend, were two sisters from the island of Kauai who were petrified by greater powers. Other myths attribute alternative origins to the stones but, whatever the explanation, they are still thought to emanate healing powers. Offerings are regularly left here. Also in Wahiawa is the **Wahiawa Botanical Garden** (1396 California Avenue; open daily 9am–4pm; tel: 621-7321).

On the north side of Wahiawa, to the left of Kamehameha Highway and just beyond Whitmore Avenue, are sacred stones of a different sort. These are the **birth stones of Kukaniloko ㉚**. This eucalyptus-fringed clearing in a pineapple field has been venerated by Hawaiians as far back as the 12th century. Wives of high-ranking chiefs bore their children on these stones' gently curved surfaces. Attendant chiefs, high priests, and physicians would gather around the infant and, during an impressive ceremony marked by great drums, chants and offerings, the royal child would be named and the navel cord cut and ritually hidden away.

From this open-air site, to the west in the direction of the Wai'anae Range, you can look up the side of Leilehua Plain to the broad **Kolekole Pass**, which was used by low-flying Japanese bombers as a convenient cover and Western approach for their sneak attacks on Schofield Barracks and adjacent **Wheeler Army Air Field**. In 1969, when the joint American-Japanese movie *Tora! Tora! Tora!* was being filmed, the sight of Japanese Zeros, Kates and Vals roaring through Kolekole and raining simulated bombs and machine-gun fire on Schofield Barracks and Wheeler Air Force Base was *déjà vu* indeed.

Pineapple fields spread across central Oahu, stretching from the Wai'anae Mountains on one side to the Ko'olau Range on the other. Europeans first came across pineapples in South America and the West Indies. Quickly adopted as a crop, they were transplanted throughout the world, reportedly in Hawaii as early as 1813. However, the commercial selling of pineapple in Hawaii did not begin until 1899, when Oahu entrepreneur James D. Dole planted 60 acres (24 hectares) of Wahiawa land with pineapple. Two years later, Dole organized the Hawaiian Pineapple Company, and by 1906 he had begun building a cannery at Iwilei, near Honolulu Harbor. Dole's father was a cousin to Sanford Dole, president of the Hawaiian Republic from 1893 to 1900 and one of the businessmen responsible for overthrowing the monarchy. Sanford Dole was reportedly against the idea of using the Dole name for a commercial enterprise.

A sample of pineapple's diversity is at the **Pineapple Variety Garden ㉛**. This very simple garden has many pineapple varieties and other bromeliads, which early Spanish explorers called the *piña* because its fruit was shaped like a pinecone. The addition of the world's largest **topiary maze** adds something unique to this otherwise overly commercialized attraction. Nearby is the **Dole Plantation**, just up the road toward Hale'iwa. ❑

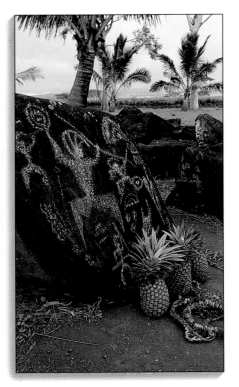

OPPOSITE: preparing flowers for sale.
BELOW: offerings at the stones of Kukaniloko.

WAI'ANAE COAST

Map, page 132

Oahu's western coast is one of the sunniest places on the island, and the locals tend to keep this a secret. They also fiercely guard their lifestyle, which sustains the coast's island feel

O ahu's Wai'anae Coast is perhaps the most misunderstood and maligned area of Oahu. It is true that this 20-mile (32-km) coastline is hotter, dustier, and drier than the rest of the island. And with the exception of the Ko 'Olina Resort at the southern end, and Makaha's golf, it does lack the usual tourist attractions. But dig deep, and you'll find that West Oahu has considerable natural and cultural beauty to offer the enlightened respectful and adventurous traveler. Even on this side of the island, however, changes are unavoidable. At its southern end, where Wai'anae meets the flat 'Ewa plains west of Honolulu, a so-called second city – Kapolei – is gradually taking shape, an ambitious attempt to relieve urban Honolulu's congestion, and to offer Oahu a resort area outside of Waikiki.

The locals eulogize

Question a long-time resident of Nanakuli, Ma'ili, Wai'anae, or Makaha about the West Side, and they might just spend hours sharing why it's paradise: "It's the closest thing to an unspoiled Hawaiian place on this island," says a truck driver from Lualualei. A Nanakuli elder states flatly that "you've never been to a real *lu'au* until you've been to a big one on this side." Indeed, wedding or first-birthday *lu'au* (feasts, *see page 117*) hosted on this side of the island are legendary, remembered fondly by the number of *kalua* pigs and kegs of beer consumed.

Just over 35,000 people live along Wai'anae's jagged shorelines and dry mountain slopes. Before the arrival of Captain Cook, the west coast of Oahu was a major center of Hawaiian civilization, probably because of the rich fishing grounds in the clear offshore waters between Nanakuli and Ka'ena Point. It was here, according to oral traditions, that the demigod Maui lived and first learned to make fire after he arrived in Hawaii. Also along this coast, several myths refer to the infamous man-pig Kamapua'a, renowned throughout Hawaii as a god who both charmed and harassed mortal worshipers with his capricious antics. As island-style a place as any to prepare for the Wai'anae Coast is **Waipahu ㉜**, which is just past Pearl City and a quick dash off the H-1 Freeway. Waipahu, over a century old, is Oahu's last big town before the freeway hooks around the southern end of the Wai'anae range; it is a town in transition. Until the middle 1970s, Waipahu was devoted to growing sugar-cane. But today, these fields of green, tassel-topped cane have been phased out to make way for a golf course and checkerboard subdivisions such as Waikele, known among locals – and Japanese visitors – for its large number of factory-outlet stores.

PRECEDING PAGES: rinsing surfboards. **OPPOSITE:** fisherman inspects his net catch. **BELOW:** fishing poles line the Wai'anae Coast.

In the heart of Waipahu, just off Waipahu Street, is **Hawaii Plantation Village** (open Mon–Sat 9am–3pm; tel: 677-0110; donations accepted). Plantation-era houses reveal the diverse cultures of eight ethnic groups in Hawaii that were a part of the sugar industry's century-long flowering. Guided tours of the 3-acre (1.2-hectare) site are offered.

Messing about in the water

The **Ko 'Olina Resort ㉝** has the requisite golf course plus a spa and a series of beach-lined lagoons. Anchoring the resort is the 'Ihilani Resort and Spa, perched on one of the lagoons and white-sand beaches. Its spa is as elegant and compre-hensive as any in the world. Each Wai'anae coast beach has its own character and devotees. 'Ewa Beach Park, for example, is famed for its abundance of *limu* (also called *ogo* in Japanese), or edible seaweed. Just outside Ko 'Olina is **Hawaiian Waters Adventure Park ㉞** (400 Farrington Way; open 10.30am–5pm daily; entrance fee; tel: 674-9283), with 25 acres (10 hectares) of waterslides and wave pools. Favored by surfers, **Kahe Point ㉟** is a beach past Ko 'Olina and opposite an electric powerplant on the main road, which parallels the western coastline. This spot is called the Kahe Point Beach Park, but locals call it Tracks because remnants of the old narrow-gauge train tracks still parallel the highway northward.

Ku'ilioloa Heiau ㊱, on the extreme fingertip of Kane'ilio Point on the south side of Poka'i Bay, is surrounded by water on three sides. This *heiau*, or temple, of coral and lava rock was built in the 15th or 16th century in honor of Ku'ili-oloa, a giant dog that often protected travelers in the area.

Protection by giant dogs was appreciated here. This area is said to have been populated in ancient times by cannibals preying on passers-by. According to J.

Gilbert McAllister, who wrote a 1933 Bishop Museum survey entitled *Archaeology of Oahu*, these highwaymen apparently hid behind high ridges and ambushed unwary victims who came their way. The largest town on this coast, Makaha, meaning fierce or savage, takes its name from these marauders.

"For many years these people preyed upon the traveler," McAllister wrote, "until at one time men from Kauai, hairless men *(olohe)* came to this beach. They were attacked by these cannibals but defeated them, killing the entire colony. Since then, the region has been safe for traveling."

Map, page 132

Surfing the waves

Several reefs and points of land along this coast have long been favored as surfing spots, but perhaps the most famous is Kepuhi Point in **Makaha ㊲**, where the annual Makaha International Surfing Championships were once held. In recent years, however, most major big-wave surfing contests have been held on Oahu's vicious North Shore, particularly at the Banzai Pipeline and Sunset Beach surf breaks. Nevertheless, an oldie-but-goodie surfing event at Makaha has caught the fancy of wave-riding old-timers: the annual Buffalo's Longboard Contest, which first began in 1978. Makaha Beach commander Buffalo Keaulana and other *kama'aina* (long-time residents) organized it to renew interest in the style of surfing that was in vogue during the 1950s and 1960s.

Wander into the back reaches of **Makaha Valley** to the impressive **Kane'aki Heiau ㊳** (open Tues–Sat 10am–2pm) restored by the National Park Service, Bishop Museum, and the Makaha Historical Society. This 17th-century *heiau*, one of the best-preserved on Oahu and tucked away in a spectacular setting alongside Makaha Stream, was rebuilt entirely by hand, using indigenous *pili*

BELOW: surfers at Makaha's Buffalo Longboard Contest.

Map,
page 132

grass, *'ohi'a* timber and lava stones much as they were utilized by ancient craftsmen. Originally, this was an agricultural *heiau* dedicated to the god Lono, but archeologists speculate that it may have been reconditioned in 1796 by Kamehameha the Great as a *luakini heiau*, or *heiau* of human sacrifice, in honor of his war god Kukailimoku. At the time, Kamehameha was amassing a huge fleet in the Makaha area in preparation for an invasion of Kauai. The fleet was forced back to Oahu by gale-force winds and raging seas, and perhaps people were sacrificed near here to appease the angry and unhelpful gods. Head up into Makaha Valley toward the Sheraton Makaha Golf Club and continue through the golf course to the gate for Mauna 'Olu Estates. The guard will direct you to the *heiau*.

Mt. Ka'ala, just east of Makaha in the Wai'anae range, is Oahu's highest point at 4,020 feet (1,225 meters) above sea level.

Hulf human-half shark

Another famous site you can walk into is about 3 miles (5 km) north of Makaha: **Kaneana ㊴**, the Cave of Kane. Although this cave is 100 ft (30 meters) high in places and about 450 ft (135 meters) deep, it is not a lava tube. Rather, it was carved out by the sea 150,000 years ago when its entrance was at or below sea level. According to a local story, this cave was occupied by a fierce character, Kamohoali'i, who was able to alternate at will between being a human and a shark. Kamohoali'i had a fondness for human flesh, so in his guise as a mortal, he would periodically jump people and then drag them into this cave for dinner. Eventually, this human disguise was discovered and Kamohoali'i had to flee into the sea, but he was captured and destroyed later by vengeful Makua residents.

BELOW: gospel shoes at a gospel church.

Makua Beach ㊵ is the photogenic area where much of the epic motion picture *Hawaii*, based on James Michener's novel of the same name, was filmed in 1965. Film producers recreated an entire set on this beach representing the old Maui whaling town of Lahaina. That set has since been carted away, but the same spectacular backdrop remains.

Moments later, Farrington Highway ends and briefly becomes a modest road that terminates at **Keawa'ula Bay ㊶**, a favorite board- and body-surfing spot known to old-timers as **Yokohama Bay**. This sandy playground received the Japanese name at the turn of the 20th century when the Oahu Railway train between 'Ewa and Hale'iwa would stop here to let off Japanese fishermen, who favored the fishing at Keawa'ula. Nobody knows who actually coined the term Yokohama Bay, but the name stuck and later became well-known in surfing circles because of popular left-slide waves that leap off a shallow reef on the bay's south side.

Beyond Yokohama Bay, the landscape loses its sandy character and turns into a jangle of black lava, thorny scrub brush, and sand dunes at **Ka'ena Point ㉔**. Like an arrow, Ka'ena points slightly to the northwest and the island of Kauai. It can be traversed on foot or bicycle. Continuing further on and around Ka'ena Point would lead to the North Shore. Ka'ena Point is now a state wildlife preserve, home to nesting albatross, the occasional Hawaiian monk seal and rare flora.

Said to be named for the brother or cousin of Pele, the fire and vocano goddess, ancient Hawaiians were reluctant to cross Ka'ena, for it was a place from which souls departed from earth – the good to the right, and the not-so good to the left. ❑

Oahu's Leeward Islands

For most travelers, Honolulu ends at the sharp, beaky tip of Ka'ena Point on northwest Oahu. Unknown to many, however, including most Honolulu residents, is that Honolulu is the most far-flung city in the world. The city's jurisdiction not only includes Oahu, but also dozens of smaller points of land that stretch some 1,400 nautical miles (2,200 km) to the northwest.

These shoals, atolls, and desert isles have names like Nihoa, Necker, French Frigate Shoals, Gardiner Pinnacles, Maro Reef, Laysan, Lisianski, Pearl and Hermes Reef, and Kure Island. The better-known Midway Islands are also within Honolulu's sprawling city limits, but they were placed under military jurisdiction at the start of the 20th century.

Collectively, these islands are often referred to as the Leeward Islands, although, officially, they are the **Northwestern Hawaiian Islands**. Eight of these islands and reefs have been combined to form the Hawaiian Islands National Wildlife Refuge.

Some 2,000 US Navy personnel and dependents – as well as hundreds of thousands of goony birds – live at Midway, but the other islets are uninhabited, except for Tern Island at French Frigate Shoals, which supports an airstrip and Loran navigation station maintained by the US Coast Guard. Midway has been partially converted to ecotourism, with twice-weekly flights from Honolulu. For information call (888) 643-9291.

Largely because of their remoteness, these isles are a favorite breeding grounds of the Hawaiian monk seal, an endangered species. This sea mammal prefers solitude over congregating in groups, hence the name "monk" seal, and can grow to over 7 feet (2 meters) in length and weigh nearly 500 lbs (230 kg).

Each spring, adult green sea turtles – Hawaiians called them *honu* – migrate to the wildlife refuge, where the females lumber ashore to lay eggs. The turtles can grow up to 4 ft (1.2 meters) in length and weigh up to 400 lbs (180 kg). They are known to bask on the beach on these uninhabited Hawaiian islets, an activity rare among sea turtles. The monk seals and green sea turtles are federally protected and should not be disturbed.

Among the interesting birds that populate these islands and excite ornithologists are Hawaiian noddy terns, sooty terns, red-footed and blue-faced boobies, Laysan albatrosses, shearwaters, frigate birds, wandering tattlers, Pacific golden plovers, Laysan honey eaters, bristle-thighed curlews and Laysan teals (said to be the rarest ducks in the world).

The two islands closest to Oahu, **Nihoa** and **Necker**, are located about 250 miles (400 km) northeast of Honolulu. They once supported small groups of pre-contact Hawaiians. On Necker, archeologists have found beautifully carved stone images, stone bowls, adzes, and other evidence of an early human presence. Nihoa is about a mile long, a quarter of a mile wide, and rises to an elevation of 900 ft (270 meters). Necker is 3,900 ft (1,100 meters) long, and has an elevation of 276 ft (84 meters). ❑

RIGHT: blue-faced boobies consider their next move, Lisianski Island.

MAUI

Crowned by Haleakala, Maui is a playful island. In its shadow, nearby Molokai and Lanai keep their own company

Perhaps Maui's most famous landmark is mighty Haleakala. This massive dormant volcano offers the adventure of lofty, sometimes snowbound, heights. In ancient times, Maui was a strong and stable island kingdom. It was the only one to successfully engineer a complete "king's highway", a paved walkway 9 ft (3 meters) wide that completely encircled the island. For a period in the late 1800s, the Maui town of Lahaina was capital of the newly united Hawaiian kingdom.

Nowadays, Maui, bolstered by a strong economy, has begun to challenge Oahu and Honolulu as Hawaii's most successful tourist destination. The economic diversification needed to compensate for declines in sugar and pineapple has sparked an interest in alternative business ventures, such as floriculture and information technology.

For a relatively small island – if it were square, it would only be 27 miles (43 km) on each side – Maui possesses an amazing natural diversity. The island is clearly composed of two entirely different volcanic masses. Eastern Maui is Haleakala, an enormous three-sided shield volcano capped with a Manhattan-sized basin, a national park, and a space-age research facility. On its western slopes, Upcountry offers productive farming and cattle ranches worked by skilled Hawaiian cowboys, or *paniolo*. Its windward slopes include one of the best windsurfing spots in the world, ancient taro-growing fields, and the notorious Hana Road. Leeward boomtown Kihei, flanked by the planned resort of Wailea, includes some of the best beaches anywhere.

West Maui is anchored by the island's older and second volcano. The "downtown" communities of Kahului and Wailuku punctuate the windward side. On the lee, colorful Lahaina and the two resort areas of Ka'anapali and Kapalua draw many of the island's visitors.

Adding to this diversity are two other neighboring islands that comprise the County of Maui – Molokai and Lanai. Together with uninhabited Kaho'olawe, this row of sheltering islands forms one side of the 'Au'Au Channel, which protects Maui's dry shores and creates a haven for humpback whales in winter.

Maui's population has doubled in the past two decades, bringing concerns about water, traffic congestion, and the risk of debasing its own fragile beauty. Popularity brings people. While its citizens struggle with their own ambitions, Maui is still one of the most popular destinations in the Pacific. ❑

PRECEDING PAGES: red sails off West Maui; beach time, Ka'anapali Beach.
LEFT: the lush cane fields and mountains of West Maui.

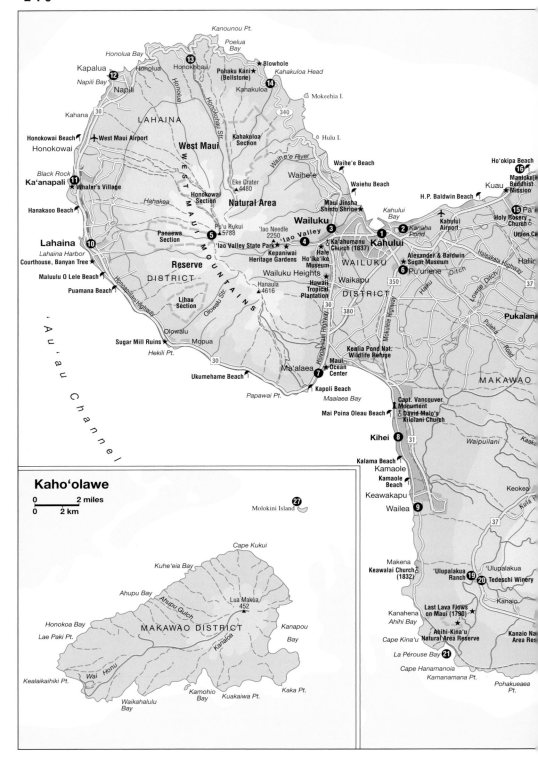

Kanounou Pt.
Poelua Bay
Honolua Bay
Kapalua ⑫ Honolua
Napili Bay
Napili
Kahana
West Maui Airport
Honokowai Beach
Honokowai
Black Rock
Ka'anapali ⑪ Whaler's Village
Hanakaoo Beach
Lahaina ⑩
Lahaina Harbor
Courthouse, Banyan Tree
Maluulu O Lele Beach
Puamana Beach

⑬ Honokohau
Pohaku Kani ★ (Bellstone)
Kahakuloa

★ Blowhole
Kahakuloa Head
⑭

Mokeehia I.
Hulu I.

LAHAINA
West Maui
Kahakuloa Section

WEST MAUI MOUNTAINS
Natural Area
Reserve
DISTRICT

Honokowai Section
Pu'u Kukui ▲ 5788
Panaewa Section
'Iao Needle 2250
'Iao Valley State Park ★★
Kepaniwai Heritage Gardens
Wailuku Heights
Hanaula ▲ 4616
Lihau Section
Olowalu Str.

Waine'e River
Waihe'e
Waihe'e Beach
Waiehu Beach

Maui Jinsha Shinto Shrine ★
Wailuku ③
'Iao Valley ④
Ka'ahumanu Church (1837) ★
Hale Ho'ike'ike Museum
Hawaii Tropical Plantation
Waikapu

Kahului Bay
① ②
Kahului
Kahului Airport
WAIKUKU DISTRICT

Ho'okipa Beach
Mantokuji Buddhist Mission ⑯
Kuau
H.P. Baldwin Beach
Holy Rosary Church ⑮
Pa'i
Union C

Alexander & Baldwin Sugar Museum
Pu'unene ⑥
Haleakala Highway
Haliʻi
Haku
Lowrie Ditch
37
Pukalani

Olowalu
Sugar Mill Ruins ★
Mopua
Hekili Pt.
Ukumehame Beach
Papawai Pt.

Ma'alaea
Maui Ocean Center ⑦
Maalaea Bay
Kapoli Beach

Kealia Pond Nat. Wildlife Refuge
MAKAWAO

350
380
Mokulele Highway
Honoapiilani Highway
30

Pulehu
Haku

Capt. Vancouver Monument
David Malo's Kilolani Church
Mai Poina Oleau Beach

Kihei ⑧
31
Kalama Beach
Kamaole
Kamaole Beach
Keawakapu
Wailea ⑨

Waipuilani
Keokea
37

Makena
Keawalai Church (1832)
Kanahena
Ahihi Bay
Cape Kina'u
La Pérouse Bay ㉑
Cape Hanamanoia

'Ulupalakua Ranch ⑲
'Ulupalakua
⑳ Tedeschi Winery
Kanaio
Last Lava Flows on Maui (1790) ★
Ahihi-Kina'u Natural Area Reserve
Kamanamana Pt.
Pohakueaea Pt.
Kanaio Na Area Res

Kala R

Kaho'olawe

0 ___ 2 miles
0 ___ 2 km

Molokini Island ㉗

Cape Kukui
Kuhe'eia Bay
Ahupu Bay
Lua Makua 452
Honokoa Bay
Lae Paki Pt.
MAKAWAO DISTRICT
Ahupu Gulch
Kanaloa
Wai Honu
Kealaikaihiki Pt.
Waikahalulu Bay
Kamohio Bay
Kuakaiwa Pt.
Kaka Pt.
Kanapou Bay

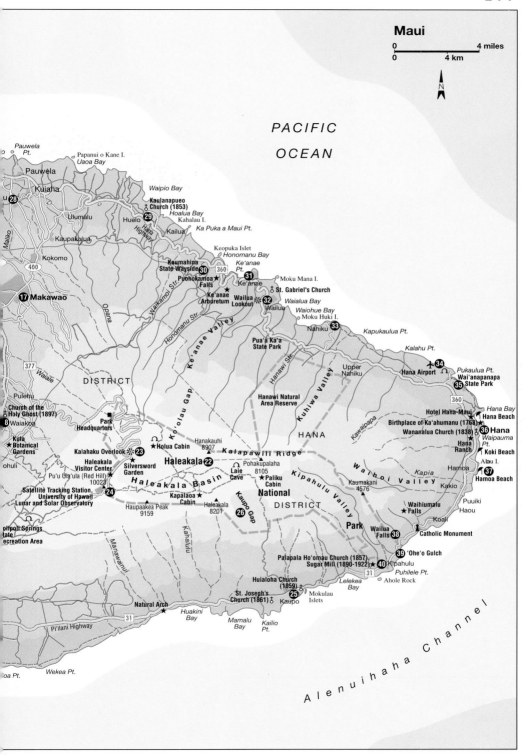

Maui

0   4 miles
0   4 km

N

PACIFIC

OCEAN

Pauwela
Pt.
Papanui o Kane I.
Uaoa Bay
Pauwela
Kuiaha
28
Waipio Bay
Kaulanapueo
Church (1853)
Hoalua Bay
Ulumalu
29
Huelo
Kahalau I.
Kailua
Ka Puka a Maui Pt.
Hana Highway
Kaupakulua
Keopuka Islet
Honomanu Bay
Kokomo
400
Kaumahina
State Wayside
30
360
Ke'anae
Pt.
Moku Mana I.
31
Ke'anae
St. Gabriel's Church
17 Makawao
Puohokamoa
Falls
Ke'anae
Arboretum
Wailua
Lookout
32
Wailua
Waialua Bay
Waiohue Bay
Moku Huki I.
Nahiku
33
Kapukaulua Pt.
Pua'a Ka'a
State Park
Kalahu Pt.
377
Waiale
Pulehu
DISTRICT
Ke'anae Valley
Honomanu Str.
Waikamoi Str.
Opana
Maliko
Hanawi Str.
Upper
Nahiku
34
Hana Airport
Pukauloa Pt.
35
Wai'anapanapa
State Park
Church of the
Holy Ghost (1897)
8 Waiakoa
Park
Headquarters
Hanawi Natural
Area Reserve
Kuhiwa Valley
360
Hana Bay
Hotel Hana-Maui
Hana Beach
Kuta
Botanical
Gardens
ohuli
Kalahaku Overlook
23
Holua Cabin
Hanakauhi
8907
HANA
Kawaipapa
Birthplace of Ka'ahumanu (1768)
Wananalua Church (1838)
36 Hana
Haleakala
Visitor Center
Haleakala
22
Kalapawili Ridge
Hana
Ranch
Waipauma
Pt.
Koki Beach
Pu'u 'Ula'ula (Red Hill)
10023
Silversword
Garden
Pohakupalaha
8105
Laie
Cave
Paliku
Cabin
Kipahulu Valley
Waihoi Valley
Kapia
Hamoa
Alau I.
37
Hamoa Beach
24
Satellite Tracking Station,
University of Hawaii
Lunar and Solar Observatory
Haupaakea Peak
9159
Kapalaoa
Cabin
Haleakala
8201
Kaupo Gap
National
Kaumakani
4576
Kakio
Puuiki
Haou
ohpili Springs
tate
ecreation Area
Kahalulu
Manawainui
26
DISTRICT
Park
Waihiumalu
Falls
Koali
Wailua
Falls
38
Catholic Monument
39
'Ohe'o Gulch
Natural Arch
31
Pi'ilani Highway
Huakini
Bay
Mamalu
Bay
Kailio
Pt.
St. Joseph's
Church (1861)
25
Kaupo
Huialoha Church
(1859)
Mokulau
Islets
Palapala Ho'omau Church (1857),
Sugar Mill (1890-1922)
40
31
Kipahulu
Puhilele Pt.
Ahole Rock
Lelekea
Bay
Pi'ilani Highway
Wekea Pt.
oa Pt.
Alenuihaha Channel

CENTRAL AND WEST MAUI

Map, page 210

The urban center of Kahului anchors the isthmus connecting the island's two volcanoes. But it is the sun and surf of the west coast – and Lahaina's whaling history – that seduces visitors

Honolulu   Maui

The central isthmus connecting Haleakala with the West Maui Mountains is Maui's prime agricultural region. It was created when lava flows from the Haleakala volcano filled in the gap between it and the much older West Maui volcano. Erosion of the West Maui Mountains blanketed the isthmus with fertile soil. Although agriculture is declining in importance elsewhere in Hawaii, both pineapple and sugar-cane production remain important here today.

Anchoring central Maui is **Kahului ❶**, Maui's deep-water port on the north side and the site of Maui's primary airport. Kahului is Maui's commercial hub, with shopping malls, a community college, and the **Maui Arts and Cultural Center** (Kahului Beach Road; tel: 242-2787). Created by a heroic grass-roots fund-raising campaign, the center includes the elegant, 1,200-seat Castle Theater, several smaller performing spaces, an amphitheater, and an art gallery and public installations by local artists. Other than shopping in Kahului and going to the cultural center, travelers have little reason to linger in the town, and most don't. Just off the highway between the airport and downtown Kahului is **Kanaha Pond ❷**, the state's most important waterfowl sanctuary and the home of several endangered species of native birds.

Wailuku ❸ is perched in the western foothills above Kahului like an older and wiser sibling. Once centered around a now-defunct sugar mill, Wailuku is the seat of the Maui County government, administering not only Maui, but the islands of Molokai, Lanai, and the contentious but uninhabited Kaho'olawe.

In Wailuku's historic district in the central area of town is **Ka'ahumanu Church**, built in 1876 of white-painted wood and plastered stone to honor Queen Ka'ahumanu, who played an important role in establishing Christianity in the islands. An early example of Western architecture touched with Hawaiian influences is **Hale Ho'ike'ike** (daily except Sun, 10am–4pm; entrance fee; tel: 244-3326), a small museum operated by the Maui Historical Society. Previously called the Bailey House, it was built in 1841 for Edward Bailey, headmaster of the former Wailuku Female Seminary. The museum conveys the spirit of missionary life and exhibits paintings of old Maui by Bailey himself.

OPPOSITE: 'Iao Needle and stream. **BELOW:** interior of Hale Ho'ike'ike.

West Maui Mountains

Beyond Wailuku at the end of the road are the wet, lush remnants of the West Maui crater and **'Iao Valley ❹** (pronounced *ee-ow*, meaning "cloud supreme"). At the valley's mouth is **Kepaniwai Heritage Gardens**, a country park with gardens and pavilions representing the many ethnic groups that have settled in Maui. It was established in counterpoint to an historic and vicious

Hawaiian battle waged in the area. During the battle of 'Iao Valley, Kamehameha's forces pushed Maui warriors back into the valley and slaughtered them, choking the river with their lifeless bodies. Kepaniwai means "water dam."

Next to Kepaniwai is the **Hawaii Nature Center** (open daily, 10am–4pm; entrance fee; tel: 244-6500), an environmental education project with particular emphasis on programs for children. The new Interactive Science Arcade offers 30 hands-on exhibits that teach Hawaii's natural history. The center also leads daily guided nature hikes in the afternoons.

Further upwards, the scenic road ends in **'Iao Valley State Park**, a lush mountain terrain dominated by **'Iao Needle**, an old cinder cone's exposed dike that rises 1,200 ft (364 meters) above the stream at its base. There is a parking lot at the end of the road, and a path leads down to the stream and up to various sheltered spots for a view of the valley. Surrounding this compact and spectacular valley are the walls of **Pu'u Kukui ❺**, 5,788 ft (1,756 meters) in altitude, the summit of the eroded remains of the West Maui volcano and one of the wettest places in the islands with more than 400 inches (1,000 cm) of rain annually.

On the isthmus

Just to the east of Kahului is the plantation town of **Pu'unene ❻** and a sugar mill that is still in operation. The former plantation manager's house next to the mill is now the **Alexander & Baldwin Sugar Museum** (open daily, 9.30am–4.30pm; entrance fee; tel: 871-8058), with working exhibits and an informative look at the lives of early migrant laborers on Hawaii's sugar plantations.

On the south side of the central isthmus is **Ma'alaea ❼**, a small coastal village and harbor and a departure point for fishing and whale-watching charters, with

If the heat and slow traffic get to you, especially on the cliffside highway into Lahaina, watch for the remnants of the old stagecoach road, which parallels the highway in some places; the trip to Wailuku used to take all day.

BELOW: Maui marlin and Wailea Beach.

one of the best surf breaks on the island. Ma'alaea's star attraction is the **Maui Ocean Center** (open daily, 9am–6pm; tel: 270-7000; entrance fee), a brilliantly designed aquarium dedicated to the Hawaiian marine environment. Exhibits include a gigantic walk-through open-ocean tank, a turtle pool, and a touch pool.

Due south along the western coast here are two resort areas often mocked by Hawaii residents elsewhere but which are popular with visitors and essential to Maui's tourism industry. **Kihei** ❽ is a long strip of condominium rentals and shopping centers with little esthetic appeal, but the beaches are actually quite decent and offer spectacular sunset views and whale-watching during winter months. There are also excellent windsurfing sites along the coast. Past Kihei are the resorts of **Wailea** ❾ and Makena, with a series of crescent beaches, five 18-hole golf courses, shops, and luxury hotels and condominiums.

Lahaina

After Honolulu, **Lahaina** ❿ is Hawaii's best-known town, partly for the nearby beaches of Ka'anapali, partly for its history, and nowadays for its party - atmosphere. In the early 1820s, Kamehameha III made Lahaina the capital of his kingdom, and it remained so until 1845. By then, New England whaling ships had begun visiting. Missionaries followed in 1823, sponsored by Queen Keopuolani, mother of Kamehameha II and Kamehameha III. She helped the missionaries establish a grass church called Waine'e, the site of today's Waiola Church. Keopuolani is buried at the site, on Waine'e Street in Lahaina.

By the 1840s, Hawaii had become the principal forward station of the American whaling fleet. Lahaina was a favorite port-of-call because of its protected offshore waters in **'Au'au Channel** that are sheltered by nearby

Map, page 210

Print of sperm whaling, 1839.

BELOW: Pioneer Inn and *Carthaginian II.*

Humpback Whales

The estimated 500–600 humpback whales that visit Hawaii each winter spend their summers in Alaska, where the rich waters fatten the whales with krill, a type of shrimp. Around November, the whales start heading for Hawaii's warmer waters, where they mate and give birth. By the end of May, they have disappeared again, having eaten little in Hawaii's nutrient-poor waters.

Although humpback whales tend to congregate in large numbers off Maui – in the protected waters between Maui, Lanai, and Molokai – they are found throughout the islands. Long endangered, the number of humpback whales wintering in Hawaii may be increasing, but no one knows for sure. In fact, only recently have researchers undertaken detailed studies of the whales' local behavior, previously having spent more time studying larger Pacific migratory patterns.

Male humpbacks sing songs in a behavior possibly related to mating. (Not all whale species, however, have songs.) It is not known whether the information contained in the songs is simple or complex. What is known is that during the winter season, males repeat the song in precise sequence. Over time, the whale song changes and evolves.

The songs are composed of thematic sets sung repeatedly in a specific order. The average song session lasts maybe a quarter of an hour, although they have been known to last as long as 22 hours. Whale songs sound like creaks and groans of different lengths in many pitches. Because sound travels well underwater, it's easy to hear these enchanting tunes if the whales are singing nearby.

When the humpbacks leave Hawaiian waters in spring, the singing stops, to resume again the following winter in almost exactly the same spot in the song as where they broke off months earlier. Humpbacks in Hawaii sing the same evolving song as humpbacks in Mexico, indicating communication between regional whale "cultures."

Humpbacks give clues regarding their moods. Slapping the long front flippers – called pectoral fins – on the water is affectionate behavior, perhaps a whale hug or a kind of caress. A tail, or fluke, slapping the water is defensive or aggressive behavior indicating a boat, a low-flying airplane, or another whale that may be too close. Whale fact: Each fluke is unique, a whale "fingerprint." Researchers photograph the flukes to track the mammals.

No one knows why humpback whales (as do some others) leap from the water in displays called breaches. But if whales breach offshore, keep watching the spot; they often do it several times before quitting. Around January, it's common to see baby whales breaching over and over next to their mothers.

Whales can easily be seen from the shore or from charter boats, and are easily located when they spout – inhaling and exhaling on the surface – and when they fluke, spy hop, (spin vertically into the air), and breach.

Humpback whales like privacy. Federal and state laws require 300 ft (100 meters) in distance for whale watchers in Hawaii. The law is strictly enforced by arrest. ❑

LEFT: humpback whales are able to dive to great depths, but must eventually surface for air.

Molokai and Lanai. Seamen took liberty from their ships and prowled the streets of Lahaina. The whaling ships have long disappeared from Lahaina, but this waterfront town continues to preserve the raucous spirit and look of the salty 1800s – although sometimes with a decidedly commercial or Hollywood veneer. It's a superb walking town, nonetheless, compact and manageable for any traveler, whatever their condition.

The heart of Lahaina lies along **Front Street**, between Shaw and Papalaua streets, parallel to the waterfront. The narrow streets that Mark Twain and Herman Melville walked are now lined with gourmet cafés and restaurants (some perched over the water in weathered buildings), art galleries, T-shirt boutiques, and fashionable shops. In 1962, the town was designated a National Historic District, and since then, the Maui County Historic Commission and the non-profit Lahaina Restoration Foundation have worked to encourage the preservation of older buildings and the construction of harmonious new ones. The result is a blend of seaport nostalgia and contemporary living, peppered nonetheless with some gaudy schlock, found nowhere else in Hawaii.

The **Pioneer Inn ⒶA**, built on the harbor in 1901 and wedged between Wharf and Front streets, is nothing if not nostalgic. On its walls are fading photographs of early ships and sailors, whaling equipment, and other memorabilia, including the original house rules: "Women is not allow in you (sic) room; if you burn you bed you going out; only on Sunday you can sleep all day." Downstairs is a veranda restaurant and a popular and noisy bar.

Kamehameha's Brick Palace once stood nearby; it is thought to have been Hawaii's first Western-style building. Built around 1798 of locally produced brick, it was commissioned by Kamehameha the Great using the labor of two ex-convicts from a British penal colony in Australia. Sadly, all traces of the ruins have disappeared.

Berthed in the harbor directly in front of the Pioneer Inn is the *Carthaginian II* **B** (open daily 10am–4.15pm; entrance fee; tel: 661-3262), a replica of a typical 19th-century freight-carrying brig. This floating museum includes a whaling exhibit. In a plaza next to the Pioneer Inn is the expansive **Banyan Tree**, planted in 1873 by the town sheriff. It is the largest known banyan tree in the islands: more than 60 ft (18 meters) high and covering ⅔ acre (0.25 hectares) with its canopy. Next to it is the old courthouse building, now an art gallery and information center. Opposite the Pioneer Inn on Front Street is the **Baldwin House C** (open daily, 10am–4.15pm; entrance fee; tel: 661-3262). Formerly the home of Dwight Baldwin, a Protestant medical missionary, it was a focus of Lahaina missionary life in the mid-19th century. The house has been fully restored and is now a museum.

Hale Pa'ahao D (lit. "stuck-in-irons house") is the old prison, located a few blocks up – where else? – Prison Street. It's a worthwhile stop just for its cool, quiet courtyard. Step inside one of the whitewashed cells and imagine a confined life in paradise. The prison had inmates convicted of the usual perfidy, including some convicted of "furious riding" – 89 in 1855 but just 48 in 1857. In that same year, one person was imprisoned for "neglect of parent to send children to school."

Herman Melville, author of Moby Dick, *unsuccessfully looked for work in Lahaina. He finally found a job in Honolulu as a store clerk and then as a pin-setter in a bowling alley. He later went home to Boston, never to return to the Pacific.*

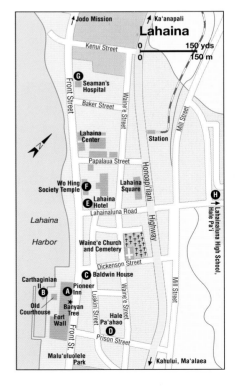

Door to one of the prison cells at Hale Pa'ahao, the Stuck-in-Irons House.

BELOW: Wo Hing Society Temple.

A few blocks to the east is **Malu'uluolele Park**, once a pond with an island where Maui chiefs lived. Kamehameha III enjoyed showing visitors the ornate coffins and burial chamber embellished with mirrors, royal feather standards, and velvet drapes. A well-known *mo'o*, or lizard god, inhabited the pond. Today, the place is a neglected ball park.

From Front Street, go half a block up Lahainaluna Road, which eventually continues toward the mountains and Lahainaluna School, until you reach the **Lahaina Hotel** ⓔ, with period furnishings. There are no televisions in the rooms and no children are permitted.

Continuing north along Front Street, the **Wo Hing Society Temple** ⓕ (open daily, 10am–4.15pm; admission fee; tel: 661-3262) is a fascinating museum of early Chinese life in the islands. The early 1900s-era building was a cultural and social home for Chinese immigrants, mostly male and single. In the former cook house next door, old Thomas Edison movies are shown amongst the pots and pans. Farther up Front Street is the restored **Seaman's Hospital** ⓖ (closed to the public), built in 1833 as a retreat for Kamehameha III. It was leased to the American government in 1844 as a hospital for seamen from the visiting whaling ships. At the north end of Front Street is the seaside **Jodo Mission Buddhist Cultural Park**, with the largest Buddha outside of Asia.

Lahainaluna High School ⓗ is located up Lahainaluna Road and behind the now defunct Pioneer Sugar Mill. It opened as a general academic school in 1831 under the name "Lahainaluna Seminary". This is the oldest American high school west of the Rockies. Californians once sent their children here rather than to East Coast schools, which ran the risk of Indian attack. The original printer's shop, **Hale Pa'i** (open Mon–Fri, 10am–4pm; donation suggested; tel: 667-7040), is where the first Bible in the Hawaiian language was published.

Ka'anapali

When the **Ka'anapali Resort** ⓫ began to be developed during the early 1960s, Maui entered the global visitor industry and began a growth spurt that has since doubled the island's population. This complex of hotels, shopping centers, golf courses, and condominiums also lays claim to what some people consider to be Hawaii's finest beaches: 2-mile (1.6-km) long beaches separated by a promontory made of a lava rock. Hotels already line the South beach, with the less-urbanized North beach poised for future development.

The **Whaler's Village** shopping center includes the **Whale Center of the Pacific** (open daily, 9am–5pm), a small but sophisticated museum with wonderful exhibits, including one of the country's best collections of baleen, the stringy plates in a whale's upper jaw used to strain tons of micro-organisms out of sea water for food. A rebuilt 1890s-vintage sugar-cane train, the **Lahaina, Ka'anapali & Pacific Railroad**, puffs over a 6-mile (10-km) route between Lahaina and Ka'anapali, transporting tourists through cane fields. Narrow-gauge tracks follow the haul-line road that was used by the Pioneer Mill until the early 1950s.

The first of Ka'anapali's hotels, the Sheraton Maui, opened in 1963 and then rebuilt and reopened in 1998,

sits at the northern end of Ka'anapali Beach at a rocky point called **Black Rock**, or **Pu'u Keka'a** (literally "the rumble"). This was one of ancient Hawaii's most important *'uhane lele*, or sacred places, where the souls of the dead departed for ancestral spirit worlds. Whether you are staying at one of the Ka'anapali deluxe resorts lining the beach – which include the Hyatt Regency Maui, Westin Maui, and Maui Marriott – or just passing through, don't miss a walk along Ka'anapali Beach.

Maps pages 210 & 217

Northward

From Ka'anapali, Honoapiilani Highway passes through the beach communities of **Honokowai**, **Kahana** and **Napili**, a clustering of condominiums and apartment hotels. Just beyond Napili Bay is **Kapalua Resort** ⓬, renowned for its golf courses, along with its luxury accommodations such as the Kapalua Bay Hotel, the Ritz-Carlton Kapalua and the Kapalua Villas.

Beyond Kapalua, the road arcs eastwards over the northern end of the West Maui Mountains, passing the fine snorkeling possibilities and a beach at the **Honolua/Mokule'ia Marine Preserve**, a destination visited by catamaran. Park roadside (the long line of cars make the site obvious) and it is then only a short hike down to the beach.

Situated nearby is the small bay of **Honokohau** ⓭. Beyond the Marine Preserve, the landscape becomes wilder, with beautiful panoramic coastal and mountain views. Even though the route is paved, narrow and curving, it is possible to navigate all the way to **Wailuku**. Make sure you stop in the rustic town of **Kahakuloa** ⓮, a scenic rural enclave where taro is still grown and the lifestyle is quintessentially Hawaiian. ❑

BELOW: Ka'anapali Beach couple.

Map,
page 210

HALEAKALA AND UPCOUNTRY

Think "Hawaii" and tropical weather comes to mind. But on the slopes of Maui's main volcano, the air is cool and often crisp. At the summit, it can be frigid, but the beaches below are usually in sight

O f the sunrise from atop Maui's Haleakala, Mark Twain wrote: "It was the sublimest spectacle I ever witnessed, and I think the memory of it will remain with me always." Travelers continue to be awed by the sunrise from the 10,023-ft (3,040-meter) summit of **Haleakala**, meaning "house of the sun." But from a distance, this gently sloping shield volcano, which is dormant, not extinct, lacks pretension. The first European to sight Haleakala, Captain James Cook, wrote simply of Haleakala as "an elevated hill… whose summit rose above the clouds." Indeed, as with the Big Island's Mauna Kea and Mauna Loa, also shield volcanoes, Haleakala carries its enormous size – 2 miles (3 km) above sea level and another 3½ miles (6 km) below – with modesty. The exact dimensions of Haleakala weren't fully known until 1841, when an American expedition surveyed the summit basin: 3,000-ft (910-meters) deep and 19 square miles (49 sq km) in area, with a 21-mile (34-km) circumference.

The island's namesake, the demigod Maui, was a magician and mythical figure in Polynesia long before the Hawaiian Islands were inhabited. According to legend, the sun was fond of sleeping late and then racing across the sky to make up time. With the short days, Hina, Maui's mother, had trouble drying

BELOW: windsurfing at Ho'okipa Beach.

kapa cloth that she pounded from the bark of the mulberry. Noticing that the sun appeared each morning over Haleakala, Maui wove a rope of coconut fiber and climbed up to the summit basin's edge one night to await dawn. When the sun awoke, Maui lassoed its rays and threatened to kill it. The sun begged for mercy and promised to behave more responsibly. For most contemporary travelers watching the sun rise or set from the summit of Haleakala, it still moves too fast. To witness the sunrise or sunset from atop Haleakala, one must first ascend the lower slopes of the volcano, an area commonly called **Upcountry**.

Upcountry

Say that you're heading Upcountry and envious listeners will know that shortly you'll be smelling eucalyptus suspended in cool air and following rolling grassy contours you'd expect to see in Ireland. Upcountry is the lower-slope area of Haleakala that overlooks the narrow isthmus connecting the volcano with West Maui. Far below one can see the white ribbons of beaches, but in Upcountry, there are farms, flowers and fireplaces. There are two gateways to Upcountry: from Kahului on the Haleakala Highway or, preferably, through Pa'ia.

Once a sugar town, **Pa'ia** ⓯ has been changed in large part by the winds and waves at **Ho'okipa Beach** ⓰, one of the world's finest windsurfing places. Pa'ia now reflects a demographic shift from plantation worker to windsurfer and artisan. Just outside of Pa'ia is the **Mantokuji Mission**, a Japanese Buddhist temple with an oceanfront cemetery of more than 600 burial markers, most of them traditional Japanese. Higher up, **Pukalani** (Heavenly Gate) and **Makawao** ⓱ (Forest Beginning) lie at the geographical entrance to Upcountry. Makawao and surrounding villages were once home for both sugar plantation laborers and

TIP

It can be quite cool in Upcountry – many homes have fireplaces – and increasingly colder as one ascends the slopes of Haleakala. In mornings and late afternoons, the winds atop Haleakala are often cold if not frigid.

BELOW: Makawao Rodeo and *paniolo* cowboy.

Church of the Holy Ghost, near Waiakoa.

cattle cowboys. Previously in decline, Makawao has been resuscitated by a diverse collection of newcomers, ranging from upscale professionals to counter-culture refugees. Even with the influx of cafés and boutiques, Makawao has retained a rough-hewn rustic feel from its days as a ranch. On the July 4th weekend, a wide variety of people turn out for the annual Makawao parade and rodeo.

Beyond Makawao and Pukalani, the **Kula** area is blessed with a mild climate and rich, deep soil. As a result, its agriculture is probably the most diversified in Hawaii. During the California gold-rush days of the mid 1800s, Kula farmers grew potatoes, corn, and wheat for export to California. Nowadays, farmers harvest lettuce, cabbage, turnips, carrots, and peas. Most delectable, claim the gourmets, are the extra-sweet Kula onions, which are said to be unparalleled. Flowers of all colors and purposes are yet another Upcountry product, including many of the exquisite tropicals like heliconia, bird-of-paradise, and protea.

There is a high road in Kula that leads to the turn off for Haleakala National Park. The sturdy road ascends from Upcountry to the summit of Haleakala in over 30 switchbacks with exquisite scenery. Continuing onward through Upcountry on the main road, near **Waiakoa** is the **Church of the Holy Ghost** ⓭. This octagonal church from the late 1890s was built by Portuguese families who had settled on Maui two decades earlier. Parishioners gave this building a full restoration in 1992.

Beyond Kula and **Keokea** (a good place to stop for coffee) on a narrow two-lane road, the 18,000-acre (7,300-hectare) **'Ulupalakua Ranch** ⓮ marks a terrain shift from green and cool to brown and hot. Started as a sugar plantation in the 1850s, 'Ulupalakua is a working cattle ranch of about 5,000 head, with additional sheep and elk. The ranch's general store offers paniolo gear and a

BELOW: a rare silver-sword plant, and Kalahaku Overlook.

Map, page 210

deli. 'Ulupalakua Ranch is also home to Hawaii's only commercial vineyard, **Tedeschi Winery** ㉑, which produces a rather diverse collection, from pineapple wine to champagne. A 20-acre (8-hectare) vineyard of Carnelian grapes thrives here. The vineyard offers free tastings, tours and a small museum.

From the winery at 'Ulupalakua Ranch, the view downslope south to the coast and **La Pérouse Bay** ㉑ is as unobstructed as one could want. Extending north from La Pérouse Bay along the coast are Wailea and Kihei. Unfortunately, there is no public road descending from here down to the coast. One must return through Makawao or Pukalani. The first Westerner to land on Maui, La Pérouse of France (Cook had sailed past without stopping), wrote in 1786 that "during our excursion we observed four small villages of about 10 or 12 houses each, built and covered with straw." Shortly after his departure, the area was covered by lava from Haleakala's last volcanic eruption, around 1790.

Atop Haleakala

More than half a million people visit **Haleakala National Park** ㉒ annually, many venturing into the basin by foot or on guided horseback trips along a 30-mile (50-km) trail system. The park extends down Haleakala's southeast flank to the Hana Coast and the 'Ohe'o Gulch (Seven Pools), embracing along the way the **Kipahulu Valley**, a research reserve of indigenous plant and animal species and closed to the public. The National Park Service maintains two campgrounds and three cabins in the basin for visitors and another coastal campsite adjacent to 'Ohe'o, which is approximately 10 miles (17 km) past Hana.

Park Headquarters (open daily, 7.30am–4pm; tel: 572-4400) offers information and a telephone, but no gas or food, and the **Visitor Center** (open daily,

Wine from Tedeschi.

BELOW: hiking the Sliding Sands Trail.

Map, page 210

Although the vast depression atop Haleakala is usually called a crater, it is actually a basin or caldera created by the collapse and erosion of the summit rim.

OPPOSITE: paragliding in Upcountry. **BELOW:** Huialoha Church.

sunrise–3pm) at the summit has displays, restrooms, and shelter from the high-altitude cold winds. There are good overlooks of the summit basin itself at several spots along the way to the summit. At the **Kalahaku Overlook ㉓**, one can see the striking Haleakala silversword, a native member of the sunflower family. The mature silversword stands from 3 to 8 ft (1 to 2.4 meters) high, with a central stem covered with yellow and reddish-purple florets – these flower from June through October, after which time the plant dies. **Pu'u 'Ula'ula ㉔** (Red Hill), the summit of Haleakala, has a space-age tenant. Here at **Science City**, scientists track satellites across the sky and bombard the heavens with laser beams, while University of Hawaii researchers operate lunar and solar observatories. Both military and civilian facilities are closed to the public.

The back side of Haleakala

Beyond 'Ulupalakua Ranch, the Pi'ilani Highway begins a slow descent, rounding the southwest ridge of Haleakala and cutting across dry open range where cattle roam. Pastures are scarred by lava flows and abandoned stonework. Now parched and uninhabited, this vast leeward side of Haleakala once supported dryland forests and a population of Hawaiians. Sandalwood cutting and ranching have bared these rugged slopes to steady winds, creating a landscape of dramatically stark panoramas that are well worth a visit.

In **Kaupo ㉕**, approximately 5 miles (8 km) of the road are unpaved, and most rental car contracts explicitly prohibit driving the unpaved sections. The road is driveable, however, and many rental cars make their way every day without problems. Kaupo is about 1½ miles (2.5 km) past pavement's end (coming from Upcountry) and situated just past **St. Joseph's Church**, built in 1861. A well-defined trail winds up the southern slope and through the 8,200-ft (2,500-meter) **Kaupo Gap ㉖** into the basin atop Haleakala.

The road beyond Kaupo continues to Kipahulu and the Hana Coast, and eventually back to Pa'ia. Even if you were planning to turn around here, consider going a little further to the windswept setting of **Huialoha Church**, built in 1859.

Molokini and Kaho'olawe

Looking seaward from the high road at 'Ulupalakua, it is impossible to miss the small crescent island of **Molokini ㉗**, an eroded tuff cone whose submerged crater offers spectacular snorkeling. Boats to Molokini depart from south-coast resort areas. Past Molokini, low and red on the horizon, lies uninhabited **Kaho'olawe**, the smallest of Hawaii's eight major islands. The ancient Hawaiians used Kaho'olawe as a center of religious practices and a navigational school. Sites on the island have been placed on the National Register of Historic Places.

Before World War II, however, the US Navy appropriated the island for use as a gunnery range. Native Hawaiian rights activism in the 1970s resulted in the return of the island to the state. A major rehabilitation program, involving the removal of debris and unexploded ordinance, has been underway for several years, and is not likely to be complete until at least 2005. ❑

THE HANA COAST

Map, page 210

Tucked away on the rainy side of Haleakala is Hana. It is so removed from the rest of Maui that in ancient times it was often the domain of Big Island chiefs. A famous road winds its way there

Honolulu   Maui

Both geography and climate have conspired to keep the Hana district, the east-facing bulge of Haleakala, a separate world. Between Hana and the rest of Maui stretches the windward face of the mountain, and in Hawaii that means the rainy side of the island. Hana is so separate from Maui proper that ruling chiefs from the Big Island often claimed it as their own and defended it successfully against the challenges of Maui chiefs. Lovely, rounded Hana Bay, certainly one of the most serene places in all of nature, was the site of some fierce fighting in the old days.

The road to Hana twists through jungle, over bridges, past waterfalls, and along cliff-edges for 35 miles (56 km), finally straightening out in the town itself. It slices through a landscape so scoured by water, cut with deep gulches, and choked with the enthusiastic flora of the rainforest that any car feels like an unreliable toy. If driven efficiently, this stretch of the road takes about two hours. Most visitors keep going at least another 30 minutes to Haleakala National Park at 'Ohe'o Gulch, promoted, erroneously, as the "Seven Sacred Pools". At that point, one can turn back or else continue on through Kaupo to completely circle Haleakala. Either way, start early and plan to put in a long day. Remember that local people drive the road every day. They know every twist and turn, and they usually have a good reason to keep moving. It's polite to use the passing places and let *kama'aina*, or residents, go by.

Today, the road to the Hana side is well maintained, and although narrow, twisting, and full of surprises that demand a driver's constant attention, it's easy enough to travel in any car. Still, for many travelers the road seems to hypnotize, and visitors often feel they've been transported to a world that's dreamier and softer than any they've known before.

The road to Hana

Properly speaking, the **Hana Road** begins at the one-mile marker (look for the green rectangular signs on the roadside) at the bottom of Kaupakalua Road in **Ha'iku** ㉘. The gateway to the Hana Coast and the winding road is the quiet community of **Huelo** ㉙, with its small Congregational church, **Kaulanapueo** (lit. "owl perch"), built in 1853. Maui's mood and *'aina* – land – begin to shift here, with the present slipping away in the tropical wetness. From this point on, you'll be driving slowly for most of the way, as pasture and open forest give way to ever-thickening jungle. Many of the bridges offer easy turnouts and places to swim. The best of these is the pool at mile 11, with a waterfall and covered pavilion.

Another good resting spot is at **Kaumahina State Wayside** ㉚. The park's carefully tended grounds, with restrooms and picnic tables, include labeled examples of plants common to this coast. You can retrace your steps a few hundred yards/meters for a refreshing swim at **Puohokamoa Falls**. Or from the Kaumahina parking lot, hike to the upper left side of the park and experience a spectacular view of the **Ke'anae Peninsula**. The view here is due east, which may explain the name Kaumahina, or Rising Moon.

The road next drops into spectacular **Honomanu** (Bird Bay), with a rocky, black beach and canyon walls choked with flowering trees. Just after Honomanu,

TIP

Souvenir T-shirts promote the drive to Hana as if it were a transcontinental expedition. It's not; it's just a slow, winding road. It is narrow, sometimes with one-lane bridges. If cars pile up behind you, pull over and let them past.

PRECEDING PAGES: a suggested way to enjoy Hana. **LEFT:** beachless coast of Hana.

Flowering vines cling to the cliffs along the Hana Highway.

at about mile 16, is **Ke'anae** ❸❶, a community of taro farmers who still maintain *lo'i*, or irrigated fields, that were first established over 500 years ago.

A narrow road leaves the highway and curves ½ mile (800 meters) down to a scattering of houses, a tiny cemetery, and a Congregationalist church built in 1860. Decades ago, when only a horse trail connected Ke'anae and Hana, there were two country grocery stores here, and the field behind the church was a baseball diamond. The school building used to face in the opposite direction, but a lethal tidal wave in 1946 spun it around on its foundations.

Near the turn off to Ke'anae is the **Ke'anae Arboretum**, which offers a look at taro cultivation and pleasant walks among tropical and Hawaiian native plants.

A Cultural Landscape area

Three miles farther is **Wailua** ❸❷, another traditional taro-growing region. The state has designated this entire area as a Cultural Landscape, and life here follows patterns established in pre-discovery Hawaii. Wailua's tiny **St. Gabriel's Church** was one of the first to be built on this coast. The lookout on the Hana Highway above Wailua has picnic benches and a captivating view.

Continuing toward Hana, the highway offers another popular roadside stop, **Pua'a Ka'a** (Rolling Pig) **State Park**, between mile markers 22 and 23. Located here, just where one least expects it, are a pay telephone, restrooms, and picnic tables, along with a natural waterfall and pool. By now you are approaching **Nahiku** ❸❸, the wettest stretch of this windward coast. At the end of the 19th century, Nahiku was the home of America's first rubber plantation, with thousands of acres of rubber trees. The once-vigorous community was even serviced by a small railroad and barges.

BELOW: Wailua nestles in verdant splendor.

The most impressive accomplishment along this coast, however, is still active and clearly visible along the roadside as flumes, tunnels, engineered ditches, and watergates. In the late 19th century, the East Maui Irrigation Company built a water-delivery system that is arguably the boldest engineering accomplishment in post-discovery Hawaii, especially considering the awesome logistics of transporting all construction materials by horse, mule, and human power. The waterworks transformed Maui's arid central plain into verdant and extremely productive sugar-cane fields.

The road begins to relax at about mile 30. The **Hana Airport** ❸, which has a limited commuter service to Honolulu and Kahului, is just beyond. One mile later, **Wai'anapanapa State Park** ❸ offers a lava coastline ornately sculpted by nature, including one of Maui's best campsites, hiking trails, cabins, and good swimming along a jet-black sand beach. Inland are some caves. Water in the caves of Wai'anapanapa (Glistening Water) is said to run red with the blood of a cruel chief's errant wife, killed for her infidelity. In fact, the effect is caused by swarms of tiny red shrimp. The caves are invigorating places to swim.

Hana

Finally, the tortuous road unravels into the rolling hills and ranch pastures of **Hana** ❸. Hawaiians say that "the sky comes close to Hana," and, indeed, moody clouds often hang low off the hills here. A local legend tells of a deity who once stood atop **Ka'uiki Hill**, the prominent cinder cone that forms the right flank of Hana Bay, and who was able to throw his spear right through the sky. Ka'uiki (The Glimmer) served as a fortress during the wars with Kamehameha the Great. A cave here, now marked with a plaque, was the 1768 birthplace of Queen

Map, page 210

BELOW: the black sands of Wai'anapanapa State Park.

Ka'ahumanu, later the favorite of Kamehameha's many wives. Nearby, pay a visit to the **Pi'ilanihale heiau**, one of the largest built. The rock platform of the *heiau* overlooks the coast and is part of either an escorted or a self-guided tour of **Kahanu Gardens** (open Mon–Fri, 10am–2pm; tel: 248-8912).

Directly above the bay and to the right, the **Hana Cultural Center** (open daily, 10am–4pm; tel: 248-8622) offers a small but thought-provoking glimpse into the area's history. Next to the museum is the small former courthouse dating to 1871, and a recently constructed *kauhale* – a compound of authentic thatch buildings constructed in the ancient style of this region. Several historic 19th-century churches add to Hana's appeal.

Exploring the trails of the Hana Ranch.

For a magnificent view of the Hana area, hike through the pasture above the town to the large stone cross on the hill; the cross is a memorial to Paul Fagan, the founder of the 3,000-acre (1,200-hectare) **Hana Ranch**, which owns much of the land in these parts. Pedestrian access to this memorial is from the parking lot across from the **Hotel Hana-Maui**, a low-profile luxury retreat. A trail from the hotel's Sea Ranch cottages leads to the isolated red sands of Kahailulu. In addition to the hotel, camping and bed-and-breakfast accommodations are options for an overnight stay in Hana. It's worth consider spending the night in Hana, for the place is bewitching in the evening hours after the tourist traffic has vanished for the day.

There are two markets in Hana. One of them is the well-known Hasegawa General Store. Rural Hawaii grew up on family-owned stores like this, established a generation or two ago by descendants of Japanese immigrants. Like most of these stores, Hasegawa Store employs a hall-closet system of inventory control, and the Hasegawa family is seldom stumped on unusual requests.

BELOW: rocky pools at 'Ohe'o Gulch.

Beyond Hana

The road beyond Hana passes through several miles of grassy ranchland. Watch for the next big cinder cone, Ka'uiki's twin, **Kaiwio Pele** (Pele's Bone), site of a legendary battle-to-the-death between Pele, the volcano goddess, and the earth deity Kamapua'a, a pig-man. Tiny **'Alau Island**, just offshore, marks the spot where Maui, the demigod, fished the Hawaiian Islands out of the sea with a magic hook. The spur road that curves down to the sea here passes two of Hana's most accessible beaches. **Koki Beach**, at the foot of the cinder cone, is shallow and sandy for a long way out, and is great for body surfing, but watch for rip tides. As the road bends back to the main highway, it passes **Hamoa Beach** ㉗, a favorite of James Michener. The Hotel Hana-Maui maintains facilities for its guests here, but the beach is open to the public.

From here to the Kipahulu district, the road encounters deep glades, sheer cliffs, and cascading waterfalls. **Wailua Falls** ㉘ is the most accessible. Then, 13 miles (21 km) out of Hana, the road enters the lower portion of **Haleakala National Park** and crosses an arched, stone bridge that overlooks **'Ohe'o Gulch** ㉙, a common turnaround spot for drivers heading back the way they came.

The parking lot, with restrooms, is just past the bridge. A trail leads down to the lower pools, which are wonderful swimming holes. Be aware that 250 inches (635 cm) of rain falls annually in the forests above, and the stream and pools quickly can become raging torrents. Near the bottom-most pools and along the cliffs fronting the ocean are the stone foundations of an ancient fishing village. Just south of this area is a campground, with tent sites along the dramatic basalt cliffs. Campers may stay for up to three days at a time. Fires are forbidden, but some barbecue pits are provided, as well as restrooms. Bring your own water, however.

Map, page 210

TIP

If you like quiet, and you want a special place mostly for yourself, spend the night in Hana. After the tourist herds leave in late afternoon, Hana becomes even more heavenly.

BELOW: the stone foundations of 'Ohe'o fishing village.

Map,
page 210

One of the most rewarding hikes on the island begins directly across the road from the parking lot: a 2-mile (3.2-km) jaunt inland to **Waimoku Falls**. Rangers have built two mildly spectacular bridges, and also a boardwalk to keep the ground virginal while passing through the heart of an enormous bamboo forest. Waimoku Falls is high (400 ft/121 meters), sheer, and powerful enough to keep observers at a distance. Afternoon showers in the hills can mean flash flooding.

Kipahulu and Kaupo

Beyond 'Ohe'o Gulch is the drier, grassy Kipahulu district and the village of **Kipahulu** ㊵. About a mile past the pools lie the ruins of the **Kipahulu Sugar Mill**, a relic of the early part of the 20th century. Below the ruins, a narrow but paved road leads toward the ocean and to tiny **Palapala Ho'omau Church**, erected in 1857. This is the burial place of aviation pioneer Charles Lindbergh, the first person to fly solo from Paris to New York. The church is open to visitors who respect the surrounding property and homes. However, the Lindbergh family and local residents don't intend the area to become a tourist must-see.

Polynesian mailbox.

BELOW: exposed roots of a young banyan tree.
RIGHT: the road's bridge over the 'Ohe'o pools.

The road beyond is paved except for about 5 rugged miles (8 km) of jaw-rattling dirt toward Kaupo; driving on the unpaved sections of the road is prohibited by most car rental companies. It's all quite passable when dry, however, and the grand scenery keeps changing in climate as you move from the windward to leeward side around the mountain.

The road breezes past the soft pastures of Kipahulu, touches a cove, then climbs a spine-tingling cliff-side grade into the sterner landscape of Kaupo. Cattle guards mark the entrance to **Kaupo Ranch**, a large cattle operation since the late 19th century. A windswept and surf-pounded peninsula juts out below the road, where **Huialoha**, a restored old Congregational circuit church is sited. Huialoha was built in 1859, a time when Kaupo was almost totally isolated and accessible only by sea and a primitive trail. The crumbling walls behind the church were once a school. There is an unlocked gate at the road leading down to the church. Offshore is an ancient surfing area once known as **Mokulau**, or "many islets," named for the lava islets sprinkled just offshore. The winds here seem nonstop.

The small store in **Kaupo** ㉕ was once the only local source of food and supplies on this part of the island, but it now caters mostly to travelers in rental cars and minivans. From here, the road continues to Upcountry.

Mauka, or toward the mountain, the slopes of Haleakala rise to a deep slash at the top called the **Kaupo Gap** ㉖, 8,200 ft (2,500 meters) above sea level, which opens into Haleakala basin. In ancient times, the gap was the primary route taken by Hawaiians traversing Maui on foot. It was easier to climb the mountain than to bushwhack through the coastal jungle. Horseback trips are available; hikers also make the climb, though it's nearly all uphill and can be jarring on joints.

Kipahulu Valley, on the Hana side of the gap, is closed to the public and is a protected natural science reserve. Untouched by introduced species of flora or fauna, the reserve shelters vast expanses of native trees like *koa* and *'ohi'a,* and endangered birds like the Maui parrotbill and Maui *nukupu'u.* ❑

MOLOKAI

Map,
page 240

*Overshadowed by nearby Maui, Molokai retains a distinctive
ambiance of "being Hawaiian." Still noted for its historic leprosy
colony, it is equally known for its rugged terrain and rural lifestyle*

Long overlooked by most travelers, Molokai has gained prominence not because of its dramatic ocean cliffs (the world's tallest)
along the northern coast, but because of an historic leprosy
colony on its northern shores. Still, travelers have had varied responses
to the colony. For example, nowhere in his travel letters from Hawaii
did Mark Twain mention leprosy, now called Hansen's disease, or the
colony on Molokai. Two decades later, however, Robert Louis Stevenson was not so timid. In a public letter, written in 1890, Stevenson
defended a Catholic priest, Father Damien, who had been criticized by a Protestant minister in Honolulu as "a coarse, dirty man, headstrong and bigoted… not
a pure man in his relations with women". Father Damien had died earlier, in
1888, of Hansen's disease, while helping the patients at the Molokai leprosy colony
of exile. Molokai certainly wasn't the "friendly island", as it's now nicknamed
in a public relations move, for many during those early years of Damien's time.

Volcanic origins

On a map, Molokai appear to be shaped like a slender slipper, 37 miles (60 km)
long and 10-miles (16-km) wide. The island has three geological anchors, each
created by volcanic activity millions of years ago. **Mauna
Loa**, a 1,380-ft (419-meter) tableland at the western end
of the island (not to be confused with the active volcano
of the same name on the Big Island), was noted in
ancient times for an adze quarry, *holua* slides (snowless
toboggans), and as a source of wood for sorcery images.

Later, the east Molokai volcano erupted, and **Mauna
Kamakou** was pushed up to 4,970 ft (1,508 meters) to
become the island's highest point. Kalaupapa Peninsula,
occasionally called Makanalua, was born even more
recently, when 400-ft (120-meter) **Kauhako**, a small
shield volcano, poured forth its lava to shape a flat
tongue of land in the center of the northern coast. It is
separated from the rest of the island by a fortress-like
barrier of *pali,* or high cliffs, perfect for isolating a
colony of exiles.

Molokai's land is primarily agricultural, and development has been limited. And, perhaps best of all for
the adventurous traveler, tourists are few. Travelers will
find that only a few paved roads transit Molokai. Many
of Molokai's spectacular sights and archeological interests require a four-wheel-drive vehicle.

Ho'olehua Airport ❶ is 7 miles (11 km) from the
town of **Kaunakakai ❷**, which is on the southern
coast. More than half of the island's 6,700 people live
near Kaunakakai. Ala Malama, the main street, contains
ramshackle buildings that have probably changed very
little since the "Cockeyed Mayor of Kaunakakai," made

PREVIOUS PAGES:
sunset over
Molokai, from Maui.
LEFT: just another
Molokai evening.
BELOW: fishermen
carrying hand nets.

famous in a *hapa-haole* (semi-Caucasian) song popular during the 1930s, strolled along its streets. While in Kaunakakai, stop by the Nature Conservancy Office (tel: 553-5236) for information about hikes through the Kamakou Preserve, which protects more than 2,000 acres (800 hectares) of pristine rainforest.

A wharf extends several hundred yards out to sea at Kaunakakai; barges were loaded with pineapple here until the plantations closed in the 1970s and 1980s. The focus is now on crops such as corn, watermelon, soybeans, hay, coffee, and onions. Close to the wharf once stood Kamehameha V's summer home. Before becoming king in 1863, Kamehameha spent his summers on Molokai. In the 1860s, he planted nearby **Kapuaiwa** (Mysterious Taboo) **Coconut Grove**, in which there were originally 1,000 coconut trees on 10 acres (4 hectares) of land. The grove that remains is a great spot for watching the sunset.

Kamehameha V.

Central Molokai

An interesting side-trip begins with a gravel-road turn off just south of the junction of Maunaloa Highway and the highway to Kaunakakai. Nine miles (14 km) ahead on this bad but scenic road is the curious **Sandalwood Boat ❸**, actually a hole in the ground roughly the size and shape of a 19th-century sailing ship's hold. Hawaiians used the crater to measure the amount of sandalwood that these ships could carry before selling it to Western traders. Sandalwood was once common throughout the Hawaiian islands, but demand from China, where it was appreciated for its fragrance, encouraged the Hawaiian king to harvest it until there was no more left.

Hidden from the gaze of casual visitors is one of the most sacred spots in Hawaii. Dedicated to Laka, the goddess of hula, a difficult-to-find *heiau* (tem-

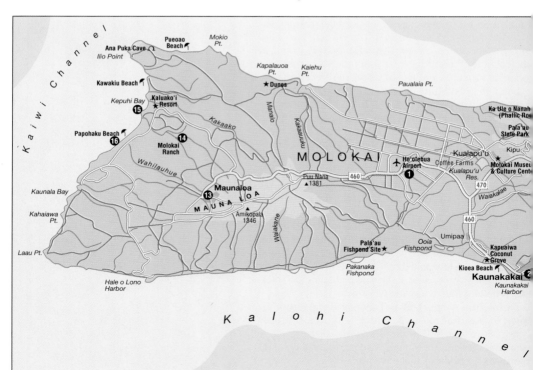

ple) is said to be the birthplace of this ancient dance form. *Halau hula* (hula school) students and their *kupuna* (ancestors) gather at this spot to make offerings before performing at the annual Molokai Ka Hula Piko festival in May.

Back out on the highway, heading north leads to **Kualapu'u**, an old Del Monte company town, and **Pala'au State Park ❹**. The park road passes through an attractive forested area of *koa*, paperbark, ironwood, and cypress trees. A small arboretum with more than 40 species of trees and a picnic area await at the end of the road. From the parking lot, it's a short walk and a slight climb to **Ka Ule o Nanahoa** (Penis of Nanahoa), a phallic rock 6 ft (1.8 meters) high and once visited for curing infertility; Nanahoa is a legendary character of sexuality.

The **Kalaupapa Overlook ❺** offers a spectacular view from atop the 1,600-ft (485-meter) high cliffs above the former leprosy colony on the **Makanalua Peninsula ❻** (often referred to as the **Kalaupapa Peninsula**, after the settlement). In his 1959 novel *Hawaii*, James Michener described the peninsula as "a majestic spot, a poem of nature… In the previous history of the world no such hellish spot had ever stood in such heavenly surroundings."

In 1866, the year of Mark Twain's visit to Molokai, the Hawaiian government began transporting victims of Hansen's disease, or leprosy, to Molokai. The exiles were literally pushed from the boat into the peninsula's rough coastal waters, and over the years, more than 8,000 people were exiled to Kalaupapa. During Father Damien's time, more than a thousand exiles lived here. Now there are fewer than 100 residents in Kalaupapa. All live there voluntarily.

Father Damien (formerly Joseph De Veuster) arrived in the islands in 1864 from Belgium. He came to Molokai in 1873 and remained in the colony until his death from leprosy 16 years later. Damien organized the colony into a true

Map, page 240

Ka Ule o Nanahoa (Penis of Nanahoa), a rock once believed to cure infertility.

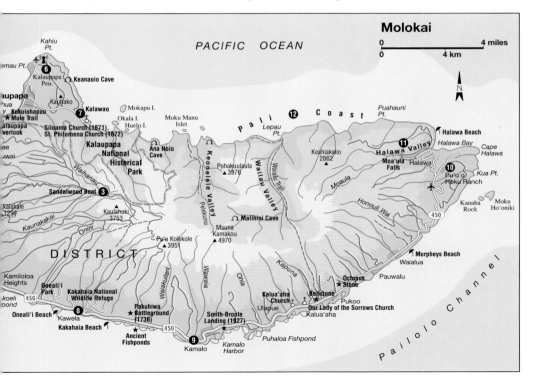

In 1936, as the Catholic Church considered Damien's candidacy for sainthood, the priest's remains were returned to Belgium. Sixty years later, a relic – his hand – was returned to Hawaii. After a ceremonial tour of the islands, it was reinterred at his former burial site in Kalaupapa.

BELOW: Damien's former grave, and an ancient fish pond.

community, establishing a church and small clinic. Land was cleared, crops were grown, and a modern water system installed. By 1883 Damien had contracted Hansen's disease and six years later he died, just 49 years old. (Not until the late 1940s was Hansen's disease brought under control.) He was buried in Kalaupapa, but his body was returned to Belgium in 1936. In 1907, the writer Jack London traced the priest's footsteps around Kalaupapa, writing a number of short stories about Hansen's disease after his visit, including a chapter in *The Cruise of the Snark* about the Kalaupapa residents.

Today, Kalaupapa is protected by the **Kalaupapa National Historical Park**, established in 1980 and jointly administered by the National Park Service and the State of Hawaii. Permission to visit is easily obtained through airlines or Damien Tours (tel: 567-6171), or by contacting the Hawaii State Department of Health in Honolulu or Molokai. Children under 16 are not permitted.

There are two ways to arrive: by air to a small airport on the peninsula, or from the top of the cliffs down the steep trail that Damien took in the late 1800s. The most colorful way to manage the trail, which drops 1,800 ft (550 meters) to the peninsula, is on the back of a nimble-footed mule, courtesy of the Molokai Mule Ride (daily except Sun, 8.30am–3.30pm; tel: 567-6088; www. muleride.com; fee). Visitors to Kalaupapa must be escorted by a resident of Kalaupapa, which usually means Damien's Tours. State law prohibits photographing residents without their permission. Although some residents still suffer from Hansen's disease, they are no longer confined to the island; they live here by choice. The disease can now be controlled by medication, and it is not contagious.

East across the peninsula is the abandoned settlement of **Kalawao ❼**, site of the original colony. **Siloama Church**, the Church of the Healing Spring, was

built here by Protestants in 1871. The Catholic church nearby, **St. Philomena's**, has a monument to Father Damien marking his original burial spot. The Hawaii Department of Health and the National Park Service are jointly committed to maintaining the settlement until the last resident dies or willingly moves away.

Eastern Molokai

East from Kaunakakai, the Kamehameha V Highway runs 30 miles (48 km) along the southern coast to Halawa. There is much to see along this road, the second half of which is a narrow lane twisting along the coast. It is a long and slow drive. Just a few miles past Kaunakakai is **Oneali'i Park** (Royal Sands), with campsites. For a small daily fee, campers may stay for two weeks but must renew their permit every three days.

Along this southern coastal road are numerous **ancient fish ponds** dating back as far as the 15th century. These were built in order to supply food for the families of chiefs. Such ponds are found on all of the Hawaiian islands, but the largest concentrations were on Oahu and the south coast of Molokai. Several of the ponds have been restored and stocked, in the hope of developing aquaculture.

Above **Kawela ❽** is a battlefield where Kamehameha the Great won an early skirmish. It's been said that his war-canoe fleet landed upon the beach here in an assault wave 4-miles (6-km) long. In 1736, two decades before Kamehameha's birth, an invading war fleet from Oahu battled combined armies from Molokai and the Big Island here. The Oahu chief was killed and his army defeated. Appropriately, perhaps, Kawela means "the heat."

Visitors should stop at **Kamalo ❾**, where Father Damien built the second of his two churches on this side of the island. He constructed this white, wood-

Map, page 240

Fishponds were enclosed by walls of coral blocks and basalt stones, rising up to 6 feet (1.8 meters) above water. Wooden gratings allowed small fish to enter from the sea. Once fattened, they were too large to escape.

BELOW: The Makanalua Peninsula and settlement seen from the top.

frame structure in 1876 and dedicated it to St. Joseph. Nearby is the spot where Ernest Smith and Emory Bronte ended the first civilian flight from the mainland by crashing their plane into a *kiawe* thicket in 1927. An earlier military attempt at flying to Hawaii from the mainland fell, literally, 300 miles (480 km) short of Hawaii. At **Kalua'aha** is the restored **Our Lady of Sorrows Church**, built by Damien in 1874. There is a wooden statue of the famous priest in the pavilion, and the grounds are well kept and pleasant to visit. Also at Kalua'aha is the **Kalua'aha Church**, which was constructed by Congregationalist missionaries in 1844 but is now in ruins.

Three miles after passing **Waialua**, the road twists inland and begins winding up to **Pu'u o Hoku Ranch ⑩**. Looking back down the mountain from Pu'u o Hoku (Hill of Stars), the scenery is spectacular. Across the **Pailolo Channel** is Maui, a little over 10 miles (16 km) away, and the great dome of Haleakala. Closer is tiny 10-acre (4-hectare) **Moku Ho'oniki** (Pinch Island, as a lover would pinch). Nicknamed Elephant Rock by inter-island pilots, it looks like a pachyderm lying at rest in the ocean, its trunk stretched out toward Maui. Just past the ranch entrance is the sacred *kukui*-tree grove of **Kalanikaula**, or the Royal Prophet. These silvery-leafed trees once encircled the home of Lanikaula, a local seer who was a lizard-god-killing prophet and *kahuna* (priest) who lived here. Hawaiian laborers once refused to help Del Monte clear the area because of Lanikaula's *mana*, and a non-Hawaiian grower who cut down some trees to plant pineapple here found that his crop wilted. Travelers speak of seeing torch lights moving through the grove at night, said to be spirits returning to Kalanikaula.

The road ends at a park and sandy shoreline on deep **Halawa Bay**, the mouth of 4-mile (6.4-km) long **Halawa Valley ⑪**. Although beautiful, the ocean cur-

BELOW: Halawa Bay.

rents at the stream's mouth can be tricky, so exercise caution. Additionally, Portuguese man-of-war jellyfish are frequently swept into the bay by offshore winds. Hundreds of fishing and farming families once lived here, but only a handful remain. At the rear of the valley are two waterfalls that feed a stream flowing into the sea. The longest is 250-ft (76-meter) **Moa'ula Falls**, legendary home of a giant sea dragon. According to tradition, you will want to find out if the *mo'o* (dragon or lizard demigod) is home before swimming: toss a ti leaf into the water, and if the leaf sinks, come back later. Upon Queen Emma's death in 1885, storms pushed beach sand up the valley to the pool at Moa'ula's base. The valley is off limits unless you sign up for one of Filipo Solitario's excellent tours (tel: 553-4355) .

From Halawa Bay, boats take visitors along the northern **Pali Coast** ⑫ to Kalaupapa. It's as beautiful and as rugged as you'll find anywhere in the world, with several 1,000-ft (300-meter) waterfalls. As with Halawa, the two deep valleys along this shore, **Wailau** and **Pelekunu**, are now off-limits to hikers. The expensive way to see them is by helicopter or from an offshore boat.

Western Molokai

Back through Kaunakakai and up past Ho'olehua Airport, the Maunaloa Highway runs through a dry landscape for about 10 miles (16 km). **Maunaloa** ⑬, itself a former plantation town, lies at the end of the road.

Much of this dry leeward side of the island is grazing land owned by the 40,000-acre (16,000-hectare) **Molokai Ranch** ⑭, the largest local landowner. When Dole closed down its pineapple operations here in 1976, the company returned almost 10,000 acres (4,000 hectares) to the ranch, much of which has been planted with commercial hay. Cattle continues to be the mainstay of the ranch's operation, which currently runs as many as 8,000 head across its arid pasture lands.

Three "wilderness campsites" have opened at the ranch, all of which are sophisticated yet rustic properties in distinctive settings. Each has 40 tent bungalows, with solar-heated water, pool and communal dining hall, and activities include mountain biking, kayaking, and cultural hikes. At **Kolo Camp**, next to the ocean, there is a unique ropes course that allows those brave enough to traverse the wild terrain by climbing and sliding down ropes. At **Paniolo Camp**, near Maunaloa Town, visitors can join a cattle round-up. The town itself has been gentrified, and features the island's only movie theaters, restaurants, and an elegant lodge. The camps offer a unique way to experience Hawaii.

A number of secondary spurs branch off the main highway and wind down to the coastline. Kaluako'i Hotel and Golf Resort, the island's only luxury hotel, is located at **Kepuhi Bay** ⑮ near the northwestern tip. The beach is good and on clear nights the roller-coaster lights of Oahu and Diamond Head are visible across the 26-mile (42-km) wide Kaiwi Channel.

Only the strongest swimmers should venture into the ocean along the beach. Nicknamed the Oahu Express, the treacherous current and pounding waves can sweep the unwary out to sea. Camping is allowed by permit at **Papohaku Beach Camp** ⑯, also on the western end of the island. ❏

Map, page 240

Molokai's population has Hawaii's highest percentage of Native Hawaiians.

BELOW: dunes and freshwater pool.

Map,
page 246

LANAI

Privately owned but open to visitors, Lanai was once a plantation island with nothing to offer but pineapples. Pineapples are history now, replaced by exclusive hotels and tourist dollars

Honolulu
Lanai

Seen from West Maui, the island of Lanai seems both close and infinitely far away. It's only 9 miles (14 km) from Maui, but the island presents a bumpy face that's as featureless as the moon. Some 18 miles (29 km) long and 13 miles (21 km) wide, Lanai is the sixth-largest of the Hawaiian islands. It buckles upward along its windward, Maui-facing ridge to a height of 3,370 ft (1,020 meters). From there, the land drops and tapers to the west, sloping gradually to the sea.

The Maui sun sets over Lanai, giving the island center stage in a much-watched spectacle of otherworldly radiance. It's not so surprising, then, that the ancient Hawaiians felt Lanai was inhabited by spirits. According to legend, people stayed away from the island until one day a hero named Kaulula'au, the son of a chief from Lahaina, crossed the channel and rid the place of danger.

The first Western residents were Mormons, who in the mid 1850s arranged generous lease terms with chief Ha'alelea of Oahu. Agriculture thrived at first, but three years later drought and insects ruined the crops. The settlement was abandoned, only to be purchased by an idealist and adventurer named Walter Murray Gibson, who used church money for the purchase of the land to his own advantage. He left Hawaii just one day ahead of a lynching.

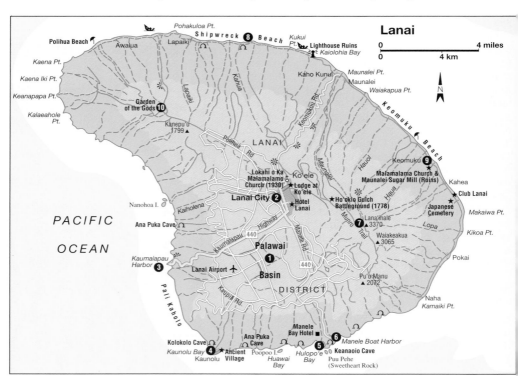

Lanai

0 ———————————— 4 miles
0 ———————————— 4 km

PACIFIC

OCEAN

LANAI

Pineapples arrive on the island

After James Dole, a persevering businessman from Boston, purchased Lanai in 1922 for $1.1 million, mules dragged anchor chains across Palawai Basin to clear it of cactus so that the land could be plowed and planted with pineapple. Using boulders from Palawai Basin, Dole then created a deep-water harbor at Kaumalapau and laid out a nearby town for the Japanese and Filipino immigrants who came to work on his Lanai plantation.

Lanai's trademark tree, the tall and dark Cook Island pine, creates water for the thirsty island. Mists collect in the trees' tight branches and drip like rain. One tree can produce as much as 40 gallons (150 liters) a day.

Dole's Hawaiian Pineapple Company prospered and was later purchased by one of Hawaii's original "Big Five" *kama'aina* (resident) corporations, Castle & Cooke, which kept Dole's name and operated the plantation as the Dole Pineapple Company. In 1987, California investor David Murdock bought controlling interest of Castle & Cooke. Like Dole, Murdock moved quickly, building two world-class hotels, two golf courses, new homes for the island's residents, and a recreational complex in the middle of Lanai City. Stunning the locals but acting pragmatically given the competition of cheaper Asian pineapples, he plowed up more than 13,000 acres (5,200 hectares) of what was once the world's largest pineapple plantation. Fewer than 500 acres (200 hectares) of pineapple land remains on Lanai – token fields to provide pineapples for the island's three hotels. Other fields are being replaced by experimental crops such as citrus, onions, papayas, macadamia, coffee, and grains used for cattle and other livestock feed.

To stay in either of the two luxury hotels (the island's third hotel, in Lanai City, is simple) is to vanish into Sybaritic privacy. The almost surreal isolation makes even nearby Maui seem like "the madding crowd" and tempts visitors to stick close to the resorts in oblivious retreat. But a rented four-wheel-drive vehicle opens the whole island for exploration – dirt roads, ancient sites, and remote beaches without a footprint in sight. There are only about 25 miles (40 km) of paved roads on Lanai.

BELOW: Kaumalapau Harbor's workers no longer load pineapples for export.

The heart of the island is a lone volcanic crater, **Palawai**, long extinct and weathered into a subtle depression surrounded by a great saucer of fertile but dry farmland. The **Palawai Basin ❶** once sustained the largest pineapple plantation in the world; today, its fields glimmer quietly in the soft, muted light.

Lanai City ❷, built by Dole in the early 1920s, is home to virtually all 2,500 residents of the island. Located inland at the base of the Lana'ihale ridge, it's a classic plantation town – quiet and orderly, designed around rectangular Dole Park rimmed with stores, the headquarters of the Lanai Company, and the vintage 10-room **Hotel Lanai**. Nearby is The Lodge at Ko'ele, one of the two award-winning luxury resorts that now sustain the island's economy. Three paved roads connect Lanai City with the coast. The busiest is the southwestern highway leading down to **Kaumalapau Harbor ❸**. When the pineapple was king on Lanai, more than a million pineapples a day were loaded onto barges here for shipment to the Honolulu cannery 60 miles (100 km) away. Now, infrequent incoming barges are filled with supplies for the island.

A very rough road off the highway leads down to **Kaunolu Bay**, but plan to hike more than 3 miles (5 km) of rocky trails; it is off-limits for rental vehicles, four-wheel-drive or otherwise. At the hike's end are the

hard-to-locate ruins of **Kaunolu ❹**, an ancient fishing village, Kamehameha's summer residence. Kaonolu is rich with the *mana*, or spiritual power, of old Hawaii. Nearby is Kahekili's Leap, a scenic lookout named after the Maui chief renowned for diving into the waters below. The coastal views from here are breathtaking.

Hulopo'e marine life

It's a far easier 20-minute drive on paved road from Lanai City to **Hulopo'e Bay ❺**. The bay, a nature conservation district that's off-limits to nearly all boats, is home to spinner dolphins, turtles, and an abundance of other marine life. Hulopo'e is the best place on the island to swim and snorkel. You can also hike along the eastern coast to reach the panoramic lookout that takes in Sweetheart Rock, with Maui rising majestically above the horizon. Conveniently, the Manele Bay Hotel stands in a commanding position directly over Hulopo'e Bay; guests can walk down from the hotel. Frequent shuttles carry people from The Lodge at Ko'ele, a 20-minute drive away. Visitors even come over for the day from Maui, and the state allows camping at six sites on the grass above the beach. Permits are available from Lanai Company for a maximum stay of seven days.

Just around an easterly point from Hulopo'e Bay is **Manele Boat Harbor ❻**. Here, sailboats can often be seen bobbing at anchor during stopovers between Maui and Oahu. A ferry from Lahaina (45 minutes) stops here several times daily. There's excellent snorkeling just outside the harbor's breakwater, or you can take a snorkel cruise to the clear waters off Lanai's south coast with Adventure Lanai Ecocenter (tel: 565-7373), which offers other adventure activities.

Lanai's most unique touring route is surely the **Munro Trail**. This is a four-wheel-drive dirt track that climbs along the island's eastern ridge, cresting at

BELOW: affluent
visitors now define
Lanai, not farming.

Lana'ihale ❼, the island's high point at 3,370 ft (1,020 meters). On a clear day, all the major Hawaiian islands except Kauai and Ni'ihau can be seen on the horizon. The Munro Trail continues down past **Ho'okio Gulch**, scene of a 1778 battle involving Kamehameha the Great, to Ko'ele and back to Lanai City. Start from the Manele Road end, because it's easier to be descending on the mushy, slippery Ko'ele side. The trail is impassable during rainy weather.

Map, page 246

Another popular excursion heads out to the island's convex northeast coast. It can be reached by following Keomuku Road until it forks near the shoreline. To the left is a track to **Shipwreck Beach ❽**, so named because of the rusting hulk of the *Helena Pt. Townsend*, a tanker that has sat impaled upon a reef in 12 ft (4 meters) of water for over 50 years. To the right is a better road to the abandoned village of **Keomuku ❾** and Club Lanai, a fantasy-resort day-camp, generally accessed by boat on day trips from Lahaina. Both require at least an hour's traveling time and are unreachable by road during rainy weather. Keomuku village was abandoned after the 1901 collapse of the Maunalei Sugar Company. A wooden church has survived the fickle fates of both people and weather. A short distance down the road is an oblong stone marker, a sad memorial to the Japanese immigrant workers who died of a plague during Keomuku's plantation days. Just a few steps beyond are the snorkel gear, hammocks, and tall, cool drinks of Club Lanai.

Shipwreck Beach.

The **Garden of the Gods ❿** can be reached by driving northwest along the Polihua Road, which turns into a dirt track that passes through grasslands. This is a strange playground of strewn boulders and disfigured lava formations. The route to Garden of the Gods also passes one of the largest examples of a dry-land forest in Hawaii. Protected by high fences, the forest at nearby **Kanepu'u** has been donated to the Nature Conservancy to preserve its native vegetation. ❏

BELOW: Garden of the Gods.

THE BIG ISLAND: HAWAII

*Appropriately named, the Big Island seduces with
its Sybaritic resorts and with the hot passion of Kilauea*

The island of Hawaii, more commonly called the Big Island, reveals its fiery soul slowly, distracting mere mortals with its intense beauty and the startling diversity of its landscape. Ride a bike on empty roads around steaming cinder cones or through crumbling fields of black lava, hike into a misty rainforest filled with towering tree ferns, ride on horseback across a spreading plain where cattle roam untethered, or strike a dimpled golf ball across the greenest-of-green golf courses.

Geologically the youngest of the Hawaiian islands and twice the size of all the others combined, the Big Island is a geological exhibit of considerable proportions. In Hawaii Volcanoes National Park, since 1983 the volcano goddess Pele has brought Kilauea to life, pouring ribbons of crimson lava from rifts and vents on the southeastern coast. Amidst billowing clouds of steam, lava hits the ocean, bursting into glistening fragments that pile up into new beaches.

A half-hour's drive to the northeast is rustic Hilo, the island's seat of government. On the island's wet side, Hilo is a quiet town, with much of its charm originating in its quiet, unassuming residents. North of Hilo is the lush Hamakua Coast, where sugar plantations once reigned. One can continue beyond Hamakua and cross over through the highland town of Waimea to Kohala and the western coast.

On the dry western side, upscale resorts stretch from Kohala in the north to Kona in the south. Save for the lushness of North Kohala, where Kamehameha the Great was born, most of the land on the island's western side is dry and expansive, and peppered with petroglyphs, ancient fish ponds, and other archeological treasures. It was here that Kamehameha the Great planned his island conquests in the 18th century.

To the south, Kona is the Big Island's center of tourism and play. Once the playground of Hawaiian royalty, the sun-washed town today is crowded with boutiques, hotels, condominiums, and tourists. Down by the waterfront, delve into history at Hulihe'e Palace, 'Ahu'ena Heiau, and Moku'aikaua Church – built of black stone from an abandoned *heiau* and cemented with white coral.

Continuing south, the highway rounds the southern part of the island at South Point, or Ka Lae, the southernmost point in both Hawaii and the United States. When the wind whistles across the grasslands, one can easily picture the original Polynesian seafarers landing at this point, a feat that archeologists think may have occurred over 1,500 years ago. ❏

PRECEDING PAGES: Pu'uhonua 'O Honaunau National Historical Park; Kalapana.
LEFT: honeymoon couple at St. Peter's Church, in Kona.

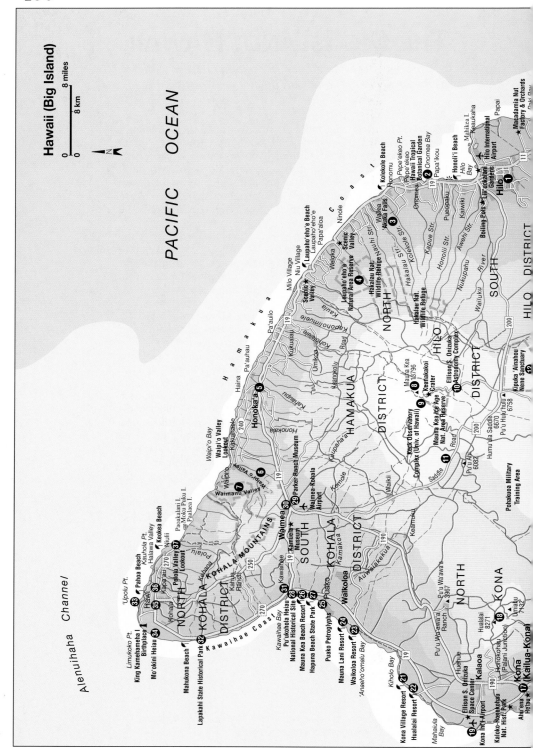

Hawaii (Big Island)

0 — 8 miles
0 — 8 km

N

PACIFIC OCEAN

Alenuihaha Channel

'Upolu Pt.
Limukoko Pt.
King Kamehameha I Birthplace
Mo'okini Heiau
Mahukona Beach
Lapakahi State Historical Park 32
Pololu Valley Lookout 37
Pahoa Beach 33
Hawi 35
Kapa'au 270 36
Niuli'i
Kauhola Pt.
Keokea Beach
Halawa Valley
Paoakalani I.
Moku Puku I.
Pa'alaea I.
34 Kohala
Kawaihae 270
Kawaihae Bay
Pu'ukohola Heiau National Historical Site 31
Mauna Kea Beach Resort 30
Hapuna Beach State Park 25
Puako Petroglyphs 28
Waikoloa Resort 23
Mauna Lani Resort 24
Puako 26 27
Waikoloa 29
Kiholo Bay
'Anaeho'omalu Bay
Kawaihae Coast

KOHALA MOUNTAINS

Kohala
NORTH KOHALA DISTRICT
Kamuela
Kahua Ranch
250
SOUTH KOHALA DISTRICT
Kamakoa
Kemole
Waikii
Keamoku
190
Auwaiakekua

Waimea 30
Waimea-Kohala Airport
Hamakua Museum
Waimanu Valley 7
Waipi'o 6
Waipi'o Valley Lookout 19
Waimanu Valley
Honoka'a 5
Parker Ranch Museum 29
240
Haina
Pa'auilo
Pa'auhau
Kukuihaele
Kukuiau
Honoka'a
Kalopa
Kapulena
Kalopa
Umikoa
Umikoa
Kalaoa
Kaohe
Kahanalu

HAMAKUA DISTRICT

KONA
NORTH KONA
SOUTH KONA

Pu'u Wa'awa'a 3967
Pu'u Wa'awa'a Ranch
Hualalai 8271
Huehue
Honokohau (Palani Junction)
190
Ellison S. Onizuka Space Center 19
Kona Village Resort 21
Hualalai Resort 22
Kona Int'l Airport 19
Kona (Kailua-Kona) 17
Kaloko-Honokohau Nat. Hist. Park
Ahu'ena Heiau 17
Kalaoa
Keahole
Umialu 182
10
Mahaiula Bay

Mauna Kea 13,796 8
Keanakakoi Crater
Keck Observatory Complex (Univ. of Hawaii) 9
Mauna Kea Ice Age Nat. Area Reserve 11
Pu'u Hulu'hulu 6758
Pu'u Oo 6082
Humu'ula Saddle
Pohakuloa Military Training Area
Pu'u Kolekole 6670
200
Saddle Road
Kipuka 'Ainahou Nene Sanctuary 12
200

HILO DISTRICT
NORTH HILO
SOUTH HILO

Ellison S. Onizuka Astronomy Complex 10

Wailuku River
Nukupanu
Puueoako
Kaiwiki
Boiling Pots
Lili'uokalani Gardens
Hilo 1
Hilo Bay
Mahikea I.
Keaukaha
Hilo International Airport
Macadamia Nut Factory & Orchards
Papai
19

Honomu
Kolekole Beach
Pepe'ekeo Pt.
Pepe'ekeo
Hawaii Tropical Botanical Garden 2
Onomea Bay
Papa'ikou
Honoli'i Beach
Honoli'i

Wailea 3
Akaka Falls
Ninole
Papa'aloa
Laupaho'eho'e Beach
Laupaho'eho'e
Scenic Valley
Laupaho'eho'e Natural Area Reserve 4
Weloka
Milo Village
Niu Village
Ka'awali'i
Honoli'i Str.
Nauhi Str.
Kolekole Str.
Kapue Str.
Aweni Str.
Hakalau Nat. Wildlife Refuge
Hakalau Nat. Wildlife Refuge

Hamakua Coast

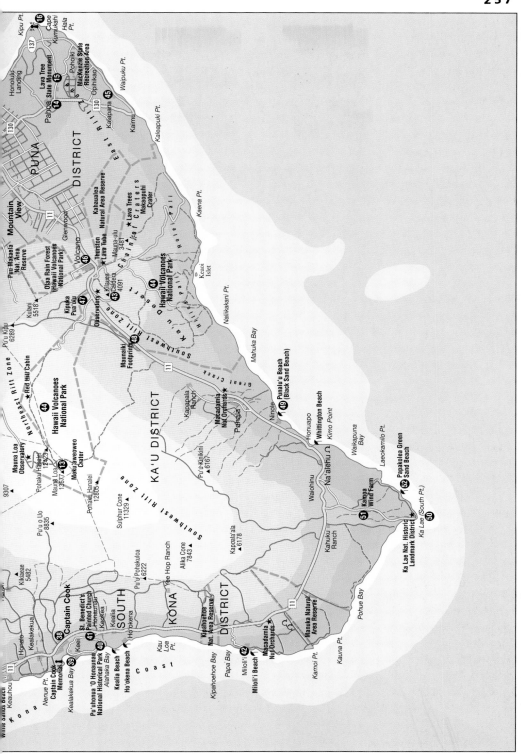

HILO AND
THE WINDWARD SIDE

Map,
page 256

*On the Big Island's wet side, Hilo is a classic, friendly island town.
To its north is the lush Hamakua Coast. To the south are the dry
Puna lands. Inland, volcanic heights beckon*

Honolulu

Big Island

Wet, warm, and sensuous in its appeal, **Hilo ❶** is undeniably a
tropical city. Unpretentious and subtle, it can yield its charm
quickly or take forever, depending upon a traveler's receptive-
ness. Named for the first night of a new moon, or possibly for an
ancient Polynesian navigator, Hilo has been a center of trade since
ancient Hawaiian times. At the **Wailuku River**, which spills into **Hilo
Bay** at the northwest end of today's Hilo, ancient Hawaiians shouted
their bargains across the rapids and gingerly made their exchanges.
Later, foreign ships found deep anchorage between the coral heads of its wide
bay, and eventually a channel was dredged so that larger steamships could
anchor. Blacksmiths, missionaries, farmers, jewelers, tailors, teachers, and den-
tists dropped anchor in Hilo, opening shops and churches, offices and schools.

Japanese foundations

The Japanese especially embody Hilo's growth. The first generation that came
as sugar-cane laborers raised English-speaking children, the *nisei,* or second
generation, who flocked not to the plantations for work
but to government service and free enterprise. Respectful of their parents, the *nisei* and later *sansei* – third generation – descendants have run the island with particular
sensitivity to the needs of older people.

The history of Hilo revolves around its harbor, just as
does most of the city's life today, whether for residents
or for visitors staying at one of its hotels around the rim
of Hilo Bay. Hilo's downtown buildings are dilapidated,
although several are quite beautiful; wooden awnings
overhang the sidewalks as shelter from the rain. Along
Waianuenue Avenue, iron rings to which horses were
once tethered are still embedded in the curb.

Downtown once stretched along the black-sand harbor, and so Hilo was nicknamed the Crescent City. But
in 1946, a tidal wave, or *tsunami*, swept half the town
inland, then dragged the debris seaward. Hilo was
rebuilt, and a stone breakwater was constructed across
the bay to shield the harbor. But in 1960 another
tsunami broke through and blasted the shore. This time
there was no rebuilding. Lowland waters were drained
and a hill of 26 ft (8 meters) was raised above sea level,
where city planners built a new government and commercial center, calling it **Kaiko'o,** or the strong seas.
The old buildings that survived form a historical downtown district with a time-worn veneer that makes Hilo
unique; the so-called Renaissance-Revival style was
obviously popular for buildings from the early 1900s.

LEFT: red ginger
and Hawaiian-style
house.
BELOW: friendly
smile from a local.

Downtown Hilo has undergone a partial restoration, and a fine walk that mixes old plantation ambiance with trendy hipness awaits in the central area, bordered by Kino'ole Street, Furneaux Lane, Kamehameha Avenue, and Waianuenue Avenue.

A few blocks inland is the **Lyman Mission House and Museum Ⓐ** (open Mon–Sat 9am–4.30pm; entrance fee; tel: 935-5021), a reminder of the island's early missionary days. Built in 1839, the house is the oldest frame building in Hilo and has been faithfully restored. Next door, a newer museum complex features Hawaiian and other ethnic history exhibits, and upstairs is a world-class shell-and-mineral collection.

At the other end of the harbor to the east is the venerable **Banyan Drive Ⓑ**, a crescent road lined with voluptuous banyan trees shading most of Hilo's finer hotels. Japanese-style **Lili'uokalani Gardens Ⓒ**, nearby and off Banyan Drive, has stone bridges, lanterns, and a tea ceremony pavilion. Toward Kilauea are the flower gardens of Nani Mau and Mauna Loa Macadamia Nut Farm Visitor Center.

From the Hawaii Naniloa Hotel, one of several Hilo hotels with superb harbor views, 13,796-ft (4,185-meter) Mauna Kea dominates the western horizon. Dark forests circle the mountain above bright-green sugar cane, thinning out as the altitude rises and finally vanishing – along with shrubs, grasses, and bird life – at the alpine heights where snow in winter gives the mountain its Hawaiian name, White Mountain. A long and broad saddle separates Mauna Kea, the island's older main volcano, from Mauna Loa, or Long Mountain.

Perhaps once in a generation Mauna Loa erupts. In 1975, after a quarter-century of dormancy, the volcano sent a thin stream of lava down to the north-east and into the saddle. Had the flows continued their natural course, Hilo, directly downstream, would have been inundated. It wasn't the first time lava

I realize more fully the beauty of Hilo, as it appeared in the gloaming. The rain had ceased, cool breezes rustled through the palm groves and sighed through the foliage of the pandanus.

— ISABELLA BIRD
19TH-CENTURY TRAVELER

BELOW: warm water, and Hilo Harbor.

Map, page 261

had come dangerously close to the city. In the late 1880s, a perilous flow from Mauna Loa headed toward Hilo, stopped only, it is said, when the volcano goddess Pele heeded pleas from a high princess. In 1942, American military aircraft dropped water and explosives on the leading edge of a similar flow to halt the lava.

Like the town itself, nearby scenic sites are quiet and contemplative places. **Rainbow Falls** in the **Wailuku River State Park ⓓ** sports a prismatic halo in early mornings and late afternoons, when the sun is oblique to its cascade. Further upstream are the odd **Boiling Pots ⓔ**, a section of bubbling water at the base of Pe'epe'e Falls.

North of Hilo

When sugar was king along the **Hamakua Coast** north of Hilo, a railway carried cane, freight, and commuters between the sugar mills of Hamakua and Hilo. A simple, winding road between the workers' camps carried cars and horse-drawn carts, with palm trees for fence posts along the sea cliffs. After the 1946 tsunami undercut most of the railway bridges, the tracks were torn up. Trucks took over, clogging the old road until a new highway was built.

You can return to plantation times and enjoy a glimpse of an old-fashioned part of Hawaii by driving along the deserted road, using the main highway to bridge its gaps. A turn-off leads to **Honoli'i**, a river estuary and beach park with the only reliable, year-round surfing waves in the Hilo vicinity. It's also where the demigod Maui came to his end while chasing a young maiden up a tree. He had turned himself into an eel during the pursuit, but a passing *kahuna* killed him.

After picking up the highway, a right turn past **Papa'ikou** marked "Scenic Drive" follows a beautiful 4-mile (6-km) stretch along the coast past **Onomea**

A note of caution if you are traveling to the Big Island in April, around Easter. Hilo is the site of the state's most popular hula competition and performance, the annual Merrie Monarch Festival. Hotel rooms for this week are reserved a year in advance. Book ahead if you can *(see page 339 for further details.)*

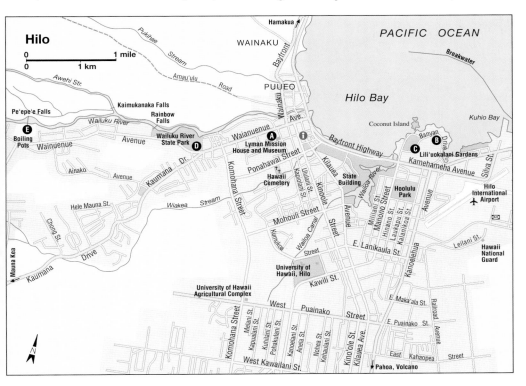

Bay, once a major sugar port. **Hawaii Tropical Botanical Garden** ❷ (open daily, 9am–4pm; entrance fee; tel: 964-5233) is a 17-acre (7-hectare) privately owned preserve with 2,000 species of plants and flowers, including palms, bromeliads, ginger, heliconia and orchids along shaded pathways in an oceanside rainforest.

The old road rumbles over single-lane wooden bridges covered with bright-red African tulip flowers in spring and squashed guavas in autumn. Plantation workers have, by and large, left the camps to buy homes on company land. Near **Pepe'ekeo**, their fine gardens and flower beds are turning old cane fields into lush, warm neighborhoods. At the town of **Honomu**, a spur road leads to the thin 400-ft-plus (120-meter) **'Akaka Falls** ❸, and its neighbor, **Kahuna Falls**. Somewhere in the area is a special rock, a stone of the fire goddess Pele, which causes the sky to cloud over and rain whenever struck by a branch of the *lehua 'apane*.

Easy living

Change comes so slowly to Hamakua that few people notice it. A new house, a new car, a new storefront appear, but never anything startling. Towns like **Papa'aloa**, **Laupaho'eho'e**, **Pa'auilo**, and **Pa'auhau** look and feel much as they have for generations. On weekends, families secretly wager on the cock-fights brought from their home islands in the Philippines. Fathers and sons take their dogs into the muddy forests on pig-hunting expeditions. Children and old men play softball in the parks. The paternal mills and the fraternal labor unions made Hamakua's plantation workers the highest-paid agricultural workers in the world. But as elsewhere in Hawaii, sugar died here. The largest mill and employer closed in 1996, and the fields of untended cane have rapidly vanished. What will replace the fields and the jobs remains to be seen. Some agribusi-

BELOW: Honomu, on the Hamakua Coast, and an illegal cockfight.

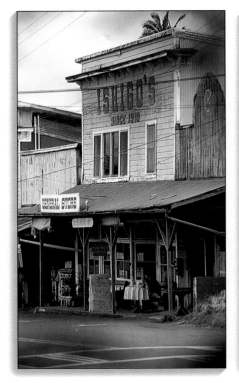

nessmen have hedged their bets by planting macadamia nuts. The trees mature late but bear fruit for decades, annually dropping hundreds of nuts with incredibly hard shells that enclose sweet white meat. It is a lucrative market, but the competition from foreign producers is fierce. Another alternative to sugarcane is a fast-growing eucalyptus tree, which is harvested for paper, wall board, and as a source of fuel.

Slicing through the Hamakua coast are three great gulches: Maulua, Laupaho'eho'e, and Ka'awali'i. The streams that cut through these volcanic channels have their sources far uphill where few people venture. With permission from neighboring ranchers to unlock their gates, the occasional hunter or forester rides up into the high terrain of the **Laupaho'eho'e Natural Area Reserve ❹**, which protects the watershed of the island's windward side, a landscape misty in summer and frosty in winter. Here, the tall indigenous *koa* and *'ohi'a* trees stand. Some are selectively logged, then trucked to Hilo to be cut and kiln-dried; others are being slowly choked by non-indigenous vines that the foresters desperately fight to cut back. Hidden in the reserve are some cold-weather trees that were planted in the 1920s by foresters: spruce, cypress, maple, Dutch elm, redwood.

Nine miles (14 km) beyond **Honoka'a ❺**, a rustic former sugar town, **Waipi'o Valley ❻** is broad and deep, the first of several windward valleys in North Kohala and a center of cultural and political life before the first European contact. It was home to thousands, including fishermen and farmers who built irrigated terraces to grow taro in the rich earth, which was said to have become red when Kanaloa, one of the four primary gods, beat Maui against the rocks.

Waipi'o's **Hi'ilawe Falls** fed a river stocked with fish that skilled men and women would catch with their bare hands. The black sand beach knew the keels

Map, page 256

BELOW: Saturday conference at the local park.

of dozens of canoes that crossed treacherous currents to trade with neighboring valleys, but by the early 20th century, young people had moved away to work on the plantations, and rice replaced taro in the fields. After World War II, two *tsunami* flooded the valley floor and it was abandoned. Today, a few families call Waipi'o home; the valley is accessed via a steep dirt road, off-limits by rental car contract. Hike in from the impressive end-of-the-road lookout, or contact Waipi'o on Horseback (tel: 775-7291) or Valley Wagon Tours (tel: 775-9518) for escorted tours.

In the 1960s, the Peace Corps, newly initiated by President Kennedy, trained volunteers here to prepare them for life in rural Asia. Today, the Peace Corps village is gone, but visitors may pitch a tent a short hike away from a natural swimming hole below 300-ft (100-meter) Hi'ilawe Falls. Dedicated hikers can cross the beach and scale the trail on the far side toward **Waimanu Valley ❼**, 7 miles (11 km) north over mostly irregular terrain.

The highest point in Hawaii

The older of the two largest Big Island volcanoes, **Mauna Kea ❽**, towers over the Pacific at 13,796 ft (4,185 meters). It is the highest point in Hawaii and the Pacific Basin. Measured from its base below the ocean's surface, it is the tallest mountain on earth at more than 30,000 ft (9,100 meters). Now a dormant volcano, Mauna Kea last erupted 3,500 years ago.

Those numbers are impressive on their own, but consider this: more than 15,000 years ago, a glacier chilled the slopes of Mauna Kea. Today, a continual layer of permafrost sustains **Lake Wai'au**, close to the summit. Poli'ahu, the snow goddess and enemy of the fire goddess Pele, is said to live atop the volcano. An early non-Hawaiian mountain climber, a missionary priest, was told

BELOW: Hi'ilawe Falls, Waipi'o.

that when the gods disapproved of someone's presence on the mountain, they would turn him or her into stone; there are a lot of stones on the mountain.

It was a special type of stone that attracted pre-contact Hawaiians to Mauna Kea's slopes: a dense and fine-grained basalt for use in adzes. The basalt is harder than some types of steel. The Mauna Kea adze quarry, eternally frozen at 11,000 ft (3,337 meters) above sea level, is a National Historic Landmark and the only one of its type in the US. It covers nearly 8 sq miles (21 sq km). The site contains 40 *heiau* (temples) and other shrines, and a trail leads to Lake Wai'au.

Map,
page 256

Stargazing

For an astronomer, no site in the Northern Hemisphere is so high, so clear, so free from light and heat, and so easily accessible as Mauna Kea's summit. The University of Hawaii and the governments of the United States, Canada, Japan, and the UK have built 13 giant telescopes on summit cinder cones. The **Keck Observatory** ❾ is the most powerful optical telescope in the world. Costing $70 million, it uses a number of mirror segments aligned by computer to create an effective light-gathering surface of 33 ft (10 meters). Four-wheel-drive vehicles are necessary to make the trek up a road that angles off Highway 20 toward the peak of Mauna Kea. (For details, call Mauna Kea Support Services, tel: 961-2180.) At a lower elevation, the **Ellison S. Onizuka Astronomy Complex** ❿ (variable opening hours; tel: 961-2180), with evening stargazing and displays in honor of Hawaii's first astronaut, who was killed in the 1986 *Challenger* space shuttle disaster, is open to visitors (no reservations necessary).

The Hilo and Kona sides of Hawaii have never been directly linked. The only overland road through the center of the Big Island, winding between Mauna Kea

TIP

No lifts, so no lines. But to reach Hawaii's finest snow skiing, found only on Mauna Kea, you'll have to walk or take a four-wheel-drive most of the way up. Ski season is December through February.

BELOW: Snow's up! March skiing on Mauna Kea.

and Mauna Loa, is the **Saddle Road** ⓫, which bypasses Kona and connects Hilo with Kohala. (Most rental car companies prohibit travel on the Saddle Road.)

An upgrade of the roads is in the planning stage, but completion is years away. A Kona-Hilo road has long been in the pipeline. In 1849, a prominent *haole* (Caucasian) doctor persuaded King Kamehameha III to let him survey and build a road over Crown lands directly from Kona, the seat of government, to Hilo, the only deep-water port. Convict laborers began at the edge of the forest and followed the nearly straight line the doctor drew on the map. After 10 years they had reached about halfway to Hilo when Mauna Loa erupted. A broad river of lava poured down the mountain and covered part of the road; it was never completed.

A scant quarter-mile from the edge of that flow, high up in what's called the **Saddle**, stands the stone remains of a monument to a 16th-century king, 'Umi, the first known king of the Big Island. He completed his military unification of Hawaii here on a desolate plateau inland behind dormant Hualalai, at 8,271 ft (2,059 meters), the island's third-largest volcano. At this location there is an auspicious optical illusion: Mauna Kea, Mauna Loa, and Hualalai appear nearly the same size. 'Umi, according to some stories, ordered a census. Stones were used to represent people, animals, and units of land. These heaps of stones were fashioned into a place of worship, Ahua 'Umi Heiau, and probably decorated with offerings. It has been 500 years since ancient armies bivouacked on the plain in this geographical center of the island, but only a few miles away in the Saddle at **Pohakuloa**, the American military practices war games. Near the Saddle's high point is the **Kipuka 'Ainahou Nene Sanctuary** ⓬, one of the preserves where Hawaii's indigenous geese, or nene, are protected. They are also protected in Haleakala National Park, on Maui and Koke'e on Kauai.

The Hawaiian goose, or nene, never sets its clawed (not webbed) feet in water. It's found only in Hawaii at higher elevations on the Big Island and Maui.

BELOW: colors on the Saddle.

Mauna Loa

Unlike its neighbor, Mauna Kea, Hawaii's southern volcano, **Mauna Loa** ⓭, is not yet dormant. Indeed, the Big Island districts of Kona, Ka'u, Hilo, and Puna remain vulnerable to a possible eruption of large magnitude. Mauna Loa's last eruption was a 1984 fountain inside the summit caldera, or crater, of **Moku'aweoweo**, a name referring to the *'aweoweo* fish whose red color has obvious volcanic parallels. In fact, Mauna Loa has erupted 36 times since European contact with Hawaii. Several times in the 20th century, it threatened Hilo city, situated on the volcano's northeast flank, most recently during the 1984 eruption, when flows stopped just 5 miles (8 km) away.

Mauna Loa is a classic shield-dome volcano, its bulk growing through the accumulative stacking of thin lava flows of 10–15 ft (3–4.5 meters) at a time. This relatively benign process gives a shield volcano a gentle convex curvature, in contrast to dramatic and explosive volcanoes such as Mt. Fuji and Mt. St. Helens. Shorter, at 13,679 ft (4,149 meters), than Mauna Kea, Mauna Loa (Long Mountain) has more mass than any other mountain on the planet, with more volume (almost 10,000 cubic miles/40,000 cubic km) than the entire Sierra Nevada range in California.

From the summit caldera, two prominent rift zones, which are fractured areas of weakness, extend deep into the ocean. The first rift zone passes through South Point at the bottom of the island, and the second, the northeast rift zone, extends toward Hilo.

Map,
page 256

South of Hilo: Puna

Travelers often bypass the **Puna** area south of Hilo along Highway 130 on the way to Kilauea and Hawaii Volcanoes National Park. The road that once linked Puna to Hawaii Volcanoes National Park was closed in 1994 after lava covered much of it. Scores of homes, as well as the village of Kalapana and several historic sites, have been destroyed by the slow-moving flows of Kilauea. In late 2001 a road to the coastal lava flows was re-opened to the public.

The gateway to the Puna area is the town of **Pahoa ⓮**, once a major supplier of *'ohi'a* wood to the railroads, which used the wood for ties. Its small downtown is interesting, with raised wooden sidewalks and an unusually high number of old buildings along its main street. The agricultural area surrounding Puna is known for producing tropical flowers, papaya, and illegal *pakalolo* (marijuana).

In 1790, lava flows flooded then drained a rainforest, leaving shells of solidified lava around now-vaporized trees. These lava-tree mold forests of **Lava Tree State Monument ⓯**, especially when in early mornings before the mists have lifted, are eerie. Further along the road is the island's westernmost point, **Cape Kumukahi ⓰**, which grew dramatically after eruptions in 1955 and 1960. The Cape's namesake was one of two men: a chief who mocked Pele or a migratory traveler originally from Tahiti. Either way, Kumukahi means "first beginning." Partially covered by the recent flows is a cemetery for Japanese immigrants. The coastline of Puna is decidedly volcanic and rough, with few satisfactory beaches. ❑

Cemetery marker on Cape Kumukahi that survived a 1960 lava flow over the Japanese cemetery there.

BELOW: road near Lava Tree National Monument, and Big Island palms.

KONA AND KOHALA

The Big Island's western coast is anchored by the town of Kailua-Kona, and peppered with some of the world's finest resorts. Still, there are ancient haunts on this drier side of the island

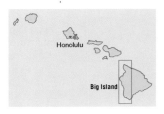

Map,
page 256

The Kona and Kohala coasts of the Big Island are on its leeward side. Like all of the Hawaiian islands, this is the island's dry side because central mountains catch the moisture-rich trade winds from the northwest and release their rain on the island's windward side. To put it simply, west coasts in Hawaii are usually the dry and sunny coasts. On the Big Island, this makes Kohala and Kona prime destinations with some of the world's finest resort hotels. The northern part of this side of the Big Island is called Kohala, while the central part is known as Kona. In the past, the only way to drive from Kohala to Kona was along a narrow road far uphill from the ocean. Today, however, a highway named for Queen Ka'ahumanu, wife of Kamehameha the Great, connects Kawaihae in Kohala with Kailua-Kona. The highway passes through some of the driest land in Hawaii, where tiny beaches and archeological sites are strung along the coast like beads. This open country is gritty, broad, and windy.

Kona

To confuse matters, the main town on this side of the Big Island known to locals usually as **Kailua**, the district being called **Kona ⑰**, is known to the post office as **Kailua-Kona**. Generally, they're interchangeable, but Kona is commonly used for the town, district, and the coast.

Dominating North Kona is 8,271-ft (2,509-meter) **Hualalai ⑱**, an awesome volcano that last erupted in 1801. The **Kona International Airport ⑲** lies on one of its lava flows at Keahole. Legend has it that an 1801 eruption of Hualalai was initiated by Pele, the fire goddess, mostly out of jealousy for the successful Kamehameha the Great. When Kamehameha followed the advice of a *kaula*, a seer, and made offerings to Pele, the eruption ceased. Today, Hualalai is home to game birds, and sheep and goats wander over its dormant heights foraging on dry shrubs and grasses.

Pu'uwa'awa'a, a pumice cone around 100,000 years old, rises abruptly 4,000 ft (1,200 meters) on the flanks of Hualalai. The typical lava flow in Hawaii is 15 ft (5 meters) thick, but flows from Pu'uwa'awa'a reached 900 ft (270 meters) in thickness. Obsidian glass, used for making sharp tools and weapons, is found here. The only other place in the Hawaiian islands where obsidian is found is on the island of Kaho'olawe. On Hualalai's southwest flank, at about 1,500 ft (457 meters), is **Holualoa ⑳** village, home to those seeking refuge from the jumble of Kailua-Kona below. On the high road, it sits amidst coffee plants and wonderful views. A growing number of visitors are discovering the town's small galleries.

The town of Kailua-Kona is one of those places noted for sun and night life – with the sun outshining the night life by far. **Kailua Bay**, a harbor skirted by Ali'i Drive and a seawall, is the downtown focus. At the north end on the grounds of King Kamehameha's Kona Beach Hotel is an ancient temple or *heiau*, **Ahu'ena**, once used for human sacrifices. It was later restored by Kamehameha the Great and used as his personal *heiau*, when he settled here at the royal compound called **Kamakahonu**, or "turtle eye".

This is where Kamehameha the Great retired and later died in 1819. Loyal attendants hid his bones, lest they be defiled by his enemies or the *mana*

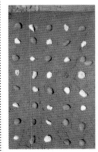

A chess-like game played by Hawaiians before Captain Cook's arrival in Hawaii.

LEFT: ancient foot trail and petroglyphs along the Kohala coast, near Mauna Lani.

(spiritual essence) abused. Occasionally, someone claims to have found the burial site – caves were traditional burial locations – but it remains undiscovered. Possibly it was sealed by a lava flow, or it may even be under water, as the island's west coast has sunk an average of 9 inches (23 cm) every 100 years for the past eight centuries. The Ahu'ena *heiau* site, which was partially demolished to build the Kona Pier, was later restored. The site provides a unique perspective for those on the nearby beach.

Ali'i Drive leads south along the harbor past the Royal Kona Resort, which is hard to miss as it juts into the ocean, and through a jungle of condominiums and apartments. The harbor area along Ali'i Drive, situated between the King Kamehameha and Royal Kona hotels, is a fine walking district for both shoppers and those interested in the history of the stretch.

The charming **Hulihe'e Palace**, built in 1838 by the brother of Queen Ka'ahumanu, sits right on the ocean just down from Ahu'ena *heiau*. Restored in 1927, it is a wonderful museum evoking the old days when it served as a royal getaway. Opposite the palace on Ali'i Drive, **Moku'aikaua Church** was built in 1837. The original church, with a pandanus roof and foundations of old *heiau* stones, was dedicated in 1823 but destroyed in 1835.

Sheltered from the prevailing trade winds, the waters off the Kona Coast are home to game fish considered among the best in the world. Each summer in late July or August, the Hawaiian International Billfish Tournament is staged here. More than a dozen blue marlin weighing 1,000 lbs (450 kg) have been caught within an hour's run from the pier. *Ahi* (tuna), *ono* (bonefish), *ulua* (jack crevalle), *mahimahi* (dolphin fish), and swordfish are now caught regularly by anglers from Europe, North America, Australia, and Japan.

BELOW: Hulihe'e Palace and fragrant plumeria.

North of Kona

North of the Kona International Airport is a one of a kind among Hawaii's resorts: the low-profile **Kona Village Resort** ❹, wrapped in a mystique that's in sharp contrast to the fantasy mega-resorts built in Hawaii during the 1980s. From the main highway, a string of what look to be simple thatched huts line the ocean. In fact, they are luxury *hale*, or bungalows, without televisions, telephones, or anything else that disrupts the serenity of the setting.

Kona Village was started in the early 1960s by Johnno and Helen Jackson, who wanted to recreate the old Hawaiian village, Ka'upulehu, that once stood on Kahuwai Bay. Sailing up the Kona coast on their schooner *New Moon*, the Jacksons dropped anchor in the bay and set out to clear the thick *kiawe*, or mesquite, covering an 1801 flow from Hualalai volcano. The result is an idyllic escapist resort, where days flow effortlessly by. The petroglyphs and beach-front *tiki* (carved Hawaiian god figure) add a sense of Hawaiian authenticity. Modernity has, however, come to the area, in the shape of the elegant **Hualalai Resort** ❷, with its Four Seasons Hotel, 18-hole golf course and condominiums. Its lovely rooms, complex of oceanside swimming pools, and impressive cultural center make it as desirable a neighbor as Kona Village could have hoped for.

Another good collection of ancient petroglyphs can be found at the Waikoloa Resort at **'Anaeho'omalu** ❷, where they have been joined by both golf course and relatively modern petroglyphs from the late 1800s that include English words, and figures bearing rifles. Also well preserved here are ancient fish ponds on the ocean side of the Outrigger Waikoloa Resort. One of Hawaii's most ambitious hotels, the Hilton Waikoloa Village, bears the signature of Chris Hemmeter, a developer who constructed fantasy destination resorts throughout Hawaii during

Map, page 256

Rock grafitti, or maybe a wistful valentine.

BELOW: Waikoloa hotel with Mauna Kea in background.

the 1980s, of which the 1,200-room Hilton is the most extravagant. Three small hotels-within-a-hotel are connected by mechanically guided boats in a canal, a sleek electric train and a mile-long walkway lined with Asian and Pacific Island art.

Kohala

A few minutes' further north is **Mauna Lani Resort** 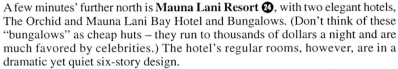, with two elegant hotels, The Orchid and Mauna Lani Bay Hotel and Bungalows. (Don't think of these "bungalows" as cheap huts – they run to thousands of dollars a night and are much favored by celebrities.) The hotel's regular rooms, however, are in a dramatic yet quiet six-story design.

In earlier days, Mauna Lani was known as Kalahuipua'a, a site of aquaculture ponds that the Mauna Lani Hotel has preserved. A walking trail leads from the hotel toward Keawanui Bay and the ponds. There are six major ponds, the largest about 5 acres (2 hectares) in size and 18 ft (6 meters) deep. A spur trail heading inland past the ponds opens onto a lava field, where excavated caves have yielded an ancient canoe paddle and large fishhooks, probably for catching sharks.

Kamehameha the Great maintained a canoe landing here, marked now by a replica of an old canoe shed; inside is a full-sized replica of an outrigger canoe. Uncovered at low tide, just *makai* (toward the ocean) of the shed, is a *papamu* petroglyph for playing a checkers-like game called *konane*. Beyond is the Eva Parker Woods Cottage Museum, built in the 1920s and later moved to its current seaside location. Ancient Hawaiian artifacts are displayed inside.

A 5-minute walk up the coast, in **Pauoa Bay** fronting the Orchid at Mauna Lani, is a submarine freshwater spring. Ancient Hawaiians would dive to the spring's opening and fill gourds with fresh drinking water.

Child's fish story.

BELOW: lobby of the Mauna Lani Hotel, and tuna catch.

North toward ancient petroglyphs

The shoreline trail to the south follows an ancient footpath that connected fishing villages in pre-contact Hawaii. Along the path are ancient fishing platforms, a house site, and some anchialine pools – low-sited caves that were once flooded with sea water. Brackish water now fills these natural depressions in the lava.

The west coast of the Big Island has a number of these ponds, unique in the United States. Some have been preserved, like these at Mauna Lani, where five shrimp species thrive. To the south at the sprawling Hilton Waikoloa Village, anchialine pools were intentionally destroyed during the resort's construction to make way for artificial lagoons, although others were preserved.

Just north of the Mauna Lani Resort is one of Polynesia's best collections of petroglyphs, the **Puako petroglyph field** ㉕. Years ago, access was through the village of Puako. Now a well-marked road at the Mauna Lani Resort ends in a parking lot, where a self-guided trail leads to a field of several thousand petroglyphs etched into the lava. The age of these petroglyphs has not been determined. Many are of uncertain meaning; others, like the circles with a dot inside, called *piko* (navel) holes, are known to have been receptacles for the umbilical cords of newborn children. Most Hawaiian petroglyphs were chiseled into smooth *paho'eho'e* lava along major trails.

The low roads in both North and South Kohala are lined with *kiawe* trees and prickly-pear cacti. The *kiawe* tree is burned into first-rate charcoal, and the cactus blooms develop into a sweet, blood-red fruit. On land found too dry for cattle, Laurence Rockefeller commissioned a luxury resort in the 1960s, the **Mauna Kea Beach Resort** ㉖, piping in water for its grounds and golf course all the way from Waimea. For more than a quarter of a century, Mauna Kea was the

Map, page 256

The most profitable agricultural crop on the Big Island is marijuana, known in Hawaii as pakalolo *(lit. "numbing tobacco"). The so-called Kona Gold is a cash crop, estimated as surpassing coffee and sugar in net revenue. It is illegal in Hawaii.*

BELOW: Puako petroglyphs.

standard by which other Hawaii resorts were measured. It is still noted for its lovely crescent beach, its exquisite, comprehensive collection of Asian antiquities, and for its fine design.

Although the Mauna Kea once imported sand to widen its beautiful beach, considered one of the Big Island's best, half a mile south lies **Hapuna Beach State Park ㉗**, with the island's largest natural white-sand beach. In 1991, at a re-dedication of the site, descendants of the once-warring clan were reconciled in an impressive 'awa ceremony, complete with costumed pageantry. The Hapuna Beach Prince Hotel opened in 1994 at the northern end of Hapuna Beach, and local people continue to use the popular public beach side by side with visitors.

The lava flows of Kona and Kohala are rich with petroglyphs. Although carved in rock, they are fragile.

A shrine to Kamehameha's war god

Continuing northward, hot, dusty, and dry South Kohala looks like parts of the western United States – rock-strewn grasslands but with a seacoast, and with fewer than 9 inches (23 cm) of rain a year. Where Highways 270 and 19 from North Kohala and Waimea meet and continue south stands the largest restored *heiau* in Hawaii: **Pu'ukohola ㉘** (open daily, 7.30am–4pm; tel: 882-7218), rebuilt in 1791 by Kamehameha the Great for his war god, Kuka'ilimoku, in hopes of successful military conquests. To dedicate the shrine after it was finished, he invited his main Big Island rival and cousin, the high chief Keoua, to a ceremony at the *heiau* as a guest, where he was killed as a sacrificial offering. Pu'ukohola (Whale Hill) is now protected as a National Historic Site.

Captain George Vancouver and other early Europeans introduced goats, sheep, and cattle to the newly united island kingdom of Kamehameha the Great. The traditional low stone walls of the Hawaiians were unable to contain these domes-

BELOW: hiking the trails of Lapakahi.

Map,
page 256

ticated stock animals, and in less than a decade, feral herds were ravaging cultivated farmlands and gnawing down young indigenous trees and plants.

In the early 1880s, a New England farmer named John Palmer Parker offered to round up the troublesome animals in exchange for homestead land. Kamehameha gave him 2 acres (1 hectare) in the Kohala. These 2 acres grew to become what was at one time the largest privately owned ranch in America. Today, the cowboys of **Parker Ranch** run some 50,000 head of cattle over 210,000 acres (85,000 hectares) of pasture. Although the ranch is administered by a trust today, the Parker name continues to be nearly ubiquitous in Kohala, the Big Island's northern district. At **Parker Ranch Visitor Center and Museum** ㉙ (open daily 9am–5pm; entrance fee; tel: 885-7655) in Waimea/Kamuela, visits to the century-old family home, Mana, and a second, more modern home, Pu'uopelu, which contains an extensive art collection, can be arranged.

As with the sugar barons during the 19th century, Parker had to import workers for his ranch, primarily Spanish-speaking cowboys from Mexico who were called *paniolo* (derived from the word *españa*) by Native Hawaiians. Today, all cowboys in Hawaii are called *paniolo*, and ranchlands are known as *paniolo*-country. In later years, Portuguese joined them, and local men were trained as ranch hands, too, as were Asian immigrants. Today, *paniolo* has no racial or ethnic identity.

The gateway to Kohala and Kona

When coming from Hilo, **Waimea** ㉚ is the gateway to Kohala and to Kona beyond. Waimea, sometimes called **Kamuela** (Hawaiian for Samuel, one of the Parkers), grew in tandem with the Parker family's increasing fortune. It's a cool and often misty town at nearly 3,000 ft (910 meters) above sea level. At the western edge of town, where Highway 250 to North Kohala branches off from Highway 19, is **Kamuela Museum** (open daily 8am–5pm; entrance fee; tel: 885-4724). The museum holds an eclectic and completely unrelated collection of ancient Hawaiian artifacts, antique American furniture, and surprises like a Viet Cong flag and rare Chinese porcelain.

Parker Ranch supplied most of the locally produced beef in Hawaii, butchering it at a company-owned slaughterhouse in Honolulu. Until a port was built, cattle were herded to the surf at **Kawaihae** ㉛ and forced to swim through the ocean to waiting ships, which hauled them aboard in slings. Nowadays, they are driven through gates onto enclosed barges. In the 1960s, Parker's descendant Richard Smart sold large, unproductive coastal tracts in South Kohala to resort developers.

In 1968, archeologists excavated a 600-year-old Hawaiian fishing village, Lapakahi, near Highway 270 that skirts North Kohala's coastline. The area is protected as **Lapakahi State Historical Park** ㉜ (open daily, 8am–3.30pm except holidays). The park, which offers self-guided tours, preserves the foundations and stone enclosures of this commoners' fishing village.

This northern tip of the Big Island, **North Kohala**, is one of those windswept, wide-open places enveloped in mysticism. Literally at the end of the road is the Big Island's northernmost point, **'Upolu Point** ㉝ (named for an island in Samoa). Past the small airfield there is

BELOW: rodeo at Waimea.

well-preserved and partially restored **Mo'okini Heiau** ㉞, built around 800, it's said, by a *kahuna* (priest) from Tahiti. Today, a *kahuna* from the Mo'okini family of North Kohala still maintains the *heiau*. Within sight of the *heiau* is the **birthplace of Kamehameha the Great**, *circa* 1752. Signs mark both Mo'okini Heiau and Kamehameha's birthplace, with the *heiau* in particular well worth the short side trip on an unpaved road.

The backbone of North Kohala

Defining North Kohala are the **Kohala Mountains**, the remains of an extinct 700,000-year-old volcano. In addition to the coastal road on the west side, Highway 250 ascends from Waimea to the ridge line and then through ranch land and groves of trees planted decades ago as windbreaks. The winds, called *'apa'a-pa'a*, that whip across the Kohala ridge are powerful and persistent.

At the north end of the peninsula is **Hawi** ㉟, an old sugar town long suspended in the past. In adjacent **Kapa'au** ㊱, in front of the town's unassuming civic center, is the original **Kamehameha the Great statue**. It was lost at sea off the Falkland Islands and later recovered and taken to the Big Island town of Kapaau. Its replacement stands opposite 'Iolani Palace in Honolulu.

In the 1880s, Kohala led the island in sugar production. Chinese laborers were hired by a businessman to construct a narrow-gauge railway from **Niuli'i**, beyond Kapa'au, to the port of Mahukona, on North Kohala's western coast. Formally opened by King Kalakaua, the railroad was abandoned half a century later when trucks replaced trains. Male Chinese laborers founded the Kohala Tong Wo Society ("together in harmony") in 1886, the last of many Chinese societies established on the Big Island. In China, the Tong Wo Society had emerged in 16th-century China to overthrow the Manchus, and later flourished overseas wherever Chinese settled. Members identified one another by passwords, special gestures, and manipulations of chopsticks. Sun Yatsen came to Hawaii in the 1880s, and again in the early 1900s, seeking help from the societies to finance his efforts to overthrow the Qing dynasty in China.

The **Kohala Tong Wo Society building** was the social center of Kohala's early Chinese society. At night, the men gambled or climbed a rope ladder for opium breaks in the loft. As a man neared death from old age, he moved to the "death house" on the society grounds, for it was bad luck to die at home. The hillside sloping down from the building is dotted with aged Chinese headstones. The main building was restored and re-dedicated in 1971. Scrollwork link the beams and posts, and plaques engraved with proverbs and phrases surround the doors and windows.

Beyond the Tong Wo building and at the end of the road, **Pololu Valley Lookout** ㊲ offers expansive views of the **Hamakua Coast** and its repeating cliffs and surf. A steep trail leads down to the rocky beach that is partially visible from the lookout or you can join Hawaii Forest and Trail (tel: 800-464-1993) on a memorable horseback or hiking excursion into the valley.

Dense forests cover the round, eroded highlands of Kohala, scarred by deep-cleft valleys and ravines.

BELOW: purple jacaranda trees.

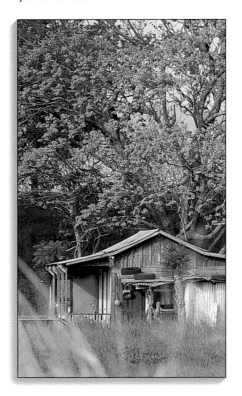

Along their eastern ocean faces, water seeps out of cracks in the cliffs and plunges a thousand feet to the sea. At the turn of the 20th century, a technique for tapping this mountain water was established. Christened in 1906, the **Kohala Ditch** was a water course 18 miles (29 km) long that funneled the headwaters of Waimanu Valley to Honokane, terminating in an 850-ft (260-meter) long artificial waterfall. Immigrant Japanese laborers bored and blasted 44 tunnels 8 ft (2.4 meters) wide and 7 ft (2 meters) high; the longest tunnel was nearly ½ mile (1 km) long. At least six men died and countless others suffered from exposure and chills while working in the icy darkness of the flooded tunnels. A completely safe kayak trip through the ditch's flumes and tunnels, and through rainforest and pastures, is offered by Flumin Da Ditch (tel: 877-449-6922 toll free).

South of Kona

Up above Kailua on the slopes of Mauna Loa, the climate is cooler. Moist air, bright sunshine, and porous volcanic soil produce one of the world's finest gourmet coffees. Schools in **South Kona** used to close during coffee-bean harvest season so that children could help their families fill burlap sacks of the bright-red beans for delivery to the local mill. The coffee industry faltered in the 1970s and 1980s, but the most recent explosion of coffee drinking throughout the country has brought a revival of Kona coffee. There are numerous boutique mills throughout the Kona region that welcome visitors. All along the upcountry stretch of highway south of Kailua-Kona in the small villages clustered around the town of **Captain Cook** ⓴ are tasting rooms where various types of Kona coffee are sold.

South Kona has diversified, both in spirit and in economics, since the 1960s, when the area was a haven for self-exiled counterculture types, then later for

Map, page 256

TIP

Kona coffee is popular with *kama'aina* and visitors alike. A Kona blend, however, is legally required to contain only 10 percent Kona beans. One hundred percent Kona sells at premium prices, but it's well worth it.

BELOW: Kealakekua Bay.

Map,
page 256

*Carved image at the
ancient place of
refuge, Pu'uhonua
'O Honaunau.*

BELOW: St.
Benedict's. **RIGHT:**
northern coast.

artisans and craftspeople. Other newcomers settled here to become farmers by leasing land from large estates and buying up farmlands. Much of that new farm land went not into coffee production, but into vegetables, citrus fruits, and cocoa, with beans that, when processed, compare with the finest European chocolate.

Higher up Mauna Loa's slopes are forests of native trees. Around their trunks, wild *maile* wraps itself. *Maile* is prized for making *lei,* but with an increasing population, *maile* has become scarce and expensive, with much of it imported from other Pacific islands. Sandalwood once covered many of these slopes; today, few trees remain. Whole forests of the creamy, aromatic wood were cut and sold by Kamehameha the Great and his heirs for profitable shipment to China.

The site of Cook's demise

Far below today's coffee and cocoa farms, Captain James Cook met his untimely death along the shore of **Kealakekua Bay ㊲**, now a state marine conservation district. Visitors arrive on day-cruises to this bay from Kailua-Kona, or else drive to it on a paved road descending through relatively recent lava fields. Inaccessible except by water, a white obelisk, on a parcel that is officially British territory, marks the spot where Cook and some of his crew died. Archeological surveys between Kealakekua Bay and Kailua-Kona have mapped at least 40 *heiau* in the area, with one of the best preserved at Napo'opo'o overlooking a small sand beach that offers welcome relief from the midday heat.

A traveler cruising by boat south along the coast from Kealakekua Bay would be startled at **Honaunau Bay** by the sight of fierce, hand-carved, wooden *ki'i* (sacred sculptures), and an immense stone platform with walls 6 ft (2 meters) thick topped by thatched roofs. In this ancient *pu'uhonua,* or place of refuge, now known as the **Pu'uhonua 'O Honaunau National Historical Park ㊵**, ancient Hawaiians pardoned violators of *kapu* (taboos) and war criminals who reached sanctuary here, but only if they committed themselves to the mercy of priests and vowed to do penance.

Over the centuries, this *pu'uhonua* gained importance and accumulated *mana,* or spiritual power, as more and more chiefs were buried here. Meticulously and accurately restored, it's a wonderful place with the *heiau* and the 1,000-ft (300-meter) long Great Wall, which is 10 ft (3 meters) high and 17 ft (5 meters) wide.

Near the main road and up from the historical park, the old **St. Benedict's "Painted" Church ㊶** is one of Hawaii's special little places. The inside of the church is painted with biblical scenes and motifs. A bust of Father Damien, the priest who helped in the Molokai leprosy colony, stands outside *(see page 143).*

South along this jagged Kona shore, the people of **Miloli'i ㊷** still fish for a living. In few places is there a feeling of neighborliness so strong as in this little village of hand-built stone walls topped with night-blooming cereus. Further south along the main highway, lava flows from the 1920s lift the road higher onto Mauna Loa's lower slopes and toward **Ka Lae ㊿**, or **South Point**, the southernmost tip of the Big Island and the United States. Past South Point, the road turns northeast and ascends to Hawaii Volcanoes National Park and eventually to Hilo. ❏

VOLCANO AND KA'U

Near the community of Volcano, a real volcano – Kilauea – has erupted for over a decade in Hawaii Volcanoes National Park. To the southwest, South Point was where the first Polynesians landed

Maps, pages 256 & 283

Honolulu

Big Island

ere on the Big Island is nature at its most awesome. Allow yourself time to absorb views of searing, red-hot lava flowing down the side of Kilauea; canopied, misty rainforests filled with giant tree ferns; barren lava flows; and the windswept deserts of Ka'u. Few visitors can ignore the primal pull originating on the southeastern slopes of **Mauna Loa**, still an active volcano. An 18-mile (29-km) trail to the summit of Mauna Loa is a difficult and unforgettable hike. It takes half a day just to reach the **Red Hill** cabin at 10,000 ft (3,030 meters), and most of the next day to attain the summit cabin that overlooks the steaming summit crater, Makua we'o we'o. Here, the unspoiled colors of the lava gleam brilliantly, snow glints from cracks in the rock – it is the only source of water – and the thin air makes sturdy travelers light-headed and the surroundings mystical.

A continually erupting volcano

On Mauna Loa's slopes is a rift zone, where lava that sometimes feeds the summit crater oozes from cracks lower on the mountain. This is the Big Island's biggest draw, along with the beaches of Kohala and Kona. All of the current activity is from **Kilauea ㊾**, youngest of Hawaii's volcanic mountains, which has been erupting steadily since 1983, the longest continuously erupting volcano in the world. Like all Hawaiian volcanoes, Kilauea is a dome-like shield volcano with gentle slopes. It rises off the southeast slopes of Mauna Loa more than 20,000 ft (6,000 meters) above its base on the ocean floor.

All of this and much of the surrounding area is part of the **Hawaii Volcanoes National Park ㊿** (open daily; entrance fee; tel: 985-6000). Created in 1916, the national park once included Maui's Haleakala, which was made into its own national park in 1961. At the **Kilauea Visitor Center Ⓐ** (open daily 7.45am–5pm; tel: 985 6011), the latest information regarding eruptions, road closures, and flow activity is displayed on maps, information boards and on film.

From the visitor center, the 11-mile (17-km) **Crater Rim Drive** passes over some of the Pacific's most bizarre scenery as it skirts past wheezing steam vents at **Steaming Bluff (Sulfur Banks) Ⓑ**, where seeping ground water hits hot rock; there are several breathtaking lookouts above the caldera. Lava flows in the caldera just below the first stretch of road and the Volcano House hotel date from 1919.

The **Hawaiian Volcano Observatory Ⓒ** (open by appointment, tel: 935-3371), operated by the US Geological Survey, is one of the world's premiere volcanology and geophysical research centers. Next door, the **Thomas A. Jaggar Museum Ⓓ** (open daily

LEFT: a fountain from Kilauea.
BELOW: a tenacious plant takes root in lava.

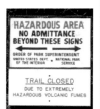

Heed the signs and warnings at Halema'uma'u and elsewhere in the national park.

8.30am–5pm; tel: 967-7643) has informative exhibits and presentations. Near the observatory, but inaccessible to visitors, is the site of one of only two *heiau* (temples) believed to have been situated near the caldera, on the bluff of Uwekahuna, "the place of priestly weeping." Apparently a house was built over a pit here. A *kahuna* (priest) waited for unsuspecting visitors to enter the house, when he yanked ropes that opened up the floor to send visitors to their death. A timely hero set the house alight, causing the *kahuna* to weep.

The primary vent of Kilauea

The road slips into the Southwest Rift zone, crossing lava flows from 1971, 1974, and 1921 to an overlook of **Halema'uma'u Crater ❸**, the collapsed depression within Kilauea Caldera. From the parking lot near the crater, whiffs of sulfuric gases escaping the earth along the short trail are reminders that all is not finished down below. Halema'uma'u is the primary vent of Kilauea. The crater of Kilauea is 2½ miles (4 km) by 2 miles (3.2 km) in size, its walls a set of step-like fault blocks that form cliffs as high as 400 ft (120 meters). From the early 1820s until 1924, Halema'uma'u was a lake of active lava, but today steam is more evident than molten lava. Still, Halema'uma'u is said to be the fire goddess Pele's current home. At the crater's rim, offerings of *lei*, ti-wrapped stones, and money are left for Pele's appeasement.

Compared to explosive volcanoes in the Mediterranean or around the Pacific Rim, Hawaii's volcanoes are relatively benign, allowing visitors "drive-through" access to eruptions and lava flows. Only twice in recorded history have explosive eruptions occurred in Hawaii. The latest was in 1924, when steam pressure expelled Kilauea volcano's plug and enlarged Halema'uma'u's diameter from

BELOW: crater of Halema'uma'u.

1,200 ft (360 meters) to 3,000 ft (900 meters), and left a hole 1,300 ft (400 meters) deep. An eight-ton block of basalt was tossed 3,000 ft (900 meters) from Halema'uma'u's center. Dust clouds rose to 20,000 ft (6,000 meters).

Map, page 283

A parasitical shield dome

The **Chain of Craters Road** ❻ cuts off the rim road and descends along the East Rift, passing prehistoric pit craters and heading toward the ocean down an immense fault scarp covered with lava flows that look like black molasses.

In recent decades, Kilauea's eruptions have been primarily along the Southwest Rift and the East Rift zones, structural weaknesses in the shield volcano. The Southwest Rift extends through Ka'u, and the East Rift to Puna. Since 1969, a number of eruptions on the East Rift have built a new "parasitic" shield dome called **Mauna-ulu** ❼, the "growing mountain." Among its achievements, Mauna-ulu has buried 12 miles (19 km) of park road, some of it under 300 ft (100 meters) of lava, and added more than 600 acres (243 hectares) of land to the Big Island.

Kilauea is famous for its "curtains of fire" – walls of flaming, gushing fountains that erupt along well-known rift zones. A typical eruption begins with a change in the pressure of the underground plumbing, then a crack or rift opens on top. Fountains dozens or hundreds of feet high squirt flaming rock into the air. Puddles collect and form a lake. Heat blasts from the surface, sucking up the colder air, which flings stinging cinders and sharp ashes into a whirlwind.

Kilauea Iki Crater ❽ was where a 2,000-ft (600-meter) volcanic geyser erupted in 1959, possibly the highest volcanic fountain ever recorded. Nearby, a popular stop is the **Thurston Lava Tube** ❾, where a short trail weaves through primal groves of fern to a short lava tube. Lava tubes, which are like perfectly

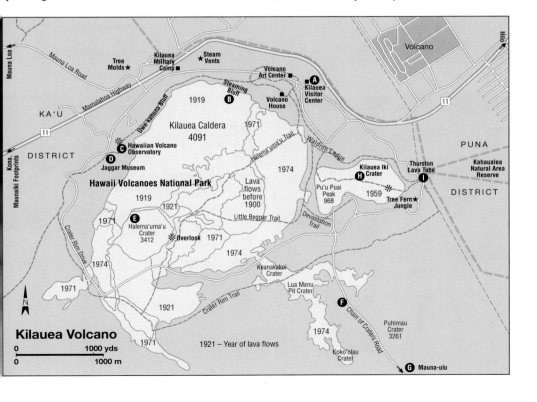

Kilauea Volcano

0 — 1000 yds
0 — 1000 m

1921 – Year of lava flows

round tunnels in a cooled lava flow, form when a *paho'eho'e* lava flow starts to cool on its outer edges. A channel forms, and the cooling edges meet and create a tunnel, through which flows continue to move while the surrounding flow cools. If Kilauea's active flows have reached the ocean, steam plumes rise ahead at road's end. Check with the park's headquarters for the location of accessible eruption zones if the volcano is erupting when you visit.

It was once possible to continue along this road into Hilo via the Puna district. In the late 1980s and early 1990s, lava flows obliterated scores of homes, the village of **Kalapana** ㊺, ancient archeological sites, the road itself, and the national park's Waha'ula Visitor Center. In 1997, **Waha'ula**, a *luakini* or *heiau* for human sacrifices, was finally swallowed up by a rapidly moving flow of lava. Waha'ula was first established by a Tahitian priest in the 13th century, and later used by Kamehameha the Great for Kuka'ilimoku, his war god. According to a legend, when a young chief passed through the smoke coming from the *heiau* – a taboo, as the smoke was considered a shadow of the *heiau*'s god – he was killed and his bones were thrown in a refuse pit. About 25 miles (40 km) out at sea, 3,000 ft (900 meters) below sea level, a new island-to-be, **Lo'ihi**, is slowly developing on the East Rift. Tens of thousands of years from now, it may finally surface, either as a new island or, if it keeps building, an extension of the Big Island itself.

Volcano

Just outside of the national park boundary, on the road to Hilo and not far from the Kilauea Visitors Center, **Volcano** ㊻ is a small town amidst forests and mists situated 3,700 ft (1,100 meters) above sea level. There are several bed-and-breakfast guest houses in the town for those wanting to stay up here, rather than

BELOW: solidified lava covers a road near Kalapana.

returning the same day to Hilo or Kona. The well-appointed Kilauea Lodge, with its reputable and popular restaurant, is well worth an overnight stay.

The Volcano area attracts artisans, writers, and craftspeople. Many of their works are offered for sale at the **Volcano Art Center** (open daily 9am–5pm; tel: 967-7511) next to the Hawaii National Park headquarters and housed in the old **Volcano House**, built in 1877. The earliest Western visitors to Kilauea stayed in a thatched hut near the caldera's edge. In 1877, a master carpenter was hired by a steamship company to build a real hotel, Volcano House. The original building was eventually moved back from the crater's edge and restored as the Volcano Art Center. The current hotel, overlooking Halemaumau and a short walk from the visitor and art centers, is comfortable though rustic. During the day, it's crowded with visitors, but in the evenings it's quiet and pleasant. The lunch buffet at the restaurant is tourist fare, but dinner is adequate.

From the main highway and still inside the national park, a side road leads to **Kipuka Pua'ulu** (Bird Park), an idyllic hideaway with a nature trail through meadows and one of the thickest concentrations of native plants in Hawaii.

A *kipuka* is an isolated ecosystem created when a lava flow shunts around an "island" of older growth or a habitat, isolating it. These *kipuka* are important biological research areas where native species continue to flourish independent of outside influences. Biologists often create artificial *kipuka* for research. In 1968, the National Park Service isolated an area near the coast with fences, protecting it from the wild pigs and goats that roam the Big Island. Something grew within the fenced *kipuka* that had never been seen before by modern scientists: a large bean plant with purple flowers. Until the fence was put up, island goats had eaten the bean plants before they could mature.

Map, page 256

TIP

If hiking in Hawaii Volcanoes National Park, don't be fooled by the visual ruggedness of the land. Its surface is fragile, as is the flora that grow from it. Please stay on trails.

BELOW: new beach near Kalapana.

Map,
page 256

Ka'u

To the southwest of Kilauea and Volcano is **Ka'u Desert**, downwind from the summit and where noxious gases and dehydrated breezes inhibit vegetation. In 1790, a freak eruption of gas and dust suffocated a phalanx of warriors opposing Kamehameha the Great. Those who were able to flee left footprints in the clay-like mud that fell. Today, those **Maunaiki footprints**  have solidified. Some are preserved under glass at the end of a mile-long trail, accessed from the main highway coming from South Point.

There are actually other footprints to be found off the trail, but the environment here is exceedingly fragile, as are the footprints, and a ramble through the bush may not only damage the delicate plants and soil, but also some of these ancient footprints that remain unprotected. Stay on the trail.

From the national park, the road descends southwesterly along the Southwest Rift of Kilauea. **Punalu'u Beach** is a popular black-sand beach near the small Sea Mountain Resort, complete with golf course. Beyond is **Na'alehu**, a pleasant and traditional Hawaiian town with a bakery renowned for its sweet bread.

Turning off the main highway, a dead-end road traverses about 12 miles (19 km) of cattle range southward to **Ka Lae** (The Point), or **South Point**. Along the way, the road passes the *swoosh-swoosh-swoosh* of three dozen immense electricity-generating windmills, spinning in the unceasing winds that have whipped this cape for eons. Privately owned **Kamoa Wind Farm** feeds electricity into the island's main power grid. (Another wind-generating project on Oahu's North Shore has closed, proving over the years to be less than profitable.)

Somewhere along South Point, the first Polynesian voyagers landed in Hawaii, calling it Ka Lae. The modern-day visitor senses somehow that this is a special place. Clear, blue waters smash against the 50-ft (15-meter) high basalt cliffs. Small fishing boats are often tied up below. The ocean is tempestuous, the wind forceful, and the isolation nearly complete. The ancient Hawaiians built the **Kalalea Heiau**, a temple dedicated to fishing, right on the cliff's edge. Today, this is the southernmost place in the United States. Due south is Tahiti.

A 3-mile (5-km) hike east from South Point through dry and grassy plain leads to the unique **Papakolea Green Sand Beach**. Here, an entire cinder cone of olivine has collapsed into a little bay and been reduced into polished sand by the surf.

Moving northward up through **Ka'u District**, one encounters an increase in the expanse of gray and black lava – the Mauna Loa lava flows of 1907, 1919, 1926, and 1950. Where the local microclimate has permitted, lichens, grass and 'ohi'a – usually the first tree to appear in lava flows – sprout from the new earth. This is one of the least-populated places in Hawaii.

During the 1950s and 1960s, however, unscrupulous real estate salesmen trafficked in these raw and barren lava acres, hawking them sight-unseen through newspaper advertisements to buyers in North America as properties in paradise. Nevertheless, some of those living here came knowing full well how barren the land was going to be and they have come to like it, even if swaying palm trees and white-sand beaches are distinctly lacking nearby. ❑

BELOW: perhaps a little too close for safety.
RIGHT: some of the youngest land on Earth.

A STATE OF FIRE IN THE PACIFIC OCEAN

Hawaii is one of the few places in the world where one may literally drive to a volcanic eruption and watch it in relative safety. It's not to be missed.

The islands of Hawaii sit almost in the middle of the Pacific Plate, a piece in the giant jigsaw puzzle that is the earth's crust. This Pacific Plate is moving slowly to the northwest. Each of the 132 islands in the Hawaiian chain, from the smallest atoll in the northeast to the Big Island, was formed as the plate moved over a "hot spot" 50 miles (80 km) deep in the earth's mantle and from where molten lava periodically welled up from inside the earth.

The oldest Hawaiian islands are in the northeast near Midway Island; erosion and sinking has reduced them to coral atolls. The process of island growth continues. Kilauea Volcano, on the Big Island, offers the world's most active continuing eruption, since 1983. Lo'ihi, an erupting seamount 20 miles (30 km) southeast of the Big Island and 3,000 ft (900 meters) below sea level, is growing and may one day surface.

VOLCANO CREATION

Hawaii's volcanoes, because they resemble the shield carried by medieval Germanic warriors, are called shield or dome volcanoes. Shield volcanoes form in massive but gently rising circular shapes because they are fed by lava flowing repeatedly through a conduit, slowly and benignly. In contrast, Fuji and Vesuvius, with more classical conical shapes, arose through explosive eruptions.

Two Hawaii volcanoes, Mauna Loa and Kilauea, have summit calderas, created when lava drains from an underground magma chamber, causing the volcano summit to sink. In contrasst, Maui's Haleakala has neither crater nor caldera, but rather a summit basin created by erosion.

Mauna Kea is the world's tallest volcano, measured from its base 18,000 ft (5,400 meters) below sea level. Mauna Loa, also on the Big Island, is the planet's most massive mountain, at 10,000 cubic miles (16,000 cu km) in volume.

△ **FOUNTAIN**
Most spectacular at the Kilauea Volcano, in Hawaii Volcanoes National Park on the Big Island, is when a rift opens and lava spurts into the air in a fountain. These happen sporadically and often don't last long, but if you are anywhere nearby when one does occur, rush, don't walk, to the national park.

▷ **SLOW MOVING**
The lava flows from Kilauea volcano have a grace to them that betrays their heat and mass. An extremely dangerous reality to those who dare to explore these new fields is that beneath a thin crust of what seems to be solid footing is yet masses of uncooled lava.

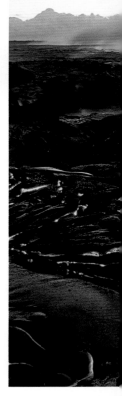

△ **GENTLE FLOWS**
The eruptions of Kilauea are quite benign and lacking the explosive destruction of other volcanoes. Still, lava flows such as this not only create new land, but also destroy nearly everything in their path.

◁ **PELE AT HOME**
Contemporary sculpture of Pele, the goddess of fire, carved out of lava from Kilauea.

PELE: GODDESS OF HAWAII'S FIRE

Stay in Hawaii long enough and you'll encounter the name of Hawaii's goddess of fire, Pele, probably the best-known of Hawaii's deities to contemporary traveler and resident alike.

Pele is responsible for the current eruptions of Kilauea. However, she did not create the Hawaiian islands, as many tend to believe. Nomadic by disposition, Pele arrived in Hawaii from Tahiti in a canoe provided by the god of sharks. After arriving in Ni'ihau, a small island to the east of Kauai, she traveled along the islands looking for a volcano to call home.

The only suitable location was the Big Island. Arriving there, she went after the reigning fire god, Aila'au, hoping to move in with him. Her reputation had preceded her, especially the stories about her awesome power and rather tempestuous personality. By the time Pele reached Kilauea, Aila'au had already fled.

A visit to Hawaii Volcanoes National Park will reveal the reverence that many contemporary Hawaiians have for Pele. Offerings pepper the caldera rim of Halema'uma'u. Even outsiders learn of her power. Tourists who've taken lava souvenirs home later return them to national park authorities, hoping to rid themselves of the bad luck that suddenly befalls them.

◁ NEW LAND, NEW LIFE
The ropy, smooth character of *paho'eho'e* lava, seen along the Chain of Craters Road near Kilauea, is easily distinguished from the jagged and rough textures of *a'a* lava. Both types are a challenge to the survival of flora.

▽ EXPLOSIVE SPRAY
Kilauea's usually passive flows can take on explosive force when reaching the cooler ocean or during the more spectacular fountaining.

◁ KALAPANA DESTRUCTION
Flows from Kilauea follow gravity to the ocean, destroying both modern housing estates and ancient *heiau* along the way. The destruction can be capricious: a house can go up in flames while a neighbor's is spared.

KAUAI

*Long the most reclusive and independent of Hawaii's islands,
lusciously sculpted Kauai bides on its own time*

The historian Edward Josting called Kauai a "separate kingdom" when he detailed the history of this idyllic island, for it remained stubbornly independent after all the other Hawaiian islands had succumbed to Kamehameha the Great's conquest in the 1790s.

Kauai does not disappoint. Remember Elvis in *Blue Hawaii*, or *South Pacific*, or *Jurassic Park* and *The Lost World?* Oldest and northernmost of all inhabited islands in the Hawaiian chain, Kauai is rimmed by perfect, white-sand beaches that are strung like seductive gems from Ha'ena Point on its northern coast to the ever-sunny resort of Po'ipu on its southern shore, to broad and beautiful Polihale Beach lying in indolent splendor. The inaccessibility of Kauai's most stunning terrain undoubtedly adds to its mystical appeal, and anchoring this nearly circular island is reportedly the wettest place on earth – the summit of Wai'ale'ale. (But not Kauai's highest point, which is nearby Kawaikini.)

On the southeastern coast is Lihu'e, Kauai's largest urban center and main airport. Northward from Lihu'e, the road passes through the green and wet windward coast to the spectacular north shore, where Hanalei Bay and Lumahai Beach seduce even hardened cynics. The road stops here. Beyond is the Na Pali coast, inaccessible except by foot or boat. In the westward direction from Lihu'e is the dry side of the island, along with some of Kauai's most important historical sites. At Waimea, Captain James Cook first set foot in the Hawaiian Islands. Nearby, an ascending road leads inward along spectacular Waimea Canyon to Koke'e, where mists compete with the sun.

The people of Kauai, some 50,000, are for the most part unassuming and hardworking individuals justifiably proud of their *'aina*, or land. More than half of this 550-sq mile (1,430-sq km) island is reserved for conservation and preservation. Alaka'i Swamp, a boggy dwarf forest in the verdant interior, provides safe harbor for a number of endangered plants and birds. Elsewhere are many nature preserves and sanctuaries. Retreat to the seemingly silent places of Kauai, and sometimes you'll hear the song or catch a flash of the red or yellow feathers of a rarely seen *'apapane* or *'akialoa*, two types of Hawaiian honeycreepers.

Kauai remains a separate kingdom from the rest of Hawaii. Even more secluded is barren Ni'ihau, a small privately owned island in the dry rain shadow of Kauai, and populated by a couple of hundred people of Hawaiian blood. Life on the island is said to be simple and lacking in amenities. ❑

PRECEDING PAGES: looking for easy fish, Hanalei Bay, on the northern shore.
LEFT: looking for an easier life, Princeville Resort, northern shore.

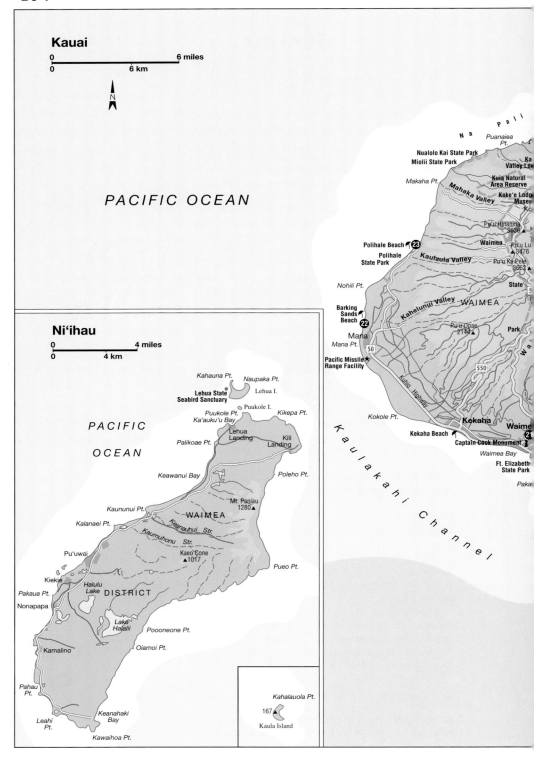

Kauai

0 — 6 miles
0 — 6 km

N

PACIFIC OCEAN

Ni'ihau

0 — 4 miles
0 — 4 km

PACIFIC OCEAN

Kahauna Pt.   Naupaka Pt.
Lehua State   Lehua I.
Seabird Sanctuary
                Puukole I.
Puukole Pt.   Kikepa Pt.
Ka'auku'u Bay
            Lehua   Kili
Palikoae Pt.   Landing   Landing

Keawanui Bay   Poleho Pt.

                    Mt. Paniau
                    1280 ▲
Kaununui Pt.   WAIMEA
Kalanaei Pt.   Keanauhui Str.
        Kaumuhonu Str.
                   Kaeo Cone
Pu'uwai   ▲1017   Pueo Pt.

Kiekie
Pakaua Pt.   Halulu   DISTRICT
            Lake
Nonapapa
                Lake
                Halalii   Poooneone Pt.
                        Oiamoi Pt.
Kamalino

Pahau
Pt.
    Leahi   Keanahaki
    Pt.   Bay
        Kawaihoa Pt.

Kahalauola Pt.
167 ▲
Kaula Island

Na Pali
            Puanaiea
            Pt.
Nualolo Kai State Park   Ka
Miolii State Park   Valley Lo
Makaha Pt.   Mahaka Valley   Kuia Natural
                            Area Reserve
                        Koke'e Lodg
                        Muse
                            Ko
                    Pu'u Hinahina ▲
                        3636 ▲
Polihale Beach ⛵ ㉓   Waimea   Pu'u Lu
    Polihale   ▲3476
    State Park   Kaulaula Valley   Pu'u Ka Pele
                            3662 ▲
Nohili Pt.   State
        Kahelunui Valley   WAIMEA
Barking
Sands   Pu'u Opae
Beach   2144 ▲   Park
    ㉒
    Mana
Mana Pt.   50
Pacific Missile ★   Kuhio Highway   550
Range Facility
                Kokole Pt.   Kekaha   Waime
                    Kekaha Beach ⛵   ④
                    Captain Cook Monument
                        Waimea Bay
                        Ft. Elizabeth
                        State Park
                            Paka

Kaulakahi Channel

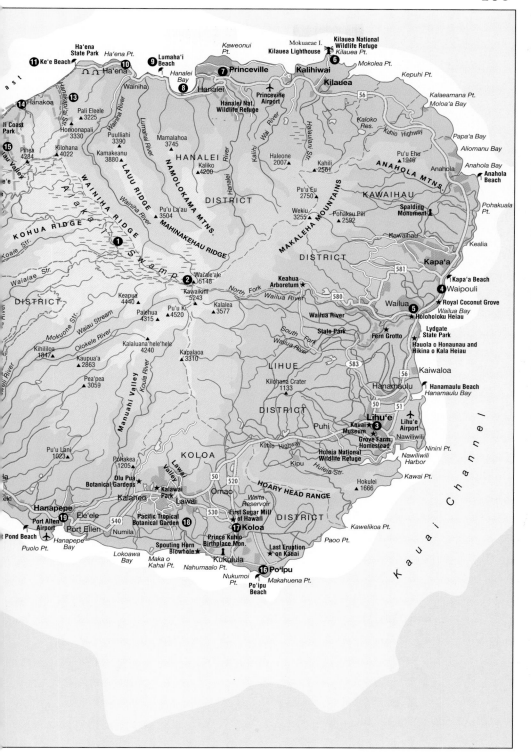

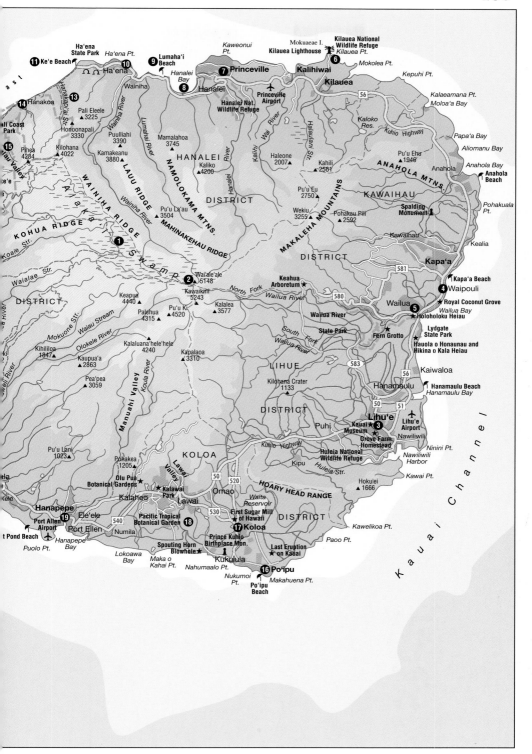

Ha'ena
State Park   Ha'ena Pt.
11 Ke'e Beach   **10**
Ω Ω **Ha'ena**
9 Lumaha'i
Beach

Kaweonui
Pt.

Mokuaeae I.   Kilauea National
Wildlife Refuge
Kilauea Lighthouse   **6**
Kilauea Pt.

Mokolea Pt.

Kepuhi Pt.

14 Hanakoa   **13**
Wainiha
Hanapēpē Str.

Hanalei
Bay   **7** **Princeville**
8 Hanalei

Kalihiwai
Kalihiwai
Kilauea

Kalaeamana Pt.
Moloa'a Bay

Pali Eleele
▲ 3225
Honoonapali
3330   Puulliahi
3390
Kamakeanu
3880 ▲

Mamalahoa
3745   **HANALEI**
Kaliko
▲ 4200

Princeville
Airport
Hanalei Nat.
Wildlife Refuge

56

Kaloko
Res.   Kuhio Highway

Pu'u Ehr
▲ 1946'

Papa'a Bay
Aliomanu Bay

Anahola Bay
Anahola   Anahola
Beach

I Coast
Park
15 Pihea
4284   Kilohana
▲ 4022

LAUU RIDGE   **NAMOLOKAMA MTNS.**

Pu'u La'au
▲ 3504

DISTRICT

Haleone
2007▲   Pu'u Eu
2750▲
Wekiu
3255▲   Pohakau Pili
▲ 2592

MAKALEHA MOUNTAINS

Kahili
▲ 2561

ANAHOLA MTNS.

KAWAIHAU

Kawaihau
Kealia

Spalding
Monument   Pohakuala
Pt.

1   **WAINIHA RIDGE**   **MAHINAKEHAU RIDGE**

2   Wai'ale'ale
▲ 5148

Keapua
4440 ▲   Kawaikini
5243   North Fork
Kalalea
▲ 3577   Keahua
Arboretum   Wailua River   580

581   **Kapa'a**

4 Waipouli
Royal Coconut Grove

Palehua
4315 ▲   Pu'u Ki
▲ 4520

Kalaluana'hele'hele
4240   Kapalaoa
▲ 3310   South Fork   Wailua River   **Wailua River
State Park**
Fern Grotto   Wailua Bay
Holoholoku Heiau
Lydgate
State Park
Hauola o Honaunau and
Hikina o Kala Heiau

DISTRICT

5

Kihililoa
1847▲   Kaupua'a
▲ 2863
Pea'pea
▲ 3059   **Manuahi Valley**   Olokele River   **LIHUE**
Kilohana Crater
1133   583   Kaiwaloa

Hanamaulu   Hanamaulu Beach
Hanamaulu Bay

Pu'u Lani
1023▲   Pohakea
1205▲   **KOLOA**   **DISTRICT**
Puhi
Kuhio Highway
Kipu   **Kauai
Museum**   **3**   Grove Farm
Homestead
Huleia National
Wildlife Refuge   **Lihu'e**   50
51
**Lihu'e
Airport**
Nawiliwili
Ninini Pt.
Nawiliwili
Harbor
Kawai Pt.

56

Olu Pua
Botanical Gardens   Lawai
Valley   Kalawai
Park   Lawai   50   520   **HOARY HEAD RANGE**   Hokulei
▲ 1666

Huleia Str.

Hanapēpē   **19** Ele'ele
Port Allen
Airport   Port Ellen   540   Numila   Kataheo
Pacific Tropical
Botanical Garden   **18**   Omao
Waita
Reservoir   530   First Sugar Mill
of Hawaii   **17 Koloa**
DISTRICT

Kawelikoa Pt.

Paoo Pt.

t Pond Beach   Hanapēpē
Bay   Puolo Pt.   Lokoawa
Bay   Maka o
Kahai Pt.   Spouting Horn
Blowhole ★   Prince Kuhio
Birthplace Mon.   Last Eruption
on Kaua'i
Nahumaalo Pt.   Kukuiula
16 **Po'ipu**
Nukumoi
Pt.   Po'ipu
Beach   Makahuena Pt.

Kauai Channel

KAUAI AND NI'IHAU

The shyest of the four main Hawaiian islands, Kauai and its people dictate the terms for appreciating the island. Not that the scenery is lacking. In fact, it is perhaps the most beautiful island

Map, page 294

An island of exceptionally lush tropical beauty, Kauai offers high valleys and remote forests and beaches that are a last refuge for endangered endemic plants and native birds. Of all the islands, Kauai has lost the fewest of its native feathered creatures. At the heart of the nearly circular island of Kauai is a virtual jungle of vegetation and fauna unique in the world, nestled in a narrow bowl that is suspended a mile (1.6 km) high amid thin, jagged ridges that rim deep valleys and canyons. Within this depression is **Alaka'i Swamp ❶**, 10 miles (16 km) long and 2 miles (3 km) wide. It is a sanctuary for endangered species of flora and fauna. But this refuge is also changing with the advance of civilization – and the devastation wrought by Hurricane 'Iniki, which in 1992 stripped and opened wide sections of the native forest, the virgin interior of Kauai is vulnerable to invasions by alien plants and animals. At the eastern end of the swamp is what is said to be the wettest spot on earth, **Wai'ale'ale ❷**, actually the second-highest point on Kauai at 5,148 ft (1,569 meters), exactly in the island's center and where 300–500 inches (760–1,270 cm) of rain fall annually. The highest point is nearby **Kawaikini** at 5,243 ft (1,598 meters). At the northern end are the precipitous ridges and valleys called Na Pali, meaning, literally, the cliffs.

Wet, warm trade winds that gather moisture from the vast Pacific are caught in a funnel over Kauai formed by the **Anahola Mountains** lying to the northeast and the **Ha'upu Mountains** to the east. The breezes carry the clouds to Wai'ale'ale, where the altitude and the colder temperature make them surrender their moisture. The rains fall all along the slopes leading to Wai'ale'ale and then over the central area of Alaka'i Swamp northwest to Na Pali. By the time the winds reach the north and west side of the island, they are dry. Thus, while Wai'ale'ale tends to be drenched, Kekaha, on the far west side of the island, gets little more than 12 inches (30 cm) of rain each year. The road that circles most of the island terminates at either end of the Na Pali, on the north coast. These isolated, roadless 13 miles (20 km) are flanked by Polihale Beach Park on the west and Ha'ena Beach Park on the north. Most of Na Pali is under state jurisdiction.

Ringing the entire island are beaches with names that roll off the tongue like a Hawaiian chant: Po'ipu, Kalapaki, Hanama'ulu, Waipouli, Kapa'a, Anahola, Kauapea, Lumahai, Ha'ena, Ke'e, Hanakapi'ai, Kalalau. These are only a few of the better-known white-sand beaches. Some are easily accessible, some require hiking, some can be reached only by boat or helicopter, and some require the permission of the owner of an adjacent property to gain access. But as everywhere in the state, all beaches are public and access can't be denied.

It is said that Kauai is one of the planet's wettest places, and the island's countless waterfalls suggest so.

Mysterious little people

Theories differ as to how and when Kauai, Hawaii's oldest main island, geologically speaking, was first inhabited, but fables regarding the *menehune,* a group of legendary Polynesian people *(see page 26),* provide fanciful explanations. Legend describes the *menehune* as a race of little people, like leprechauns. Seldom seen, they worked only after dark. In a single night, they would perform prodigious works, accepting in payment only a single shrimp per worker. Among the construction projects attributed to these pygmies are the Menehune Ditch near

LEFT: Hanalei Valley and Bay.

TIP

The astounding
amount of rainfall
makes much of the
area surrounding
Wai'ale'ale nearly
impassible to hikers.
Stay on authorized
trails – not because
you might sink into the
boggy ground, but
because the ecosys-
tem is fragile.

BELOW: Po'ipu
Beach.

Waimea on the leeward coast, which exhibits a knowledge of stonework not seen elsewhere in Hawaii, and the 'Alekoko Fishpond, also called the Menehune Fishpond, near Lihu'e's Nawiliwili Harbor on the southern coast.

Kauai remains a rural island, despite the increasing traffic congestion, and farmers and fishermen provide a balance to tourism. Farmers grow taro at Hanalei, Waimea, and a few other places, and papayas at Moloa'a along the main highway between Anahola and Kilauea. Sugar-cane still waves in the trade winds over much of the dry southern and western sections of the island, but the wetter east-side fields are being abandoned. Tropical flowers and crops thrive on small farms, and local fresh produce is often sold in the weekly markets held across the island.

A few large commercial fishing operations remain in business, but the majority of Kauai's fishing is done by individuals with their own small boats who fish on days off from their regular jobs. Some of the commercial fishing docks have been taken over by sport-fishing boats, which take visitors out hunting for deep-sea prizes like marlin, *aku, kawakawa,* and *mahimahi.* But the newest form of fishing on Kauai follows the form of traditional Hawaiian fish ponds. In old Hawaii, large ponds were built along the shoreline to form enclosures in which fish were raised and harvested for eating. On Kauai, the best example of such a pond is a rare one built in a river instead of on the shoreline. The aforementioned 'Alekoko, or Menehune Fishpond, at Lihu'e was built by cutting off an elbow of the Hule'ia River with a stone dam. It is no longer farmed for fish, but it is a much-admired scenic spot. Kayakers, both escorted and on their own, make their way to the Hule'ia Nature Preserve and beyond.

Kauai's people are low-key and guarded about their lives and about the island's more private and especially beautiful places. But that doesn't mean that

tourism is shunted aside. Indeed, Kauai is visited by around 1 million people annually. Some visitors arrive in the morning to climb into tour buses that stop at scenic areas, then leave for Honolulu in the evening: others spend time becoming acquainted with the island. The primary tourist centers are Kauai Lagoons, Lihu'e, Po'ipu, Kapaa/Wailua and Princeville/Hanalei.

The island has long attracted escapists – tourists, and travelers of limited resources who make Kauai their home in paradise, lured by Kauai's rugged beauty and langorous pace of life. In the 1970s, Woodstock-generation dropouts and wanderers were an established part of the scene, and several communities of transients settled on the island. The best known was Taylor Camp, on the far north side near Ha'ena: the mostly young visitors constructed houses of driftwood, bamboo, and plastic amidst the trees. Sixty or more people lived in homes shaded by Java plum trees and flanked by the small, clear Limahuli Stream; their front yard was a magnificent white-sand beach. Taylor Camp took its name from the property's owner, Howard Taylor, the brother of actress Elizabeth Taylor. In the mid 1970s, the state bought the land for part of the planned Ha'ena State Beach Park, but it took years of legal wrangling to move the transients, who claimed squatters' rights. Finally, with court actions complete, the state evicted the squatters and burned the houses.

Lihu'e

On the island's southeast coast, **Lihu'e** ❸ is the seat of county government, the island's major business district and shopping area, and the site of Kauai's jet airport. Nearby, **Nawiliwili Harbor**, the island's major port, plays host to a growing number of cruise ships on inter-island and trans-Pacific itineraries.

Map,
page 294

BELOW: planting taro, and a beach on the western coast of Kauai.

The Lihu'e area is home to the **Kauai Lagoons Resort**, an elegant spread that includes two magnificently scenic golf courses and the Kauai Marriott, a large property featuring a grand classically Roman-style pool, impressive grounds and the sands of Kalapaki Beach, which faces the beautiful Hoary Head mountains and Nawiliwili Harbor.

Since the 1850s Kauai has been a sugar-producing island, and the history of sugar's heyday can be studied at two highly recommended museums in Lihu'e. In the center of town, on Rice Street, **Kauai Museum** (open Mon–Sat; entrance fee; tel: 245-6931) occasionally offers courses in such activities as *lau hala* weaving and *lei*-making. A gallery upstairs frequently displays the work of local artists, and many excellent books and maps may be found in its gift shop. Located off Nawiliwili Road (Hwy 58), also in Lihu'e, is the **Grove Farm Homestead** (tours Mon, Wed, Thur, 10am and 1pm; entrance fee; tel: 245-3202). For close to a century this was a plantation-owner's home; today it provides insights into the era of plantation agriculture in Hawaii. Reservations are required. **Kilohana**, another restored plantation-era home, includes shops and Gaylords, one of Kauai's best restaurants. You can also take a ride around the grounds in a horse-drawn carriage.

Both museums offer a good introduction to the contributions made by Kauai's elite *kama'aina* (long-time resident) families, with names that become more familiar during one's stay on the island: Rice, Wilcox, Sinclair, Gay, and Robinson. Many had missionary roots but later made their fortunes in sugar and ranching. Some of these *kama'aina*, such as William Harrison Rice and his son, William Hyde Rice, had a strong affinity for the Hawaiian people and their culture, and did a great deal to keep the language and legends alive. Kauai Museum

BELOW: storefront lure, and Kauai Museum, Lihu'e.

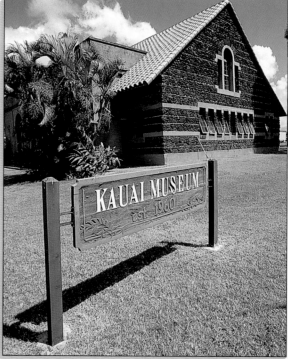

was founded by Rice's progeny, while Grove Farm Homestead was established by George N. Wilcox, whose parents were among the earliest American Protestant missionaries to Hawaii; they left a legacy of land and sugar.

The Wilcox holdings comprise some of the largest privately owned land on Kauai. With the decline of the sugar industry, Grove Farm has branched into land development, including Kukui Grove, Kauai's largest shopping mall. The Wilcox family also retains extensive holdings on the North Shore and developed a shopping center in Hanalei. The Sinclair-Robinson-Gay clan, which purchased the tiny island of Ni'ihau in 1864, continues to be active in cattle ranching and sugar cultivation. The Robinsons, who manage Ni'ihau, are also perhaps the most secretive of the *kama'aina* families.

Map, page 294

North from Lihu'e

Along the eastern shore from Lihu'e, sometimes called the Coconut Coast in its lower extent, a string of bays and beaches, resort hotels and condominiums runs from **Waipouli ❹** to Kapa'a.

Kauai legends and oral traditions are among Hawaii's richest. They often concern the activities of *kahuna,* a class of elite professionals, priests, or wise men. In the past decade or so, visible remnants that embody ancient Hawaiian culture have become popular with travelers, including a large gathering of rocks at **Wailua ❺**, a few hundred yards up Kuamo'o Road toward the mountains and Opaeka'a Falls. Here are the Wailua Golf Course, a municipal 18-hole facility; Wailua Beach; the Wailua River, which carries tour boats to the **Fern Grotto**, a popular though commercialized wedding site; and the modern Coconut Plantation Marketplace.

BELOW: Fern Grotto.

Two stones, a birthstone and a *piko* (navel) stone (30), make Wailua a sacred place. Women of high rank bore their children at the birth stone to ensure their babies would be chiefs, then disposed of the umbilical cord at the piko stone, or *pohakuho'ohanau*. According to legend, the umbilical cords of the newly born were wrapped in a cloth and hidden in narrow cracks in the stone, a common practice throughout the islands. They were secreted in this manner because ancient chants suggest that if a rat were to steal the cord, the child would grow up a thief.

Further north is the small town of **Kilauea**. Sea birds are protected at the **Kilauea National Wildlife Refuge** ➏, where visitors can follow trails around the refuge and tour the lighthouse on the point. It was built in 1913 and is a National Historic Landmark (open daily 10am–4pm; entrance fee).

The coastline cliffs at the Kilauea National Wildlife Refuge make excellent breeding grounds for assorted birds.

The lush Princeville area

A few miles beyond is **Princeville** ➐, a 2,000-acre (800-hectare) resort area containing several golf courses and a large clubhouse, airport, shopping center, private houses, several luxurious condominium projects, and the elegant Princeville Hotel. Princeville offers striking views of Hanalei Bay and the sheer mountains at Hanalei, which is one of the wettest and greenest parts of the island. When rain mists the mountains, countless waterfalls hang like strands of silk thread from the dark green cliffs. It was in these lush mountains that films such as *Jurassic Park* and *Raiders of the Lost Ark* were filmed. In the distance, near where the sun sets, is the so-called Bali Hai, a small peak that rises where the mountains enter the ocean. Beginning at Princeville and continuing to the end of the road at Ha'ena are several valleys, each fronted by a curved, white, and sandy beach.

BELOW: not a golf course, but an open range along Kauai's northern shore.

Hanalei Bay , the largest bay on Kauai, is a favorite spot for yachts in summer. In winter, when big surf from the north makes anchorage unsafe, the Bay's outer reef provides a challenge for the island's surfers. Waves generated by storms in the north Pacific can reach 30 ft (9 meters) when they break on the reefs of the north shore, although surf of 10–20-ft (3–6-meters) are more common. From fall to spring, the huge waves create clouds of floating sea mist known as *'ehukai* all along the north shore. In late afternoon, the descending sun gives the mist a golden cast.

Further north along the Hanalei Bay coastline is a photogenic series of beaches called **Lumaha'i** ❾, where brilliant white sands are interspersed with black-lava rock promontories. The blue of the sea shimmers beyond the sand, and the green of *hala* trees glows behind it. Access to the beach is down a short dirt trail overhung with exotic hala trees (also known as pandanus). This is the beach where Mitzi Gaynor sang to the world in the movie *South Pacific* that she'd "wash that man right out of my hair." Lumaha'i Beach, like the rest of Kauai, continues to be known for its dramatic, rich beauty, an attribute that justifiably adds to Kauai's reputation as the most romantic island of all.

The Na Pali Coast

The volcano goddess, Pele, was associated with Kauai long before she established her current home at Kilauea on the Big Island. One famous story about Pele places her at beautiful **Ha'ena** ❿, beyond Hanalei Bay and at the end of the road before the Na Pali, during a big hula festival. In order to join the dancing, Pele took the form of a beautiful young woman, then fell in love with a handsome Kauai chief, Lohi'au. The remnants of the hula platform can still

Map, page 294

BELOW: Princeville resort, and Lumaha'i Beach.

be found on the hillside, to the west of **Ke'e Beach ⑪**, where the road ends. It's a popular spot that marks the start of **Na Pali Coast ⑫**, perhaps one of the world's most exquisite places. A foot trail starts at Ha'ena – there is no vehicular access to Na Pali – then rises on a ridge and drops into lush **Hanakapi'ai ⑬**, which has a lovely pool and waterfall at the back of the valley reached by a 2-mile (3-km) loop trail, and a crescent of white sand at its mouth during the summer months. The ocean here is often treacherous and, though public nudity is illegal in Hawaii, many visitors bathe in the buff when the park rangers are not around.

From Hanakapi'ai, the Na Pali trail zigzags a heart-thumping course upwards and scurries in and out of valleys and across a sheer cliff face to **Hanakoa ⑭**, a "hanging" valley. Like several other valleys here, Hanakoa sweeps from the heights in a flourish of vegetation and ends abruptly, hanging over the ocean, its stream turning into a misty waterfall that falls on the rocks and sea below.

A rough trail shelter is well used by hunters at Hanakoa, and from it the jungle-shaded trail wanders out and along the shallow valleys and cliffs until it drops and then ends in **Kalalau Valley ⑮**, the largest of Na Pali's valleys and visible from an overlook near Koke'e.

A once-inhabited valley

Hikers can camp at Kalalau, Hanakoa, and Hanakapi'ai with a permit from the state parks office in Lihu'e; hikers who venture beyond Hanakapi'ai also need permits. The state maintains portable toilets in Hanakapi'ai and Kalalau, but there's no safe drinking water. If you plan to use stream water, first boil it or use purification tablets. There are no cabins and only the occasional usable cave. Kalalau has a stream at one end of the valley mouth and a waterfall at the other joined by a beach. And at the back of Kalalau are fruit trees, creeks, and the remains of ancient house sites and stone-lined taro patches used by Hawaiians who lived here until the early years of the 20th century.

BELOW: harvesting taro.

Today there is little to indicate the large numbers who once inhabited Na Pali's valleys. House platforms, stone walls, irrigation ditches, coffee, taro, and even the trail itself were built and planted by families that settled in what is now a wilderness. However, in the valleys, some remnants of the old civilization still remain.

Extensive stonework that formed the taro paddies of Nu'alolo-aina (*'aina* means fertile land), a hanging valley, and the remains of a fishing village at Nu'alolo-kai (*kai* means sea) survive. The people of Nu'alolo-aina had access to the sea, and the people of N'alolo-kai had little land or fresh water, so each group worked with what it had. They formed a trading relationship, a single community built of necessity in two valleys.

In centuries past, the people who lived here maintained trails, but they are impassable today. A tree trunk that spanned a section of cliff between Honopu and Awa'awapuhi has rotted, and a ladder that once connected the upper and lower sections of the Nu'alolo-aina and Nu'alolo-kai trail is gone. A hardy hiker can reach Kalalau Valley from Ha'ena in six to eight grueling hours, but you need a kayak, boat or helicopter to get to most of the rest of Na Pali's valleys and beaches; helicopters are controversial because of the noise they generate.

Westward from Lihu'e

On Kauai's southernmost point southwest of Lihu'e, **Po'ipu** ⓰ is the sunniest of
the island's districts. It has several large hotels, plus many smaller hotels and
condominiums; all of them face the ocean and have sandy beaches and generally
calm and multi-hued water. There are several scenic spots in the area, such as
the **Spouting Horn**, a water spout in the shoreline rocks of an old lava flow, and
Brennecke's Beach, a spot renowned for its sometimes perfect bodysurfing
waves. This portion of the island suffered most from the 1992 hurricane's wrath,
with its strong winds and huge waves. Although many homes, especially those
along the coastline leading to Spouting Horn, were destroyed, they have all been
rebuilt, as has a visitor center for the National Tropical Botanical Garden.

The coast westward from Lihu'e, the dry leeward side, might as well be a
different island from the opposite side. Little rain falls here; moisture is extracted
from the air by the heights of Wai'ale'ale in the center of the island.

Kauai's "Hawaiianness" is obvious, but since 1835, when Hawaii's first commercial sugar plantation was started at **Koloa** ⓱, the island's ethnic character
has gone through radical and charming changes. As in other parts of Hawaii,
sugar attracted a diverse set of people willing to work in its dusty, itchy fields and
pungent mills. First came the Chinese, then the Japanese, Portuguese, Puerto
Ricans and lastly, the Filipinos. Thus many of Kauai's communities developed
as plantation towns, with the different races separated into camps. Koloa is one
of these towns, welcoming visitors with rustic charm and a cluster of shops and
restaurants. The town also has a monument to its plantation past, a Buddhist
temple and several historic churches to add flavor to a visit. Today, many of the
sugar firms that started the towns are gone or have merged with other companies,

Map,
page 294

BELOW: sugar-cane
fields, and making
sandcastles, Po'ipu.

but the communities themselves persist. Waimea, Numila (the Hawaiian pronunciation of New Mill), Puhi, Kealia, and Kilauea are a few of the towns that have lost the plantations which helped build them. Only three sugar mills now remain on the island, and five sugar-growing companies.

Botanical Gardens

The prestigious **National Tropical Botanical Garden** ⓲ (open Mon–Sat 9am–4pm; entrance fee, reservations essential; tel: 332-7361) in Lawa'i Valley is a congressionally chartered facility which saves endangered tropical plants and locates and grows flora of medicinal and economic importance. In recent years, the garden has begun collecting and propagating Hawaii's endemic plants, which are found nowhere else on the planet. The gardens also include **Lawa'i Kai**, the verdant estate of John Gregg Allerton, who willed his estate to the National upon his death. Lawa'i Kai is a wonderland of vegetation and statuary at the base of Lawa'i, where it meets the sea in a clean, white-sand beach. The estate's lovely gardens and buildings, including Queen Emma's summer home, were devastated by a 30-ft (9-meter) wave generated by Hurricane 'Iniki, but have been restored and re-opened to the public (tours at 9am, 10am, 1pm, 2pm). A satellite garden at **Limahuli** (open Tues–Fri, Sun, 9.30am–4pm; entrance fee), on the island's North Shore, is dedicated almost entirely to native plants and includes a 900-acre (360-hectare) natural preserve that encompasses much of this striking valley. Walking tours of the gardens are conducted daily, but it's a good idea to call ahead for reservations.

On the ocean side of sleepy **Hanapepe** ⓳ town are a group of pre-contact salt ponds that have been worked by local Hawaiian salt gatherers for generations.

Japanese immigrant working in a sugar plantation, circa *1910.*

BELOW: sugar-cane plantation workers.

Here, along the seaside just off Highway 543, members of the Hanapepe Salt Makers Group still gather salt in the old Hawaiian way during the spring and summer months by filling small, mud-lined ponds with sea water and letting the sun cause the water to evaporate, leaving behind heavy salt crystals.

On the south bank of the Waimea River is the old Russian **Fort Elizabeth ⑳**, now protected as a state park. In 1816, an agent of the Imperial Russian government came to Kauai to recover the cargo of a ship that had broken up on the island's shore. The agent, Dr. Anton Sheffer, convinced Kauai's King Kaumuali'i that together they could conquer the rest of the islands. Sheffer's Machiavellian bid for Hawaiian power failed miserably, but ruins of the fort, named after the czar Nicholas's queen, remain as a testimonial to Sheffer's adventurism and folly.

Between Hanapepe and Waimea, just past mile marker 19, ancient monkeypod trees line the nameless road that leads to the Gay & Robinson mill and plantation tour. Kauai's only remaining sugar plantation (one of two left in Hawaii) was founded in 1889. The two-hour commentated tour includes a visit to the mill and canefields. Reservations are required for the 8.45am and 12.45pm tours, offered weekdays only. The small visitor center displays artifacts of the plantation's long history.

The people of old Hawaii took full advantage of the island's often drastic climatic variations. Chiefs sometimes moved their courts from the warmth of leeward **Waimea ㉑** to cooler Wailua on the east side of the island. When Captain Cook arrived at Waimea in 1778, there were no chiefs in residence. Historians suggest that the *ali'i*, or royalty, were holding court at Wailua on the other side of the island. Cook left Waimea before the chiefs could return to greet him. He eventually found his welcome, and end, on the Big Island.

Map, page 294

BELOW: net fishing near Hanapepe, and an anthurium blooms.

Ni'ihau

Across the **Kaulakahi Channel** from Kauai's west side, Ni'ihau rises dimly through sea mists like some slumbering prehistoric creature 17 miles (27 km) away. It is denied rain because it falls in the lee of Kauai, whose mountains collect most of the moisture. The mystique of this windswept, privately owned island, whose estimated 200 residents are seemingly caught in a 19th-century time warp, has been perpetuated by the owner's patriarchal restriction on visitors.

Owned by the Robinson family since 1864, Ni'ihau has been cloaked in myth from the time the first Polynesian explorers came upon the 6 x 18-mile (10 x 29 km) sliver of arid land. Early chants relay that Ni'ihau and its tiny islet neighbors, **Lehua** and **Ka'ula**, were triplet siblings born to the ancestral gods Papa and Wakea.

Another chant postulates that Pele chose Ni'ihau as her first home. Interestingly, many volcanologists now theorize that Ni'ihau was

the first of the current Hawaiian islands to break the surface of the ocean. Seventh largest in the chain, its highest point is 1,281 ft (390 meters) above sea level.

Ni'ihau was Captain James Cook's second stop (following Kauai) in the islands during his voyage of exploration in 1778. In 1864, King Kamehameha V sold it to Elizabeth (McHutcheson) Sinclair, widow of a Navy officer who had perished, along with their eldest son, in a shipwreck. Mrs. Sinclair saw Ni'ihau lush after two years of abundant rainfall and believed it would make a good ranch home for her remaining five children. For her $10,000, she acquired not only an island, but also the 300 Hawaiians living on it. Today, family heirs Keith and Bruce Robinson manage the ranch and island. They continue to guard the privacy of Ni'ihau's Hawaiian populace to the extent that the island is one of the last true enclaves of a lifestyle that has long since disappeared elsewhere. Life on the island, however, is quite unembellished and without frills.

Ni'ihau is the only island in Hawaii where Hawaiian is the primary language. Today, children attend a grammar school with three classrooms in **Pu'uwai**, the island's only village. Though many homes do not have electricity and most do not have indoor plumbing or telephones, the school has solar-powered computers. Other schools for Ni'ihau's children are on Kauai, where kids go to live with relatives. They must go to Kauai or Oahu to attend high school.

State education officials and tax officers visit the island, and a couple of doctors make infrequent checks on the populace. Otherwise, access is limited to visitors who pay for an expensive helicopter tour or less costly day-long snorkeling tours to remote southern and northern ends of the island. There are virtually no county services, no county roads, and no sewers. Few people use cars; horses and bicycles are more common.

Nearly all residents still work for the Robinsons, rearing cattle and sheep, making charcoal from *kiawe* trees and gathering honey. Twice a week a barge arrives at Ka'auku'u Bay to carry goods across the sea to market and to deliver mail and other necessities. ❏

LEFT: rare Ni'ihau-shell *lei* are made by Ni'ihau residents, who find the shells on the beach.

Map, page 294

Kauai provided its residents with many avenues to the sea, as the island is ringed with sandy beaches. The largest is the stretch of nearly unbroken sand along the western coast, from Waimea northward more than 15 miles (24 km) along Highway 50 through sugar plantations and shorefront property. Along the beach north of Waimea is the Pacific Missile Range Facility at **Barking Sands ㉒**, which has been the site of controversial military testing. At the end of the highway – and at the end of this long stretch of sand and cane fields – is **Polihale ㉓**. A state park, the beach is Hawaii's longest at over 15 miles (24 km), it is usually empty, and often dramatically draped with the shifts of weather and ocean. Polihale offers campsites and showers; permits are available from the state parks office in the state office building in downtown Lihu'e. Hidden in the cliffs at the Na Pali coast end are a couple of *heiau*, or temples. Unless you know exactly what you're looking for, however, you'll not find them. There is no public access trail from here to join the hiking trail along the Na Pali coast.

All along this western coast of Kauai, the modest rise of **Ni'ihau** breaks the horizon less than 20 miles offshore. Because the island sits on the leeward side and so in the rain shadow of Kauai, desert-like Ni'ihau receives very little rain.

Barking Sands got its name from the sound made – something like a tired barking dog – when walked upon. The unusual structure of the grains of sand generate the sound.

Waimea

Back down the coast from Polihale, at both Kekaha and Waimea, roads lead up into the high central regions of the island. Winding upward into the interior is **Waimea Canyon ㉔**. This roseate canyon's headwaters are high in the bogs of the Alaka'i Swamp. Waterfalls tumble from here into deep valleys carpeted in green. As the plum- and guava-dotted valleys converge into gorges, a change in flora occurs. The wetness of the swamp is left behind as the vegetation becomes sparse.

BELOW: crescent-shaped Lehua and Ni'ihau.

Map,
page 294

Downstream, the *'ohi'a* gives way to *kukui,* the candlenut tree. The gorges meet with the main canyon, and the *kukui* yields to dry country trees: the native *wiliwili* and introduced *kiawe* (mesquite) and *lantana.* The weather lower down is hot and dry, and the streambed holds the only moisture. Red dust blows from barren hillsides; by the time the **Waimea River** meets the sea at Waimea town, its currents carry a heavy suspension of red earth.

Mark Twain wrote well of Waimea Canyon, but the modern traveler should arrive early before the mists have cleared and before the rainbows have had time to form. The caravans of other tourists in rental cars, not to mention tour buses, can get tedious, too. But whenever one visits, the scenery is elegant and primal.

Waimea Canyon Drive runs up from Waimea, while Highway 550 from Kekaha goes up to Koke'e, where residents from around the state have vacation cabins on leased state land.

Koke'e

Situated at the western end of the Alaka'i Swamp, **Koke'e ㉕** is the only inhabited place in Kauai's higher elevations. Also here are a dozen state-owned cabins that anyone can rent as long as reservations are made well in advance. The cabins, which are very basic and rustic, are managed from **Koke'e Lodge**, which offers facilities including a restaurant, bar, convenience store, and information center. Educational activities are also run from here.

Next to the lodge is the **Koke'e Museum** (open daily 10am–4pm; donation requested; tel: 335-9975) with displays depicting the natural history of Kauai and the other islands. Prints and living examples of important native plants are on display, and maps and guidebooks are for sale. Also on exhibit are the birds found in the wild, a three-dimensional map of Kauai, and a wild boar's head. Located in the state park, the lodge and museum are fronted by a spreading lawn where protected *moa,* or wild Hawaiian chickens, strut.

Great hiking in the Koke'e area includes the **Iliau Nature Loop** for casual strolling. For the more experienced hiker, there is the **Kukui Trail**, which drops in a steep, zigzagging course down the side of the remarkable Waimea Canyon. If you're in the mood for less strenuous activity, a drive to **Kalalau Valley Lookout ㉖** at the end of the road reveals one of the world's finest views on a clear day: the panorama of Kalalau Valley, the largest valley along the Na Pali Coast. The view from that 4,000-ft (1,200-meter) high lookout will more than reward the trials of the twisting drive to Koke'e. Low clouds sometimes obscure the view of the valley, but the lookout offers a fine opportunity to see some of Kauai's native birds, such as the red-and-black *'apapane* and vermilion-colored *'i'iwi*, which frequents the *'ohia* tree.

From the town of Waimea, the main road skirts the renowned **Menehune Ditch**. It is not terribly exciting to see and it really is not worth the extra effort trying to find it. In fact, without the metal plaque that marks a part of it along the road, you might not even notice the ditch. However, the idea is still a provocative one: tunneling through rock to make water channels before the time of modern drilling equipment. ❑

Opposite: Waimea Canyon.
Below: water lily.

INSIGHT GUIDES

TRAVEL TIPS

New Insight Maps

Maps in Insight Guides are tailored to complement the text. But when you're on the road you sometimes need the big picture that only a large-scale map can provide. This new range of durable Insight Fleximaps has been designed to meet just that need.

Detailed, clear cartography
makes the comprehensive route and city maps easy to follow, highlights all the major tourist sites and provides valuable motoring information plus a full index.

Informative and easy to use
with additional text and photographs covering a destination's top 10 essential sites, plus useful addresses, facts about the destination and handy tips on getting around.

Laminated finish
allows you to mark your route on the map using a non-permanent marker pen, and wipe it off. It makes the maps more durable and easier to fold than traditional maps.

The first titles
cover many popular destinations. They include Algarve, Amsterdam, Bangkok, California, Cyprus, Dominican Republic, Florence, Hong Kong, Ireland, London, Mallorca, Paris, Prague, Rome, San Francisco, Sydney, Thailand, Tuscany, USA Southwest, Venice, and Vienna.

🗿 INSIGHT GUIDES

The world's largest collection of visual travel guides

CONTENTS

Getting Acquainted

GEOGRAPHY

Honolulu's location is 21°18'30"N, 157°52'15"W, nearly 1,500 miles (2,400 km) north of the equator. Thus, contrary to popular belief, Hawaii is not in the South Pacific. (It is, however, part of Polynesia, most of which is in the South Pacific.)

The two points in Hawaii farthest apart are Cape Kumukahi, on the east coast of the Big Island, and Kure Atoll, at the northwest end of the Hawaiian archipelago. The antipode of Honolulu – the point on the opposite side of the globe equidistant from Honolulu in all directions – is the African country of Botswana. (Hawaii is the only place in the United States with an antipode on land.)

The ocean depth of the Kauai Channel, 72 miles (115 km) wide between Oahu and Kauai, is 10,890 ft (3,320 meters). The deepest Hawaiian channel is between Lisianski Island and Hermes Atoll, at 17,400 ft (5,300 meters). The deepest harbor is Honolulu Harbor at 40 ft (12 meters).

In comparison with the other American states, Hawaii is 4th in coastline miles, 14th in land owned by the federal government and 43rd in total land area.

Distance in miles (km) from Honolulu to:

Hilo	214 (344)
Kailua-Kona	168 (270)
Kahului, Maui	98 (158)
Lanai	72 (116)
Molokai	54 (87)
Lihu'e, Kauai	103 (166)
Midway Is.	1,309 (2,106)
Kure Atoll	1,367 (2,200)
Anchorage	2,781 (4,475)
Auckland	4,393 (7,068)
Equator	1,470 (2,352)
Hong Kong	5,541 (8,915)
London	7,226 (11,627)
Los Angeles	2,557 (4,114)
Manila	5,293 (8,516)
New York	4,959 (7,979)
North Pole	4,740 (7,631)
San Francisco	2,397 (3,857)
Papeete, Tahiti	2,741 (4,410)
Tokyo	3,847 (6,190)
Vancouver	2,709 (4,359)

Hawaii is + 10 hours GMT.
Pacific Standard Time + 2
Central Standard Time + 4
Eastern Standard Time + 5
As Hawaii does not adjust to daylight savings time, add 1 hour to the time difference from April through October, when in effect.

Island High Points

Big Island/Mauna Kea
13,796 ft (4,205 meters)
Maui/Haleakala
10,023 ft (3,055 meters)
Kauai/Kawaikini
5,243 ft (1,598 meters)
Molokai/Kamakou
4,961 ft (1,512 meters)
Oahu/Ka'ala
4,020 ft (1,220 meters)
Lanai/Lana'ihale
3,366 ft (1,026 meters)
Kaho'olawe/Pu'u Moaulanui
1,483 ft (452 meters)
Ni'ihau/Pani'au
1,250 ft (381 meters)
Kure Atoll
20 ft (6 meters)

There are seasons in sub-tropic Hawaii, it just takes time to recognize them. Most of Hawaii experiences balmy 73°F–88°F (23°C–31°C) weather from April through October, and cooler, wetter 65°F–83°F (18°C–28°C) weather from November through March. Rarely does the mercury drop below 60°F (15°C), nor go higher than about 90°F (32°C).

While sunbathing is a common activity here, don't overdo it. Slowly create a tolerance for Hawaii's strong sunlight by taking no more than 30 minutes of direct sun exposure the first day, 40 minutes the second day, 50 minutes the third day and so on. To prevent sunburn, be sure to wear sunscreen and keep applying it – you will find instructions on use on the container.

The surrounding sea and northeasterly trade winds are a natural air-conditioning system. However, when the trade winds stop, and less frequent southerly winds take over, the result is often sticky and humid.

Certain areas on each island – usually on the windward side of mountains – receive more rainfall than others. One of the wettest spots on Earth is Mount Wai'ale'ale on Kauai, which has been drenched by as much as 486 inches (1,234 cm) of rain in a year.

In higher places such as Upcountry and Haleakala on Maui, and Koke'e on Kauai, temperatures range from 48°F to 72°F (9°C–22°C), and in mountainous parts of the Big Island the average temperature drops to 31°F to 58°F (-1°C–14°C) during the winter and at night. Snow falls on Mauna Kea (and sometimes Haleakala on Maui) in the winter, so bring warm clothing if you intend to tour these areas.

Sometimes when there is a volcanic eruption on the Big Island, a smoky pall lingers over the islands for a few days, especially in the Kona area. Islanders call this volcanic haze "vog," or volcanic smog. People suffering from asthma or other respiratory problems may wish to take extra precautions during "voggy" weather.

The People

POPULATION

Details of Hawaii's wide diversity of peoples and cultures are covered in the main text of this book *(see pages 87–94)*. But for those with a knack for statistics… Compared with the rest of the United States, Hawaii is second in people per household; third in the number of marriages per 1,000; 14th in number of persons per square mile; 30th in divorces per 1,000 people; 37th in percentage of residents below poverty level; 39th in infant mortality; 42nd in the rate of violent crimes; and 48th in the rate of deaths from cancer.

Population (2000 census)

Total population	1,211,537
Oahu	876,156
Big Island	148,677
Maui	117,644
Kauai	58,303
Molokai	7,404
Lanai	3,193
Ni'ihau	160

Ethnicity (2000 census)

The 2000 census used different categories to the 1990 census, therefore, the tally adds up to more than 100 percent with some people claiming more than one racial background, i.e. both Japanese and of mixed ancestry.

Asian/Pacific		48 percent
	Japanese	16.5 percent
	Filipino	14 percent
	Hawaiian	6.5 percent
	Chinese	5 percent
	Korean	2 percent
Caucasian		24 percent
Black		2 percent
Mixed race (includes some people identified in the above racial categories)		55 percent

Culture & Customs

Aloha Friday

Friday is usually greeted in the islands with aloha wear, where even businessmen don aloha shirts of bright and cheerful Hawaiian prints instead of formal suits and ties. Ladies often tuck a fragrant plumeria behind their ear, or drape a *kukui* nut or flower *lei* on their shoulders. These are appropriate accessories for their *mu'umu'u*. This is a Friday custom that has become *de rigueur* here, even in state, federal and business offices and at public schools. And in most businesses, it is no longer limited to Friday only.

Hawaiian Time

Time in the islands is not noticeably defined by the four seasons, and Hawaii's balmy tropical climate tends to warp any rigid schedule. Islanders can be lax about time, especially when going on dates and to meetings outside of strictly commercial business circles. This habit of being "fashionably late" by around 10 minutes is generally known as being on "Hawaiian time."

The Economy

For a century, agriculture dominated the economy of Hawaii. Sugar was king of the islands, followed by pineapple. (Both crops are introduced species to the islands). But after World War II, the structure of Hawaii's economy began a slow shift, and by statehood in 1959, Hawaii was ready to begin a new economic era: tourism. Hawaii's sugar and pineapple industries have in fact been in steady decline: In 1972, there were 230,000 acres (93,078 hectares) under sugar cultivation; over three decades later, there are fewer than 70,000 acres (28,328 hectares). And perhaps no island demonstrates the decline of Hawaii's pineapple industry better than Lanai. Once known as the Pineapple Island, Lanai is now an upscale resort destination – its once-thriving 16,000-acre (6,475-hectare) pineapple plantation has been decimated. Today, the five big industries in Hawaii are tourism, the military, sugar, pineapple and diversified agriculture.

Considering tourism's importance to Hawaii's economy, it's no wonder that the islands' hotels and resorts spare no expense to provide high-quality visitor accommodations. According to reader surveys of major travel publications, Hawaii repeatedly ranks top or near the top as a tropical resort destination. The island of Maui has topped *Conde Nast Traveller's* list of the top 20 islands in the world more than once, often followed closely by Kauai; the Big Island, Lanai and Oahu also came high on the list. Two Hawaii spas were named on the list of the world's top 10 spas – Grand Wailea Resort came first, while 'Ihilani was placed third.

In 1971, there was an average of 41,000 tourists in Hawaii on any given day. During 2000, the average rose to 190,000, with 3.9 million tourists annually from the Mainland, 1.8 million from Japan, and 330,000 from Canada. Oahu is the most visited island, followed by Maui, the Big Island, Kauai, Lanai and then Molokai.

The largest single source of jobs is in the service industry – the hotels and other tourist-related businesses. After that comes the retail trade, government and the self-employed.

No matter where they make their money, Hawaii residents need every penny of it. Hawaii is 16th in average annual income in the United States, but has an above-average cost of living. Paradise doesn't come cheap.

The Government

The structure and hierarchy of Hawaii's local government is simple. The governor of Hawaii is popularly elected, as are the lieutenant governor, state legislators, and county mayors and councils. The state Legislature convenes in Honolulu each January for a 60-day session. The Legislature is bicameral, comprised of the Senate (with 25 members) and the House of Representatives (51 members). The dominant political party in Hawaii has been the Democratic Party, although a Republican resurgence has recently begun a return to a more balanced two-party system.

The state is divided into four counties, with a mayor for each one: Honolulu, Hawaii (Big Island), Maui and Kauai. The City and County of Honolulu – the only officially incorporated city in the state – includes Oahu and a 1,200-mile (1,930-km) long string of Islands that lead to Midway Island. The County of Maui includes Molokai, Lanai and the uninhabited island of Kaho'olawe. The County of Kauai includes the privately owned island of Ni'ihau, which has a Hawaiian population of 230.

The last of the 50 states to be admitted to the American union (in 1959), Hawaii has a congressional delegation of four in Washington, DC: two senators and two representatives.

Planning the Trip

What to Bring

Electrical Goods & Adapters
Standard US 110–120 volts, 60 cycles AC. Large hotels are usually able to provide voltage and plug converters.

What to Wear

Dress is cool and casual in Honolulu and even more so beyond the city proper. Light, loose garments are suitable for the summer months. Hawaiian-print *mu'umu'u* and aloha shirts are practical all-round garments (just don't wear matching prints with your partner.) Thongs, flip-flops, slippers, *zoris* – all different names for the same thing – are ideal for pacing the pavement or at the beach.

A few exclusive restaurants and nightclubs require a coat, maybe a tie, and definitely shoes, but they are the exceptions. Leather sandals and shoes are appropriate for night life. In most island homes, shoes are removed at the entrance.

For the cooler, wetter months, pack a sweater and an umbrella. A parka and heavy jacket are advised to keep you warm when hiking in mountainous areas on Maui, Kauai and, particularly, on the Big Island.

Entry Regulations

VISAS & PASSPORTS

Whatever requirements are necessary for entry to the United States are necessary for Hawaii. Visitors from most foreign countries need to show a valid passport with a US visa.

US Passport Agency, tel: 522-8283.
US Customs, tel: 522-8060.
US Immigration, tel: 532-3721.

ANIMALS & AGRICULTURE

Hawaii is free of rabies, snakes and poison ivy, and state officials work hard to keep it that way. Incoming animals are placed in quarantine for 120 days at the owner's expense, although recent legislation now permits dogs and cats that meet certain pre- and post-arrival requirements to be quarantined for only 30 days.

Baggage is inspected coming and going through the airport. Papayas, avocados and bananas must be treated before being exported. Coconuts and pineapples do not need treatment.

US Dept of Agriculture, tel: 861-8490.
State Dept of Agriculture, tel: 948-0145.
Animal Quarantine Station, tel: 483-7171.
Plant Quarantine Station, tel: 586-0844.

Currency

Hawaii uses standard US currency and coins in all denominations. $1 = 100 cents. All major credit cards are accepted, including American Express, Visa, MasterCard, Discover, JCB and, to a lesser degree, Diners Club. Most car rental companies require a credit card. Cash machines (ATMS) are everywhere, especially at banks and shopping centers; ATMS accept bank cards from the mainland and are accessible 24 hours a day.

Currency Exchange
Currency conversion is readily available at Honolulu International Airport, in the customs area and at most major banks in Hawaii. Currency exchange is also available at most hotels, although the rate tends to be a little less favorable than at a bank.

Normal banking hours are Monday to Thursday 8am–3pm, and Friday 8am–6pm. Some banks open at 8.30am, others stay open later on select days. Note that there are no street money changers in Hawaii.

Holidays

Hawaii observes all the US national holidays, plus three state holidays – Prince Kuhio Day, Kamehameha Day and Admission Day.

On national holidays, all government offices, banks, post offices and most businesses, except shops, close. On state holidays, local government offices and banks close, but federal offices and post offices remain open.

Public Holidays

- **New Year's Day** January 1
- **Martin Luther King Day** third Monday in January
- **Presidents' Day** third Monday in February
- **Prince Kuhio Day** March 26
- **Good Friday** Friday preceding Easter Sunday
- **Memorial Day** last Monday in May
- **Kamehameha Day** June 11
- **Independence Day** July 4
- **Admission Day** third Friday in August
- **Labor Day** first Monday in September
- **Columbus Day** October 12
- **Veterans Day** November 11
- **Thanksgiving Day** fourth Thursday in November
- **Christmas Day** December 25

Getting There
BY AIR

Hawaii is regularly serviced from the US mainland, Canada, Europe, the South Pacific and Asia. Arriving aircraft at **Honolulu International Airport** touch down on a reef runway, completed in 1977 on a shallow reef-lagoon between Honolulu Harbor and Pearl Harbor.

The airport's interior is adorned with Hawaiian arts and crafts created by top local artists. (In 1967, a Hawaii legislative act designated one percent of all appropriated public works funds for the purchase of artwork for state buildings, including the airport.) Japanese, Hawaiian and Chinese gardens also enhance the terminal's promenade areas.

Located at the center of the airport's main concourse is the **Pacific Aerospace Museum** (open daily 8.30am–6pm), a 6,500-sq-ft (604-sq-meter), $3.8-million museum that highlights the many aviation and aerospace achievements in Hawaii and the Pacific region. It's a worthwhile visit, especially if you have some time to kill while waiting for a flight.

Some airlines fly directly from the US mainland to Hawaii's neighbor islands, particularly Maui, Kauai and the Big Island. If you're traveling on a full-fare round-trip ticket from the US mainland or Canada, inquire about discount tickets that allow travel from Oahu to any of the neighboring islands. This bargain, designed to serve as an island-hopping incentive, is available in cooperation with Aloha Airlines and Hawaiian Airlines, the state's inter-island carriers.

Leaving the airport
A yellow-brown-and-orange striped bus – **TheBus** (sic) – departs frequently from Honolulu Airport to Waikiki via downtown and Ala Moana Shopping Center. Exact change (currently $1.50) is required. Passengers are limited to one carry-on bag small enough to be held on the lap or placed under the seat. No exceptions. If you have more than a small carry-on piece of luggage, forget the bus – it's better to take a taxi into Waikiki and pick up a rental car from there, if you need one. You can also rent cars from the airport, although the busy 20–30 minute drive into town can be tiring.

Airport, tel: 836-6411.
Information, tel: 836-6413.

BY SEA

Arriving by ship at Oahu's picturesque Honolulu Harbor was once the way to reach the islands, but today only a few passenger liners make Honolulu a port of call. A few lucky souls, of course, arrive by private yacht.

Useful Phone Numbers

Tourist Information
Hawaii Visitors and Convention Bureau, tel: 923-1811.
Hawaii Tourism Office, tel: 973-2255.
Airport visitor information, tel: 836-6413.

TheBus
Customer service, tel: 848-4500.
Schedule and route info, tel: 848-5555.
Lost and found, tel: 848-4444.
24-hour recorded information, tel: 296-1818 (then enter 8287).

International Airlines
Air New Zealand, tel: (800) 262-1234.
American Airlines, tel: 833-7600.
Canadian Airlines, tel: 877-359 2263.
China Airlines, tel: 955-0088.
Continental Airlines, tel: 523-0000.
Delta Airlines, tel: (800) 221-1212.
Japan Airlines, tel: 521-1441.
Korean Air Lines, tel: (800) 438-5000.
Northwest Airlines, tel: 800-225 2525.
Philippine Airlines, tel: (800) 435-9725.
Pleasant Hawaiian Holidays (via American Trans Air), tel: (800) 2 Hawaii.
Qantas Airways, tel: (800) 227-4500.
TWA, tel: (800) 221-2000.

United Airlines,
tel: (800) 241-6522.

Inter-Island Airlines

Aloha Airlines
Oahu, tel: 484-1111.
Maui, tel: 244-9071.
Big Island, tel: 935-5771.
Kauai: 245-3691; toll free from the
US mainland, tel: (800) 367-5250.

Aloha Inter-Island Air
Oahu, tel: 484-2222.
Toll-free from neighbor islands,
tel: (800) 652-6541.
Toll-free from US mainland,
tel: (800) 323-3345.

Hawaiian Airlines
Toll free from neighbor islands,
tel: (800) 882-8811.
Toll free from US mainland,
tel: (800) 367-5320.

Reference

University of Hawaii,
tel: 956-8111.
UH Information Center,
tel: 956-7235.
UH Bookstore, tel: 956-6884.
Library recorded information,
tel: 956-7204.
Hamilton Library reference desk,
tel: 956-7214.
Hawaii State Library,
tel: 586-3500.

Customs and Immigration

US Passport Agency,
tel: 522-8283.
US Customs/24 hour,
tel: 522-8060.
US Immigration,
tel: 532-3721.

Miscellaneous

Time of Day,
tel: 983-3211.
Governor's Office,
tel: 586-0034.
Honolulu Mayor's Office,
tel: 523-4141.
Office of Consumer Protection,
tel: 586-2630.
Police (Honolulu) lost and found,
tel: 529-3283.

Cultural

Neal S. Blaisdell Center
(ticket office), tel: 591-2211

Honolulu Symphony
(ticket office), tel: 538-8863
Aloha Stadium
(ticket office), tel: 486-9300
Waikiki Shell
(ticket office), tel: 924-8934

Internet Sites

● **General**
www.planet-hawaii.com
www.gohawaii.com
www.bestofhawaii.com
www.hawaiiguide.com
www.search-hawaii.com
www.discoveringhawaii.com
www.gohawaiianvacations.com
www.travel-kauai.com
www.bestplaceshawaii.com
● **Hotels & Restaurants**
www.hi-inns.com
www.hotel-in-hawaii.com
www.hawaiihotelsontheweb.com
www.hawaii-hotels.com
www.hawaiihotels.com
● **Links and Indexes**
www.hawaii.com or
www.hawaii.net
● **Bishop Museum**
www.bishop.hawaii.org

Practical Tips

Emergencies

SECURITY & CRIME

Hawaii has earned a reputation for
hospitality and all the good cheer
that the word *aloha* implies. However,
travelers should be warned that all
types of crime – including burglaries,
robberies, assaults and rapes – do
occur on the islands. On the whole,
however, Honolulu is one of the
safest cities in North America.

Follow the usual precautions as
when traveling anywhere else. Use
common sense. Don't carry jewelry,
large amounts of cash or other
valuables. In areas far from
population centers, car break-ins and
beach thefts of unattended personal
property are becoming common,
even at popular tourist sites.

Emergency Phone Numbers
Fire, Police, Ambulance,
tel: 911.
Coast Guard Search and Rescue,
tel: (800) 552-6458.
Poison Center, tel: 941-4411.

MEDICAL SERVICES

Most of the larger hotels have a
physician on call. Other medical
services can be obtained at several
main Honolulu hospitals:
Kaiser-Permanente
(clinics throughout Hawaii), 1010
Pensacola Street.
Tel: 593-2950
Kaiser's Urgent Care Clinic, 2155
Kalakaua Avenue.
Tel: 597-2860.
**Kapi'olani Medical Center
for Women and Children,** 1319
Punahou Street. Tel: 983-6000.

Queen's Medical Center, 1301
Punchbowl Street. Tel: 538-9011.
Straub Clinic and Hospital, 888 S.
King Street. Tel: 522-4000.

*Other Emergency Services
(Oahu)*
American Red Cross,
tel: 734-2101.
Dental emergency service,
tel: 944-8863.
FBI, tel: 566-4300.
Lifeguard Service,
tel: 922-3888.
Sex Abuse Treatment Center,
tel: 524-7273.
Suicide & Crisis Center,
tel: 521-4555.
US Secret Service,
tel: 541-1912.

FLASH FLOODS

In the mountain areas, intense rain
can cause flash floods. If you are
hiking in valleys, take care during
heavy rains in the mountains, as
flash floods can occur without
warning.

If a flash flood watch has been
issued by the National Weather
Service, be alert: flooding is
possible. A warning means that
flooding is imminent or already
occurring. If you are in a flood-prone
area, get to higher ground
immediately.

HURRICANES

Hawaii lies in Pacific storm tracks.
Hurricanes are infrequent in Hawaii,
but when they do touch the islands,
they generally hit hard. Take all
warnings seriously. Phone
directories contain detailed
information, including flood and tidal
wave zones for each island, and
public shelter locations.

The hurricane season is from
June through November. In general,
Pacific storms do more damage
when coming from the south than
from other directions. There are
several classifications of storms, up
to hurricane status.

• Tropical depressions are low-
pressure systems with sustained
winds of less than 40 miles (60
km) per hour.
• Tropical storms are cyclones with
winds of 40–75 mph (60–120
kph).
• A hurricane is declared when a
tropical cyclone has winds greater
than 75 miles (120 km) per hour.
When a tropical depression forms,
the National Weather Service issues
a series of advisories, based on the
position and strength of the
approaching storm. If a hurricane
watch has been issued, a hurricane
is expected within 36 hours. A
hurricane warning means a hurricane
is expected within 24 hours.

When the civil defense sirens
sound, tune to local radio or
television stations for emergency
disaster instructions. Stay indoors
during high winds, and evacuate
areas that may flood. Evacuation
orders by authorities must be
followed at all times.

CIVIL DEFENSE

The Emergency Alert System,
which warns of natural disasters or
a nuclear holocaust, are tested
at 11.45am on the first business

Tsunami (tidal waves)

Earthquakes, particularly on the
Big Island, sometimes forebode a
tsunami, the correct term for a
seismic or tidal wave. Earthquakes
elsewhere, including Alaska, can
send a *tsunami* to Hawaii. They
can occur with little warning or
time for preparation. When a
tsunami warning is issued, leave
coastal areas immediately. Use
the *tsunami* evacuation maps
published in island telephone
directories. Should civil defense
sirens sound, tune in to a radio or
TV for instructions. If outside of
the danger zones indicated in the
telephone directory maps, remain
there. If you are in a flood-prone
area, head for higher ground.

day of every month. In the event
of an actual emergency, civil
defense instructions are broadcast
on all radio, TV and cable TV
systems.

Telephone Numbers
State Civil Defense,
tel: 733-4300.
Oahu, tel: 523-4121.
Big Island, tel: 935-0031.
Maui County, tel: 243-7285.
Kauai, tel: 241-6336.

Tipping

Tipping for service is expected in
Hawaii, as tips are considered part
of a service worker's overall salary.
In general, airport porters'
baggage-handling fees run at
roughly $1 per bag, and taxi drivers
are usually tipped 15 percent in
addition to about 25¢ per bag. A
15–20 percent tip at a fine
restaurant is the norm, and at
other eating establishments you
should tip whatever you feel is fair,
typically 15 percent.

Religious Services

Bethany Assembly of God
(Assembly of God), 98-1125
Moanalua Road, 'Aiea.
Tel: 488-3231.
Cathedral of Our Lady of Peace
(Roman Catholic), Fort Street Mall at
Beretania Street, downtown
Honolulu. Tel: 536-7036.
Central Union Church (United
Church of Christ), 1660 S. Beretania
at Punahou Street, Honolulu. Tel:
941-0957.
Chabad of Hawaii (Jewish),
3432 East Manoa Road, Honolulu.
Tel: 988-1004.
Church of Jesus Christ
of the Latter Day Saints (Mormon),
1500 Beretania Street, Honolulu.
Tel: 942-0050.
Daijingu Temple of Hawaii (Shinto),
61 Pu'iwa Road, Honolulu.
Tel: 595-3102.
First Church of Christ Scientist
Honolulu (Christian Scientist), 1508
Punahou Street, Honolulu.
Tel: 949-8403.

First Presbyterian Church of Honolulu, 1822 Ke'eaumoku at Nehoa Street, Honolulu. Tel: 532-1111.

Greek Orthodox Church of Sts Constantine & Helen, 930 Lunalilo Street, Honolulu. Tel: 521-7220.

Hare Krishna Temple, 51 Coelho Way, Nu'uanu. Tel: 595-4913.

Honpa Hongwanji Mission (Buddhist), 1727 Pali Highway, Nu'uanu. Tel: 522-9200. Services in both English and Japanese.

Jehovah's Witness Central Kingdom, 1228 Pensacola Street, Honolulu. Tel: 521-7372.

Kawaiaha'o Church (Congregational), 957 Punchbowl at King Street, downtown. Tel: 522-1333. Services in Hawaiian and English.

Korean Buddhist Dae Won Sa Temple of Hawaii, 2420 Halela'au Place, Honolulu. Tel: 735-7858.

Nichiren Shoshu Honseiji (Buddhist), 44-668 Kane'ohe Bay Drive, Kane'ohe. Tel: 235-8486.

Prince of Peace Church (Lutheran), Princess Kaiulani Hotel, Waikiki. Tel: 922-6011.

Religious Society of Friends (Quakers), 2426 Oahu Avenue, Manoa Valley. Tel: 988-2714.

St Andrew's Cathedral (Episcopalian), Corner of Queen Emma and Beretania Streets, downtown. Tel: 524-2822.

St Augustine's Church (Catholic), 130 'Ohua Avenue, Waikiki. Tel: 923-7024.

Seventh Day Adventist Church, 2313 Nu'uanu Avenue, Honolulu. Tel: 524-1352.

Temple Emanuel (Jewish), 2550 Pali Highway, Nu'uanu. Tel: 595-7521.

Todaiji Hawaii Bekkaku Honzan (Buddhist), 426 Luakini Street, Nu'uanu. Tel: 595-2083.

United Methodist Church, 20 S. Vineyard, Honolulu. Tel: 536-1864.

Waikiki Baptist Church, 424 Kuamo'o Street, Waikiki. Tel: 955-3525.

Media

NEWSPAPERS & MAGAZINES

Hawaii has a handful of island daily and weekly newspapers, and numerous magazines. The two statewide circulated major dailies are *The Honolulu Advertiser*, a morning newspaper, and *The Honolulu Star-Bulletin*, an afternoon independent newspaper. Neighbor islands also have their own daily newspapers, with circulation restricted to that island. A variety of other newspapers are published by ethnic groups, the military, religious organizations, and by the tourism and business industries. The Associated Press maintains a bureau in Honolulu to cover both Hawaii and the Pacific.

RADIO

Honolulu's listeners tune in to some 30 radio stations, with programs ranging from Top 40 hits, jazz, classic rock and Hawaiian music to news, talk and sports. Foreign-language programs are available on certain stations. Check newspaper listings.

TELEVISION

There are more than 10 broadcast TV channels that originate in Hawaii. They include channels 2 (KHON-FOX); 4 (KITV-ABC); 5 (KFVE); 9 (KGMB-CBS); 11 (KHET-PBS); and 13 (KHNL-NBC). For broadcasts originating in Honolulu, relay transmitters serve the neighbor islands, and private companies provide cable television programming by subscription only. The majority of hotels offer cable TV viewing to guests.

Postal Services

Normal American postal rates apply. From Honolulu, it costs the same price to mail a letter to Maui as it does to New York City.

Honolulu District Office (at the airport), 3600 Aolele Street. Tel: (800) 275-8777; Window service: Monday–Friday 7.30am–8.30pm. **Waikiki**, 330 Saratoga Road. Tel: (800) 275-8777. There are also sub-stations at several locations in Waikiki.

Customer information, tel: (800) 275-8777.

Telecoms

Area code: 808
AT&T access code: 1-800 CALL ATT
Sprint access code: 1-800 877 8000
MCI access code: 1-888 757 6655

From the middle of the Pacific, you can dial directly to almost anywhere in the world. Because of underwater fiber-optic cables, the quality to both Asia and North America is excellent.

Both inter-island and mainland/international calls are usually discounted in the evening and at night. Many hotels charge $0.75–$1 for local calls. Public telephones cost $0.35 for local calls.

Dialing Codes
Same-island calls: dial number.
Inter-island (direct):
1 + 808 + number.
Inter-island (operator assisted):
0 + 808 + number.
Mainland (direct dial):
1 + area code + number.
Mainland (operator assisted):
0 + area code + number.
International (direct dial):
011 + country + city + number.
International (operator assist):
01 + country + city + number.
Home-country direct: Operators in some countries can be called directly from Hawaii by special toll-free 800 numbers. Call 643-1000 for a list of numbers and foreign countries where service is available.

Directory Assistance
Operator assistance: dial 0.
Same-island: 1 + 411.
Inter-island: 1 + 808 + 555-1212.
Mainland: 1 + area code + 555-1212.
Verizon consumer line: 643-3456.

Consulates

American Samoa, tel: 847-1998.
Australia, tel: 524-5050.
Japan, tel: 543-3111.
Korea, tel: 595-6109.
Philippines, tel: 595-4316.
Taiwan, tel: 595-6347.
Thailand, tel: 845-7332.
Tonga, tel: 521-5149.

Tourist Offices

In Hawaii

There are no longer visitor-focused tourist offices for Hawaiian tourism – rather, they concentrate on developing corporate tourism. But you can contact the office below, who will field questions. For brochures, call 0800 60 HAWAII toll-free.
● **Hawaii Visitors & Conventions Bureau**, 1801 Kalakaua Avenue, Honolulu 96815.
Tel: 973-2255; fax: 973-2253
   Hilo, tel: 961-5797.
   Kona, tel: 886-1655.
   Kauai, tel: 245-3971.
   Maui, tel: 244-3530.
   www.hawaii.gov.tourism

Offices Abroad
● **Canada**
1260 Hornby Street,
Suite 104, Vancouver BC,
Canada, V6Z1W2.
Tel: 1-800 464-2924.

Getting Around

Island Hopping

BY SEA

For seafaring types, **American Hawaii Cruises** offers inter-island cruises on several passenger liners, with ports of call in Lihu'e, Kauai; Kahului, Maui; and Hilo and Kona on the Big Island. There are sails weekly to and from Honolulu. Week-long voyages as well as three- and four-day trips are available. Bus excursions are optional, and rental cars are also available in each port for those passengers who require a more leisurely pace. Contact travel agents for current schedules and a list of prices.

There is no inter-island ferry service, although there are daily runs between Lahaina, Maui; Manele and Lanai, and, despite setbacks, a regular commuter service is scheduled to begin between Ewa and Honolulu.

BY AIR

Flights between islands are frequent, typically every half hour or hour. There are two primary carriers, **Aloha** and **Hawaiian Airlines**, using jets between all major airports. In addition, **Aloha Island Air**, a subsidiary of Aloha Airlines, uses small prop craft to smaller airports like Princeville on Kauai. There are also fixed-wing and helicopter flights for inter-island travel.

With the exception of morning and late afternoon commuter times, when local workers and business-people are returning to

their home islands, you can usually get a seat at short notice. If one flight is full, there is another flight in about 30 minutes to an hour. However, weekends and holidays are busy times; reserve ahead if possible. Inter-island flights are short, from 20 to 45 minutes, depending on the route.

Both Aloha and Hawaiian Airlines offer hotel and rental car deals with their flights, again often on very short notice. The first couple of early-morning flights and the last couple of flights at night are sometimes also discounted.

Inter-Island Airlines
Aloha Airlines

A jet fleet operates to all main islands from Honolulu. There are select flights between neighbor islands.
Oahu, tel: 484-1111.
Maui, tel: 244-9071.
Big Island, tel: 935-5771.
Kauai: 245-3691; or toll-free from US mainland,
tel: 800-367 5250.

Aloha Island Air
Mid-size propeller aircraft with services to Honolulu, Molokai, Lanai, West Maui and Hilo, on the Big Island.
Oahu, tel: 484-2222.
Toll-free from neighbor islands, tel: 800-652 6541.
Toll-free from US mainland, tel: 800-323 3345.

Hawaiian Airlines
The jet fleet operates to all the main islands from Honolulu. There are also select flights between some of the neighbor islands.
Toll free from neighbor islands, tel: 800-882 8811.
Toll-free from US mainland, tel: 800-367 5320.

Pacific Wings
A commuter-carrier serving the resorts of Honolulu, Lanai, Molokai and Hana, and Kapalua on Maui.
Call toll-free from the Mainland and the Islands, tel: 888-575 4546.

Public Transportation

BY BUS

Oahu is the only Hawaiian island with a mass transit system. (On the neighboring islands, bus transportation, other than tour buses, is not an available option.) With more than 65 routes that cover the entire island, **TheBus** (sic) system is a convenient and affordable way to get around. TheBus Gazebo is at Ala Moana Center, and the staff here are very helpful.

Multi-day passes, which are available at the ubiquitous ABC stores, are recommended if you're likely to use TheBus to get around. Up-to-date maps and bus schedules are available free of charge.

Printed schedules are also available at all satellite City Halls on Oahu.

Customer service,
tel: 848-4500.
Schedule and route information,
tel: 848-5555.

Orientation

Local folks share a common vernacular for directions, which has nothing to do with cardinal directions or where the sun rises and sets. Rather, it deals with *local* geographical features. The two most common directional terms are *mauka* ("upland" or "towards the mountain") and *makai* ("towards the sea"). In Honolulu, directions are also given in relation to *'Ewa*, a plantation town just west of Pearl Harbor, and to *Diamond Head*, the famous landmark to the east side of Waikiki. Those four orientations – *mauka*, *makai*, *'Ewa* and *Diamond Head* – are regularly used among residents. Say north, south, east or west and you'll receive looks of bewilderment.

24-hour recorded information, includes information on attractions accessible by TheBus.
tel: 296-1818 (then enter 8287).
Lost and found/bus pass,
tel: 848-4445.

BY TAXI

Although a taxi service is available on all islands, if you are traveling beyond local destinations it generally becomes cheaper to rent a car. All taxis are metered, although most are available for sightseeing at a fixed rate. Honolulu, of course, has the most taxis, but don't expect to flag one down on the street. If a taxi is required, go to a nearby hotel. Elsewhere on Oahu, call one of the companies listed below or check the yellow pages under the heading "Taxicabs."

Aloha State Cab, tel: 847-3566.
Charley's Taxi, tel: 531-1333.
Sida Taxi, tel: 836-0011.

Where to Stay

Choosing a Hotel

Hawaii abounds in accommodations of every persuasion. There are four types of places to stay: hotels (including small, classy inns), rental condominiums, bed-and-breakfasts and campsites.

Many of the international luxury hotel chains have resorts in Hawaii. If you can afford them, you'll probably know what you're looking for. But for those on a budget or wanting to visit on an extended stay, the multitudinous offerings of economical and mid-range hotels can be intimidating.

You can take a gamble and book a hotel room based on price without seeing it. Another way is to arrive with a confirmed reservation for a day or two, and look for a suitable place for later. Depending on the season, you might be successful – or you might end up sleeping on the beach in the rain.

Another option is the resort management companies that manage a string of properties – some offer only hotels, some split between hotels and condominiums, and others offer only condominiums. Most of their properties are quite satisfactory, with quality and amenities usually in direct proportion to the price. Call one of the companies below and tell them what you're looking for.

If you are particular about exact location, you should either confirm the location with the property or call the reservations company. Mailing addresses sometimes don't reflect the true location of a hotel or condominium. Lahaina, for example, is often the mailing post office for places across West Maui.

Holiday villas beyond indulgence.

BALEARICS ~ CARIBBEAN ~ FRANCE ~ GREECE ~ ITALY ~ MAURITIUS
MOROCCO ~ PORTUGAL ~ SCOTLAND ~ SPAIN

If you enjoy the really good things in life, we offer the highest quality holiday villas with the utmost privacy, style and true luxury. You'll find each with maid service and most have swimming pools.

For 18 years, we've gone to great lengths to select the very best villas at all of our locations around the world.

Contact us for a brochure on the destination of your choice and experience what most only dream of.

INTERNATIONAL
CHAPTERS

Live it up!

Ride through the **past** in a **trishaw** and be welcomed into the **future** by **lions**.

For the time of your life, live it up in Singapore!
Explore historic back lanes and shop in malls of the future. Take part in a traditional tea ceremony at a quaint Peranakan house, then tee off for a birdie at one of our challenging golf courses.

Spice things up with some hot Pepper Crab and unwind in a world-class spa. Join a Feng Shui Tour to harness positive energy and later channel it into a night on the town. Come to Singapore and catch the buzz and excitement of Asia's most vibrant city.

Singapore NEW ASIA

www.newasia-singapore.com

For more information, mail to: Singapore Tourism Board, Tourism Court, 1 Orchard Spring Lane, Singapore 247729 or Fax to (65) 736 9423.

Name: _____   Address: _____

Email: _____

Aston Hotels & Resorts
2155 Kalakaua Avenue, Suite 500,
Honolulu, HI 96815
Tel: 931-1400
Fax: 922-8785
Toll free: 800-922 7866.
Castle Resorts & Hotels
2032 S. Beretania Street,
Honolulu, 96826
Tel: 955-6221
Fax: 800-477 2320
Toll free: 800-367 5004.
Colony Resorts
Worldwide Reservation Center,
11340 Blondo Street,
Omaha, NE 68164
Fax: 402-501 9166
Toll free: 800-777 1700.
Marc Resorts Hawaii
2155 Kalakaua Avenue, Suite 318,
Honolulu, HI 96815
Tel: 922-9700
Fax: 922-2421
Toll free: 800-535 0085.
Outrigger Hotels & Resorts
Denver Reservations Center, 3443
S. Galena Street, Denver, CO 80231
Tel: 303-743 3201
Fax: 303-369 9403
Toll free: 800-688 7444.
Starwood Hotels & Resorts
This, the world's largest hotelier, has
Sheraton, West In, Luxury Collection
and W- Hotel brands in Hawaii.
Tel: 800-325 3535.

Bed & Breakfast

Bed-and-breakfast places were slow
to catch on in Hawaii. There is little
regulation of B&Bs, so standards
vary. The reservation companies
below book for most of the islands.

**Affordable Paradise Bed &
Breakfast**
332 Ku'ukama Street, Kailua,
HI 96734
Tel: 261-1693.
All Islands Bed & Breakfast
463 'Iliwahi Loop, Kailua,
HI 96734-1837
Tel: 263-2342
Toll free: 800-542 0344.
Bed & Breakfast Hawaii
PO Box 449, Kapa'a, HI 96746
Tel: 822-7771
Toll free: 800-733 1632.

Bed & Breakfast Honolulu
3242 Ka'ohinani Drive, Honolulu,
HI 96817
Tel: 595-7533
Toll free: 800-288 4666.
**Hawaiian Islands Bed & Breakfast
and Vacation Rentals**
572 Kailua Road, Suite 201, Kailua,
HI 96734
Tel: 261-7895
Toll free: 800-258 7895.
Hawaii's Best Bed & Breakfasts
PO Box 563, Kamuela, HI 96743
Tel: 885-4550
Toll free: 800-262 9912.

Price Categories

$$$$$	=	US$200 and up
$$$$	=	US$150–US$200
$$$	=	US$100–US$150
$$	=	US$50–US$100
$	=	below US$50

Hotels

The following listings are not
comprehensive and they do not
carry endorsements. An
establishment not listed –
especially in bed-and-breakfasts
and rental condominiums – could be
just as satisfactory as those listed.
For travelers wanting a more
inclusive and comprehensive
listing, telephone the **Hawaii
Visitors Bureau** on 923-1811 for a
current *Accommodations and Car
Rentals* guide or visit:
www.gohawaii.com.

Notes on Room Rates
It is difficult to give exact price
categories for hotels in Hawaii.
There are simply too many variables:
season, packages, corporate
discounts. Nobody pays a full rack
rate in Hawaii. Prices fluctuate with
the seasons and the type of
accommodation. An individual hotel
can have rooms ranging from $100
to $1,000.
   Our pricing notations – $ (budget)
to $$$$$ (luxurious) – are intended
only as a relative guide of a hotel's
cost compared to others. Bargains,
discounts, packages and seasonal

deals abound and should be
pursued through travel agents,
airlines or brokers.

OAHU

Hotels
$$$$$
Halekulani
2199 Kalia Road, Honolulu,
HI 96815-1988
Tel: 923-2311
Toll free: 800-367 2343
Fax: 926-8004.
Centrally located on Waikiki Beach,
quiet, crisply elegant, chic and
expensive, with stress on
personalized service; 456 rooms,
fitness center and beach service
center.
J.W. Marriott 'Ihilani Resort & Spa
92-1001 Olani Street, Kapolei,
HI 96707
Tel: 679-0079
Toll free: 800-626 4446
Fax: 679-0080.
Located in West Oahu at Ko Olina
Resort, about a 30-minute drive
from Honolulu International Airport.
'Ihilani has 387 rooms. Spa placed
third among world's best spas,
according to *Condé Nast Traveller*.
Area is quiet with a secluded beach
and lagoons adjacent to the hotel.
Spacious rooms with private roofed
verandas.
Royal Hawaiian Hotel
2259 Kalakaua Avenue, Honolulu,
HI 96815
Tel: 923-7311
Toll free: 800-325 3535
Fax: 924-7098.
The "Pink Palace of the Pacific" is a
landmark on Waikiki Beach with its
familiar coral-pink stucco and
Moorish-Spanish design. "Old
Hawaii" ambiance. Home of
Waikiki's only beachfront *lu'au*
(traditional feast). Steps away from
the Royal Hawaiian Shopping
Center.
Sheraton Moana Surfrider
2365 Kalakaua Avenue, Honolulu,
HI 96815
Tel: 922-3111
Toll free: 800-325 3535
Fax: 923-0308.

Built in 1901; still retains its nostalgic, early 20th-century ambiance and first-class service. Enjoy tea-time on the hotel's veranda surrounding a huge banyan tree.

$$$$

Hawaii Prince Hotel
100 Holomoana Street, Honolulu, HI 96815
Tel: 956-1111
Toll free: 800-321 OAHU
Fax: 946-0811.
Luxury hotel overlooking Ala Wai Yacht Harbor. Within walking distance of Ala Moana Center. 521 rooms, most with ocean views, in two towers. Gourmet American and Japanese dining; don't miss the great buffets.

Hilton Hawaiian Village
2005 Kalia Road, Honolulu, HI 96815
Tel: 949-4321
Toll free: 800-HILTONS
Fax: 951-5458.
Largest hotel in Hawaii with 2,970 rooms in five towers. Good for families; hotel includes penguin habitat, video arcade, children's programs. For business travelers, there are tele-conferencing services and a 24-hour business center. Also includes a shopping mall with designer boutiques. Friday night fireworks show.

Hyatt Regency Waikiki
2424 Kalakaua Avenue, Honolulu, HI 96815
Tel: 923-1234
Toll free: 800-233 1234
Fax: 926-3415.
Centrally located just across the street from Waikiki Beach. Large, 1,230-room hotel takes up an entire block along Waikiki's main street. Expansive lobby and shopping area.

Kahala Mandarin Oriental
5000 Kahala Avenue, Honolulu, HI 96816
Tel: 739-8888
Toll free: 800-367 2525
Fax: 739-8800.
This 370-room hotel (formerly the Kahala Hilton) is a 10-minute drive east of Waikiki. Tucked away in the upscale residential area of Wai'alae-

Kahala, it is especially valued for its secluded oceanfront location away from Waikiki. The dolphin lagoon is home to Atlantic bottlenose dolphins and tropical fish.

Turtle Bay Resort
57-091 Kamehameha Highway, Kahuku, HI 96731
Tel: 293-8811
Toll free: 800-203 3650
Fax: 293-9147.
Located on the North Shore of Oahu. This relaxing and quiet 485-room hotel with suites and cottages has many activities to choose from including golf, tennis, horseback riding. Great surfing spots nearby.

W Honolulu-Diamond Head Hotel
2885 Kalakaua Avenue, Honolulu, HI 96815
Tel: 924-3111
Toll free: 888-627 7816
Fax: 791-5110.
A 50-room hotel situated on the oceanside border of Kapiolani Park. Elegant and in a quiet setting within a short walk of central Waikiki. The service is first rate and personal; the rooms are nicely decorated.

$$$

Ala Moana Hotel
410 Atkinson Drive, Honolulu, HI 96814
Tel: 955-4811
Toll free: 800-367 6025
Fax: 944-2974.
Conveniently located next to Ala Moana Center, one of the largest open-air shopping malls in the world. Approximately a five-minute drive from Waikiki. Ala Moana Beach Park is just one block away. Rumours nightclub is popular with young *kama'aina* and visitors for dancing.

'Ilikai Renaissance Waikiki Hotel
1777 Ala Moana Boulevard, Honolulu, HI 96815
Tel: 949-3811
Toll free: 800-245 4524
Fax: 947-4523.
A 10-minute walk from Ala Moana Shopping Center, on the outskirts of Waikiki. Overlooks the Ala Wai Yacht Harbor. The 800-room complex includes hotel rooms and condominium rentals. Its tennis courts and golf practice range are

unique for Waikiki. Many dining options in and around the hotel.

Marriott Waikiki Beach Resort
2552 Kalakaua Avenue, Honolulu, HI 96815
Tel: 922-6611
Toll free: 800-367 5370
Fax: 921-5255.
Across the street from Waikiki Beach. Large complex with 1,346 rooms and a mall of shops. Renovated in 2001–2002.

New Otani Kaimana Beach Hotel
2863 Kalakaua Avenue, Honolulu, HI 96815
Tel: 923-1555
Toll free: 800-356 8264
Fax: 922-9404.
Oceanfront on Sans Souci Beach, at the foot of Diamond Head in Waikiki. Relatively small with just 125 rooms. Hau Tree Lanai restaurant has stunning ocean and sunset view. Close to Kapi'olani Park, Waikiki Aquarium and Honolulu Zoo.

Outrigger Waikiki Hotel
2335 Kalakaua Avenue, Honolulu, HI 96815
Tel: 923-0711
Toll free: 800-688 7444
Fax: 921-9749.
Located on the beach at Waikiki. This 530-room hotel is the best known of the Outriggers on Oahu. The 600-seat showroom features the Society of Seven, a popular local band. Check out the good food and contemporary Hawaiian music at Duke's Canoe Club.

Pacific Beach Hotel
2490 Kalakaua Avenue, Honolulu, HI 96815
Tel: 923-4511
Toll free: 800-367 6060
Fax: 922-0129.
Two towers with 831 rooms. Located in Waikiki, across from the beach. The centerpiece of hotel is a spectacular 3-story, 280,000-gallon

Price Categories

$$$$$	=	US$200 and up
$$$$	=	US$150–US$200
$$$	=	US$100–US$150
$$	=	US$50–US$100
$	=	below US$50

indoor oceanarium tank filled with stingrays, angel fish and other marine life, which is visible from the hotel's three restaurants.

Sheraton Waikiki
2255 Kalakaua Avenue, Honolulu, HI 96815
Tel: 922-4422
Toll free: 800-325 3535
Fax: 922-7708.
Large hotel with 1,852 rooms, many with perfect Diamond Head views. Take the glass elevator to the Hanohano Room for fine dining and spectacular views of Waikiki. Lovely beachfront location.

Waikiki Beachcomber Hotel
2300 Kalakaua Avenue, Honolulu, HI 96815
Tel: 922-4646
Toll free: 800-622 4646
Fax: 923-4889.
Great central location. Shopping at International Marketplace and Royal Hawaiian Shopping Center nearby. Home of the legendary Don Ho show.

Waikiki Parc Hotel
2233 Helumoa Road, Honolulu, HI 96815
Tel: 921-7272
Toll free: 800-422 0450
Fax: 923-1336.
Relatively small for a Waikiki hotel with 298 rooms. Affordable sister hotel to Halekulani, which is located across the street on Waikiki Beach.

$$
Best Western Plaza Airport Hotel
3253 N. Nimitz Highway, Honolulu, HI 96819
Tel: 836-3636
Toll free: 800-800 4683
Fax: 834-7406.
A 274-room hotel near the Honolulu International Airport. Primarily used by business travelers, and visitors with late-night or early-morning flights.

Manoa Valley Inn
2001 Vancouver Drive, Honolulu, HI 96822
Tel: 947-6019
Fax: 946-6168.
Eight-room country-style inn. Located in a residential neighborhood, close to the

University of Hawaii at Manoa. Victorian inn filled with antique furniture. Built in 1912 and listed in the National Register of Historic Places.

Outrigger Islander Waikiki
270 Lewers Street, Honolulu, Hawaii, HI 96815
Tel: 923-7711
Toll free: 800-688 7444
Fax: 924-5755.
A very convenient and well-priced hotel located within an elevator-ride of shops and restaurants. Pleasant rooms with up-to-date decor add to the hotel's appeal.

Pagoda Hotel & Terrace
1525 Rycroft Street, Honolulu, HI 96814
Tel: 923-4511
Toll free: 800-367 6060
Fax: 955-5067.
A 362-room hotel with affordable rates. Very popular with residents traveling inter-island. A five-minute drive from Ala Moana Center, it is set amidst high-rise apartment buildings and strip malls. The Pagoda restaurant is surrounded by ponds filled with large, colorful *koi*.

Queen Kapi'olani Hotel
150 Kapahulu Avenue, Honolulu, HI 96815
Tel: 922-1941
Toll free: 800-367 2317
Fax: 922-2694.
This 315-room hotel is located at the Diamond Head end of Waikiki. Across the street is Kapi'olani Park and the Honolulu Zoo. Basic accommodations. Within walking distance of Waikiki Beach.

Royal Garden at Waikiki
440 Olohana Street, Honolulu, HI 96815
Tel: 943-0202
Toll free: 800-367 5666
Fax: 946-8777.
Located several blocks *mauka* of Waikiki Beach. Elegant surroundings and friendly staff. Mediterranean and Japanese dining available.

Waikiki Joy Hotel
320 Lewers Street, Honolulu, HI 96815
Tel: 923-2300
Toll free: 800-922 7866
Fax: 924-4010.

This 93-room boutique hotel is located on a side street in Waikiki. Karaoke studio; shops, restaurants and movie theaters nearby.

Condominiums
$$$$
Aston Waikiki Beach Tower
2470 Kalakaua Avenue, Honolulu, HI 96815
Tel: 926-6400
Toll free: 800-922 7866
Fax: 926-7380.
Luxurious and spacious 140-suite hotel with four suites per floor. Paddle tennis court on property.

$$$
Aston at the Waikiki Banyan
201 'Ohua Avenue, Honolulu, HI 96815
Tel: 922-0555
Toll free: 800-922 7866
Fax: 922-0609.
Located on Diamond Head side of Waikiki. Pleasant family resort, one block from the beach. Children's playground, tennis courts and barbecue area.

Outrigger at the Waikiki Shore
2161 Kalia Road, Honolulu, HI, 96815
Tel: 952-4500
Toll free: 800-367 2353
Fax: 808-971 4580.
The only condominium resort located on Waikiki Beach. Roomy studios fitted with air-conditioning.

HAWAII (BIG ISLAND)

Hotels
$$$$$
Four Seasons Resort at Hualalai
PO Box 1269, Kailua-Kona, HI 96745
Tel: 325-8000
Toll free: 888-340 5662
Fax: 325-8100.
Located on 625 acres (253 hectares) on the Kohala Coast, just a seven-minute drive from Keahole-Kona Airport. Thirty-six low-rise ocean-view bungalows house 243 rooms and suites. Serene, intimate atmosphere.

Informative exhibits are on view at the resort's Hawaiian Interpretive Center. Natural anchialine ponds and oceanfront pools, plus a championship golf course carved out of lava rock.

Kona Village Resort
PO Box 1299, Kailua-Kona,
HI 96745
Tel: 325-5555
Toll free: 800-367 5290
Fax: 325-5124.
On the beach at Ka'upulehu, just 5 miles (8 km) north of the airport. Unique resort with 125 individual thatched *hale* (huts or bungalows). Oceanfront units are the ultimate in romance. Pure bliss for visitors seeking a total escape from reality (there's no in-room TV, radio or telephone).

Mauna Kea Beach Hotel
1 Mauna Kea Beach Drive,
Kamuela, HI 96743
Tel: 882-7222
Toll free: 800-882 6060
Fax: 882-5700.
Kohala Coast landmark. The hotel's look and Hawaiian-style atmosphere were enhanced by a 1995 facelift. With 314 units, a great beach for lounging, swimming and snorkeling. Also has golfing facilities.

Mauna Lani Bay Hotel & Bungalows
68-1400 Mauna Lani Drive, Kohala Coast, HI 96743
Tel: 885-6622
Toll free: 800-367 2323
Fax: 885-1484.
This 350-unit, beachfront full-service resort scores highly for its elegant-yet-comfortable ambiance and is located conveniently near a golf course. Hosts the annual "Cuisines of the Sun," a food symposium spotlighting cuisines from sunny climates.

The Orchid at Mauna Lani
One North Kaniku Drive,
Kohala Coast, HI 96743
Tel: 885-2000
Toll free 800-845 9905
Fax: 885-1064.
A wonderfully elegant 537-unit hotel with a great beach and spacious rooms that reveal a Ritz-Carlton pedigree. The Hawaiian program is a plus.

$$$$
Hapuna Beach Prince Hotel
62-100 Kauna'oa Drive, Kohala,
HI 96743
Tel: 880-1111
Toll free: 800-882 6060
Fax: 880-3112.
With 350 units, this oceanfront resort is a half-hour's drive from the Keahole-Kona Airport. Younger sibling property of the Mauna Kea Beach Hotel. Full-service resort with upscale amenities and fine service. Great golf course nearby.

Hilton Waikoloa Village
425 Waikoloa Beach Drive,
Waikoloa, HI 96743
Tel: 885-1234
Toll free: 800-445 8667
Fax: 886-2900.
Formerly the Hyatt Regency Waikoloa, this 1,238-room resort (a 30-minute drive from the airport) is an expansive Hawaiian playground with championship golf, fabulous frolicking dolphins and wall-to-wall extravagance.

$$$
Hale Ohia
PO Box 758, Volcano, HI 96785
Tel: 967-7986
Toll free: 800-455 3803
Fax: 967-8610.
This 8-unit bed-and-breakfast includes rooms in the vintage 1930's main house as well as adjacent cottages.

King Kamehameha's Kona Beach Hotel
75-5660 Palani Road, Kailua-Kona,
HI 96740
Tel: 329-2911
Toll free: 800-367 6060
Fax: 329-4602.
Full-service, 460-unit hotel. Slightly dated but on an historic site and conveniently situated by Kona's beach and pier.

Royal Kona Resort
75-5852 Ali'i Drive, Kailua-Kona,
Hi 96740
Tel: 329-3111
Toll free: 800-22 ALOHA
Fax: 329-9532.
Formerly the Kona Hilton, this 452-room hotel is within easy walking distance of Kailua-Kona town. It overlooks Kailua Bay.

Outrigger Waikoloa Beach
69-275 Waikoloa Beach Drive,
Waikoloa, HI 96738
Tel: 886-6789
Toll free: 800-688 7444
Fax: 886-7852.
A 20-minute drive from Keahole Kona Airport. Most rooms have ocean views. The hotel is bordered by royal fishpond and beach. Frequent Hawaiian arts and crafts demonstrations.

$$
Hawaii Naniloa Hotel
93 Banyan Drive, Hilo, HI 96720
Tel: 969-3333
Toll free: 800-367 5360
Fax: 969-6622.
Located at Hilo Bay, just a few minutes from Hilo Airport and adjacent to a popular nine-hole golf course; 325 units with a pleasant atmosphere and great bay views.

Hilo Hawaiian Hotel
71 Banyan Drive, Hilo, HI 96720
Tel: 935-9361
Toll free: 800-272 5275
Fax: 961-9642.
Bayside 290-unit hotel. Spectacular views and friendly kama'aina service. Home of Hilo's best buffet.

Holualoa Inn
76-5932 Mamalahoa Highway,
Holualoa, HI 96725
Tel: 324-1121
Toll free: 800-392 1812
Fax: 322-2472.
Quaint, 6-unit country inn located just a few minutes from Kailua-Kona. Tranquil atmosphere. Great for rest and relaxation.

Kamuela Inn
65-1300 Kawaihae Road, Kamuela,
HI 96743
Tel: 885-4243
Toll free: 800-555 8968
Fax: 885-8857.
Unassuming 31-unit inn set in the rolling paniolo countryside of Kamuela (also known as Waimea).

Kilauea Lodge
PO Box 116, Volcano, HI 96785
Tel: (866) 967-7366
Fax: 967-7366.
A cozy 13-unit lodge set in Volcano, near the southeast portion of the Island.

Ohana Keauhou Beach Hotel
78-6740 Ali'i Drive, Kailua-Kona,
HI 96740
Tel: 322-3441
Toll free: 800-462 6262
Fax: 322-3117.
Oceanfront hotel with 310 units on
Kailua-Kona's main artery. Features
nightly buffets with friendly service.

Uncle Billy's Hilo Bay Hotel
87 Banyan Drive, Hilo, HI 96720
Tel: 961-5818
Toll free: 800-367 5102
Fax: 935-7903.
On the waterfront at Hilo Bay.
Gracious hospitality. Free hula show
nightly.

Uncle Billy's Kona Bay Hotel
75-5739 Ali'i Drive, Kailua-Kona,
HI 96740
Tel: 961-5818
Toll free: 800-367 5102
Fax: 329-9210.
In the heart of Kailua-Kona, across
from Kailua Bay. Friendly, casual
atmosphere.

Volcano House
PO Box 53, Hawaii Volcanoes
National Park, HI 96718
Tel: 967-7321
Fax: 967-8429.
Valued for its location inside the
Hawaii Volcanoes National Park near
Kilauea. Small and cozy place to
stay. Has 42 rooms.

$
Manago Hotel
PO Box 145, Captain Cook-Kona,
HI 96704
Tel: 323-2642
Fax: 323-3451.
Family-run hostel located in Captain
Cook. Small hotel with 64 rooms.

Condominiums
$$$$
The Shores at Waikoloa
69-1035 Keana Place, Waikoloa,
HI 96743
Tel: 886-5001
Toll free: 800-922 7866
Fax: 886-8414.
Luxury condominium resort on
Kohala Coast. Next to Waikoloa Golf
Club's famed Beach Course. Well-
appointed suites with gourmet
kitchens.

Price Categories

$$$$$	=	US$200 and up
$$$$	=	US$150–US$200
$$$	=	US$100–US$150
$$	=	US$50–US$100
$	=	below US$50

$$$
Kanaloa at Kona
78-261 Manukai Street, Kailua-
Kona, HI 96740
Tel: 322-9625
Toll free: 800-688 7444
Fax: 322-3818.
Oceanfront condominium bordered
by a championship golf course and
Heeia Bay. Elegantly furnished
suites with garden or ocean views.
Edward's at the Terrace is a popular
restaurant with a pleasant
atmosphere.

Kona by the Sea
75-6106 Ali'i Drive, Kailua-Kona,
HI 96740
Tel: 327-2300
Toll free: 800-922 7866
Fax: 327-2333.
Intimate oceanfront resort, just
south of Kailua-Kona town.
Comfortable rooms, each with a
private *lanai* (roofed balcony).

$$
Outrigger Royal Sea Cliff Resort
75-6040 Ali'i Drive, Kailua-Kona,
HI 96740
Tel: 329-8021
Toll free: 800-688 7444
Fax: 326-1887.
Relaxed, oceanfront, garden setting
on the Kohala Coast. With 148 one-
and two-bedroom studios with
complete kitchens and spacious
lanais. Tennis courts and pools.

KAUAI

Hotels
$$$$$
Hyatt Regency Kauai
1571 Po'ipu Road, Koloa,
HI 96756
Tel: 742-1234
Toll free: 800-233 1234
Fax: 742-1557.

Large, 600-room hotel located on
the oceanfront in sunny Po'ipu. Early
20th-century ambience.

Princeville Resort
5520 Kahaku Road, Princeville,
HI 96722
Tel: 826-9644
Toll free: 800-826 1260
Fax: 826-1166.
Attractive and luxurious 252-room
property set on a cliff overlooking
Hanalei Bay. Excellent food,
wonderful views, great ambiance.
Worth the drive.

$$$$
Kauai Marriott Resort
Kalapaki Beach, Lihu'e, HI 96766
Tel: 245-5050
Toll free: 800-220 2925
Fax: 245-5049.
Set along Kalapaki Beach, fronting
Nawiliwili Bay. Located a mile from
Lihue Airport. Elegant 356-room
property within Kauai Lagoons
Resort.

$$$
Kauai Coconut Beach Resort
PO Box 830, Kapa'a, HI 96746
Tel: 822-3455
Toll free: 800-760 8555
Fax: 822-1830.
Great central location in Kapa'a.
Reasonably priced hotel offering a
full-range of resort services
including a nightly *lu'au* (traditional
feast) and torchlighting ceremony.

Radisson Kauai Beach
4331 Kauai Beach Drive, Lihu'e,
HI 96766
Tel: 245-1955
Toll free: 800-333 3333
Fax: 246-9085.
A 341-room beachfront hotel near
Wailua River, 4 miles (6 km) from
Lihue Airport. Secluded beach for
sunbathing.

Waimea Plantation Cottages
9400 Kaumuali'i Highway, Waimea,
HI 96796
Tel: 338-1625
Toll free: 800-9 WAIMEA
Fax: 338-2338.
Seaside cottages set amidst a 27-
acre (11-hectare) coconut grove just
outside Waimea. Renovated and
updated former homes of sugar

plantation workers. Perfect place to relax and unwind.

$$

Kauai Coast Beachboy Resort
4-484 Kuhio Highway, Kapa'a,
HI 96746
Tel: 822-3441
Toll free: 877-977 4355
Fax: 822-0843.
Centrally located. Adjacent to Coconut Marketplace, a popular open-air shopping mall. With 243-rooms in three low-rise buildings. Situated on Waipouli Beach.

Koloa Landing Cottages
2704B Ho'onani Road, Koloa,
HI 96756
Tel: 742-1470
Toll free: 800-779 8773.
Five comfy cottages including a studio. Lovely friendly and relaxed atmosphere.

Condominiums
$$$$

Kiahuna Plantation
2253 Po'ipu Road, Koloa,
HI 96756
Tel: 742-6411
Toll free: 800-688 7444
Fax: 742-1698.
Located on Po'ipu Beach. Laid-back ambiance. Plantation-style buildings. One- and two-bedroom units with full kitchens, ceiling fans and *lanai* (balconies). Across from Po'ipu Shopping Village. Minimum stay of 2 nights.

$$$

Embassy Vacation Resort
1613 Pe'e Road, Koloa, HI 96756
Tel: 742-1888
Toll free: 800-349 4720
Fax: 742-1924.
Luxury oceanfront condominium on Po'ipu Coast with 209 rooms. Tropical gardens and lily ponds on property. Facilities include a fitness center, sauna, steam room and two hydrospas.

Hanalei Colony Resort
PO Box 206, Hanalei, HI 96714
Tel: 826-6235
Toll free: 800-628 3004
Fax: 826-9893.
Located on the beach in Ha'ena in

northern Kauai. Comfy two-bedroom units with views of Hanalei Bay or mountains. Low-rise property. Close to Na Pali Coast. No TVs, stereos or phones in room.

$$

Aston Kaha Lani
4460 Nehe Road, Lihu'e, HI 96766
Tel: 822-9331
Toll free: 800-922 7866
Fax: 822-2828.
On the beach. Roomy one-, two- and three-bedroom suites. Next to Wailua Golf Course and Lydgate Park.

Lae Nani
410 Papaloa Road, Kapa'a,
HI 96746
Tel: 822-4938
Toll free: 800-688 7444
Fax: 822-1022.
A five-minute drive from Wailua Falls, this is a 70-unit beachfront property on Kauai's east shore within walking distance of Coconut Marketplace. Self-guided tours of nearby oceanside *heiau* (temples).

Nihi Kai Villas
1870 Hoone Road, Po'ipu,
HI 96756
Tel: 742-7220
Toll free: 800-742 1412
Fax: 742-8612.
Across Brennecke's Beach in Po'ipu. Intimate, tropical condominium resort. Minimum stay of 3 nights.

Po'ipu Kapili
2221 Kapili Road, Koloa, HI 96756
Tel: 742-6449
Toll free: 800-443 7714
Fax: 742-9162.
Located in popular Po'ipu Beach Resort community. Spacious with magnificent ocean views. Features 60 luxury oceanfront units. Also equipped with Championship tennis courts. Visitors must stay for a minimum of 3 nights.

Price Categories

$$$$$	=	US$200 and up
$$$$	=	US$150–US$200
$$$	=	US$100–US$150
$$	=	US$50–US$100
$	=	below US$50

MAUI

Hotels
$$$$$

Four Seasons Wailea
3900 Wailea Alanui, Wailea,
HI 96753
Tel: 874-8000
Toll free: 800-334 MAUI
Fax: 874-2222.
Located in Wailea on one of the most beautiful beaches in Maui. Most rooms have ocean views. Elegant furnishings. Tranquil surroundings with gardens, waterfalls, fountains and pools.

Grand Wailea Resort
3850 Wailea Alanui Drive, Wailea,
HI 96753
Tel: 875-1234
Toll free: 800-888 6100
Fax: 874-2442.
With 737 ocean-view suites and a 2,000-ft (610-meter) water feature with slides, waterfalls, caves and grottoes. The Spa Grande at the Grand Wailea is one of the largest hotel spas in the nation with water therapies, *lomi lomi* massage (traditional Hawaiian) and various other beauty and body treatments.

Hotel Hana-Maui
PO Box 9, Hana, HI 96713
Tel: 248-8211
Toll free: 800-321 HANA
Fax: 248-7202.
Intimate, secluded, 96-unit hotel located in Hana surrounded by ranch land. Warm, friendly staff.

Kapalua Bay Hotel
One Bay Drive, Kapalua, HI 96761
Tel: 669-5656
Toll free: 800-367 8000
Fax: 669-4690.
Located in Kapalua on Maui's northwest shore. Low-key elegance with 194 plantation-style rooms and 15 villas with views of Molokai and Lanai. Lovely beach.

Ritz-Carlton
One Ritz-Carlton Drive, Kapalua,
HI 96761
Tel: 669-6200
Toll free: 800-262 8440
Fax: 665-0026.
This 37-acre (15 hectare) lush, oceanfront resort located on Maui's northwest shore has 548

rooms with spacious *lanais* (balconies). With a 143-seat amphitheater, large air-conditioned fitness center and spa. Hiking and nature programs available to guests on request.

$$$$
Embassy Suites
104 Ka'anapali Shores Place, Lahaina, HI 96761
Tel: 661-2000
Toll free: (800) GO-2-MAUI
Fax: 667-5821.
A 413 unit, all-suite hotel located in Ka'anapali. Miniature 18-hole golf course on hotel rooftop. Swimming pool with water slide and complete fitness center.

Hyatt Regency Maui
200 Nohea Kai Drive, Ka'anapali, HI 96761
Tel: 661-1234
Toll free: (800) 233-1234
Fax: 667-4714.
An 815-room oceanfront resort in Ka'anapali. Collection of exotic and tropical birds and penguins. Spectacular "Drums of the Pacific" *lu'au* (traditional feast).

Kea Lani Hotel & Villas
4100 Wailea Alanui Drive, Wailea, HI 96753
Tel: 875-4100
Toll free: (800) 882-4100
Fax: 875-1200.
Oceanside in Wailea. A 450-suite luxury resort with striking Moorish design. Beautiful landscaping. Spacious and luxurious suites and villas.

Maui Marriott Resort
100 Nohea Kai Drive, Lahaina, HI 96761
Tel: 667-1200
Toll free: 800-763 1333
Fax: 667-8192.
720 units with large rooms, located in Lahaina. Tropical gardens, *koi* ponds, fountains and waterfalls. Tennis courts and a beach activities center.

Maui Prince Hotel
5400 Makena Alanui, Kihei, HI 96753
Tel: 874-1111
Toll free: 800-321 MAUI
Fax: 879-8763.

Located near Makena Beach, south of Wailea. Set apart from the other resorts in Kihei. Scenic views of neighboring islands.

Outrigger Wailea Resort
3700 Wailea Alanui, Wailea, HI 96753
Tel: 879-1922
Toll free: 800-367 2960
Fax: 875-4878.
Located oceanfront at Wailea. Spacious rooms with private *lanais* (balconies). Grounds contain lush, tropical foliage.

Renaissance Wailea Beach
3550 Wailea Alanui Drive, Wailea, HI 96753
Tel: 879-4900
Toll free: 800-992 4532
Fax: 879-6128.
Luxury hotel on pristine Mokapu Beach in Wailea with a tropical, airy feel. Elegant 347-room resort. Many recreational amenities including fitness center, two fresh-water swimming pools, basketball court, shuffle board (point-scoring Hawaiian game), ping pong and beach activity center. There are tennis and golf facilities located nearby.

Sheraton Maui
2605 Ka'anapali Parkway, Lahaina, HI 96761
Tel: 661-0031
Toll free: 888-625 4988
Fax: 661-0458.
Reopened in late 1996 after a two-year, $150 million redevelopment. Low-rise buildings with 492 guest rooms. Focal point of hotel is a 142-yard freshwater swimming lagoon. Nightly torchlighting and cliff diving ceremony. Within walking distance of Whalers Village Shopping Center.

Westin Maui
2365 Ka'anapali Parkway, Lahaina, HI 96761
Tel: 667-2525
Toll free: 800- WESTIN 1
Fax: 661-5831.
Located along the Ka'anapali coast, this 761-unit hotel has Asian influences and artwork throughout. Beautiful landscape with many waterfalls and lagoons.

$$$
Diamond Resort
555 Kaukahi Street, Wailea, HI 96753
Tel: 874-0500
Toll free: 800-800 0720
Fax: 874-8778.
Nestled on the slopes of Haleakala with panoramic views of Wailea beaches, Haleakala or Wailea golf courses. With 72 one-bedroom suites in 18 two-story buildings. Quiet and secluded.

Ka'anapali Beach Hotel
2525 Ka'anapali Parkway, Lahaina, HI 96761
Tel: 661-0011
Toll free: 800-262 8450
Fax: 667-5978.
Adjacent to Ka'anapali golf courses and Whalers Village Shopping Center. A 423-room oceanfront hotel on the beach at Ka'anapali. Comfortable, airy rooms with private *lanais*. Hawaiian arts and crafts classes and demonstrations.

Royal Lahaina Resort
2780 Keka'a Drive, Lahaina, HI 96761
Tel: 661-3611
Toll free: 800-447 6925
Fax: 661-6150.
On the beach at Ka'anapali, a 592-room resort adjacent to Ka'anapali's North and South golf courses. Quaint wedding gazebo in courtyard.

$$
Kula Lodge (cottages)
RR 1, Box 475, Kula, HI 96790
Tel: 878-2517
Toll free: 800-233 1535
Fax: 878-2518.
Located in lush, rural Upcountry Maui. Five units in two cozy wooden cabins surrounded by forest. No phones or televisions in rooms. Be prepared for cool nights.

Lahaina Inn
127 Lahainaluna Road, Lahaina, HI 96761
Tel: 661-0577
Toll free: 800-669 3444
Fax: 667-9480.
Downtown Lahaina, near waterfront. Restored 1860s boutique hotel located off Front Street in Lahaina.

Twelve-room property with antique furnishings.

Maui Lu Resort
575 S. Kihei Road, Kihei, HI 96753
Tel: 879-5881
Toll free: 800-922 7866
Fax: 879-4627.
Affordable units situated on 28 lush oceanfront acres (11 hectares) with private beach coves. Operated by Aston Hotels and Resorts.

Silver Cloud Ranch
RRII Box 201, Kula, HI 96790
Tel: 878-6101
Toll free: 800-532 1111
Fax: 878-2132.
The setting says it all – spectacular views and a pleasant ranch-style inn. Breakfast served but no other on-property meals,

Condominium Rentals
$$$$
Ka'anapali Ali'i
50 Nohea Kai Drive, Ka'anapali, HI 96761
Tel: 661-3339
Toll free: 800-642 6284
Fax: 667-1145.
With 264 units in four buildings, 209 of which are for rental. Condominum resort in the middle of Ka'anapali's resort hotels. Tennis courts plus exercise/weight room on property.

$$$
The Whaler on Ka'anapali Beach
2481 Ka'anapali Parkway, Lahaina, HI 96761
Tel: 661-4861
Toll free: 800-922 7866
Fax: 661-8315.
Located on Ka'anapali Beach next to Whalers Village Shopping Center and 36-hole Ka'anapali Golf Courses. There are 360 units with ocean and garden views.

$$
Aston Ka'anapali Shores
3445 Honoapi'ilani Highway, Lahaina, HI 96761
Tel: 667-2211
Toll free: 800-922 7866
Fax: 661-0836.
Oceanfront, 463-room condominium resort on the north end of Ka'anapali Beach.

Kamaole Sands
2695 S. Kihei Road, Kihei, HI 96753
Tel: 874-8700
Fax: 879-3273.
Located at the foot of Haleakala, across the street from Kihei Beach, with 315 condominium units. Tennis and pool on property. Golf nearby.

Mana Kai Maui Resort
2960 S. Kihei Road, Kihei, HI 96753
Tel: 879-1561
Toll free: 800-367 5242
Fax: 874-5042.
Located on the beach in Kihei. Modest 126-unit accommodation with great ocean views.

MOLOKAI & LANAI

$$$$$
The Lodge at Ko'ele
PO Box 630310, Lanai City, HI 96763
Tel: 565-3800
Toll free: 800-321 4666
Fax: 565-3868.
Cool mountain retreat in the uplands of Lanai. This 102-room country estate-like hotel is surrounded by pine trees. The hotel's Formal Dining Room is superb. Activities include horseback riding, tennis, golf and Lanai Pine Sporting Clays.

Manele Bay Hotel
PO Box 630310, Lanai City, HI 96763
Tel: 565-3800
Toll free: 800-321 4666.
Set on a cliff overlooking pristine Hulopo'e Bay. Views of the ocean and the island of Maui. Amenities include health club, tennis courts, beach and a pool.

$$$$
Molokai Ranch & Lodge
PO Box 259, Maunaloa, HI 96770
Tel: 531-0158
Toll free: 800-877 PANIOLO
Fax: 534-1606.
This 54,000-acre (21,850-hectare) working cattle ranch has a luxurious 22-room lodge. Great for both adventure holidays and romantic

getaways, the Molokai Ranch offers a blend of white-sand beaches, dramatic cliffs and lush, green valleys.

$$$
Ke Nani Kai
PO Box 289, Maunaloa, HI 96770
Tel: 552-2761
Toll free: 800-535 0085
Fax: 800-633 5085.
Property surrounded by Kaluakoi golf course. A few minutes away from secluded beach. Of the 120 units, 35 are available to rent. Facilities include parking, TV, swimming pool, tennis court, golf, jacuzzi; minimum stay of 2 nights.

Price Categories

$$$$$	=	US$200 and up
$$$$	=	US$150–US$200
$$$	=	US$100–US$150
$$	=	US$50–US$100
$	=	below US$50

Camping

Campgrounds are run by the National Park Service, the State of Hawaii, and the four island counties. Plan outings ahead of time, as campsites are usually very popular. Conditions and rates vary, so refer to current maps, brochures and proper agencies for information.

Haleakala National Park
Haleakala National Park
PO Box 369, Makawao, HI 96768
Tel: 572-9306.
Haleakala weather forecast
Tel: 877-5111.

There are two drive-in campgrounds near the summit, and one in Kipahulu, at 'Ohe'o Pools near Hana. For the two near the summit, permits are required and are issued on arrival at the park. Sites are first-come, first-served. In Haleakala basin itself, there are three cabins available, accessible by hiking and assigned by lottery reservations. It is recommended that applications are made three months in advance.

Hawaii Volcanoes National Park
Hawaii Volcanoes National Park
PO Box 52, Hawaii Volcanoes
National Park, HI 96718
Tel: 985-6000.

There are three drive-in
campgrounds. Permits are not
required, as the sites operate on a
first-come, first-served basis. There
are also privately operated cabins,
which are rustic, utilitarian and
without windows, available at
inflated prices at the Namakani
Paio campground; arrangements
and payment of the fee should be
made at the Volcano House hotel, in
the park. Bedding is provided.

STATE PARKS

There are more than 60 state parks
throughout Hawaii. Some are well
developed, others are primitive and
rustic; many are true gems. Many
have simple cabins available for
rent. Permits are required but there
are no fees for camping.

Camping permits, Ohau, tel: 587-
0300; City & County of Honolulu,
tel: 523-4527.
Hiking, tel: 587-0166.
Fishing licenses, tel: 587-0109.

Regional Offices
Big Island
Department of Land and Natural
Resources, Division of State Parks,
PO Box 936, Hilo, HI 96720
Tel: 974-6200.
Kauai
Department of Land and Natural
Resources, Division of State Parks,
3060 Eiwa, #306, Lihu'e, HI 96766
Tel: 274-3444; Koke'e State Park
(cabins), Manager, Koke'e Lodge,
PO Box 819, Waimea, HI 96796
Tel: 335-8405.
Maui (includes Molokai)
Department of Land and Natural
Resources, Division of State Parks,
54 High Street, Wailuku, HI 96793
Tel: 984-8109.
Oahu
Department of Land and Natural
Resources, Division of State Parks,

1151 Punchbowl, Honolulu, HI
96813
Tel: 587-0300.

COUNTY PARKS

Hawaii (Big Island)
Department of Parks and
Recreation, 25 Aupuni Street, Hilo,
Hawaii 96720
Tel: 961-8311.
13 county beach parks plus tent and
vehicle camping. Both permits and
fees are required.
Honolulu/Oahu
Department of Parks and
Recreation, 650 S. King Street,
Honolulu, HI 96813
Tel: 523-4525.
13 beach parks, tent and vehicle
camping. Permits required, no fee.
Kauai
Department of Parks and
Recreation, 4444 Rice, Suite 150,
Lihu'e, HI 96766
Tel: 241-6660.
Seven county parks, both beach and
inland. Permits and fees are
required.
Maui (including Molokai)
Department of Parks and
Recreation, 1580 Ka'ahumanu
Avenue, Wailuku, HI 96793
Tel: 270-7389.
One county park, situated inland.
Permits and fees are required. On
Molokai: seven parks, permits and
fees are required.

Where to Eat

How to Choose

Forget all about dieting while in
Hawaii. There are simply far too many
good restaurants on the islands to
pass up the chance of a meal here.
   One problem in describing
Hawaii's restaurants – and in effect
it's a delightful problem – is that
chefs here enjoy experimenting,
adding a little Asian to Continental,
or Italian to Pacific. The results are
excellent, including the popular
"Pacific Rim" cuisine that has gained
international respect. So, when you
go to an Italian restaurant in Hawaii,
you might find touches of Asian
cuisine; likewise, in a Continental
restaurant, embellishments from the
Pacific region are likely.

The Lu'au
A unique form of Hawaiian nightlife
that generally begins at sundown is
the *lu'au*, traditionally a feast, a
celebration of life. There is a wide
range of *lu'au* offerings and styles,
from the Hollywood-tinsel
"Polynesian" revue with the
requisite drums, fire dancers, and
shimmering hula dancers, to some
quite authentic presentations,
mostly on the neighbor islands.
Whatever type you choose, it's
usually worth the $50 or so per
person, which includes copious
amounts of food and a satisfying
show of varying authenticity.
   Check with your hotel for the
nearest *lu'au* options. Several
hotels also hold nearly authentic
lu'au themselves.
   The listing below is intended to
make the traveler's transition to
island life a little easier, but it is
anything but comprehensive.
Exclusion from this list indicates

nothing about an establishment's quality or cuisine; there are simply too many restaurants to list. For a more comprehensive listing, a copy of the Hawaii Visitors and Convention Bureau Entertainment and Dining Guide includes everything from *lu'aus* to fast-food joints.

These price listings are broad guides for relative costs of an average meal and have nothing to do with subjective evaluations of quality or menu offerings. Breakfast: B; lunch: L; dinner: D.

Price Categories

$$$ = more than US$50
$$ = US$25 to US$45
$ = less than US$25

Oahu

$$$

Alan Wong's Restaurant
1857 S. King Street (3rd flr), Honolulu
Tel: 949-2526.
A Honolulu hot spot for Hawaiian Regional Cuisine. D

Chef Mavro
1969 S. King Street, Honolulu
Tel: 944-4714.
Contemporary elegance and the masterful French-Hawaiian culinary artistry of chef George Mavrothalassitis make this one of Hawaii's best restaurants. LD

Hoku's, Kahala Mandarin Oriental Hawaii
Tel: 739-8888.
Quiet setting with an appealing contemporary elegance. The fusion cuisine is deliciously prepared and beautifully presented. D

$$

Chai's
Aloha Tower Marketplace, Honolulu
Tel: 585-0011.
Lovely flowery setting with great melt-in-the-mouth fusion foods and a Thai twist.

Compadres
Ward Centre, Honolulu
Tel: 591-8307.
Mexican. Popular and lively hangout. LD

Crouching Lion
51-666 Kamehameha Highway, North Shore
Tel: 237-8511.
Notable North Shore fixture, serving *kama'aina* before other customers. LD

Indigo
1121 Nu'uanu Avenue, Honolulu
Tel: 521-2900.
Downtown favorite offering Eurasian cuisine. LD

Keo's Thai Cuisine
2028 Kuhio Avenue
Tel: 951-9355.
Thai food in a lively setting. Popular with locals and celebrities. Another branch at Ward Centre. D

Legend Seafood
100 N. Beretania Street, Honolulu
Tel: 532-1868.
Bustling Chinese eatery specializing in dim sum. LD

Roy's Restaurant
6600 Kalaniana'ole Highway, Hawaii Kai
Tel: 396-7697.
Nouvelle cuisine with global flourishes. LD

Sam Choy's Diamond Head
449 Kapahulu Avenue, Kapahulu
Tel: 732-8645.
Hawaii Regional Cuisine in generous portions from the renowned chef. D

3660 On The Rise
3660 Wai'alae Avenue, Kahala
Tel: 737-1177.
Eurasian Pacific Rim. Popular, trendy eatery with pleasant ambiance. D

$

A Little Bit of Saigon
1160 Maunakea Street, Honolulu
Tel: 528-3663.
Vietnamese. A Chinatown favorite with a solid following. LD

Andy's (aka Manoa Health Market)
2904 E. Manoa Road, Honolulu, Manoa Valley
Tel: 988-6161.
Vegetarian. Family-run, simple seating with diverse menu, bakery. BL

Auntie Pasto's
559 Kapahulu Avenue, Honolulu
Tel: 739-2426.
Italian cuisine. Highly popular local eatery; no reservations, so expect a wait in line. LD

Eggs N Things
1911-B Kalakaua Avenue
Tel: 949-0820.
Old-time Honolulu diner that remains popular among locals. BL

Garden Cafe
Honolulu Academy of Arts, 900 S. Beretania Street, Honolulu
Tel: 532-8734.
Island cuisine. Pleasant, open-air spot for lunch. L

Irifune
563 Kapahulu Avenue
Tel: 737-1141.
Japanese cuisine. No-frills diner, but the food is excellent. LD

Jameson's by the Sea
Kamehameha Highway, Hale'iwa
Tel: 637-4336.
American. Great seafood, even better sunset views. BLD

Krung Thai
1028 Nu'uanu Avenue, Honolulu
Tel: 599-4803.
Superb Thai cuisine; this is one of downtown Honolulu's best-kept secrets. L

Makai Market
Ala Moana Shopping Center, Honolulu
Tel: 955-9517.
A lively, crowded food court offering a wide variety of ethnic foods. LD

Maple Garden
909 Isenberg Street, Honolulu
Tel: 941-6641.
Szechuan cuisine. A *kama'aina* favorite. LD

Maunakea Market Place
1120 Maunakea Street, Honolulu
Tel: 524-3409.
Chinatown marketplace lined with ethnic foods of all types. D

Ono Hawaiian Food
726 Kapahulu Avenue
Tel: 737-2275.
Tasty Hawaiian cuisine, reasonable prices. Very popular, so expect to wait in line. LD

Waikiki

$$$

Bali by the Sea
Hilton Hawaiian Village, 2005 Kalia Road, Waikiki
Tel: 941-BALI.
Continental. Open-air, upscale

restaurant with touches of both the Pacific and Asia on menu. BLD

Hanohano Room
Sheraton Waikiki, 2255 Kalakaua Avenue
Tel: 922-4422.
Elegant and classy establishment. BD

La Mer
Halekulani Hotel, 2199 Kalia Road
Tel: 923-2311.
French. Very upscale, with touches of the Pacific on the menu. Jacket required. D

$$

Caffélatte
339 Saratoga Road
Tel: 924-1414.
Italian. Family-run, small and classy; located at the quiet 'Ewa end of Waikiki. D

Ciao Mein
Hyatt Regency Waikiki, 2424 Kalakaua Avenue
Tel: 923-2426.
Chinese/Italian. An upscale blend of East and West. D

Duke's Canoe Club
Outrigger Waikiki Hotel, 2335 Kalakaua Avenue
Tel: 922-2268.
American. Casual and trendy steak-and-seafood place. BLD

Golden Dragon
Hilton Hawaiian Village, 2005 Kalia Road
Tel: 946-5336.
Award-winning upscale Cantonese cuisine. D

Hau Tree Lanai
New Otani Kaimana Beach Hotel, 2863 Kalakaua Avenue
Tel: 921-7066.
American. On the beach, outside the site where poet Robert Louis Stevenson once sat. Fabulous sunset views. BLD

Parc Cafe
Waikiki Parc Hotel, 2233 Helumoa Road
Tel: 931-6643.
Asian/Pacific. Changing gourmet buffets, quality entrées with unique offerings. BLD

Prince Court
Hawaii Prince Hotel, 100 Holomoana Street
Tel: 944-4494.

Regional. Emphasis on local ingredients, blending East and West. BLD

$

Arancino
255 Beach Walk
Tel: 923-5557.
Small hole-in-the-wall eatery. There may be lines but the Italian specialties are worth the wait. LD

Hawaii (Big Island)

$$$

CanoeHouse
Mauna Lani Bay Hotel and Bungalows, South Kohala
Tel: 885-6622.
Pacific Rim. Beautiful open-air views of the Pacific Ocean and Kohala sunset. D

Merriman's
Opelo Plaza, Highway 19, Waimea
Tel: 885-6822.
Regional. Renowned chef Peter Merriman's Hawaiian-and-Pacific menu. LD

Roussels
Waikoloa Village Golf Club
Tel: 883-9644.
French Creole. Good Cajun. LD

$$

Café Pesto
308 Kamehameha Avenue, Hilo
Tel: 969-6640.
Popular Italian café. Traditional and nouveau establishment. Another branch in Kohala, tel: 882-1071. LD

Edelweiss
Highway 19, Waimea
Tel: 885-6800.
Relaxed atmosphere, continental offerings. LD

Jameson's by the Sea
77-6452 Ali'i Drive, Kailua-Kona
Tel: 329-3195.
American. On the waterfront, with fresh local fish and salmon. LD

Kilauea Lodge
Old Volcano Road, Volcano Village
Tel: 967-7366.
Continental. Spacious country dining, casual but upscale. D

Sam Choy's
73-5576 Kauhola Street, Kailua-Kona
Tel: 326-1545.

Pacific Rim. Dishes up hearty, local-style fare from one of Hawaii's most popular chefs. BLD

$

Aloha Angel Cafe
Highway 11, Kainaliu
Tel: 322-3383.
Particularly diverse menu with terrace seating in an old theater building. BLD

Holuakoa Cafe
76-5901 Mamalahoa Highway. Holualoa (above Kailua-Kona)
Tel: 322-2233.
Easy-going espresso bar offering light, simple meals. BL

Manago Hotel
82-6155 Mamalahoa Highway, Captain Cook, Kona
Tel: 323-2642.
American. Casual fundamentals in family-run hotel. BLD

Reuben's
336 Kamehameha Avenue, Hilo
Tel: 961-2552.
Mexican. Family-run place just like down home. Immense servings. LD

Sibu Cafe
75-5695 Ali'i Drive, Kona
Tel: 329-1112.
Low-key, laid-back café, particularly well known for its tasty Indonesian variations. LD

Kauai

$$

A Pacific Cafe
4-831 Kuhio Highway, Suite 220, Kapa'a
Tel: 822-0013.
Asian, Pacific Rim. Upscale yet the ambiance is still easy-going. D

Brennecke's Beach Broiler
2100 Ho'one Road, Po'ipu
Tel: 742-7588.
American. Seriously casual, steak and seafood on the beach. LD

Cafe Hanalei
Princeville Hotel, Princeville, North Shore
Tel: 826-9644.
Contemporary establishment overlooking Hanalei Bay. Upscale but still casual. BLD

Casa di Amici
2301 Nalo Road, Poipu, Kilauea
Tel: 742-1555.

A real gem serving excellent Italian cuisine. LD

Gaylord's at Kilohana
3-2087 Kaumuali'i Highway, Puhi, near Lihu'e
Tel: 245-9593.
Continental eatery. Situated in a restored 1935 plantation estate. Outside seating. LD

Keoki's Paradise
Po'ipu Shopping Village, Po'ipu
Tel: 742-7534.
Polynesian-style setting. Particulary notable for its seafood dishes. LD

Plantation Gardens
2253 Po'ipu Road at Kiahuna Plantation, Koloa
Tel: 742-2216.
Provides award-winning Italian cuisine and a tropical ambiance. D

Roy's Po'ipu Bar & Grill
Po'ipu Shopping Village, Po'ipu
Tel: 742-5000.
Yet more creative morsels from chef extraordinaire, Roy Yamaguchi. D

$

Roadrunner Bakery and Cafe
2430 Oka Street, Kilauea
Tel: 828-8226.
Great salads and king-sized *burritos* highlight the menu of the Mexican café. The bakery serves some fabulous pastries. BLD

Sinaloa Mexican Restaurant
1-3959 Kaumuali'i Highway, Hanapepe
Tel: 335-0006.
Good solid Mexican food in old sugar town. LD

Maui

$$$

Gerard's
Plantation Inn, 174 Lahainaluna Road, Lahaina
Tel: 661-8939.
French. Sit outdoors or inside a restored plantation home. D

Pacific Grill
Four Seasons Resort, 3900 Wailea Alanui, Wailea
Tel: 874-8000.
Pacific Rim with Asian influences. BD

Seasons
Four Seasons Resort, 3900 Wailea Alanui, Wailea
Tel: 874-8000.

Pacific Rim cuisine with French flair. Classy and upscale. D

Swan Court
Hyatt Regency Maui, Ka'anapali
Tel: 667-4420.
Continental. Top 10 romantic restaurant, according to *Lifestyles of the Rich and Famous* (once-popular Hawaiian television program). BD

Price Categories

$$$	=	more than US$50
$$	=	US$25 to US$45
$	=	less than US$25

$$

A Pacific Cafe Maui
1279 S. Kihei Road, Kihei
Tel: 879-0069.
More superb menu offerings from Chef Jean-Marie Josselin. D

David Paul's Lahaina Grill
Lahaina Hotel, 127 Lahainaluna Road, Lahaina
Tel: 667-5117.
Pacific Rim. Part of restored historic Lahaina Hotel. Casual ambiance, sophisticated food. LD

Flames of Avalon Restaurant & Bar
844 Front Street, Lahaina
Tel: 667-5559.
Inventive Asian and Pacific cuisine. Outdoors in busy courtyard. LD

Hakone
Maui Prince Hotel, 5400 Makena Alanui, Makena/Wailea
Tel: 874-1111.
Japanese elegance with authentic food and ambiance. D

Hali'imaile General Store
900 Hali'imaile Road, Makawao
Tel: 572-2666.
Eclectic American food with Asian overtones. LD

Hula Moons
Outrigger Wailea Resort, Wailea
Tel: 879-1922.
Good food served in colorful Hawaiian-style atmosphere. LD

Longhi's
888 Front Street, Lahaina
Tel: 667-2286.
Continental. Popular spot for people-watching; sometimes a celebrity hangout. BLD

Mama's Fish House
799 Poho Place, on main highway near Pa'ia
Tel: 579-8488.
Seafood/Hawaiian. A local favorite overlooking the cove. LD

The Plantation House
2000 Plantation Club Drive, Kapalua
Tel: 669-6299.
Hawaiian-Mediterranean cuisine, specializing in seafood. Casual but elegant atmosphere; excellent views of the Kapalua area. BLD

Roy's Kahana Bar & Grill
4405 Honoapi'ilani Highway, Kahana
Tel: 669-6999.
Euro-Asian cuisine. D

Siam Thai Cuisine
123 North Market Street, Wailuku
Tel: 244-3817.
Thai. A long-time favorite, with basic diner ambiance. LD

$

Casanova Italian Restaurant and Deli
1188 Makawao Avenue, Makawao
Tel: 572-0220.
Italian. Popular local hangout; good for people-watching. LD

Cheeseburger in Paradise
811 Front Street, Lahaina
Tel: 661-4855.
American. Waterfront hangout with live music. LD

Saeng's Thai Cuisine
2119 Vineyard Street, Wailuku
Tel: 244-1567.
Thai. Pleasant and friendly garden setting. LD

Lanai

$$$

Dining Room
The Lodge at Ko'ele, Lanai City
Tel: 565-7300.
Chef Andrew Manion-Copley uses local produce to create a delicious and unusual menu. D

$$

Ko'ele Terrace
The Lodge at Ko'ele, Lanai City
Tel: 565-7300.
Outstanding Hawaiian regional cuisine shares the spotlight with tranquil garden views. BLD

Attractions

Options

Beyond peeking out at paradise from behind tinted tour bus windows, you can dip in and out of fantasy settings of your choice, choosing between glider, helicopter and small-propeller plane tours; off-shore dinner and sunset "booze" cruises; catamaran and glass-bottom boat rides; and even deep-sea fishing trips.

For more information about these tours and other places of interest, consult the numerous free visitors' publications available in Waikiki, the daily newspapers' entertainment and community calendar sections, or call the **Hawaii Visitors Bureau**, tel: 923-1811, or visit the website: www.gohawaii.com.

Honolulu and Environs

Aloha Tower, Pier 9 at Honolulu Harbor. Tenth-floor observation deck open Monday–Friday 9am–4pm, Saturday 9am–10pm, Sunday 9am–6pm. Free.
Battleship US Missouri. Tel: 455-1600. The latest addition to Pearl Harbor. Shuttle from Bowfen to Missouri. Open daily 8am–4.30pm. Admission fee.
Bishop Museum & Planetarium, 1525 Bernice Street, Kalihi. Tel: (museum) 847-3511. Open 9am–5pm daily except Christmas. Free. Planetarium Show at 11.30am, 1.30pm and 3.30pm daily; Friday and Saturday also at 7pm. Free.
Contemporary Museum, 2411 Makiki Heights Drive. Tel: 526-1322. Open Tuesday–Saturday 10am–4pm, Sunday noon–4pm. Admission fee.

Foster Botanic Garden, 180 N. Vineyard Boulevard (entrance on Vineyard Boulevard at Nu'uanu Stream). Tel: 522-7066. Open daily 9am–4pm. Admission fee.
Hawaii Maritime Center, Pier 7 downtown Honolulu, adjacent to Aloha Tower. Tel: 536-6373. Open daily 8.30am–5pm. Free for children under the age of 6.
Honolulu Academy of Arts, 900 S. Beretania Street, *mauka* of Thomas Square. Tel: 532-8701. Open Tuesday–Saturday 10am–4.30pm and Sunday 1–5pm, closed on Monday. Admission fee.
'Iolani Palace, S. King Street, across from the Kamehameha statue. Tel: 522-0832. This beautifully restored palace was completed by King Kalakaua in 1882. The 90-minute tour, open Tuesday–Saturday 8.30am–2pm, includes a visit to the palace and its exhibits such as Hawaii's crown jewels. Under 5s not admitted. Admission fee.
Mission Houses Museum, 553 S. King Street. Tel: 531-0481. Open Tuesday–Saturday 9am–4pm, Tours: 11am, 1pm, 2pm. Admission fee. Guided tours last about 45 minutes.
National Memorial Cemetery of the Pacific, in Punchbowl Crater, top of Puowaina Drive. Tel: 532-3720. Open September 30–March 1, 8am–5.30pm daily, March 2–September 29, 8am–6.30pm daily, Memorial Day 7am–7pm. Free.
Queen Emma Summer Palace, 2913 Pali Highway, Nu'uanu Valley. Tel: 595-3167. Open daily 9am–4pm. Admission fee.
Royal Mausoleum, 2261 Nu'uanu Avenue, Nu'uanu Valley. Tel: 536-7602. Open Monday–Friday 8am–4.30pm, closed holidays. Advance reservations requested for groups. Free.
USS Arizona Memorial, At Pearl Harbor, conducted by the National Park Service via US Navy-operated shuttle boats. Tel: 422-0561. Open daily, except on rainy or windy days. Free.

USS Bowfin Submarine Museum & Park, at Pearl Harbor, near Arizona Memorial. Tel: 423-1341. Open 8am–4.30pm daily. Admission fee.

In Waikiki

Honolulu Zoo, Diamond Head end of Kalakaua Avenue in the Kapi'olani Park complex. Tel: 971-7171. Open daily 9am–4.30pm. Admission fee.
Kapi'olani Park, at the foot of Diamond Head across from Queen's Surf Beach. The range of features includes a 1.8-mile (3-km) jogging course, soccer field, tennis courts, picnic tables, aquarium, amphitheater, zoo and bandstand.
Pleasant Hawaiian Hula Show, off Monsarrat Avenue near the Waikiki Shell Amphitheater. Tel: 843-8002. Shows Tuesday–Thursday at 10am. Free.
US Army Museum, Kalia Road, Fort DeRussy, near Diamond Head end of the Hilton Hawaiian Village. Tel: 438-2821. Open Tuesday–Sunday 10am–4.30pm. Free.
Waikiki Aquarium, 2777 Kalakaua Avenue, opposite Kapi'olani Park. Tel: 923-9741. Open 9am–5pm daily. Admission fee.

Elsewhere on Oahu

Byodo-In Temple, 47-200 Kahekili Highway, Windward Oahu. Tel: 239-8811. Open daily 8am–4.30pm. Admission fee.
Hawaiian Waters Adventure Park, 400 Farrington Highway, Kapolei. Tel: 945-3928. Acres of slides and pools. A big hit with kids. Open 10.30am–5pm. Admission fee.
Polynesian Cultural Center, at La'ie on Oahu's North Shore. Tel: 293-3333. Open Monday–Saturday 12.30–9pm. Admission fee.
Sea Life Park, 41-202 Kalaniana'ole Highway, at Makapu'u Point. Tel: 259-7933. Open daily 9.30am–5pm. Admission fee.
Senator Fong's Plantation & Gardens, 47-285 Pulama Road, north of Kane'ohe on the Windward Side. Tel: 239-6775. Open daily 10am–4pm. Admission fee. Tours are also available.

Waimea Valley (a.k.a. Waimea Falls Park), 59-864 Kamehameha Highway, at Waimea on Oahu's North Shore. Tel: 638-8511. Open daily 10am–5.30pm. Admission fee.

Maui

Alexander & Baldwin Sugar Museum, 3957 Hanson Road, Pu'unene, near Kahului Airport. Tel: 871-8058. Open 9.30am–4.30pm daily. Admission fee. An underrated museum that not only displays the history and processing of sugar, but also the cultural and ethnic lifestyles of Hawaii's early plantation workers.

Hale Ho'ike'ike (Bailey House), 2375-A Main Street, Wailuku. Tel: 244-3326. Open daily 10am–4pm. Admission fee. Missionary home featuring a collection of Hawaiian artifacts, as well as clothes and furniture of the times.

Baldwin Home, 120 Dickenson Street, Lahaina. Tel: 661-3262. Open 10am–4pm daily. Admission fee. Learn all about missionary life in the 19th century at this 150-year-old clapboard private residence of the Rev. Dwight Baldwin.

Carthaginian II, Lahaina Harbor, Lahaina. Tel: 661-3262. Open 10am–4pm daily. Admission fee. Replica of a 93-ft (28-meter) two-masted sailing vessel used during the whaling days.

Lahaina-Ka'anapali Pacific Railroad, 957 Limahana Place, Suite 203, Lahaina. Tel: 661-0089, toll free: 800-499 2307, fax: 661-8389. Call for times. Admission fee. This 1890s locomotive, which is also known as the Sugar Cane Train, transports sightseers between Lahaina and Ka'anapali with an additional stop at Pu'ukoli'i. Narrators share the history of sugar in Hawaii.

Whalers Village Museum, Whalers Village, 2435 Ka'anapali Parkway, Ka'anapali Resort. Tel: 661-5992. Open 9am–10pm daily. Free. A very well-presented exhibit of whaling and early life in Lahaina and Maui.

Hawaii (Big Island)

Hawaii Volcanoes National Park, PO box 52, Big Island. Visitors Center open 7.45am– 5pm daily. Admission fee. The Visitors Center features displays and films about the volcanoes on the Big Isle. Information on current volcanic activity is posted.

Kamuela Museum, Junction of Routes 19 and 250, Waimea. Tel: 885-4724. Open daily 8am–5pm. Admission fee. An amazing and valuable collection with no apparent theme – like a discriminating collector's attic. Ancient Hawaiian to Viet Cong.

Lyman House Memorial Museum, 276 Haili Street, Hilo. Tel: 935-5021. Open 9am–4.30pm Monday–Saturday. Admission fee. A restored 1800s missionary house, with an adjacent museum that has some rare Hawaiian artifacts on show.

Parker Ranch Visitor Center & Historic Homes, 67-1185 Mamalahoa Highway, Waimea 96743. Tel: 885-7655. Open daily 9am–5pm; historic homes daily 10am–5pm. Admission fee. Museum of the Big Island's Parker family, owner of the largest ranch in Hawaii.

Pu'uhonua O Honaunau National Historical Park, PO Box 129, Honaunau. Tel: 328-2326. Visitors Center open daily 8am–5.30pm. Admission fee. Historic site featuring ancient artifacts, structures and the Hale O Keawe Heiau.

Kauai

Guava Kai Plantation, PO Box 80, Kilauea. Located on Kauai's north shore, 25 minutes from Lihu'e. Tel: 828-6121. Open daily 9am–5pm. Free. Self-guided tours of this 480-acre (194-hectare) guava orchard; learn about the production and processing of guava products.

Kauai Museum, 4428 Rice Street, Lihu'e. Tel: 245-6931. Open 9am–4pm Monday through Friday, 10am–4pm Saturday. Admission fee. This former library contains a wealth of geological and ethnic displays in a compact space.

Koke'e Natural History Museum, PO Box 100, Kekaha. Tel: 335-9975. Open 10am–4pm daily. Donations are appreciated. This is a small museum featuring exhibits on the natural history of the area.

Limahuli Garden, National Tropical Botanical Garden (NTBG), PO Box 808, Hanalei. Tel: 826-1053. Call for hours. Admission fee. This 17-acre (7-hectare) garden and 990-acre (400-hectare) forest preserve, located in Ha'ena, includes native Hawaiian plants and Limahuli Stream. Visits to NTBG's Lawai and Allerton Gardens are also worthwhile.

Wai'oli Mission House Museum, PO Box 1631, Lihu'e. Tel: 245-3202. Open 9am–3pm Tuesday, Thursday, Saturday. Admission fee.

Festivals

Hula Bowl: Annual college all-star football game spotlighting the top senior players in the nation. Held on Oahu for 51 years, the game relocated to Maui in 1998 and is played (usually the second or third Saturday) at the 24,500-seat War Memorial Stadium. Tel: 534-1188.
Lunar New Year: A 15-day celebration starting on the day of the second new moon after the winter solstice (around mid- to late January). Drums, firecrackers and traditional lion dances chase bad spirits out of homes and shops in Chinatown, downtown Honolulu, clearing the way for a *kung hee fat choi* (Prosperous New Year). Tel: 533-3181.
Molokai Makahiki: Friendly Isle Festival with hula performances, arts and crafts, games and food. Usually held the last Saturday in January. Kaunakakai, Molokai. Toll free: 800-800 6367.
Narcissus Festival: Five weeks of various Chinese shows, exhibits and events coinciding with Chinese New Year; topped with the coronation of the Chinese Narcissus Queen. Event continues into February. Tel: 533-3181.
Senior Skins Game: Annual golf event hosted by the Grand Wailea Resort on Maui. This two-day event, held during Super Bowl weekend, features four golf legends – Jack Nicklaus, Arnold Palmer and Lee Trevino are among past participants. Tel: 875-7450.
State Legislature Opening: Annual Legislative session is initiated in style at the State Capitol in Honolulu on the third Wednesday of January with a colorful ceremony, *lei* presentations, Hawaiian entertainment and speeches.

Great Aloha Run: Annual 8.2-mile (13.2 km) fun run on Oahu benefiting local charities. Held every President's Day; begins at Aloha Tower and finishes at Aloha Stadium. Tel: 528-7388.
Pro Bowl: Annual all-star football game featuring the top players from the National Football League. Held on Oahu at Aloha Stadium on the Sunday following the Super Bowl. Tel: 486-9300.
Punahou Carnival: Largest and most popular school carnival in the state, taking place in early February. Fruit jams, jellies and other homemade local foods on sale; white elephant tent; art sale; games; rides. Manoa Valley, Honolulu. Tel: 944-5711.

Cherry Blossom Festival: An 11-week Japanese festival of cultural demonstrations from flower arrangement and tea ceremony to martial arts and an annual Cherry Blossom Queen contest. Tel: 949-2255.
Girls' Day (Hinamatsuri) Dolls Festival: Japanese customarily honor young girls on the third of March with a gift of a doll for their heirloom collections. Several department stores feature intricate doll displays.
Hawaii International Sport Kite Championships: Kite-flying demonstrations and competitions featuring expert kite-flyers from around the world. Held in early March at Kapi'olani Park.
Kamehameha Schools Song Festival: On the Friday before spring break, a Hawaiian choral singing competition between classes for Hawaiian and part-Hawaiian youths is staged at the Neal Blaisdell Center. Tel: 842-8495.
Kuhio Day: March 26 is a state holiday honoring the birthday of Prince Jonah Kuhio Kalaniana'ole. Celebrations include parades, memorial services at the Nu'uanu Royal Mausoleum and ceremonies at Kawaiaha'o Church in downtown Honolulu. A Prince Kuhio Festival takes place on the weekend closest to his birthday on the island of his birth, Kauai. Tel: (808) 245-3971.
Polo Season: Head to the Waimanalo Polo Field, Sundays at 3pm, for a rousing match, or arrive any time after 1pm and have an alfresco picnic before the match begins.

Celebration of the Arts: Annual festival featuring hula and chant performances, art workshops and demonstrations. Held early April at the Ritz-Carlton, Kapalua on Maui. Tel: 669-6200.
Easter: Sunrise services held at the former leprosy colony of Kalaupapa, Molokai; and at the National Memorial Cemetery of the Pacific, Punchbowl Crater, Honolulu.
Merrie Monarch Festival: A *ho'olaule'a*, arts and crafts fair, and a parade highlight the week-long hula festival, which honors King David Kalakaua. The Merrie Monarch hula competition is considered Hawaii's finest and most prestigious. Hilo, island of Hawaii. Tel: 935-9168.

Boys' Day: Long, colorful paper or cloth carp are strung up on May 5 outside Island homes to honor boys in the family – so that they may pursue their goals like the strong-spirited carp that fights upstream currents. Imported from Japan.
Honoka'a Western Weekend and Rodeo: Annual Big Island festival with a rodeo, parade, ethnic foods, arts and crafts, entertainment and country dance.
Lei Day: Every May 1, people celebrate May Day island-style – dressed in cheerful, printed *mu'umu'u* and aloha shirts, lots of *leis* and smiles. Students

throughout the islands – notably at elementary school level – perform multi-ethnic dances and songs in full costume (usually on the first school day of the month). Visitors are welcome. Much happens at the Waikiki Shell at Kapi'olani Park, including a *lei*-making contest, sunset hula show and the coronation of a Lei Day Queen.

Molokai Ka Hula Piko: Annual festival celebrating the birth of the hula on Molokai. Held the third Saturday of May, the event includes a sunrise ceremonial, hula and music performances, arts and crafts, and food booths. Papohaku Beach Park, Molokai. Tel: 553-3876.

World Fire Knife Dancing Championships: Hosted by the Polynesian Cultural Center in La'ie on Oahu, this annual competition features top fire knife dancers from around the world performing amazing feats with the traditional Samoan fire knife. Tel: 293-3333.

June

50th State Fair: Hawaiian quilt-making contests, local musicians and a rainbow of ethnic dances, produce and livestock shows, food booths, carnival rides and commercial booth displays and specially scheduled entertainment; usually at the Aloha Stadium. Tel: 486-9300/949-4131.

Hawaii State Farm Fair: Midway rides, carnival games, food booths, agricultural exhibits and entertainment are featured at this annual fair – held late June or early July – at Aloha Stadium on Oahu. Tel: 848-2074.

King Kamehameha Celebration: June 11 is King Kamehameha Day, honoring Hawaii's great king who united all the Hawaiian islands under single rule. Festivities are held throughout the month. Oahu events include a *lei*-draping ceremony at the King Kamehameha Statue in downtown Honolulu, a floral parade in Waikiki and a prestigious hula competition at the Neal Blaisdell Center. Tel: 586-0333.

Pan-Pacific Festival: Also known as the Matsuri in Hawaii Festival, this event celebrates the cultures of Hawaii, Japan and the Pacific. Cultural demonstrations and entertainment take place at various sites in Honolulu, Oahu. Tel: 926-8177.

Pu'uhonua O Honaunau Festival: Week-long Hawaiian celebration at Pu'uhonua O Honaunau in Kailua-Kona on the Big Island, featuring traditional Hawaiian games, entertainment, food and cultural demonstrations. Held end of June. Tel: 328-2288.

July

Bon Odori Dance Festival: Japanese Buddhists honor deceased ancestors at this lively dance under paper lanterns and around a tower supporting a drum beater and vocalists. Temples throughout the islands hold these dances (around 7.30pm to midnight) throughout July and August, and visitors are invited to join. The season ends with the Floating Lanterns Festival at the Jodo Mission in Hale'iwa, where candlelit hexagonal lanterns are set afloat at a nearby beach. Tel: 637-4382.

Cuisines of the Sun: Annual food event spotlighting top chefs from around the world. Held at the Mauna Lani Bay Hotel and Bungalows on the Big Island. Tel: 800-367 2323.

Fourth of July: America's Independence Day is celebrated with special activities throughout the state. Check local newspaper listings. The most popular – and most crowded – event is a glorious fireworks show off Magic Island at Ala Moana Beach Park in Honolulu.

Hawaii All-Collectors Show: Collectors of things Hawaiian (and even non-Hawaiian) should not miss this annual end-of-July production at the Neal Blaisdell Exhibition Hall in Honolulu. Antique coins, postcards, dolls, toys, records, aloha shirts and more are available for sale. Tel: 941-9754.

Hawaii International Jazz Festival: Top international jazz musicians and vocalists gather on Oahu each July for a four-day jazz celebration. Various sites across Honolulu and Waikiki. Tel: 941-9974.

Kapalua Wine & Food Festival: Fine wine and sumptuous cuisine highlight this three-day event, which gathers winemakers and chefs from around the globe and includes seminars, demonstrations, tastings and spectacular evening galas. Kapalua Resort, Maui. Toll free: (800) KAPALUA.

Koloa Plantation Days: Week-long Kauai festival in July pays tribute to Hawaii's once-thriving sugar plantations. Entertainment includes sporting events, cooking demonstrations and a parade. Tel: 742-6096.

Prince Lot Hula Festival: Another popular hula event – this one isn't a competition – held at the relaxing Moanalua Gardens on Oahu. Tel: 839-5334.

August

Earth Maui: A three-day nature summit featuring hands-on environmental workshops, eco-seminars, nature exhibits and guided tours of Maui's pristine wilderness. Kapalua, Maui. Tel: 669-0244.

Hawaiian International Billfish Tournament: Held in early August; giant marlin are caught during this popular tournament at Kailua-Kona on the Big Island. Tel: 329-6155.

Maui Onion Festival: Food demonstrations (featuring the famous Maui onion), entertainment and a Maui onion cook-off highlight this festival at Whalers Village in Ka'anapali, Maui. Don't forget your breath mints. Tel: 661-3271.

Pu'ukohola Heiau Cultural Festival: Annual Hawaiian festival at Pu'ukohola Heiau National Historic Site on the Big Island. Highlights include cultural demonstrations, food tastings, arts and crafts workshops, and hula performances. Tel: 882-7218.

Queen Lili'uokalani Keiki Hula Competition: Statewide hula competition featuring Hawaii's top

young hula students. Neal Blaisdell Center, Honolulu.
Tel: 521-6905.

September

Aloha Festivals: Hawaii's biggest festival, with statewide celebrations encompassing beautiful floral parades, street parties, special ceremonies and community events to celebrate the spirit of aloha.
Tel: 589-1771.
A Day at Queen Emma Summer Palace: Hawaiian arts and crafts, entertainment plus food highlight this annual September 21 tribute to Hawaii's Queen Emma. Honolulu, Oahu. Tel: 595-6291.
Honolulu International Bed Race: Fund-raising craziness with teams pushing decorated beds down Kalakaua Avenue at Kapi'olani Park in Waikiki. Also featured are entertainment events, food booths and displays. Tel: 239-5546.
Honolulu Symphony: The symphony season generally runs from September to May with performances at the Blaisdell Concert Hall and Hawaii Theatre in Honolulu. Check newspaper listings.
Tel: 524-0815.
Okinawan Festival: Kapi'olani Park, Oahu. Labor Day weekend cultural event featuring Okinawan food demonstrations, dance and entertainment.
Tel: 676-5400.

October

Bankoh Molokai Hoe: International Molokai-to-Oahu canoe race. Event starts at Hale o Lono Harbor on Molokai and ends at Fort DeRussy Beach in Waikiki; first finishers are expected around noon–12.30pm.
Tel: 526-1969.
The French Festival, All things French add Euroflair to Hawaii, with a week of events from runway modeling to culinary events and museum exhibits. Last week of October. Honolulu. Tel: (877) THE FEST.
Halloween in Lahaina: Hawaii's biggest Halloween party takes place on Halloween night in Lahaina,

Maui, with costumed parades and plenty of raucous entertainment.
Tel: 667-9175.
Ironman World Triathlon: A 2.4-mile (4-km) open-ocean swim, followed by a 112-mile (180-km) bike ride and a full 26-mile (42-km) marathon is the order of the Kailua-Kona day.
Tel: 329-0063.

November

Grand Slam of Golf: The winners of golf's four main championships – the Masters, US Open, British Open and PGA Championship – compete for a $1-million purse. Po'ipu, Kauai.
Tel: 742-8711.
Hawaii International Film Festival: Acclaimed two-week festival features international films and celebrates an "East meets West" theme. Generally held on Oahu during the second week of November, followed by a week-long stint on the neighbor islands.
Tel: 528-3456.
Kona Coffee Festival: Week-long festivities in early November; includes judging of coffee recipes, Kona coffee-farm tours, and local parade and pageantry; Kailua, Big Island. Tel: 326-7820.
Mission Houses Museum Christmas Fair: Handcrafters' fair in late November features more than 50 of Hawaii's finest craftspeople, a special display in the 1831 Chamberlain House and much free entertainment.
Tel: 531-0481.
Na Mele O Maui Festival: Several Ka'anapali hotels participate in a celebration of Hawaiian music and dance; Maui. Tel: 661-3271.
Surfing Contests: November through February are the Big Surf months on Oahu's North Shore. Several world championship contests are scheduled each year, dates determined by the condition of the surf. The surf here at this time is regarded as the world's best, and the world's top surfers are on the beach, waiting for the perfect break. Check local newspapers for day-by-day announcements. Tel: 638-7770.

December

Festival of Art & Flowers: From floral displays of Maui-grown protea and other tropical flora to arts and crafts. There are workshops and Hawaiian music. Held in Lahaina's Banyan park. Toll free: 888-310 1117.
Honolulu City Lights: During the holiday season, downtown Honolulu dresses itself at night with bright lights and festive Christmas displays. It's a sure ooh-and-aah highlight for the kids. In the daytime, check out Honolulu Hale (City Hall), which displays specially decorated Christmas trees and wreaths. Tel: 523-4834.
Honolulu Marathon: At the crack of dawn one morning every December, thousands of dedicated runners from across the world set off from the Aloha Tower on a 26-mile, 385-yard (42.2-km) AAU-certified (American Athletic Union) marathon course along Oahu's south shore. The Honolulu marathon ends at Kapiolani Park Bandstand.
Tel: 734-7200.
Kamehameha Schools Christmas Song Festival: Comprises songs performed in both Hawaiian and English by the Kamehameha Schools' Glee Club Orchestra. Held early December at the Neal Blaisdell Concert Hall in Honolulu.
Tel: 842-8495.
Pearl Harbor Day: In memory of those who were killed during the Japanese bombing of Oahu on December 7, 1941, a memorial service is held every year at the *USS Arizona* Memorial. Tel: 422-2771.

Shopping

Cosmopolitan residents and visitors shop for a variety of international goods and domestic creations in shops throughout the islands, but Hawaii has its own distinct goods. Items range from Polynesian kitsch *tiki* gods with olivine stone eyes to fine Ni'ihau shell *lei* that may cost as much as $2,500 for four strands.

Aloha wear: Hawaii has its own fashions, the *mu'umu'u* and aloha shirt. The first *mu'umu'u*, designed and introduced by the early missionaries, was a loose, lengthy, high-necked, long-sleeved shroud. Because of variations in its style, *mu'umu'u* has come to refer to just about any casual smock, long or short, made of Hawaiian print fabric. The aloha shirt was first marketed in the 1930s by a Chinese tailor in Honolulu. It is a simple button-front shirt with short sleeves made of Hawaiian print textiles. *Mu'umu'u* and aloha shirts are sold and worn everywhere. Some island occasions, such as wedding receptions and dinner parties, specify "aloha attire" as the preferred mode of dress.

Chinese preserves: Introduced by the Chinese, these preserves have become a favorite snack treat in Hawaii and are craved by those truly accustomed to local tastes. Plums, cherries, mangos, guavas, apricots, lemons and limes are salted and preserved in the form of sweet-sour pickles known as "crack seed." Shops specializing in these pickled seeds can be found in major suburban shopping areas and downtown.

Coral jewelry: Forget coral souvenirs. Coral is a delicate yet essential component in the ocean ecosystem, especially in reef communities. Hawaii's reefs are young and fragile and taking coral is unsound.

Dried gourds: Called *ipu* in Hawaiian, the tan bottle gourd is hollowed-out and dried and used as a food and water receptacle, a drum or a hula instrument.

Feather *leis* and hat bands: Feathers of birds such as the pheasant and peacock are made into attractive *leis* and hat bands. In ancient Hawaii, items made of feathers were reserved for royalty and high-ranking *ali'i*.

Hawaiian instruments: Popular Hawaiian hula instruments include the *ipu*, *pu'ili* (slashed percussive bamboo sticks), *'uli'uli* (a feather-topped gourd rattle filled with seeds) and *'ili'ili* (small smooth stones used like castanets in a set of four). There are also the *hano* (nose flute) and *'ukulele*. All are available at island hula supply shops and some music stores.

Jellies, jams and preserves: Tropical fruits such as guava, *poha*, mango, passion fruit, papaya and coconut are made into unique, luscious spreads.

Kukui nut and seed *lei*: The tradition of stringing and wearing the brown and black-and-white *kukui* nuts, commonly called candlenuts, is still very popular. *Koa* seed *lei* are also appealing, but most of these are strung in the Philippines.

Macadamia nuts: Delicious roasted and eaten plain or chocolate-covered, this rich nut is true gourmet fare. Macadamia nut products are grown and packaged in Hawaii.

Ni'ihau shell *lei*: Small, rare shells are washed up onto the beaches of the privately owned island of Ni'ihau, where some of the 200-plus residents will gather and string them into *lei* or necklaces. There is a beautiful range of delicate, subtle colors. The *lei* are very expensive, and found only in upscale shops, especially on Kauai.

Photographs of old Hawaii: Peer into Hawaii's past. Leaf through the photo albums at the Hawaii State Archives (Tel: 586-0329), downtown off S. King Street in the 'Iolani Palace grounds. The archives are open Monday–Friday 9am–4pm. Copies are available but generally take up to two weeks for delivery (by mail). Or visit the archives at the Bishop Museum (Tel: 848-4182), by far the largest in the state with more than 500,000 images. Here, copies are more expensive, but the choice is greater.

Plants: Exotic hibiscus, anthurium, bamboo, orchid, *ti* and bird of paradise plants (and their seeds) are potted in sterile peat moss and agriculturally inspected. (Warning: Be sure they were inspected by the Agricultural Inspection Board before attempting to take them on to the mainland.) Some sellers will ship these pre-fumigated.

Scrimshaw: This Pacific art came into its own in the 1800s when bored sailors on whaling vessels scratched pictures on whale teeth. Nowadays, a number of non-endangered materials are used, such as fossilized walrus tusk. Predictably, Maui is a good place to look at and purchase scrimshaw, particularly in West Maui.

Sea shells: Forget these. A souvenir whose time has passed. Shells taken locally deprive sea life of shelter. Also, many of the shells found in souvenir shops come from places like the Philippines.

Surfboards: Custom-made fiberglass surfboards can be

Hawaii's own homegrown and roasted coffee beans are produced in Kona on the only commercial coffee plantations in the United States. This Big Island product is accorded a gourmet status in international coffee-drinking circles. Stay away from the blends, which require only 10 percent Kona beans. And there's more beyond Kona: Gourmet coffee is being grown on Molokai, Kauai and Maui as well.

adapted to your height, weight and personal taste in design by some of the finest board shapers in the world.

Tapa: Tapa (bark cloth), properly called *kapa*, is made into popular items – place mats, wall-hangings, bags and hats. However, the *tapa* for sale may not be Hawaiian *kapa*, but a related fabric made in Samoa and Tonga. The art of making real Hawaiian *kapa* was lost during the 19th century, but is now enjoying a revival with a new generation of artisans.

Wood: Monkeypod, *koa* and *milo* are three popular island woods used in the making of furniture, *calabashes* (large ceremonial bowls) and other fine wood creations. *Koa* and rosewood are also used to make quality guitars and *'ukuleles*.

Woven goods: *Lauhala* (pandanus), coconut fronds, makaloa sedge and the rootlets of the *'ie'ie* forest vine are used to weave baskets, mats, bowls, hats and more.

Shopping Areas

Waikiki

DFS **Galleria**, 330 Royal Hawaiian Avenue, at the corner of Kalakaua Avenue. The nautically themed complex, complete with a multi-level aquarium, features resort-wear, cosmetics and souvenirs.

Hyatt Regency Shopping Center, on the first three floors of the Hyatt Regency Waikiki, 2424 Kalakaua Avenue. Visit the café on the first level, next to a three-story waterfall.

International Market Place, 2330 Kalakaua Avenue, across from the Sheraton Moana Surfrider, in the heart of Waikiki. Open daily 9am–11pm. Shops and stalls with what sometimes appears to be little more than an endless array of "genuine" gold jewelry and tourist souvenirs.

King's Village, 131 Ka'iulani Avenue, behind the Hyatt Regency Waikiki. Open daily 9am–11pm. This rambling, split-level commercial complex takes its theme from the 19th century, right down to a changing of the King's Guard every night at 6.15pm.

Kuhio Mall, located behind the International Market Place on Kuhio Avenue. Open daily 10am–10pm.

Rainbow Bazaar, 2005 Kalia Road, on the grounds of the Hilton Hawaiian Village. Open 8am–11pm daily. Shops and restaurants scattered over several acres.

Royal Hawaiian Shopping Center, stretches for three blocks along Kalakaua Avenue, offering a wide variety of shops and restaurants on three levels. Daily entertainment at its central courtyard. Open daily 9.30am–10.30pm.

Oahu

Ala Moana Center, the largest mall in the state and one of the largest open-air malls in the world , housing about 200 stores (including 21 eateries) and covering 50 acres (50 hectares) across from Ala Moana Park. Free island entertainment regularly takes place on the mall's centerstage. Open Mon–Sat 9.30am–9pm, Sun 10am–7pm. Tel: 955-9517.

Aloha Tower Marketplace, located at Pier 9 near the downtown financial district. This 180,000-sq foot (16,720-sq meter) harborside complex features an interesting array of shops and restaurants. The adjacent Hawaii Maritime Center features more than 40 exhibits celebrating Hawaii's maritime heritage. Open Mon–Sat 9am–9pm, Sun 10am–6pm; restaurants and bars close later. Tel: 528-5700.

Chinatown, adjacent to downtown Honolulu and by far the most interesting shopping area in the islands. Asian immigrants have changed the look, smell and taste of this old neighborhood, but the open market ambiance is the same. Watch noodles being made, take your ailments to an acupuncturist's or herbal shop, choose from among more than 30 ethnic restaurants, or visit more than a dozen fine art galleries on side streets from Hotel Street. At night, a small section of Hotel Street retains its sailors-on-liberty flavor, with strip joints and bars that should not be entered alone.

Downtown Honolulu, on Bishop Street, which was named after the islands' first banker (Charles Bishop) and is today the financial center of Hawaii. All the major banks are here, along with many of the airlines, and a wide range of restaurants and shops. Every Friday there are free concerts at Tamarind Park, which spotlight Hawaii's very best Hawaiian, contemporary and jazz musicians. Usual business hours are 8am–5pm.

Kahala Mall, in the Kahala residential district just east of Diamond Head and Waikiki, home of the designer pizza and a movie complex. Openings are staggered, beginning at 8.30am. Most shops close at 10pm, although the supermarkets are open 24 hours. Tel: 732-7736.

Kapahulu, Avenue, which ends in Waikiki, offers an interesting selection of shops that feature collectible Hawaiiana approximately 1 mile (1.5 km) from the beach.

Pearlridge Center, 1005 Moanalua Road, in 'Aiea. A massive mall in two "phases," divided by a watercress farm whose owner refused to sell his land to the developer. (A nice reminder that Hawaii's motto says the land is perpetuated in "righteousness.") Open Mon–Sat 10am–9pm, Sun 10am–6pm. Tel: 488-0981.

Ward Centre, 1200 Ala Moana Boulevard, just a few blocks from Ala Moana Center on Ala Moana Boulevard. This center is mostly upscale, with a bookstore and several popular but semi-expensive restaurants and gourmet shops. Very good nightlife. Open Mon–Sat 10am–9pm, Sun 10am–5pm. Tel: 591-8411.

Ward Warehouse, located one block from Ward Centre. This is not a warehouse at all, but a two-level complex of affordable restaurants and almost 70 shops. Same hours as Ward Centre. Tel: 591-8411.

Maui

For those heading to Maui, Kahului is the focus of urban commerce, but don't overlook the street shopping

of historic Wailuku, just above Kahului, and of Makawao and Pa'ia, toward Upcountry. As nearly everybody visiting Maui stays in either the Wailea or Ka'anapali resorts, those two areas are rich with shopping wonders, mostly within the expansive resorts. Lahaina, of course, lives off both shopping and eating. Ramble its streets to find an abundance of cash-and-credit card opportunities.
Ka'ahumanu Center, 275 Ka'ahumanu Avenue. Tel: 877-3369. Maui's largest mall with over 75 shops and eateries. Open Mon–Fri 9.30am–9pm, Sat 9.30am–7pm, Sun 10am–5pm.
Kapalua Shops, Kapalua Bay Hotel and Villas, Kapalua, West Maui. Tel: 669-3754. Small with upscale shops, clothing to antiques. Open Mon–Sat 8am–9pm, Sun 8am–5pm.
Lahaina Cannery Mall, 1221 Honoapiilani Highway. Tel: 661-5304. West Maui's most comprehensive indoor shopping mall, north end of Lahaina. Open daily 9.30am–9pm.
Shops at Wailea, An elegant upgrade of the old shopping village, with dozens of shops and restaurants in a multi-level mall. Open daily until 9pm.
Whalers Village, Ka'anapali Resort, West Maui. Tel: 661-4567. Includes more than 50 shops, a whaling museum and a 40-ft (12-meter) sperm whale skeleton. Several popular restaurants on the beach. Outdoors. Open daily 9.30am–10pm.

Hawaii

On the Big Island, the commercial centers of Hilo and Kona are the obvious choices. Historic downtown Hilo is small, compact and undergoing a revival, and is good for quiet walking and browsing. Kona's waterfront thrives on tourism, and the offerings range – with the stress on low-end souvenirs – from T-shirts and postcards to at times dubious art. The resort hotels of Kohala – Mauna Lani, Waikoloa, Mauna Kea – have what those with gold cards are looking for.

Kings' Shops, Waikoloa Beach Resort. Tel: 885-8811. Hawaiiana exhibits throughout this shopping complex complement the nearly 40 shops and restaurants. Open 9.30am–9.30pm.
Prince Kuhio Plaza, 111 East Puainako Street, Hilo. Tel: 959-3555. Largest enclosed mall on the Big Island. Open weekdays 10am–9pm, Sat 9.30am–7pm and Sun 10am–6pm.

Kauai

In keeping with its personality, Kauai's shopping is lower-key than the other islands, but pleasurable and often unique. Commercial shopping centers are Lihu'e – including the Po'ipu, Koloa, and Kapa'a areas – and Princeville and Hanalei on the north shore. Kauai's shopping tends to be decentralized, with small (but high-quality) pockets of stores.
Coconut Marketplace, on main highway, near Kapa'a. Tel: 822-3641. Standard open-air shopping mall with 70 assorted shops. Open daily 9am–9pm.
Kilohana, Route 50, 1½ mile (2 km) north of Lihu'e. Tel: 245-5608. Plantation estate with high-quality retail shops, galleries. Open daily 9.30am–9.30pm.
Koloa/Kapaa/Hanapepe/Hanalei, Small town Hawaii with a mix of enjoyable shops.
Kukui Grove, Highway 50, near Lihu'e. Tel: 245-7784. Large standard enclosed shopping mall, Kauai's largest.
Poipu Shopping Village, 2360 Kiahuna Plantation Drive. Tel: 742-2831. Pleasant outdoor mall with shops and restaurants.

Sport

Watersports

Not surprisingly, Hawaii offers a sizable menu of watersports, including surfing, windsurfing, scuba diving, fishing, kayaking and yachting.

Most hotels can arrange any of these wet 'n' wild adventures for you, including lessons. One of the advantages of booking arrangements through a hotel is that the hotel has a stake in your satisfaction. If concerned about quality, go to one of the high-end luxury hotels and make arrangements through their activities desk. The price may be 5–10 percent higher, but those hotels have international reputations to maintain, so they won't refer guests to questionable activity operators. That's the theory, at least, and it usually works well.

Surfing

Novices can head out to Oahu's Waikiki Beach, where the waves are beginner-friendly and where bronze-skinned beachboys still offer lessons. Consult the local phone directory if you are looking for more formal lessons (under "Surfing Instruction").

WINDSURFING

Hawaii has world-class windsurfing, especially at Kailua Beach on Oahu and Ho'okipa Beach on Maui. In fact, both locations are the sites of major international competitions. Most of the activities desks at resort hotels offer lessons to both guests and non-guests. Check around for prices, and for an instructor you're comfortable with – you'll be out there with him or her in full view of everyone on the beach, and the less stress the better.

SCUBA DIVING

While the diving in Hawaii is not equal to that in Fiji or Palau, it is quite good and often unique, especially around the Big Island, which is too young for a decent coral reef but which has lots of interesting underwater lava formations. The waters are usually warm, although in winter a full wetsuit is recommended.

There are scores of dive shops and operators in Hawaii, and the problem for the visitor is finding a trip that will assure a quality experience. On Oahu, especially in the Waikiki area, a number of dive operators run their dive trips like a factory process, and the experience is thoroughly unrewarding, especially for the more advanced diver.

The activities desks of the larger hotels usually have a long-term working relationship with a single dive operator, and most of them maintain high standards in their dives.

If you're looking for diving lessons leading to certification, make sure the dive instructor is PADI or NAUI certified. Depending on the schedule used for instruction, it can take two to five days to complete the lessons. Again, hotel activity desks can set you up with lessons.

FISHING

There is not much in the way of lake or river fishing in Hawaii quite simply because there are few lakes or rivers there. However, big game fishing is another story. Hawaii is world-famous for this type of fishing, especially for catches taken off the Kona Coast of the Big

Island. There are world-class fishing tournaments there each summer.

It's all done by charter boats, most of which are located at Kona Harbor or at another harbor up near the Kona airport. Book a charter through a hotel activities desk, or go to the harbors and check out the boats and skippers in person.

YACHTING AND KAYAKING

Oddly enough, few people think of taking a yacht trip through the islands. It is pricey, perhaps, but the experience is unmatched. There are several yachts available for charters, complete with meals and captain. They can be customized for big-game fishing, scuba diving or just a leisurely holiday jaunt. The majority of them are based on the Big Island.

Kayaking is gaining popularity in the islands. River kayaking is limited mostly to Kauai, particularly on the Hanalei River. Ocean kayaking is found everywhere. Popular excursions include the Na Pali Coast of Kauai and the coast of Molokai.

Language

Words & Phrases

In its development, the Hawaiian language has acquired several interesting grammatical complications, as well as a pronunciation system known for its complex vowel combinations and small number of consonants. The Hawaiian alphabet has eight consonants, each roughly similar in pronunciation to their equivalent letter symbols in English, with the exception of w and the glottal stop: '.

h	hula	(Hawaiian dance)
k	kai	(sea)
l	lani	(heaven)
m	manu	(bird)
n	niho	(tooth)
p	pua	(flower)
w	wa'a	(canoe)
'	'ala	(fragrance)

In Hawaiian, the letter w varies in pronunciation between a w and v sound. To English speakers, w often sounds like a v after a stressed vowel, as in the place name Hale'iwa. At the beginning of a word or after an unstressed vowel, w sounds like an English w as in the place names Waikiki and Wahiawa.

Meanwhile, the consonant symbol ' – called the 'okina in Hawaiian – represents a glottal stop, which indicates a stop-start-pronunciation. Common to Hawaii, it is also found in several dialects of English such as in the Cockney pronunciation of "a little bottle of beer" (which comes out as "a li'l bo 'l a beer").

The five Hawaiian vowels come in both short and long duration forms.

Long duration vowels are marked by a bar termed the ß in Hawaiian (called a macron in English) and sometimes differ from short vowels in quality as well as duration.

Pronunciation of vowels is similar to Spanish or Japanese: no sloppy or lazy sounds as found in English.

a as in father	*nana*	(look)
e as in hay	*nene*	(goose)
i as in beet	*wiwi*	(skinny)
o as in boat	*lolo*	(feeble mind)
u as in boot	*pupu*	(snack)

If you would like more *kokua* (help) with Hawaiian language, refer to three excellent books on the subject: *Spoken Hawaiian*, by Samuel Elbert; *Let's Speak Hawaiian*, by Dorothy Kahananui and A. Anthony; and *The Hawaiian Dictionary*, by Samuel Elbert and Mary Kawena Pukui.

WORD LIST

ali'i **ancient Hawaiian royalty, nobility**
aloha **love, greeting, farewell**
'Ewa **toward 'Ewa**
hana hou **one more time, encore**
haole **technically all foreigners, now refers mainly to people of Caucasian ancestry**
hapa **half, part**
hapa-haole **part-Caucasian**
heiau **traditional Hawaiian place of worship, a temple**
ho'olaule'a **celebration, party**
imu **underground cooking oven**
kama'aina **island-born or longtime resident of Hawaii**
kanaka **man, person, especially a native Hawaiian**
kane **man**
keiki **child, children**
kokua **help, assistance**
lanai **porch, balcony, veranda**
lauhala **pandanus leaf, for weaving**
lu'au **traditional feast**
mahalo **thank you**
makai **toward the ocean**
malihini **newcomer or visitor to the islands**

mana **spiritual power**
mauka **toward the mountains**
mauna **mountain**
Mele Kalikimaka **Merry Christmas**
'ohana **family**
'okole **rear end, buttocks**
'ono **delicious, tasty**
pakalolo **marijuana**
pali **cliff, precipice**
paniolo **cowboy**
pau **finished, completed**
pau hana **end of work**
poi **food paste made from taro roots**
puka **hole, opening**
pupu **hors d'oeuvre**
shaka **slang for an island hand greeting**
wahine **woman**

Further Reading

The Art of the Hula by Allan Seiden. Honolulu: Island Heritage, 1999. Richly illustrated history of Hawaii's nature dance.
Atlas of Hawaii University of Hawaii Press, 1983. 2nd edition. The definitive reference for diverse information about the islands: environment, culture and economy.
The Betrayal of Lili'uokalani by Helena G. Allen. Glendale: Clark, 1982. All-important biography of Hawaii's last queen.
Born in Paradise by Armine Von Tempski. Duell, 1940. One of the best accounts of old Hawaii ranch life on the island of Maui.
Discovery by Bishop Museum Press. Honolulu: 1993. A superb collection of essays and photographs addressing ancient, contemporary and future Hawaii.
Hawaii 1959–89 by Gavan Daws. Publishers Group Hawaii, 1989. A thorough history of Hawaii's first 30 years of statehood.
Hawaii: A Literary Chronicle by W. Storrs Lee. Funk and Wagnalls, 1967. A collection of Hawaii impressions penned by prominent visiting authors of the late 18th and 19th centuries.
Hawaii Recalls: Selling Romance to America by Ann Ellett Brown and Gary Gienza De Soto. Honolulu: Editions Limited, 1982. Nostalgic images of the Isles, 1910–50.
Hawaii: The Royal Legacy by Allan Seiden. Honolulu: Mutual Publishing, 1993. The illustrated story of Hawaii's chiefs and Kings.
Hawaii's Birds by Hawaii Audubon Society. Honolulu, 1981. A local birdwatcher's bible.
Hawaii's Story by Hawaii's Queen by Queen Lili'uokalani of the Hawaiian Islands. Boston: Lothrop, Lee & Shepard Co., 1898; and Ruthland, Vermont & Tokyo: Charles E. Tuttle, 1990. Queen Lili'uokalani's memoirs.